Microsoft®

Excel® 2010
for Medical Professionals

Microsoft®

Excel® 2010
for Medical Professionals

ELIZABETH EISNER REDING

LYNN WERMERS

COURSE TECHNOLOGY
CENGAGE Learning

Australia • Brazil • Japan • Korea • Mexico • Singapore • Spain • United Kingdom • United States

COURSE TECHNOLOGY
CENGAGE Learning

Microsoft® Excel® 2010 for Medical Professionals
Elizabeth Eisner Reding, Lynn Wermers

Vice President, Publisher: Nicole Jones Pinard

Executive Editor: Marjorie Hunt

Associate Acquisitions Editor: Amanda Lyons

Senior Product Manager: Christina Kling Garrett

Associate Product Manager: Kim Klasner

Director of Marketing: Cheryl Costantini

Senior Marketing Manager: Ryan DeGrote

Marketing Coordinator: Kristen Panciocco

Contributing Author: Carol Cram

Developmental Editor: Karen Stevens

Content Project Manager: Heather Hopkins

Copy Editor: Mark Goodin

Proofreader: Vicki Zimmer

Indexer: BIM Indexing and Proofreading Services

QA Manuscript Reviewers: Marianne Snow

Print Buyer: Fola Orekoya

Cover Designer: GEX Publishing Services

Composition: GEX Publishing Services

For product information and technology assistance, contact us at
Cengage Learning Customer & Sales Support, 1-800-354-9706
For permission to use material from this text or product, submit all requests online at **www.cengage.com/permissions**
Further permissions questions can be emailed to
permissionrequest@cengage.com

Trademarks:

Some of the product names and company names used in this book have been used for identification purposes only and may be trademarks or registered trademarks of their respective manufacturers and sellers.

Microsoft and the Office logo are either registered trademarks or trademarks of Microsoft Corporation in the United States and/or other countries. Course Technology, Cengage Learning is an independent entity from Microsoft Corporation, and not affiliated with Microsoft in any manner.

ISBN-13: 978-0-538-74845-2
ISBN-10: 0-538-74845-1

Course Technology
20 Channel Center Street
Boston, MA 02210
USA

Cengage Learning is a leading provider of customized learning solutions with office locations around the globe, including Singapore, the United Kingdom, Australia, Mexico, Brazil, and Japan. Locate your local office at:
international.cengage.com/region

Cengage Learning products are represented in Canada by Nelson Education, Ltd.

To learn more about Course Technology, visit **www.cengage.com/coursetechnology**

To learn more about Cengage Learning, visit **www.cengage.com**

Purchase any of our products at your local college store or at our preferred online store **www.cengagebrain.com**

Printed in the United States of America
3 4 5 6 7 8 9 19 18 17 16 15 14 13 12

Brief Contents

Preface x

Office 2010

Unit A: Getting Started with Microsoft Office 2010 ....Office 1

Excel 2010

Unit A: Getting Started with Excel 2010 ....Excel 1

Unit B: Working with Formulas and Functions ....Excel 25

Unit C: Formatting a Worksheet ....Excel 51

Unit D: Working with Charts ....Excel 79

Unit E: Analyzing Data Using Formulas ....Excel 105

Unit F: Managing Workbook Data ....Excel 129

Unit G: Managing Data Using Tables ....Excel 153

Unit H: Analyzing Table Data..Excel 177

Web Apps

Appendix Web Apps: Working with Windows Live and Office Web Apps .... Web Apps 1

Glossary ....Glossary 1

Index...Index 6

Contents

Preface..x

Office 2010

Unit A: Getting Started with Microsoft Office 2010 .... **Office 1**

Understanding the Office 2010 Suite.. Office 2
    Deciding which program to use

Starting and Exiting an Office Program .... Office 4
    Using shortcut keys to move between Office programs
    Windows Live and Microsoft Office Web Apps

Viewing the Office 2010 User Interface .... Office 6
    Using Backstage view

Creating and Saving a File.. Office 8
    Using the Office Clipboard

Opening a File and Saving it with a New Name .... Office 10
    Working in Compatibility Mode
    Exploring File Open options

Viewing and Printing your Work .... Office 12
    Customizing the Quick Access toolbar
    Creating a screen capture

Getting Help and Closing a File .... Office 14
    Recovering a document

Practice.. Office 16

Excel 2010

Unit A: Getting Started with Excel 2010 .... **Excel 1**

Understanding Spreadsheet Software..Excel 2

Touring the Excel 2010 Window ....Excel 4
    Windows Live and Microsoft Office Web Apps

Understanding Formulas...Excel 6

Entering Labels and Values and Using the Sum Button ....Excel 8
    Navigating a worksheet

Editing Cell Entries...Excel 10
    Recovering unsaved changes to a workbook file

Entering and Editing a Simple Formula ....Excel 12
    Understanding named ranges

Switching Worksheet Views ....Excel 14

Choosing Print Options ....Excel 16
    Printing worksheet formulas
    Scaling to fit

Practice..Excel 18

Unit B: Working with Formulas and Functions.. **Excel 25**

Creating a Complex Formula ....Excel 26
    Reviewing the order of precedence

Inserting a Function ....Excel 28

Typing a Function ....Excel 30

    Using the COUNT and COUNTA functions

Copying and Moving Cell Entries...Excel 32

    Inserting and deleting selected cells

Understanding Relative and Absolute Cell References ....Excel 34

    Using a mixed reference

Copying Formulas with Relative Cell References...Excel 36

    Using Paste Preview

    Using Auto Fill options

Copying Formulas with Absolute Cell References ....Excel 38

    Using the fill handle for sequential text or values

Rounding a Value with a Function ....Excel 40

    Creating a new workbook using a template

Practice..Excel 42

Unit C: Formatting a Worksheet...Excel 51

Formatting Values...Excel 52

    Formatting as a table

Changing Font and Font Size...Excel 54

    Inserting and adjusting clip art and other images

Changing Font Styles and Alignment..Excel 56

    Rotating and indenting cell entries

Adjusting Column Width...Excel 58

    Changing row height

Inserting and Deleting Rows and Columns ....Excel 60

    Hiding and unhiding columns and rows

    Adding and editing comments

Applying Colors, Patterns, and Borders ....Excel 62

    Working with themes and cell styles

Applying Conditional Formatting ....Excel 64

    Managing conditional formatting rules

Renaming and Moving a Worksheet..Excel 66

    Copying worksheets

Checking Spelling..Excel 68

    E-mailing a workbook

Practice..Excel 70

Unit D: Working with Charts ....Excel 79

Planning a Chart..Excel 80

Creating a Chart ....Excel 82

    Creating sparklines

Moving and Resizing a Chart ....Excel 84

    Moving an embedded chart to a sheet

Changing the Chart Design ....Excel 86

    Creating a Combination Chart

    Working with a 3-D chart

Changing the Chart Layout ....Excel 88

    Adding data labels to a chart

Formatting a Chart ....Excel 90

    Changing alignment and angle in axis labels and titles

Annotating and Drawing on a Chart ....Excel 92

    Adding SmartArt graphics

Creating a Pie Chart ....Excel 94
    Previewing a chart
Practice ....Excel 96

Unit E: Analyzing Data Using Formulas ....Excel 105

Formatting Data Using Text Functions ....Excel 106
    Using text functions
Summing a Data Range Based on Conditions ....Excel 108
Consolidating Data Using a Formula ....Excel 110
    Linking data between workbooks
Checking Formulas for Errors ....Excel 112
    Correcting circular references
Constructing Formulas Using Named Ranges ....Excel 114
    Consolidating data using named ranges
    Managing workbook names
Building a Logical Formula with the IF Function ....Excel 116
Building a Logical Formula with the AND Function ....Excel 118
    Using the OR and NOT logical functions
    Inserting an equation into a worksheet
Calculating Payments with the PMT Function ....Excel 120
    Calculating future value with the FV function
Practice ....Excel 122

Unit F: Managing Workbook Data ....Excel 129

Viewing and Arranging Worksheets ....Excel 130
    Splitting the worksheet into multiple panes
Protecting Worksheets and Workbooks ....Excel 132
    Freezing rows and columns
Saving Custom Views of a Worksheet ....Excel 134
    Using Page Break Preview
Adding a Worksheet Background ....Excel 136
    Clipping Screens in Excel
Preparing a Workbook for Distribution ....Excel 138
    Sharing a workbook
Inserting Hyperlinks ....Excel 140
    Returning to your document
    Using research tools
Saving a Workbook for Distribution ....Excel 142
    Understanding Excel file formats
Grouping Worksheets ....Excel 144
    Adding a digital signature to a workbook
    Creating a workspace
Practice ....Excel 146

Unit G: Managing Data Using Tables ....Excel 153

Planning a Table ....Excel 154
Creating and Formatting a Table ....Excel 156
    Changing table style options
Adding Table Data ....Excel 158
    Selecting table elements
Finding and Replacing Table Data ....Excel 160
    Using Find and Select features

Deleting Table Data ....Excel 162

Sorting Table Data ....Excel 164

    Sorting a table using conditional formatting

    Specifying a custom sort order

Using Formulas in a Table ....Excel 166

    Using structured references

Printing a Table...Excel 168

    Setting a print area

Practice..Excel 170

Unit H: Analyzing Table Data ....**Excel 177**

Filtering a Table ....Excel 178

Creating a Custom Filter ....Excel 180

    Using more than one rule when conditionally formatting data

Filtering a Table with the Advanced Filter ....Excel 182

    Using advanced conditional formatting options

Extracting Table Data..Excel 184

    Understanding the criteria range and the copy-to location

Looking Up Values in a Table..Excel 186

    Finding records using the DGET function

    Using the HLOOKUP and MATCH functions

Summarizing Table Data ....Excel 188

Validating Table Data..Excel 190

    Restricting cell values and data length

    Adding input messages and error alerts

Creating Subtotals ....Excel 192

Practice..Excel 194

Web Apps

Appendix Web Apps: Working with Windows Live and Office Web Apps ....**Web Apps 1**

Exploring How to Work Online from Windows Live .... Web Apps 2

Obtaining a Windows Live ID and Signing In to Windows Live .... Web Apps 4

    Verifying your Windows Live ID

Uploading Files to Windows Live .... Web Apps 6

Working with the PowerPoint Web App .... Web Apps 8

Creating Folders and Organizing Files on SkyDrive... Web Apps 10

Adding People to Your Network and Sharing Files .... Web Apps 12

    Sharing files on SkyDrive

Working with the Excel Web App .... Web Apps 14

    Exploring other Office Web Apps

Windows Live and Microsoft Office Web Apps Quick Reference .... Web Apps 16

Glossary... **Glossary 1**

Index .... **Index 6**

Preface

Welcome to *Microsoft Excel 2010 for Medical Professionals*. This book is designed to meet the needs of students who are training for careers in medical office administration. What makes this book unique is that every lesson and exercise features a real-world spreadsheet or chart related to the medical profession. As they learn Excel skills, students work with examples they are likely to encounter in a typical medical practice, clinic, or hospital.

If this is your first experience with this book, you'll see it has a unique design: each skill is presented on two facing pages, with steps on the left and screens on the right. The layout makes it easy to learn a skill without having to read a lot of text and flip pages to see an illustration.

See the illustration on the right to learn more about the pedagogical and design elements of a typical lesson.

What's New In This Edition

- **Fully Updated.** Highlights the new features of Microsoft Excel 2010 including creating sparklines, using Paste Preview, the new Backstage view, screen clipping, and inserting an equation into a worksheet. A new appendix covers cloud computing concepts and using Microsoft Office Web Apps. Examples and exercises are updated throughout.

- **Maps to SAM 2010.** This book is designed to work with SAM (Skills Assessment Manager) 2010. **SAM Assessment** contains performance-based, hands-on SAM exams for each unit of this book, and **SAM Training** provides hands-on training for skills covered in the book. (SAM sold separately.) See page xii for more information on SAM.

Each two-page spread focuses on a single skill.

Introduction briefly explains why the lesson skill is important.

A case scenario motivates the the steps and puts learning in context.

UNIT A
Excel 2010

Editing Cell Entries

You can change, or **edit**, the contents of an active cell at any time. To do so, double-click the cell, click in the formula bar, or just start typing. Excel switches to Edit mode when you are making cell entries. Different pointers, shown in Table A-3, guide you through the editing process. ▓▓▓▓ You noticed some errors in the worksheet and want to make corrections. The first error is in cell A11, which contains a misspelled name.

STEPS

1. **Click cell A11, then click to the right of P in the formula bar**
   As soon as you click in the formula bar, a blinking vertical line called the **insertion point** appears on the formula bar at the location where new text will be inserted. See Figure A-9. The mouse pointer changes to I when you point anywhere in the formula bar.

2. **Press [Delete], then click the Enter button ☑ on the formula bar**
   Clicking the Enter button accepts the edit, and the spelling of the employee's first name is corrected. You can also press [Enter] or [Tab] to accept an edit. Pressing [Enter] to accept an edit moves the cell pointer down one cell, and pressing [Tab] to accept an edit moves the cell pointer one cell to the right.

   > **QUICK TIP**
   > On some keyboards, you might need to press an [F Lock] key to enable the function keys.

3. **Click cell C12, then press [F2]**
   Excel switches to Edit mode, and the insertion point blinks in the cell. Pressing [F2] activates the cell for editing directly in the cell instead of the formula bar. Whether you edit in the cell or the formula bar is simply a matter of preference; the results in the worksheet are the same.

   > **QUICK TIP**
   > The Undo button allows you to reverse up to 100 previous actions, one at a time.

4. **Press [Backspace], type 8, then press [Enter]**
   The value in the cell changes from 35 to 38, and cell C13 becomes the active cell. Did you notice that the calculations in cells C21 and F12 also changed? That's because those cells contain formulas that include cell C12 in their calculations. If you make a mistake when editing, you can click the Cancel button ☒ on the formula bar *before* pressing [Enter] to confirm the cell entry. The Enter and Cancel buttons appear only when you're in Edit mode. If you notice the mistake *after* you have confirmed the cell entry, click the Undo button ↺ on the Quick Access toolbar.

   > **QUICK TIP**
   > You can use the keyboard to select all cell contents by clicking to the right of the cell contents in the cell or formula bar, pressing and holding [Shift], then pressing [Home].

5. **Click cell A15, then double-click the word Juan in the formula bar**
   Double-clicking a word in a cell selects it.

6. **Type Javier, then press [Enter]**
   When text is selected, typing deletes it and replaces it with the new text.

7. **Double-click cell D18, press [Delete], type 4, then click ☑**
   Double-clicking a cell activates it for editing directly in the cell. Compare your screen to Figure A-10.

8. **Save your work**
   Your changes to the workbook are saved.

Recovering unsaved changes to a workbook file

You can use Excel's AutoRecover feature to automatically save (Autosave) your work as often as you want. This means that if you suddenly lose power or if Excel closes unexpectedly while you're working, you can recover all or some of the changes you have made since you last saved it. (Of course, this is no substitute for regularly saving your work: this is just added insurance.) To customize the AutoRecover settings, click the File tab, click Options, then click Save. AutoRecover lets you decide how often and into which location it should Autosave files. When you restart Excel after losing power, a Document Recovery pane opens and provides access to the saved and Autosaved versions of the files that were open when Excel closed. You can also click the File tab, click Recent on the navigation bar, then click Recover Unsaved Workbooks to open Autosaved workbooks using the Open dialog box.

Excel 10   Getting Started with Excel 2010

Tips and troubleshooting advice, right where you need it—next to the step itself.

Clues to Use boxes provide useful information related to the lesson skill.

Large screen shots keep
students on track as
they complete steps

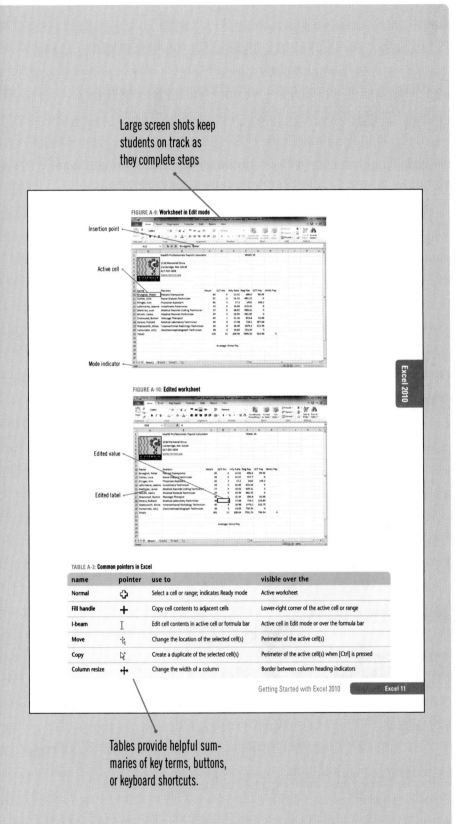

FIGURE A-9: Worksheet in Edit mode

Insertion point

Active cell

Mode indicator

FIGURE A-10: Edited worksheet

Edited value

Edited label

TABLE A-3: Common pointers in Excel

name	pointer	use to	visible over the
Normal		Select a cell or range; indicates Ready mode	Active worksheet
Fill handle	+	Copy cell contents to adjacent cells	Lower-right corner of the active cell or range
I-beam	I	Edit cell contents in active cell or formula bar	Active cell in Edit mode or over the formula bar
Move		Change the location of the selected cell(s)	Perimeter of the active cell(s)
Copy		Create a duplicate of the selected cell(s)	Perimeter of the active cell(s) when [Ctrl] is pressed
Column resize	+|+	Change the width of a column	Border between column heading indicators

Getting Started with Excel 2010

Tables provide helpful summaries of key terms, buttons,
or keyboard shortcuts.

Assignments

The lessons use Riverwalk Medical Clinic, a fictional outpatient medical facility, as the case study. The assignments on the light yellow pages at the end of each unit increase in difficulty. Assignments include:

- **Concepts Review** consist of multiple choice, matching, and screen identification questions.
- **Skills Reviews** are hands-on, step-by-step exercises that review the skills covered in each lesson in the unit.
- **Independent Challenges** are case projects requiring critical thinking and application of the unit skills. The Independent Challenges increase in difficulty, with the first one in each unit being the easiest. Independent Challenges 2 and 3 become increasingly open-ended, requiring more independent problem solving.
- **Real Life Independent Challenges** are practical exercises in which students create documents to help them with their every day lives.
- **Advanced Challenge Exercises** set within the Independent Challenges provide optional steps for more advanced students.
- **Visual Workshops** are practical, self-graded capstone projects that require independent problem solving.

xi

About SAM

SAM is the premier proficiency-based assessment and training environment for Microsoft Office. Web-based software along with an inviting user interface provide maximum teaching and learning flexibility. SAM builds students' skills and confidence with a variety of real-life simulations, and SAM Projects' assignments prepare students for today's workplace.

The SAM system includes Assessment and Training featuring page references and remediation for this book as well as Course Technology's Microsoft Office textbooks. With SAM, instructors can enjoy the flexibility of creating assignments based on content from their favorite Microsoft Office books or based on specific course objectives. Instructors appreciate the scheduling and reporting options that have made SAM the market-leading online testing and training software for over a decade. Over 2,000 performance-based questions and matching Training simulations, as well as tens of thousands of objective-based questions from many Course Technology texts, provide instructors with a variety of choices across multiple applications from the introductory level through the comprehensive level. The inclusion of hands-on Projects guarantee that student knowledge will skyrocket from the practice of solving real-world situations using Microsoft Office software.

SAM Assessment

- Content for these hands-on, performance-based tasks includes Word, Excel, Access, PowerPoint, Internet Explorer, Outlook, and Windows. Includes tens of thousands of objective-based questions from many Course Technology texts.

SAM Training

- Observe mode allows the student to watch and listen to a task as it is being completed.
- Practice mode allows the student to follow guided arrows and hear audio prompts to help visual learners know how to complete a task.
- Apply mode allows the student to prove what they've learned by completing a task using helpful instructions.

SAM Projects

- Live-in-the-application assignments in Word, Excel, Access and PowerPoint that help students be sure they know how to effectively communicate, solve a problem or make a decision. (*Note*:There are no SAM Projects that are based on the content in this book.)

Instructor Resources

The Instructor Resources CD is Course Technology's way of putting the resources and information needed to teach and learn effectively into your hands. With an integrated array of teaching and learning tools that offer you and your students a broad range of technology-based instructional options, we believe this CD represents the highest quality and most cutting edge resources available to instructors today. The resources available with this book are:

- **Instructor's Manual**—Available as an electronic file, the Instructor's Manual includes detailed lecture topics with teaching tips for each unit.

- **Sample Syllabus**—Prepare and customize your course easily using this sample course outline.

- **PowerPoint Presentations**—Each unit has a corresponding PowerPoint presentation that you can use in lecture, distribute to your students, or customize to suit your course.

- **Figure Files**—The figures in the text are provided on the Instructor Resources CD to help you illustrate key topics or concepts. You can create traditional overhead transparencies by printing the figure files. Or you can create electronic slide shows by using the figures in a presentation program such as PowerPoint.

- **Solutions to Exercises**—Solutions to Exercises contains every file students are asked to create or modify in the lessons and end-of-unit material. Also provided in this section, there is a document outlining the solutions for the end-of-unit Concepts Review, Skills Review, and Independent Challenges. An Annotated Solution File and Grading Rubric accompany each file and can be used together for quick and easy grading.

- **Data Files for Students**—To complete most of the units in this book, your students will need Data Files. You can post the Data Files on a file server for students to copy. The Data Files are available on the Instructor Resources CD-ROM, the Review Pack, and can also be downloaded from cengagebrain.com. For more information on how to download the Data Files, see the inside back cover.

Instruct students to use the Data Files List included on the Review Pack and the Instructor Resources CD. This list gives instructions on copying and organizing files.

- **ExamView**—ExamView is a powerful testing software package that allows you to create and administer printed, computer (LAN-based), and Internet exams. ExamView includes hundreds of questions that correspond to the topics covered in this text, enabling students to generate detailed study guides that include page references for further review. The computer-based and Internet testing components allow students to take exams at their computers, and also saves you time by grading each exam automatically.

Acknowledgements

Instructor Advisory Board

We thank our Instructor Advisory Board who gave us their opinions and guided our decisions as we updated our texts for Microsoft Office 2010. They are as follows:

Terri Helfand, Chaffey Community College

Barbara Comfort, J. Sargeant Reynolds Community College

Brenda Nielsen, Mesa Community College

Sharon Cotman, Thomas Nelson Community College

Marian Meyer, Central New Mexico Community College

Audrey Styer, Morton College

Richard Alexander, Heald College

Xiaodong Qiao, Heald College

Author Acknowledgements

Elizabeth Eisner Reding Creating a book of this magnitude is a team effort. I would like to thank my husband, Michael, as well as Christina Kling Garrett, the project manager, and my development editor, Karen Stevens, for her suggestions and corrections. I would also like to thank the production and editorial staff for all their hard work that made this project a reality.

Lynn Wermers Thanks to Karen Stevens for her insightful contributions, invaluable feedback, great humor, and patience. Thanks also to Christina Kling Garrett for her encouragement and support in guiding and managing this project.

Read This Before You Begin

Frequently Asked Questions

What are Data Files?

A Data File is a partially completed Excel workbook or another type of file that you use to complete the steps in the units and exercises to create the final document that you submit to your instructor. Each unit opener page lists the Data Files that you need for that unit.

Where are the Data Files?

Your instructor will provide the Data Files to you or direct you to a location on a network drive from which you can download them. For information on how to download the Data Files from cengagebrain.com, see the inside back cover.

What software was used to write and test this book?

This book was written and tested using a typical installation of Microsoft Office 2010 Professional Plus on a computer with a typical installation of Microsoft Windows 7 Ultimate.

The browser used for any Web-dependent steps is Internet Explorer 8.

Do I need to be connected to the Internet to complete the steps and exercises in this book?

Some of the exercises in this book require that your computer be connected to the Internet. If you are not connected to the Internet, see your instructor for information on how to complete the exercises.

What do I do if my screen is different from the figures shown in this book?

This book was written and tested on computers with monitors set at a resolution of 1024 × 768. If your screen shows more or less information than the figures in the book, your monitor is probably set at a higher or lower resolution. If you don't see something on your screen, you might have to scroll down or up to see the object identified in the figures.

The Ribbon—the blue area at the top of the screen—in Microsoft Office 2010 adapts to different resolutions. If your monitor is set at a lower resolution than 1024 × 768, you might not see all of the buttons shown in the figures. The groups of buttons will always appear, but the entire group might be condensed into a single button that you need to click to access the buttons described in the instructions.

COURSECASTS Learning on the Go. Always Available...Always Relevant.

Our fast-paced world is driven by technology. You know because you are an active participant—always on the go, always keeping up with technological trends, and always learning new ways to embrace technology to power your life. Let CourseCasts, hosted by Ken Baldauf of Florida State University, be your guide into weekly updates in this ever-changing space. These timely, relevant podcasts are produced weekly and are available for download at http://coursecasts.course.com or directly from iTunes (search by CourseCasts). CourseCasts are a perfect solution to getting students (and even instructors) to learn on the go!

Getting Started with Microsoft Office 2010

Microsoft Office 2010 is a group of software programs designed to help you create documents, collaborate with coworkers, and track and analyze information. Each program is designed so you can work quickly and efficiently to create professional-looking results. You use different Office programs to accomplish specific tasks, such as writing a letter or producing a sales presentation, yet all the programs have a similar look and feel. Once you become familiar with one program, you'll find it easy to transfer your knowledge to the others.  This unit introduces you to the most frequently used programs in Office, as well as common features they all share.

OBJECTIVES

Understand the Office 2010 suite

Start and exit an Office program

View the Office 2010 user interface

Create and save a file

Open a file and save it with a new name

View and print your work

Get Help and close a file

Understanding the Office 2010 Suite

Microsoft Office 2010 features an intuitive, context-sensitive user interface, so you can get up to speed faster and use advanced features with greater ease. The programs in Office are bundled together in a group called a **suite** (although you can also purchase them separately). The Office suite is available in several configurations, but all include Word, Excel, and PowerPoint. Other configurations include Access, Outlook, Publisher, and other programs. Each program in Office is best suited for completing specific types of tasks, though there is some overlap in capabilities.

DETAILS

The Office programs covered in this book include:

- **Microsoft Word 2010**

  When you need to create any kind of text-based document, such as a memo, newsletter, or multipage report, Word is the program to use. You can easily make your documents look great by inserting eye-catching graphics and using formatting tools such as themes, which are available in most Office programs. **Themes** are predesigned combinations of color and formatting attributes you can apply to a document. The Word document shown in Figure A-1 was formatted with the Solstice theme.

- **Microsoft Excel 2010**

  Excel is the perfect solution when you need to work with numeric values and make calculations. It puts the power of formulas, functions, charts, and other analytical tools into the hands of every user, so you can analyze sales projections, calculate loan payments, and present your findings in style. The Excel worksheet shown in Figure A-1 tracks personal expenses. Because Excel automatically recalculates results whenever a value changes, the information is always up to date. A chart illustrates how the monthly expenses are broken down.

- **Microsoft PowerPoint 2010**

  Using PowerPoint, it's easy to create powerful presentations complete with graphics, transitions, and even a soundtrack. Using professionally designed themes and clip art, you can quickly and easily create dynamic slide shows such as the one shown in Figure A-1.

- **Microsoft Access 2010**

  Access helps you keep track of large amounts of quantitative data, such as product inventories or employee records. The form shown in Figure A-1 was created for a grocery store inventory database. Employees use the form to enter data about each item. Using Access enables employees to quickly find specific information such as price and quantity without hunting through store shelves and stockrooms.

Microsoft Office has benefits beyond the power of each program, including:

- **Common user interface: Improving business processes**

  Because the Office suite programs have a similar **interface**, or look and feel, your experience using one program's tools makes it easy to learn those in the other programs. In addition, Office documents are **compatible** with one another, meaning that you can easily incorporate, or **integrate**, an Excel chart into a PowerPoint slide, or an Access table into a Word document.

- **Collaboration: Simplifying how people work together**

  Office recognizes the way people do business today, and supports the emphasis on communication and knowledge sharing within companies and across the globe. All Office programs include the capability to incorporate feedback—called **online collaboration**—across the Internet or a company network.

FIGURE A-1: Microsoft Office 2010 documents

Newsletter created in Word

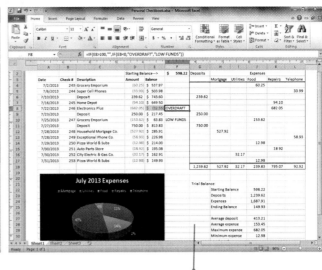

Checkbook register created in Excel

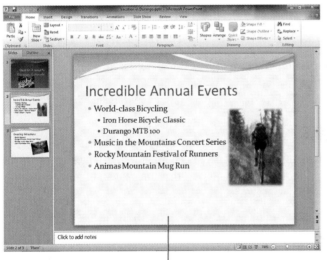

Tourism presentation created in PowerPoint

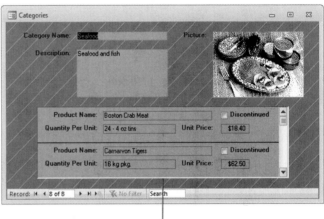

Store inventory form created in Access

Deciding which program to use

Every Office program includes tools that go far beyond what you might expect. For example, although Excel is primarily designed for making calculations, you can use it to create a database. So when you're planning a project, how do you decide which Office program to use? The general rule of thumb is to use the program best suited for your intended task, and make use of supporting tools in the program if you need them. Word is best for creating text-based documents, Excel is best for making mathematical calculations, PowerPoint is best for preparing presentations, and Access is best for managing quantitative data. Although the capabilities of Office are so vast that you *could* create an inventory in Excel or a budget in Word, you'll find greater flexibility and efficiency by using the program designed for the task. And remember, you can always create a file in one program, and then insert it in a document in another program when you need to, such as including sales projections (Excel) in a memo (Word).

Starting and Exiting an Office Program

The first step in using an Office program is to open, or **launch**, it on your computer. The easiest ways to launch a program are to click the Start button on the Windows taskbar or to double-click an icon on your desktop. You can have multiple programs open on your computer simultaneously, and you can move between open programs by clicking the desired program or document button on the taskbar or by using the [Alt][Tab] keyboard shortcut combination. When working, you'll often want to open multiple programs in Office and switch among them as you work. Begin by launching a few Office programs now.

STEPS

QUICK TIP
You can also launch a program by double-clicking a desktop icon or clicking the program name on the Start menu.

1. **Click the Start button 🌐 on the taskbar**

   The Start menu opens. If the taskbar is hidden, you can display it by pointing to the bottom of the screen. Depending on your taskbar property settings, the taskbar may be displayed at all times, or only when you point to that area of the screen. For more information, or to change your taskbar properties, consult your instructor or technical support person.

2. **Click All Programs, scroll down if necessary in the All Programs menu, click Microsoft Office as shown in Figure A-2, then click Microsoft Word 2010**

   Word 2010 starts, and the program window opens on your screen.

QUICK TIP
It is not necessary to close one program before opening another.

3. **Click 🌐 on the taskbar, click All Programs, click Microsoft Office, then click Microsoft Excel 2010**

   Excel 2010 starts, and the program window opens, as shown in Figure A-3. Word is no longer visible, but it remains open. The taskbar displays a button for each open program and document. Because this Excel document is **active**, or in front and available, the Excel button on the taskbar appears slightly lighter.

QUICK TIP
As you work in Windows, your computer adapts to your activities. You may notice that after clicking the Start button, the name of the program you want to open appears in the Start menu above All Programs; if so, you can click it to start the program.

4. **Point to the Word program button �W on the taskbar, then click �W**

   The Word program window is now in front. When the Aero feature is turned on in Windows 7, pointing to a program button on the taskbar displays a thumbnail version of each open window in that program above the program button. Clicking a program button on the taskbar activates that program and the most recently active document. Clicking a thumbnail of a document activates that document.

5. **Click 🌐 on the taskbar, click All Programs, click Microsoft Office, then click Microsoft PowerPoint 2010**

   PowerPoint 2010 starts and becomes the active program.

6. **Click the Excel program button 📊 on the taskbar**

   Excel is now the active program.

TROUBLE
If you don't have Access installed on your computer, proceed to the next lesson.

7. **Click 🌐 on the taskbar, click All Programs, click Microsoft Office, then click Microsoft Access 2010**

   Access 2010 starts and becomes the active program. Now all four Office programs are open at the same time.

8. **Click Exit on the navigation bar in the Access program window, as shown in Figure A-4**

   Access closes, leaving Excel active and Word and PowerPoint open.

Using shortcut keys to move between Office programs

As an alternative to the Windows taskbar, you can use a keyboard shortcut to move among open Office programs. The [Alt][Tab] keyboard combination lets you either switch quickly to the next open program or file or choose one from a gallery. To switch immediately to the next open program or file, press [Alt][Tab]. To choose from all open programs and files, press and hold [Alt], then press and release [Tab] without releasing [Alt]. A gallery opens on screen, displaying the filename and a thumbnail image of each open program and file, as well as of the desktop. Each time you press [Tab] while holding [Alt], the selection cycles to the next open file or location. Release [Alt] when the program, file, or location you want to activate is selected.

FIGURE A-2: **Start menu**

All programs
menu (yours
will look
different)

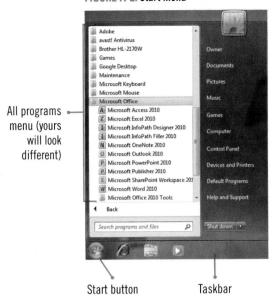

Start button   Taskbar

FIGURE A-3: **Excel program window and Windows taskbar**

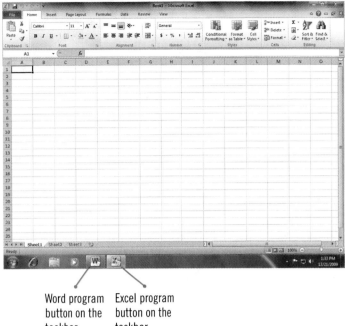

Word program   Excel program
button on the   button on the
taskbar   taskbar

FIGURE A-4: **Access program window**

File tab

Navigation bar

Exit command

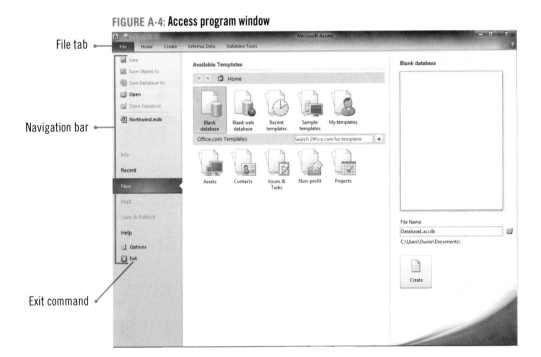

Windows Live and Microsoft Office Web Apps

All Office programs include the capability to incorporate feedback—called online collaboration—across the Internet or a company network. Using **cloud computing** (work done in a virtual environment), you can take advantage of Web programs called Microsoft Office Web Apps, which are simplified versions of the programs found in the Microsoft Office 2010 suite. Because these programs are online, they take up no computer disk space and are accessed using

Windows Live SkyDrive, a free service from Microsoft. Using Windows Live SkyDrive, you and your colleagues can create and store documents in a "cloud" and make the documents available to whomever you grant access. To use Windows Live SkyDrive, you need a free Windows Live ID, which you obtain at the Windows Live Web site. You can find more information in the "Working with Windows Live and Office Web Apps" appendix.

Viewing the Office 2010 User Interface

One of the benefits of using Office is that the programs have much in common, making them easy to learn and making it simple to move from one to another. Individual Office programs have always shared many features, but the innovations in the Office 2010 user interface mean even greater similarity among them all. That means you can also use your knowledge of one program to get up to speed in another. A **user interface** is a collective term for all the ways you interact with a software program. The user interface in Office 2010 provides intuitive ways to choose commands, work with files, and navigate in the program window. Familiarize yourself with some of the common interface elements in Office by examining the PowerPoint program window.

STEPS

1. **Click the PowerPoint program button 🅿 on the taskbar**

   PowerPoint becomes the active program. Refer to Figure A-5 to identify common elements of the Office user interface. The **document window** occupies most of the screen. In PowerPoint, a blank slide appears in the document window, so you can build your slide show. At the top of every Office program window is a **title bar** that displays the document name and program name. Below the title bar is the **Ribbon**, which displays commands you're likely to need for the current task. Commands are organized onto **tabs**. The tab names appear at the top of the Ribbon, and the active tab appears in front. The Ribbon in every Office program includes tabs specific to the program, but all Office programs include a File tab and Home tab on the left end of the Ribbon.

2. **Click the File tab**

   The File tab opens, displaying **Backstage view**. The navigation bar on the left side of Backstage view contains commands to perform actions common to most Office programs, such as opening a file, saving a file, and closing the current program. Just above the File tab is the **Quick Access toolbar**, which also includes buttons for common Office commands.

3. **Click the File tab again to close Backstage view and return to the document window, then click the Design tab on the Ribbon**

   To display a different tab, you click the tab on the Ribbon. Each tab contains related commands arranged into **groups** to make features easy to find. On the Design tab, the Themes group displays available design themes in a **gallery**, or visual collection of choices you can browse. Many groups contain a **dialog box launcher**, an icon you can click to open a dialog box or task pane from which to choose related commands.

4. **Move the mouse pointer ⌖ over the Angles theme in the Themes group as shown in Figure A-6, but do not click the mouse button**

   The Angles theme is temporarily applied to the slide in the document window. However, because you did not click the theme, you did not permanently change the slide. With the **Live Preview** feature, you can point to a choice, see the results right in the document, and then decide if you want to make the change.

5. **Move ⌖ away from the Ribbon and towards the slide**

   If you had clicked the Angles theme, it would be applied to this slide. Instead, the slide remains unchanged.

6. **Point to the Zoom slider ▽ on the status bar, then drag ▽ to the right until the Zoom level reads 166%**

   The slide display is enlarged. Zoom tools are located on the status bar. You can drag the slider or click the Zoom In or Zoom Out buttons to zoom in or out on an area of interest. **Zooming in**, or choosing a higher percentage, makes a document appear bigger on screen, but less of it fits on the screen at once; **zooming out**, or choosing a lower percentage, lets you see more of the document but at a reduced size.

7. **Drag ▽ on the status bar to the left until the Zoom level reads 73%**

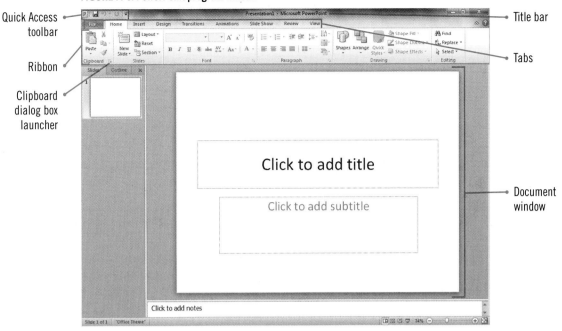

FIGURE A-5: **PowerPoint program window**

Quick Access toolbar
Ribbon
Clipboard dialog box launcher

Title bar
Tabs
Document window

Click to add title

Click to add subtitle

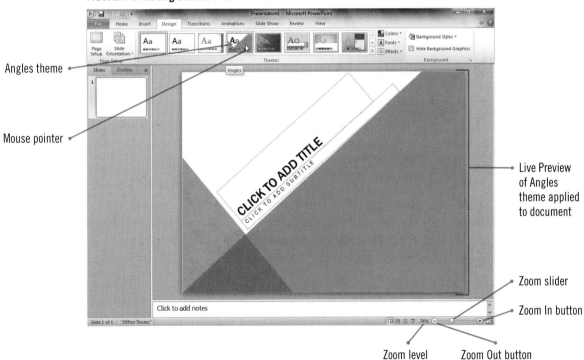

FIGURE A-6: **Viewing a theme with Live Preview**

Angles theme
Mouse pointer

Live Preview of Angles theme applied to document

Zoom slider
Zoom In button
Zoom level
Zoom Out button

Using Backstage view

Backstage view in each Microsoft Office program offers "one stop shopping" for many commonly performed tasks, such as opening and saving a file, printing and previewing a document, defining document properties, sharing information, and exiting a program.

Backstage view opens when you click the File tab in any Office program, and while features such as the Ribbon, Mini toolbar, and Live Preview all help you work *in* your documents, the File tab and Backstage view help you work *with* your documents.

Creating and Saving a File

When working in a program, one of the first things you need to do is to create and save a file. A **file** is a stored collection of data. Saving a file enables you to work on a project now, then put it away and work on it again later. In some Office programs, including Word, Excel, and PowerPoint, a new file is automatically created when you start the program, so all you have to do is enter some data and save it. In Access, you must expressly create a file before you enter any data. You should give your files meaningful names and save them in an appropriate location so that they're easy to find. Use Word to familiarize yourself with the process of creating and saving a document. First you'll type some notes about a possible location for a corporate meeting, then you'll save the information for later use.

STEPS

1. **Click the Word program button 🆆 on the taskbar**

2. **Type Locations for Corporate Meeting, then press [Enter] twice**
   The text appears in the document window, and the **insertion point** blinks on a new blank line. The insertion point indicates where the next typed text will appear.

3. **Type Las Vegas, NV, press [Enter], type Orlando, FL, press [Enter], type Boston, MA, press [Enter] twice, then type your name**
   Compare your document to Figure A-7.

> **QUICK TIP**
> A filename can be up to 255 characters, including a file extension, and can include upper- or lowercase characters and spaces, but not ?, ", /, \, <, >, *, |, or :.

4. **Click the Save button 💾 on the Quick Access toolbar**
   Because this is the first time you are saving this document, the Save As dialog box opens, as shown in Figure A-8. The Save As dialog box includes options for assigning a filename and storage location. Once you save a file for the first time, clicking 💾 saves any changes to the file *without* opening the Save As dialog box, because no additional information is needed. The Address bar in the Save As dialog box displays the default location for saving the file, but you can change it to any location. The File name field contains a suggested name for the document based on text in the file, but you can enter a different name.

5. **Type OF A-Potential Corporate Meeting Locations**
   The text you type replaces the highlighted text. (The "OF A-" in the filename indicates that the file is created in Office Unit A. You will see similar designations throughout this book when files are named. For example, a file named in Excel Unit B would begin with "EX B-" .)

> **QUICK TIP**
> Saving a file to the Desktop creates a desktop icon that you can double-click to both launch a program and open a document.

6. **In the Save As dialog box, use the Address bar or Navigation Pane to navigate to the drive and folder where you store your Data Files**
   Many students store files on a flash drive, but you can also store files on your computer, a network drive, or any storage device indicated by your instructor or technical support person.

> **QUICK TIP**
> To create a new blank file when a file is open, click the File tab, click New on the navigation bar, then click Create near the bottom of the document preview pane.

7. **Click Save**
   The Save As dialog box closes, the new file is saved to the location you specified, then the name of the document appears in the title bar, as shown in Figure A-9. (You may or may not see the file extension ".docx" after the filename.) See Table A-1 for a description of the different types of files you create in Office, and the file extensions associated with each.

TABLE A-1: Common filenames and default file extensions

file created in	is called a	and has the default extension
Word	document	.docx
Excel	workbook	.xlsx
PowerPoint	presentation	.pptx
Access	database	.accdb

Getting Started with Microsoft Office 2010

FIGURE A-7: Document created in Word

Save button

Your name should appear here

Insertion point

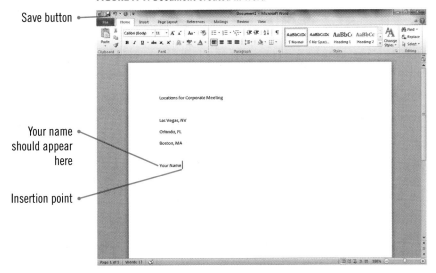

FIGURE A-8: Save As dialog box

Address bar

Navigation Pane; your links and folders may differ

File name field; your computer may not display file extensions

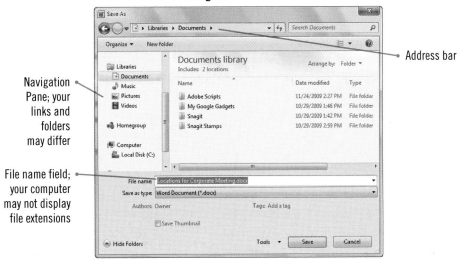

FIGURE A-9: Saved and named Word document

Filename appears in title bar

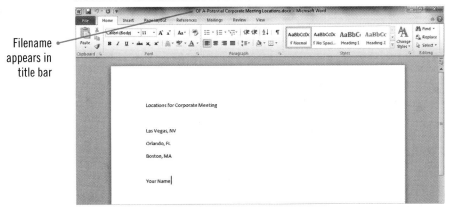

Using the Office Clipboard

You can use the Office Clipboard to cut and copy items from one Office program and paste them into others. The Office Clipboard can store a maximum of 24 items. To access it, open the Office Clipboard task pane by clicking the dialog box launcher 🔲 in the Clipboard group on the Home tab. Each time you copy a selection, it is saved in the Office Clipboard. Each entry in the Office Clipboard includes an icon that tells you the program it was created in. To paste an entry, click in the document where you want it to appear, then click the item in the Office Clipboard. To delete an item from the Office Clipboard, right-click the item, then click Delete.

Opening a File and Saving It with a New Name

In many cases as you work in Office, you start with a blank document, but often you need to use an existing file. It might be a file you or a coworker created earlier as a work in progress, or it could be a complete document that you want to use as the basis for another. For example, you might want to create a budget for this year using the budget you created last year; you could type in all the categories and information from scratch, or you could open last year's budget, save it with a new name, and just make changes to update it for the current year. By opening the existing file and saving it with the Save As command, you create a duplicate that you can modify to your heart's content, while the original file remains intact. Use Excel to open an existing workbook file, and save it with a new name so the original remains unchanged.

STEPS

QUICK TIP

Click Recent on the navigation bar to display a list of recent workbooks; click a file in the list to open it.

1. **Click the Excel program button on the taskbar, click the File tab, then click Open on the navigation bar**

   The Open dialog box opens, where you can navigate to any drive or folder accessible to your computer to locate a file.

2. **In the Open dialog box, navigate to the drive and folder where you store your Data Files**

   The files available in the current folder are listed, as shown in Figure A-10. This folder contains one file.

TROUBLE

Click Enable Editing on the Protected View bar near the top of your document window if prompted.

3. **Click OFFICE A-1.xlsx, then click Open**

   The dialog box closes, and the file opens in Excel. An Excel file is an electronic spreadsheet, so it looks different from a Word document or a PowerPoint slide.

4. **Click the File tab, then click Save As on the navigation bar**

   The Save As dialog box opens, and the current filename is highlighted in the File name text box. Using the Save As command enables you to create a copy of the current, existing file with a new name. This action preserves the original file and creates a new file that you can modify.

QUICK TIP

The Save As command works identically in all Office programs, except Access; in Access, this command lets you save a copy of the current database object, such as a table or form, with a new name, but not a copy of the entire database.

5. **Navigate to the drive and folder where you store your Data Files if necessary, type OF A-Budget for Corporate Meeting in the File name text box, as shown in Figure A-11, then click Save**

   A copy of the existing workbook is created with the new name. The original file, Office A-1.xlsx, closes automatically.

6. **Click cell A19, type your name, then press [Enter], as shown in Figure A-12**

   In Excel, you enter data in cells, which are formed by the intersection of a row and a column. Cell A19 is at the intersection of column A and row 19. When you press [Enter], the cell pointer moves to cell A20.

7. **Click the Save button on the Quick Access toolbar**

   Your name appears in the workbook, and your changes to the file are saved.

Working in Compatibility Mode

Not everyone upgrades to the newest version of Office. As a general rule, new software versions are **backward compatible**, meaning that documents saved by an older version can be read by newer software. To open documents created in older Office versions, Office 2010 includes a feature called Compatibility Mode. When you use Office 2010 to open a file created in an earlier version of Office, "Compatibility Mode" appears in the title bar, letting you know the file was created in an earlier but usable version of the program. If you are working with someone who may not be using the newest version of the software, you can avoid possible incompatibility problems by saving your file in another, earlier format. To do this in an Office program, click the File tab, click Save As on the navigation bar, click the Save as type list arrow in the Save As dialog box, then click an option on the list. For example, if you're working in Excel, click Excel 97-2003 Workbook format in the Save as type list to save an Excel file so that it can be opened in Excel 97 or Excel 2003.

FIGURE A-10: Open dialog box

Available files in this folder

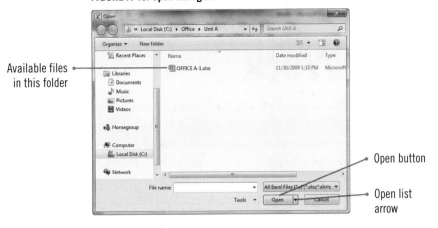

Open button

Open list arrow

FIGURE A-11: Save As dialog box

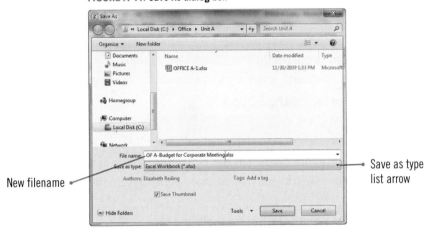

New filename

Save as type list arrow

FIGURE A-12: Your name added to the workbook

Address for cell A19 formed by column A and row 19

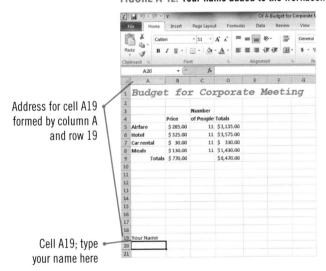

Cell A19; type your name here

Exploring File Open options

You might have noticed that the Open button on the Open dialog box includes an arrow. In a dialog box, if a button includes an arrow you can click the button to invoke the command, or you can click the arrow to choose from a list of related commands. The Open list arrow includes several related commands, including Open Read-Only and Open as Copy. Clicking Open Read-Only opens a file that you can only save with a new name; you cannot save changes to the original file. Clicking Open as Copy creates a copy of the file already saved and named with the word "Copy" in the title. Like the Save As command, these commands provide additional ways to use copies of existing files while ensuring that original files do not get changed by mistake.

Viewing and Printing Your Work

Each Microsoft Office program lets you switch among various **views** of the document window to show more or fewer details or a different combination of elements that make it easier to complete certain tasks, such as formatting or reading text. Changing your view of a document does not affect the file in any way, it affects only the way it looks on screen. If your computer is connected to a printer or a print server, you can easily print any Office document using the Print button on the Print tab in Backstage view. Printing can be as simple as **previewing** the document to see exactly what a document will look like when it is printed and then clicking the Print button. Or, you can customize the print job by printing only selected pages or making other choices. Experiment with changing your view of a Word document, and then preview and print your work.

STEPS

1. **Click the Word program button [W] on the taskbar**

   Word becomes the active program, and the document fills the screen.

2. **Click the View tab on the Ribbon**

   In most Office programs, the View tab on the Ribbon includes groups and commands for changing your view of the current document. You can also change views using the View buttons on the status bar.

3. **Click the Web Layout button in the Document Views group on the View tab**

   The view changes to Web Layout view, as shown in Figure A-13. This view shows how the document will look if you save it as a Web page.

4. **Click the Print Layout button on the View tab**

   You return to Print Layout view, the default view in Word.

5. **Click the File tab, then click Print on the navigation bar**

   The Print tab opens in Backstage view. The preview pane on the right side of the window automatically displays a preview of how your document will look when printed, showing the entire page on screen at once. Compare your screen to Figure A-14. Options in the Settings section enable you to change settings such as margins, orientation, and paper size before printing. To change a setting, click it, and then click the new setting you want. For instance, to change from Letter paper size to Legal, click Letter in the Settings section, then click Legal on the menu that opens. The document preview is updated as you change the settings. You also can use the Settings section to change which pages to print and even the number of pages you print on each sheet of printed paper. If you have multiple printers from which to choose, you can change from one installed printer to another by clicking the current printer in the Printer section, then clicking the name of the installed printer you want to use. The Print section contains the Print button and also enables you to select the number of copies of the document to print.

6. **Click the Print button in the Print section**

   A copy of the document prints, and Backstage view closes.

> **QUICK TIP**
> You can add the Quick Print button [printer icon] to the Quick Access toolbar by clicking the Customize Quick Access Toolbar button, then clicking Quick Print. The Quick Print button prints one copy of your document using the default settings.

Customizing the Quick Access toolbar

You can customize the Quick Access toolbar to display your favorite commands. To do so, click the Customize Quick Access Toolbar button [▾] in the title bar, then click the command you want to add. If you don't see the command in the list, click More Commands to open the Quick Access Toolbar tab of the current program's Options dialog box. In the Options dialog box, use the Choose commands from list to choose a category, click the desired command in the list on the left, click Add to add it to the Quick Access toolbar, then click OK. To remove a button from the toolbar, click the name in the list on the right in the Options dialog box, then click Remove. To add a command to the Quick Access toolbar on the fly, simply right-click the button on the Ribbon, then click Add to Quick Access Toolbar on the shortcut menu. To move the Quick Access toolbar below the Ribbon, click the Customize Quick Access Toolbar button, and then click Show Below the Ribbon.

FIGURE A-13: Web Layout view

Web Layout button

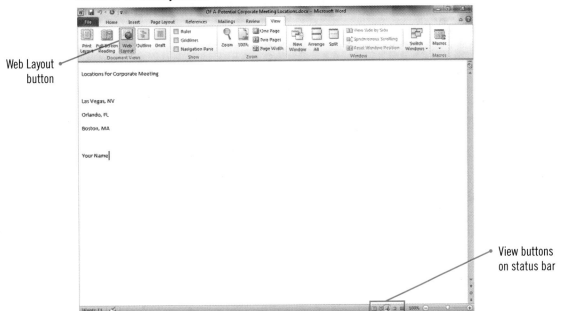

View buttons on status bar

FIGURE A-14: Print tab in Backstage view

Print button

Click to select a different installed printer

Settings section

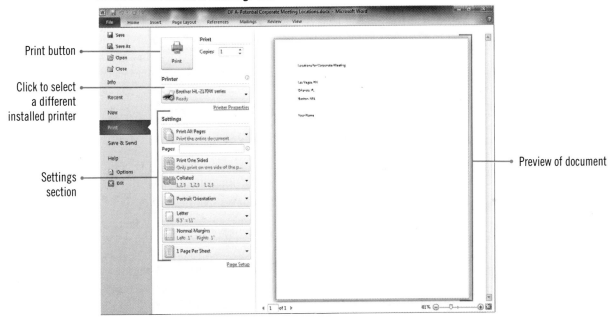

Preview of document

Creating a screen capture

A **screen capture** is a digital image of your screen, as if you took a picture of it with a camera. For instance, you might want to take a screen capture if an error message occurs and you want Technical Support to see exactly what's on the screen. You can create a screen capture using features found in Windows 7 or Office 2010. Windows 7 comes with the Snipping Tool, a separate program designed to capture whole screens or portions of screens. To open the Snipping Tool, click it on the Start menu or click All Programs, click Accessories, then click Snipping Tool. After opening the Snipping Tool, drag the pointer on the screen to select the area of the screen you want to capture. When you release the mouse button, the screen capture opens in the Snipping Tool window, and

you can save, copy, or send it in an e-mail. In Word, Excel, and PowerPoint 2010, you can capture screens or portions of screens and insert them in the current document using the Screenshot button on the Insert tab. And finally, you can create a screen capture by pressing [PrtScn]. (Keyboards differ, but you may find the [PrtScn] button in or near your keyboard's function keys.) Pressing this key places a digital image of your screen in the Windows temporary storage area known as the **Clipboard**. Open the document where you want the screen capture to appear, click the Home tab on the Ribbon (if necessary), then click the Paste button on the Home tab. The screen capture is pasted into the document.

Getting Help and Closing a File

You can get comprehensive help at any time by pressing [F1] in an Office program. You can also get help in the form of a ScreenTip by pointing to almost any icon in the program window. When you're finished working in an Office document, you have a few choices regarding ending your work session. You can close a file or exit a program by using the File tab or by clicking a button on the title bar. Closing a file leaves a program running, while exiting a program closes all the open files in that program as well as the program itself. In all cases, Office reminds you if you try to close a file or exit a program and your document contains unsaved changes. ▰▰▰▰ Explore the Help system in Microsoft Office, and then close your documents and exit any open programs.

STEPS

TROUBLE

If the Table of Contents pane doesn't appear on the left in the Help window, click the Show Table of Contents button ◈ on the Help toolbar to show it.

1. **Point to the Zoom button on the View tab of the Ribbon**

   A ScreenTip appears that describes how the Zoom button works and explains where to find other zoom controls.

2. **Press [F1]**

   The Word Help window opens, as shown in Figure A-15, displaying the home page for help in Word on the right and the Table of Contents pane on the left. In both panes of the Help window, each entry is a hyperlink you can click to open a list of related topics. The Help window also includes a toolbar of useful Help commands and a Search field. The connection status at the bottom of the Help window indicates that the connection to Office.com is active. Office.com supplements the help content available on your computer with a wide variety of up-to-date topics, templates, and training. If you are not connected to the Internet, the Help window displays only the help content available on your computer.

QUICK TIP

You can also open the Help window by clicking the Microsoft Office Word Help button ❓ to the right of the tabs on the Ribbon.

3. **Click the Creating documents link in the Table of Contents pane**

   The icon next to Creating documents changes, and a list of subtopics expands beneath the topic.

4. **Click the Create a document link in the subtopics list in the Table of Contents pane**

   The topic opens in the right pane of the Help window, as shown in Figure A-16.

QUICK TIP

You can print the entire current topic by clicking the Print button 🖨 on the Help toolbar, then clicking Print in the Print dialog box.

5. **Click Delete a document under "What do you want to do?" in the right pane**

   The link leads to information about deleting a document.

6. **Click the Accessibility link in the Table of Contents pane, click the Accessibility features in Word link, read the information in the right pane, then click the Help window Close button ╳**

7. **Click the File tab, then click Close on the navigation bar; if a dialog box opens asking whether you want to save your changes, click Save**

   The Potential Corporate Meeting Locations document closes, leaving the Word program open.

8. **Click the File tab, then click Exit on the navigation bar**

   Word closes, and the Excel program window is active.

9. **Click the File tab, click Exit on the navigation bar to exit Excel, click the PowerPoint program button 🄿 on the taskbar if necessary, click the File tab, then click Exit on the navigation bar to exit PowerPoint**

   Excel and PowerPoint both close.

FIGURE A-15: Word Help window

Help toolbar

Search field

The colors of
your links may
differ if the
links have
been visited
previously

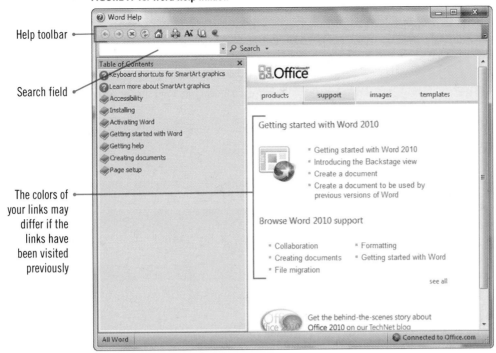

FIGURE A-16: Create a document Help topic

Print button

Icon indicates
expanded topic

Create a
document link

Create a
document
topic

Click to read
how to perform
the action
described

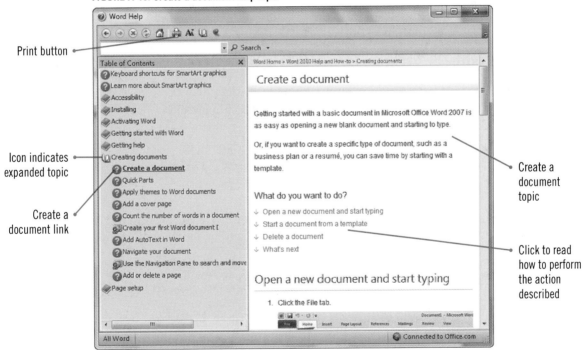

Recovering a document

Each Office program has a built-in recovery feature that allows you to open and save files that were open at the time of an interruption such as a power failure. When you restart the program(s) after an interruption, the Document Recovery task pane opens on the left side of your screen displaying both original and recovered versions of the files that were open. If you're not sure which file to open (original or recovered), it's usually better to open the recovered file because it will contain the latest information. You can, however, open and review all versions of the file that were recovered and save the best one. Each file listed in the Document Recovery task pane displays a list arrow with options that allow you to open the file, save it as is, delete it, or show repairs made to it during recovery.

Practice

Concepts Review

For current SAM information, including versions and content details, visit SAM Central (http://www.cengage.com/samcentral). If you have a SAM user profile, you may have access to hands-on instruction, practice, and assessment of the skills covered in this unit. Since various versions of SAM are supported throughout the life of this text, check with your instructor for the correct instructions and URL/Web site for accessing assignments.

Label the elements of the program window shown in Figure A-17.

FIGURE A-17

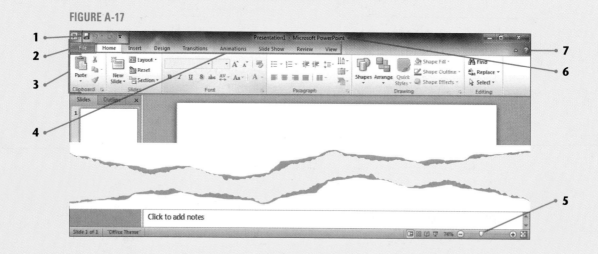

Match each project with the program for which it is best suited.

8. Microsoft Access	a. Corporate convention budget with expense projections
9. Microsoft Excel	b. Business cover letter for a job application
10. Microsoft Word	c. Department store inventory
11. Microsoft PowerPoint	d. Presentation for city council meeting

Independent Challenge 1

You just accepted an administrative position with a local independently owned produce vendor that has recently invested in computers and is now considering purchasing Microsoft Office for the company. You are asked to propose ways Office might help the business. You produce your document in Word.

a. Start Word, then save the document as **OF A-Microsoft Office Document** in the drive and folder where you store your Data Files.

b. Type **Microsoft Word**, press [Enter] twice, type **Microsoft Excel**, press [Enter] twice, type **Microsoft PowerPoint**, press [Enter] twice, type **Microsoft Access**, press [Enter] twice, then type your name.

c. Click the line beneath each program name, type at least two tasks suited to that program (each separated by a comma), then press [Enter].

Advanced Challenge Exercise

- Press the [PrtScn] button to create a screen capture.
- Click after your name, press [Enter] to move to a blank line below your name, then click the Paste button in the Clipboard group on the Home tab.

d. Save the document, then submit your work to your instructor as directed.

e. Exit Word.

Getting Started with Excel 2010

Files You Will Need:

EMP A-1.xlsx

EMP A-2.xlsx

EMP A-3.xlsx

EMP A-4.xlsx

EMP A-5.xlsx

In this unit, you will learn how spreadsheet software helps you analyze data and make business decisions, even if you aren't a math pro. You'll become familiar with the different elements of a spreadsheet and learn your way around the Excel program window. You will also work in an Excel worksheet and make simple calculations.  You have been hired as an assistant at Riverwalk Medical Clinic (RMC), a large outpatient medical facility staffed by family physicians, specialists, nurses, and other allied health professionals. You report to Tony Sanchez, R.N., the office manager. As Tony's assistant, you create worksheets to analyze data from various departments so you can help him make sound decisions on company expansion and investments, as well as day-to-day operations.

OBJECTIVES

Understand spreadsheet software

Tour the Excel 2010 window

Understand formulas

Enter labels and values and use the Sum button

Edit cell entries

Enter and edit a simple formula

Switch worksheet views

Choose print options

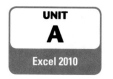
Understanding Spreadsheet Software

Microsoft Excel is the electronic spreadsheet program within the Microsoft Office suite. An **electronic spreadsheet** is an application you use to perform numeric calculations and to analyze and present numeric data. One advantage of spreadsheet programs over pencil and paper is that your calculations are updated automatically, so you can change entries without having to manually recalculate. Table A-1 shows some of the common business tasks people accomplish using Excel. In Excel, the electronic spreadsheet in which you work is called a **worksheet**, and it is contained in a file called a **workbook**, which has the file extension .xlsx. At Riverwalk Medical Clinic, you use Excel extensively to track finances and manage corporate data.

DETAILS

When you use Excel, you have the ability to:

- **Enter data quickly and accurately**

  With Excel, you can enter information faster and more accurately than with pencil and paper. Figure A-1 shows a payroll worksheet created using pencil and paper. Figure A-2 shows the same worksheet created using Excel. Equations were added to calculate the hours and pay. You can use Excel to recreate this information for each week by copying the worksheet's structure and the information that doesn't change from week to week, then entering unique data and formulas for each week. You can also quickly create charts and other elements to help visualize how the payroll is distributed.

- **Recalculate data easily**

  Fixing typing errors or updating data is easy in Excel. In the payroll example, if you receive updated hours for an employee, you just enter the new hours and Excel recalculates the pay.

- **Perform what-if analysis**

  The ability to change data and quickly view the recalculated results gives you the power to make informed business decisions. For instance, if you're considering raising the hourly rate for a medical records technician from $16.95 to $18.00, you can enter the new value in the worksheet and immediately see the impact on the overall payroll as well as on the individual employee. Any time you use a worksheet to ask the question "What if?" you are performing **what-if analysis**. Excel also includes a Scenario Manager where you can name and save different what-if versions of your worksheet.

- **Change the appearance of information**

  Excel provides powerful features for making information visually appealing and easier to understand. You can format text and numbers in different fonts, colors, and styles to make it stand out.

- **Create charts**

  Excel makes it easy to create charts based on worksheet information. Charts are updated automatically in Excel whenever data changes. The worksheet in Figure A-2 includes a 3-D pie chart.

- **Share information**

  It's easy for everyone at RMC to collaborate in Excel using the company intranet, the Internet, or a network storage device. For example, you can complete the weekly payroll that your boss, Tony Sanchez, began to create. You can also take advantage of collaboration tools, such as shared workbooks, so that multiple people can edit a workbook simultaneously.

- **Build on previous work**

  Instead of creating a new worksheet for every project, it's easy to modify an existing Excel worksheet. When you are ready to create next week's payroll, you can open the file for last week's payroll, save it with a new filename, and modify the information as necessary. You can also use predesigned, formatted files called **templates** to create new worksheets quickly. Excel comes with many templates that you can customize.

FIGURE A-1: Traditional paper worksheet

Riverwalk Medical Clinic
Health Professionals Payroll Calculator

Name	Position	Hours	O/T Hours	Hrly Rate	Reg Pay	O/T Pay	Gross Pay
Brueghel, Pieter	Patient Transporter	40	4	12.42	423.60	84.72	596.16
Cortez, Livia	Renal Dialysis Technician	35	0	14.15	495.25	-	495.25
Klinger, Kim	Physician Assistant	40	2	37.30	1,492.00	149.20	1,641.20
Lafontaine, Jeanne	Anesthesia Technician	29	0	14.46	419.34	-	419.34
Martinez, Juan	Medical Records Coding Technician	37	0	18.63	689.31	-	689.31
Mioshi, Keiko	Medical Records Technician	39	0	16.95	661.05	-	661.05
Sherwood, Burton	Massage Therapist	40	1	21.34	853.60	42.68	853.60
Strano, Richard	Medical Laboratory Technician	40	8	17.98	719.20	287.68	1,006.88
Wadsworth, Alicia	Interventional Radiology Technician	40	5	26.98	1,079.20	269.80	1,349.00
Yamamoto, Johji	Electroencephalograph Technician	38	0	19.83	753.54	-	753.54

FIGURE A-2: Excel worksheet

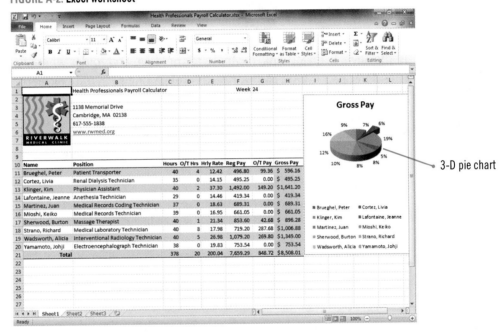

3-D pie chart

TABLE A-1: Business tasks you can accomplish using Excel

you can use spreadsheets to:	by:
Perform calculations	Adding formulas and functions to worksheet data; for example, adding a list of sales results or calculating a car payment
Represent values graphically	Creating charts based on worksheet data; for example, creating a chart that displays expenses
Generate reports	Creating workbooks that combine information from multiple worksheets, such as summarized sales information from multiple stores
Organize data	Sorting data in ascending or descending order; for example, alphabetizing a list of products or customer names, or prioritizing orders by date
Analyze data	Creating data summaries and short lists using PivotTables or AutoFilters; for example, making a list of the top 10 customers based on spending habits
Create what-if data scenarios	Using variable values to investigate and sample different outcomes; for example, changing the interest rate or payment schedule on a loan

Touring the Excel 2010 Window

To start Excel, Microsoft Windows must be running. Similar to starting any program in Office, you can use the Start button on the Windows taskbar, or you may have a shortcut on your desktop you prefer to use. If you need additional assistance, ask your instructor or technical support person. ▰▰▰ You decide to start Excel and familiarize yourself with the worksheet window.

STEPS

QUICK TIP

For more information on starting a program or opening and saving a file, see the unit "Getting Started with Microsoft Office 2010."

TROUBLE

If you don't see the extension .xlsx on the filenames in the Save As dialog box, don't worry; Windows can be set up to display or not to display the file extensions.

1. **Start Excel, click the File tab, then click Open on the navigation bar to open the Open dialog box**

2. **In the Open dialog box, navigate to the drive and folder where you store your Data Files, click EMP A-1.xlsx, then click Open**

   The file opens in the Excel window.

3. **Click the File tab, then click Save As on the navigation bar to open the Save As dialog box**

4. **In the Save As dialog box, navigate to the drive and folder where you store your Data Files if necessary, type EMP A-Health Professionals Payroll Calculator in the File name text box, then click Save**

   Using Figure A-3 as a guide, identify the following items:
   - The **Name box** displays the active cell address. "A1" appears in the Name box.
   - The **formula bar** allows you to enter or edit data in the worksheet.
   - The worksheet window contains a grid of columns and rows. Columns are labeled alphabetically and rows are labeled numerically. The worksheet window can contain a total of 1,048,576 rows and 16,384 columns. The intersection of a column and a row is called a **cell**. Cells can contain text, numbers, formulas, or a combination of all three. Every cell has its own unique location or **cell address**, which is identified by the coordinates of the intersecting column and row.
   - The **cell pointer** is a dark rectangle that outlines the cell in which you are working. This cell is called the **active cell**. In Figure A-3, the cell pointer outlines cell A1, so A1 is the active cell. The column and row headings for the active cell are highlighted, making it easier to locate.
   - **Sheet tabs** below the worksheet grid let you switch from sheet to sheet in a workbook. By default, a workbook file contains three worksheets—but you can use just one, or have as many as 255, in a workbook. The Insert Worksheet button to the right of Sheet 3 allows you to add worksheets to a workbook. **Sheet tab scrolling buttons** let you navigate to additional sheet tabs when available.
   - You can use the **scroll bars** to move around in a worksheet that is too large to fit on the screen at once.
   - The **status bar** is located at the bottom of the Excel window. It provides a brief description of the active command or task in progress. The **mode indicator** in the lower-left corner of the status bar provides additional information about certain tasks.

5. **Click cell D4**

   Cell D4 becomes the active cell. To activate a different cell, you can click the cell or press the arrow keys on your keyboard to move to it.

6. **Click cell C11, press and hold the mouse button, drag ⊕ to cell C20, then release the mouse button**

   You selected a group of cells and they are now highlighted, as shown in Figure A-4. A selection of two or more cells such as C11:C20 is called a **range**; you select a range when you want to perform an action on a group of cells at once, such as moving them or formatting them. When you select a range, the status bar displays the average, count (or number of items selected), and sum of the selected cells as a quick reference.

FIGURE A-3: Open workbook

Name box

Cell pointer indicates active cell

Formula bar

Sheet tab scrolling buttons

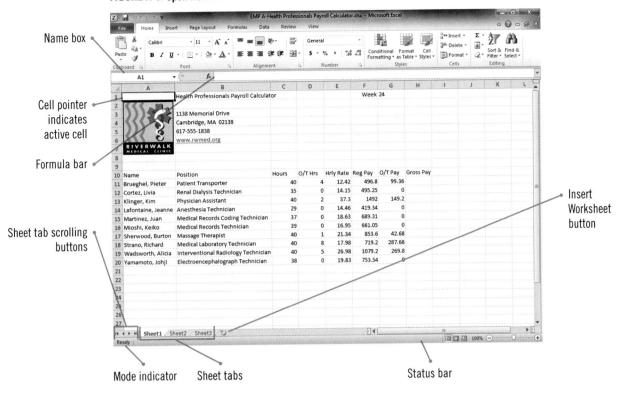

Insert Worksheet button

Mode indicator   Sheet tabs

Status bar

FIGURE A-4: Selected range

Selected cells

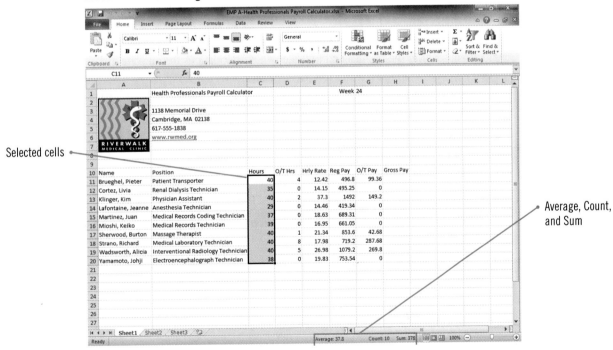

Average, Count, and Sum

Windows Live and Microsoft Office Web Apps

All Office programs include the capability to incorporate feedback—called online collaboration—across the Internet or a company network. Using **cloud computing** (work done in a virtual environment), you can take advantage of Web programs called Microsoft Office Web Apps, which are simplified versions of the programs found in the Microsoft Office 2010 suite. Because these programs are online, they take up no computer disk space and are accessed using Windows Live SkyDrive, a free service from Microsoft. Using Windows Live SkyDrive, you and your colleagues can create and store documents in a "cloud" and make the documents available to whomever you grant access. To use Windows Live SkyDrive, you need a free Windows Live ID, which you obtain at the Windows Live Web site. You can find more information in the "Working with Windows Live and Office Web Apps" appendix.

Understanding Formulas

Excel is a truly powerful program because users at every level of mathematical expertise can make calculations with accuracy. To do so, you use formulas. A **formula** is an equation in a worksheet. You use formulas to make calculations as simple as adding a column of numbers, or as complex as creating profit-and-loss projections for a global corporation. To tap into the power of Excel, you should understand how formulas work. Managers at RMC use the Health Professionals Payroll Calculator workbook to keep track of employee hours prior to submitting them to the Payroll Department. You'll be using this workbook regularly, so you need to understand the formulas it contains and how Excel calculates the results.

1. **Click cell F11**

   The active cell contains a formula, which appears on the formula bar. All Excel formulas begin with the equal sign (=). If you want a cell to show the result of adding 4 plus 2, the formula in the cell would look like this: =4+2. If you want a cell to show the result of multiplying two values in your worksheet, such as the values in cells C11 and E11, the formula would look like this: =C11*E11, as shown in Figure A-5. While you're entering a formula in a cell, the cell references and arithmetic operators appear on the formula bar. See Table A-2 for a list of commonly used arithmetic operators. When you're finished entering the formula, you can either click the Enter button on the formula bar or press [Enter].

2. **Click cell G11**

   An example of a more complex formula is the calculation of overtime pay. At RMC, overtime pay is calculated at twice the regular hourly rate times the number of overtime hours. The formula used to calculate overtime pay for the employee in row 11 is:

   O/T Hrs times (2 times Hrly Rate)

   In the worksheet cell, you would enter: =D11*(2*E11), as shown in Figure A-6. The use of parentheses creates groups within the formula and indicates which calculations to complete first—an important consideration in complex formulas. In this formula, first the hourly rate is multiplied by 2, because that calculation is within the parentheses. Next, that value is multiplied by the number of overtime hours. Because overtime is calculated at twice the hourly rate, managers are aware that they need to closely watch this expense.

In creating calculations in Excel, it is important to:

- **Know where the formulas should be**

  An Excel formula is created in the cell where the formula's results should appear. This means that the formula calculating Gross Pay for the employee in row 11 will be entered in cell H11.

- **Know exactly what cells and arithmetic operations are needed**

  Don't guess; make sure you know exactly what cells are involved before creating a formula.

- **Create formulas with care**

  Make sure you know exactly what you want a formula to accomplish before it is created. An inaccurate formula may have far-reaching effects if the formula or its results are referenced by other formulas.

- **Use cell references rather than values**

  The beauty of Excel is that whenever you change a value in a cell, any formula containing a reference to that cell is automatically updated. For this reason, it's important that you use cell references in formulas, rather than actual values, whenever possible.

- **Determine what calculations will be needed**

  Sometimes it's difficult to predict what data will be needed within a worksheet, but you should try to anticipate what statistical information may be required. For example, if there are columns of numbers, chances are good that both column and row totals should be present.

FIGURE A-5: Viewing a formula

Formula is displayed in formula bar

Calculated value is displayed in cell

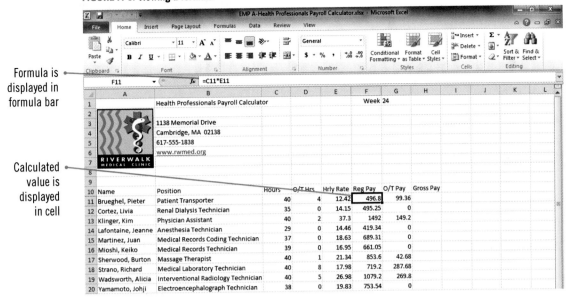

FIGURE A-6: Formula with multiple operators

Formula to calculate overtime pay

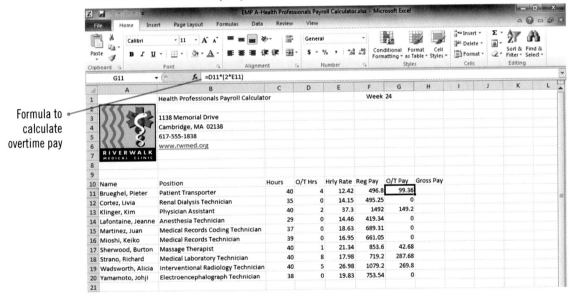

TABLE A-2: Excel arithmetic operators

operator	purpose	example
+	Addition	=A5+A7
-	Subtraction or negation	=A5-10
*	Multiplication	=A5*A7
/	Division	=A5/A7
%	Percent	=35%
^ (caret)	Exponent	=6^2 (same as 6^2)

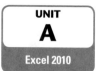
Entering Labels and Values and Using the Sum Button

To enter content in a cell, you can type on the formula bar or directly in the cell itself. When entering content in a worksheet, you should start by entering all the labels first. **Labels** are entries that contain text and numerical information not used in calculations, such as "2013 Revenue" or "Travel Expenses." Labels help you identify data in worksheet rows and columns, making your worksheet easier to understand. **Values** are numbers, formulas, and functions that can be used in calculations. To enter a calculation, you type an equal sign (=) plus the formula for the calculation; some examples of an Excel calculation are "=2+2" and "=C5+C6." Functions are Excel's built-in formulas; you learn more about them in the next unit. 🖱️ You want to enter some information in the Health Professionals Payroll Calculator workbook, and use a very simple function to total a range of cells.

STEPS

1. **Click cell A21, then click in the formula bar**

   Notice that the **mode indicator** on the status bar now reads "Edit", indicating you are in Edit mode. You are in Edit mode any time you are entering or changing the contents of a cell.

   > **QUICK TIP**
   > If you change your mind and want to cancel an entry in the formula bar, click the Cancel button ✖ on the formula bar.

2. **Type Totals, then click the Enter button ✓ on the formula bar**

   Clicking the Enter button accepts the entry. The new text is left-aligned in the cell. Labels are left-aligned by default, and values are right-aligned by default. Excel recognizes an entry as a value if it is a number or it begins with one of these symbols: +, -, =, @, #, or $. When a cell contains both text and numbers, Excel recognizes it as a label.

3. **Click cell C21**

   You want this cell to total the hours worked by all the employees. You might think you need to create a formula that looks like this: =C11+C12+C13+C14+C15+C16+C17+C18+C19+C20. However, there's an easier way to achieve this result.

4. **Click the Sum button Σ in the Editing group on the Home tab on the Ribbon**

   The SUM function is inserted in the cell, and a suggested range appears in parentheses, as shown in Figure A-7. A **function** is a built-in formula; it includes the **arguments** (the information necessary to calculate an answer) as well as cell references and other unique information. Clicking the Sum button sums the adjacent range (that is, the cells next to the active cell) above or to the left, though you can adjust the range if necessary by selecting a different range before accepting the cell entry. Using the SUM function is quicker than entering a formula, and using the range C11:C20 is more efficient than entering individual cell references.

   > **QUICK TIP**
   > You can create formulas in a cell even before you enter the values to be calculated; the results will be recalculated as soon as the data is entered.

5. **Click ✓ on the formula bar**

   Excel calculates the total contained in cells C11:C20 and displays the result, 378, in cell C21. The cell actually contains the formula =SUM(C11:C20), and the result is displayed.

6. **Click cell D19, type 6, then press [Enter]**

   The number 6 replaces the cell's contents, the cell pointer moves to cell D20, and the value in cell G19 changes.

7. **Click cell D24, type Average Gross Pay, then press [Enter]**

   The new label is entered in cell D24. The contents appear to spill into the empty cells to the right.

   > **QUICK TIP**
   > If making horizontal entries, you can also press [Tab] to complete a cell entry and move the cell pointer to the right.

8. **Click cell C21, position the pointer on the lower-right corner of the cell (the fill handle) so that the pointer changes to ➕, drag the ➕ to cell H21, then release the mouse button**

   Dragging the fill handle across a range of cells copies the contents of the first cell into the other cells in the range. In the range C21:H21, each filled cell now contains a function that sums the range of cells above, as shown in Figure A-8.

9. **Save your work**

Getting Started with Excel 2010

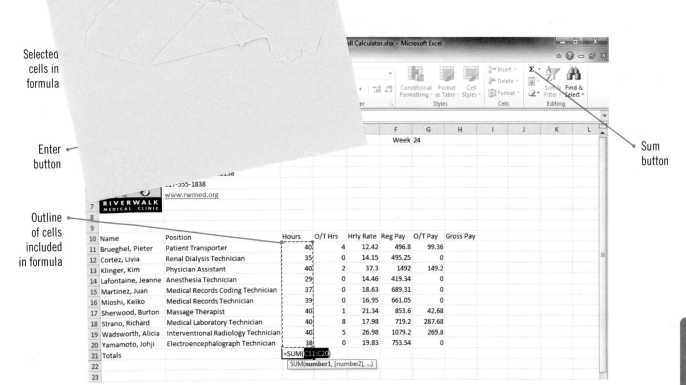

Selected cells in formula

Enter button

Outline of cells included in formula

Sum button

FIGURE A-8: Results of copied SUM functions

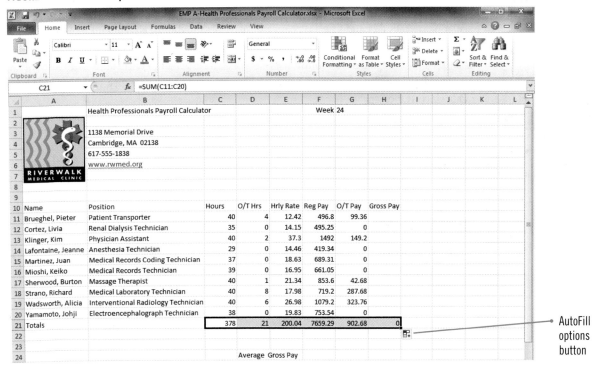

AutoFill options button

Navigating a worksheet

With over a million cells available in a worksheet, it is important to know how to move around, or **navigate**, in a worksheet. You can use the arrow keys on the keyboard [↑],[↓], [→], or [←] to move one cell at a time, or press [Page Up] or [Page Down] to move one screen at a time. To move one screen to the left press [Alt][Page Up]; to move one screen to the right press [Alt][Page Down]. You can also use the mouse pointer to click the desired cell. If the desired cell is not visible in the worksheet window, use the scroll bars or use the Go To command by clicking the Find & Select button in the Editing group on the Home tab on the Ribbon. To quickly jump to the first cell in a worksheet press [Ctrl][Home]; to jump to the last cell, press [Ctrl][End].

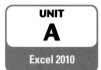

Editing Cell Entries

You can change, or **edit**, the contents of an active cell at any time. To do so, double-click the cell, click in the formula bar, or just start typing. Excel switches to Edit mode when you are making cell entries. Different pointers, shown in Table A-3, guide you through the editing process. █████ You noticed some errors in the worksheet and want to make corrections. The first error is in cell A11, which contains a misspelled name.

STEPS

1. **Click cell A11, then click to the right of P in the formula bar**

   As soon as you click in the formula bar, a blinking vertical line called the **insertion point** appears on the formula bar at the location where new text will be inserted. See Figure A-9. The mouse pointer changes to ⌶ when you point anywhere in the formula bar.

2. **Press [Delete], then click the Enter button ✔ on the formula bar**

   Clicking the Enter button accepts the edit, and the spelling of the employee's first name is corrected. You can also press [Enter] or [Tab] to accept an edit. Pressing [Enter] to accept an edit moves the cell pointer down one cell, and pressing [Tab] to accept an edit moves the cell pointer one cell to the right.

   > **QUICK TIP**
   > On some keyboards, you might need to press an [F Lock] key to enable the function keys.

3. **Click cell C12, then press [F2]**

   Excel switches to Edit mode, and the insertion point blinks in the cell. Pressing [F2] activates the cell for editing directly in the cell instead of the formula bar. Whether you edit in the cell or the formula bar is simply a matter of preference; the results in the worksheet are the same.

   > **QUICK TIP**
   > The Undo button allows you to reverse up to 100 previous actions, one at a time.

4. **Press [Backspace], type 8, then press [Enter]**

   The value in the cell changes from 35 to 38, and cell C13 becomes the active cell. Did you notice that the calculations in cells C21 and F12 also changed? That's because those cells contain formulas that include cell C12 in their calculations. If you make a mistake when editing, you can click the Cancel button ✖ on the formula bar *before* pressing [Enter] to confirm the cell entry. The Enter and Cancel buttons appear only when you're in Edit mode. If you notice the mistake *after* you have confirmed the cell entry, click the Undo button ↶ on the Quick Access toolbar.

   > **QUICK TIP**
   > You can use the keyboard to select all cell contents by clicking to the right of the cell contents in the cell or formula bar, pressing and holding [Shift], then pressing [Home].

5. **Click cell A15, then double-click the word Juan in the formula bar**

   Double-clicking a word in a cell selects it.

6. **Type Javier, then press [Enter]**

   When text is selected, typing deletes it and replaces it with the new text.

7. **Double-click cell D18, press [Delete], type 4, then click ✔**

   Double-clicking a cell activates it for editing directly in the cell. Compare your screen to Figure A-10.

8. **Save your work**

   Your changes to the workbook are saved.

Recovering unsaved changes to a workbook file

You can use Excel's AutoRecover feature to automatically save (Autosave) your work as often as you want. This means that if you suddenly lose power or if Excel closes unexpectedly while you're working, you can recover all or some of the changes you made since you last saved it. (Of course, this is no substitute for regularly saving your work: this is just added insurance.) To customize the AutoRecover settings, click the File tab, click Options, then click

Save. AutoRecover lets you decide how often and into which location it should Autosave files. When you restart Excel after losing power, a Document Recovery pane opens and provides access to the saved and Autosaved versions of the files that were open when Excel closed. You can also click the File tab, click Recent on the navigation bar, then click Recover Unsaved Workbooks to open Autosaved workbooks using the Open dialog box.

FIGURE A-9: Worksheet in Edit mode

Insertion point

Active cell

Mode indicator

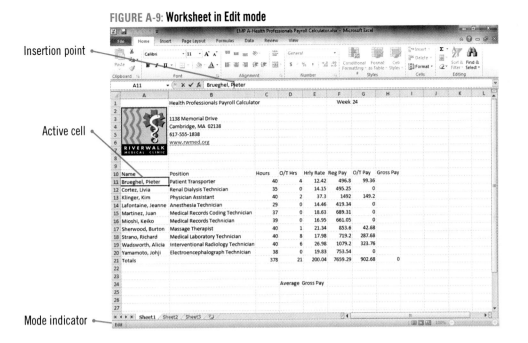

FIGURE A-10: Edited worksheet

Edited value

Edited label

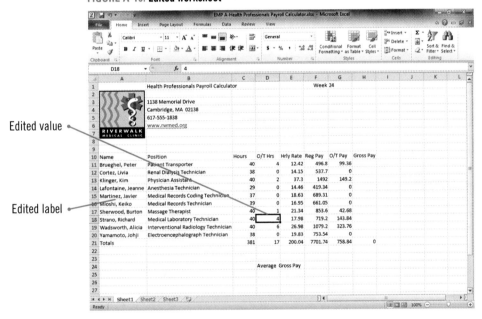

TABLE A-3: Common pointers in Excel

name	pointer	use to	visible over the
Normal	⊕	Select a cell or range; indicates Ready mode	Active worksheet
Fill handle	+	Copy cell contents to adjacent cells	Lower-right corner of the active cell or range
I-beam	I	Edit cell contents in active cell or formula bar	Active cell in Edit mode or over the formula bar
Move	⊹	Change the location of the selected cell(s)	Perimeter of the active cell(s)
Copy	⊳⁺	Create a duplicate of the selected cell(s)	Perimeter of the active cell(s) when [Ctrl] is pressed
Column resize	↔	Change the width of a column	Border between column heading indicators

Entering and Editing a Simple Formula

You use formulas in Excel to perform calculations such as adding, multiplying, and averaging. Formulas in an Excel worksheet start with the equal sign (=), also called the **formula prefix**, followed by cell addresses, range names, values, and calculation operators. **Calculation operators** indicate what type of calculation you want to perform on the cells, ranges, or values. They can include **arithmetic operators**, which perform mathematical calculations (see Table A-2 in the "Understanding Formulas" lesson); **comparison operators**, which compare values for the purpose of true/false results; **text concatenation operators**, which join strings of text in different cells; and **reference operators**, which enable you to use ranges in calculations. You want to create a formula in the worksheet that calculates gross pay for each employee.

STEPS

1. **Click cell H11**

    This is the first cell where you want to insert the formula. To calculate gross pay, you need to add regular pay and overtime pay. For employee Peter Brueghel, regular pay appears in cell F11 and overtime pay appears in cell G11.

> **QUICK TIP**
>
> You can reference a cell in a formula either by typing the cell reference or clicking the cell in the worksheet; when you click a cell to add a reference, the Mode indicator changes to "Point."

2. **Type =, click cell F11, type +, then click cell G11**

    Compare your formula bar to Figure A-11. The blue and green cell references in cell H11 correspond to the colored cell outlines. When entering a formula, it's a good idea to use cell references instead of values whenever you can. That way, if you later change a value in a cell (if, for example, Peter's regular pay changes to 500), any formula that includes this information reflects accurate, up-to-date results.

3. **Click the Enter button** ✅ **on the formula bar**

    The result of the formula =F11+G11, 596.16, appears in cell H11. This same value appears in cell H21 because cell H21 contains a formula that totals the values in cells H11:H20, and there are no other values now.

4. **Click cell G11**

    The formula in this cell calculates overtime pay by multiplying overtime hours (D11) times twice the regular hourly rate (2*E11). You want to edit this formula to reflect a new overtime pay rate.

5. **Click to the right of 2 in the formula bar, then type .5 as shown in Figure A-12**

    The formula that calculates overtime pay has been edited.

6. **Click** ✅ **on the formula bar**

    Compare your screen to Figure A-13. Notice that the calculated values in cells G21, H11, and H21 have all changed to reflect your edits to cell G11.

7. **Save your work**

Understanding named ranges

It can be difficult to remember the cell locations of critical information in a worksheet, but using cell names can make this task much easier. You can name a single cell or a range of contiguous, or touching, cells. For example, you might name a cell that contains data on average gross pay "AVG_GP" instead of trying to remember the cell address C18. A named range must begin with a letter or an underscore. It cannot contain any spaces or be the same as a built-in name, such as a function or another object (for example a different named range) in the workbook. To name a range, select the cell(s) you want to name, click the Name box in the formula bar, type the name you want to use, then press [Enter]. You can also name a

range by clicking the Formulas tab, then clicking the Define Name button in the Defined Names group. Type the new range name in the Name text box in the New Name dialog box, verify the selected range, then click OK. When you use a named range in a formula, the named range appears instead of the cell address. You can also create a named range using the contents of a cell already in the range. Select the range containing the text you want to use as a name, then click the Create from Selection button in the Defined Names group. The Create Names from Selection dialog box opens. Choose the location of the name you want to use, then click OK.

FIGURE A-11: Simple formula in a worksheet

Referenced cells are inserted in formula

Cell outline color corresponds to cell reference

Mode indicator changes to Point

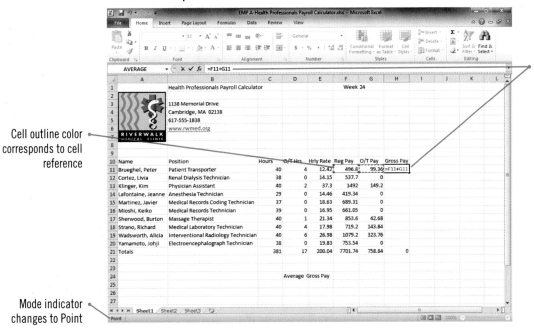

FIGURE A-12: Edited formula in a worksheet

Edited value in formula

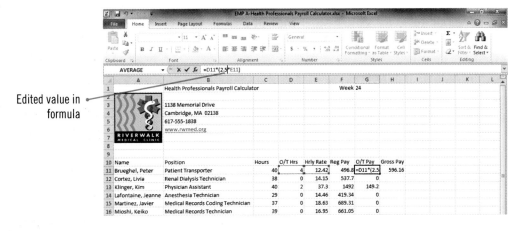

FIGURE A-13: Edited formula with changes

Edited formula results in changes to these other cells

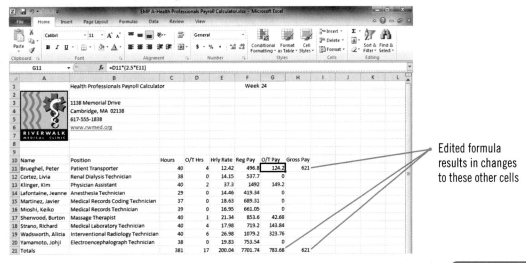

Switching Worksheet Views

You can change your view of the worksheet window at any time, using either the View tab on the Ribbon or the View buttons on the status bar. Changing your view does not affect the contents of a worksheet; it just makes it easier for you to focus on different tasks, such as entering content or preparing a worksheet for printing. The View tab includes a variety of viewing options, such as View buttons, zoom controls, and the ability to show or hide worksheet elements such as gridlines. The status bar offers fewer View options but can be more convenient to use. You want to make some final adjustments to your worksheet, including adding a header so the document looks more polished.

STEPS

QUICK TIP

Although a work-sheet can contain more than a million rows and thousands of columns, the current document contains only as many pages as necessary for the current project.

1. **Click the** View tab **on the Ribbon, then click the** Page Layout button **in the Workbook Views group**

   The view switches from the default view, Normal, to Page Layout view. **Normal view** shows the worksheet without including certain details like headers and footers, or tools like rulers and a page number indicator; it's great for creating and editing a worksheet, but may not be detailed enough when you want to put the finishing touches on a document. **Page Layout view** provides a more accurate view of how a worksheet will look when printed, as shown in Figure A-14. The margins of the page are displayed, along with a text box for the header. A footer text box appears at the bottom of the page, but your screen may not be large enough to view it without scrolling. Above and to the left of the page are rulers. Part of an additional page appears to the right of this page. If the next page did not contain any data, it would appear dimmed. A page number indicator on the status bar tells you the current page and the total number of pages in this worksheet.

2. **Drag the pointer** ▷ **over the header** *without clicking*

   The header is made up of three text boxes: left, center, and right. Each text box is highlighted blue as you pass over it with the pointer.

QUICK TIP

You can change header and footer information using the Header & Footer Tools Design tab that opens on the Ribbon when a header or footer is active. For example, you can insert the date by clicking the Current Date button in the Header & Footer Elements group, or insert the time by clicking the Current Time button.

3. **Drag the horizontal scroll bar to the left so column A is visible, click the** left header text box, **type** Riverwalk Medical Clinic, **click the** center header text box, **type** Health Prof Payroll Calculator, **click the** right header text box, **then type** Week 24

   The new text appears in the text boxes, as shown in Figure A-15.

4. **Select the range B1:G1, then press [Delete]**

   The duplicate information you just entered in the header is deleted from cells in the worksheet.

5. **Click the** View tab **if necessary, click the** Ruler check box **in the Show group, then click the** Gridlines check box **in the Show group**

   The rulers and the gridlines are hidden. By default, gridlines in a worksheet do not print, so hiding them gives you a more accurate image of your final document.

6. **Click the** Page Break Preview button 🖳 **on the status bar, then click OK in the Welcome to Page Break Preview dialog box, if necessary**

   Your view changes to **Page Break Preview**, which displays a reduced view of each page of your worksheet, along with page break indicators that you can drag to include more or less information on a page.

7. **Drag the pointer** ↔ **from the dotted vertical page break indicator to the right of** column I

   See Figure A-16. When you're working on a large worksheet with multiple pages, sometimes you need to adjust where pages break; in this worksheet, however, the information will all fit comfortably on one page.

QUICK TIP

Once you view a worksheet in Page Break Preview, the page break indica-tors appear as dot-ted lines after you switch back to Normal view or Page Layout view.

8. **Click the** Page Layout button **in the Workbook Views group, click the** Ruler check box **in the Show group, then click the** Gridlines check box **in the Show group**

   The rulers and gridlines are no longer hidden. You can show or hide View tab items in any view.

9. **Save your work**

FIGURE A-14: Page Layout view

Turns ruler on/off

Turns gridlines on/off

Workbook Views group

Header text box

Vertical ruler

Current page and total number of pages

Horizontal ruler

Additional page

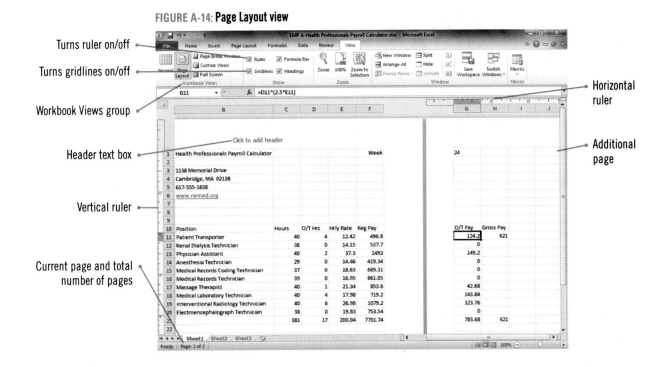

FIGURE A-15: Header text entered

Header & Footer Tools Design tab

Header text boxes

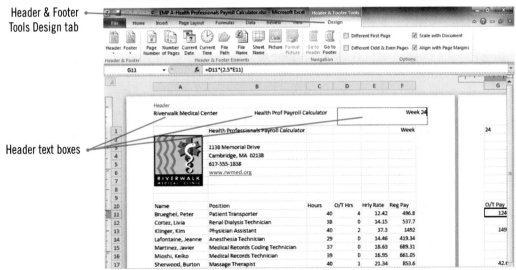

FIGURE A-16: Page Break Preview

Blue outline indicates print area

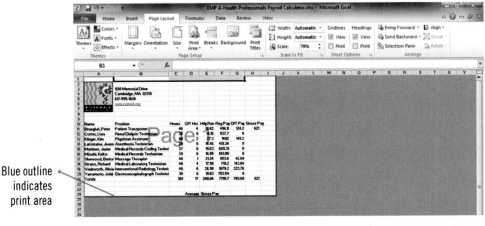

Choosing Print Options

Before printing a document, you may want to review it using the Page Layout tab to fine-tune your printed output. You can use tools on the Page Layout tab to adjust print orientation (the direction in which the content prints across the page), paper size, and location of page breaks. You can also use the Scale to Fit options on the Page Layout tab to fit a large amount of data on a single page without making changes to individual margins, and to turn gridlines and column/row headings on and off. When you are ready to print, you can set print options such as the number of copies to print and the correct printer, and you can preview your document in Backstage view using the File tab. You can also adjust page layout settings from within Backstage view and immediately see the results in the document preview. ⬛️💤💤 You are ready to prepare your worksheet for printing.

STEPS

1. **Click cell A24, type your name, then press [Enter]**

2. **Click the Page Layout tab on the Ribbon**
   Compare your screen to Figure A-17. The dotted line indicates the default **print area**, the area to be printed.

> **QUICK TIP**
> You can use the Zoom slider on the status bar at any time to enlarge your view of specific areas of your worksheet.

3. **Click the Orientation button in the Page Setup group, then click Landscape**
   The paper orientation changes to **landscape**, so the contents will print across the length of the page instead of across the width.

4. **Click the Orientation button in the Page Setup group, then click Portrait**
   The orientation returns to **portrait**, so the contents will print across the width of the page.

5. **Click the Gridlines View check box in the Sheet Options group on the Page Layout tab to deselect the check box, click the Gridlines Print check box to select it if necessary, then save your work**
   Printing gridlines makes the data easier to read, but the gridlines will not print unless the Gridlines Print check box is checked.

> **QUICK TIP**
> To change the active printer, click the current printer in the Printer section in Backstage view, then choose a different printer.

6. **Click the File tab, then click Print on the navigation bar**
   The Print tab in Backstage view displays a preview of your worksheet exactly as it will look when it is printed. To the left of the worksheet preview, you can also change a number of document settings and print options. To open the Page Setup dialog box and adjust page layout options, click the Page Setup link in the Settings section. Compare your preview screen to Figure A-18. You can print from this view by clicking the Print button, or return to the worksheet without printing by clicking the File tab again.

> **QUICK TIP**
> If the Quick Print button 🖨 appears on the Quick Access Toolbar, you can print your worksheet using the default settings by clicking it.

7. **Compare your settings to Figure A-18, then click the Print button**
   One copy of the worksheet prints.

8. **Submit your work to your instructor as directed, then exit Excel**

Printing worksheet formulas

Sometimes you need to keep a record of all the formulas in a worksheet. You might want to do this to see exactly how you came up with a complex calculation, so you can explain it to others. To prepare a worksheet to show formulas rather than results when printed, open the workbook containing the formulas you want to print. Click the Formulas tab, then click the Show Formulas button in the Formula Auditing group to select it. When the Show Formulas button is selected, formulas rather than resulting values are displayed in the worksheet on screen and when printed.

FIGURE A-17: Worksheet with portrait orientation

Dotted line surrounds print area

Your name appears here

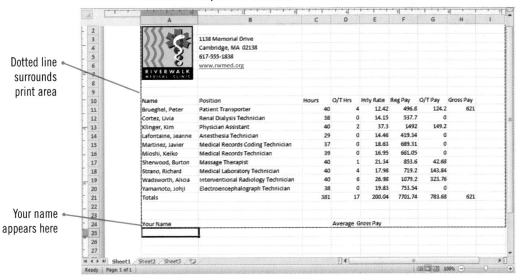

FIGURE A-18: Worksheet in Backstage view

Click to change number of copies

Print button

Active printer; yours will be different

Choose which pages to print

Click to select scaling options

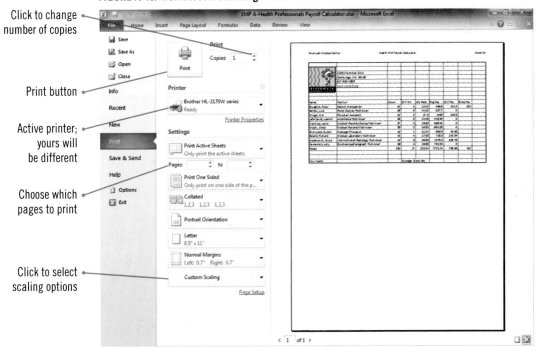

Scaling to fit

If you have a large amount of data that you want to fit to a single sheet of paper, but you don't want to spend a lot of time trying to adjust the margins and other settings, you have several options. You can easily print your work on a single sheet by clicking the No Scaling list arrow in the Settings section on the Print tab in Backstage view, then clicking Fit Sheet on One Page. Another method for fitting worksheet content onto one page is to click the Page Layout tab, then change the Width and Height settings in the Scale to Fit group each to 1 Page. You can also use the Fit to option in the Page Setup dialog box to fit a worksheet on one page. To open the Page Setup dialog box, click the dialog box launcher in the Scale to Fit group on the Page Layout tab, or click the Page Setup link on the Print tab in Backstage view. Make sure the Page tab is selected in the Page Setup dialog box, then click the Fit to option button.

Practice

Concepts Review

For current SAM information, including versions and content details, visit SAM Central (http://www.cengage.com/samcentral). If you have a SAM user profile, you may have access to hands-on instruction, practice, and assessment of the skills covered in this unit. Since various versions of SAM are supported throughout the life of this text, check with your instructor for the correct instructions and URL/Web site for accessing assignments.

Label the elements of the Excel worksheet window shown in Figure A-19.

FIGURE A-19

Match each term with the statement that best describes it.

7. Formula prefix
8. Normal view
9. Name box
10. Cell
11. Orientation
12. Workbook

a. Default view in Excel
b. Direction in which contents of page will print
c. Equal sign preceding a formula
d. File consisting of one or more worksheets
e. Intersection of a column and a row
f. Part of the Excel program window that displays the active cell address

Select the best answer from the list of choices.

13. **The maximum number of worksheets you can include in a workbook is:**
    a. 3.
    b. 250.
    c. 255.
    d. Unlimited.

14. **Using a cell address in a formula is known as:**
    a. Formularizing.
    b. Prefixing.
    c. Cell referencing.
    d. Cell mathematics.

15. **Which feature could be used to print a very long worksheet on a single sheet of paper?**
    a. Show Formulas
    b. Scale to fit
    c. Page Break Preview
    d. Named Ranges

16. **A selection of multiple cells is called a:**
    a. Group.
    b. Range.
    c. Reference.
    d. Package.

17. **Which worksheet view shows how your worksheet will look when printed?**
    a. Page Layout
    b. Data
    c. Review
    d. View

18. **Which key can you press to switch to Edit mode?**
    a. [F1]
    b. [F2]
    c. [F4]
    d. [F6]

19. **Which view shows you a reduced view of each page of your worksheet?**
    a. Normal
    b. Page Layout
    c. Thumbnail
    d. Page Break Preview

20. **In which area can you see a preview of your worksheet?**
    a. Page Setup
    b. Backstage view
    c. Printer Setup
    d. View tab

21. **In which view can you see the header and footer areas of a worksheet?**
    a. Normal view
    b. Page Layout view
    c. Page Break Preview
    d. Header/Footer view

Skills Review

1. **Understand spreadsheet software.**
   a. What is the difference between a workbook and a worksheet?
   b. Identify five common business uses for electronic spreadsheets.
   c. What is what-if analysis?

2. **Tour the Excel 2010 window.**
   a. Start Excel.
   b. Open the file EMP A-2.xlsx from the drive and folder where you store your Data Files, then save it as **EMP A-Weather Statistics**.
   c. Locate the formula bar, the Sheet tabs, the mode indicator, and the cell pointer.

3. **Understand formulas.**
   a. What is the average high temperature of the listed cities? (*Hint*: Select the range B5:G5 and use the status bar.)
   b. What formula would you create to calculate the difference in altitude between Denver and Phoenix? Enter your answer (as an equation) in cell D13.

4. **Enter labels and values and use the Sum button.**
   a. Click cell H8, then use the Sum button to calculate the total snowfall.
   b. Click cell H7, then use the Sum button to calculate the total rainfall.
   c. Save your changes to the file.

Skills Review (continued)

5. Edit cell entries.

  a. Use [F2] to correct the spelling of SanteFe in cell G3 (the correct spelling is Santa Fe).

  b. Click cell A17, then type your name.

  c. Save your changes.

6. Enter and edit a simple formula.

  a. Change the value 41 in cell C8 to **52**.

  b. Change the value 37 in cell D6 to **35.4**.

  c. Select cell J4, then use the fill handle to copy the formula in cell J4 to cells J5:J8.

  d. Save your changes.

7. Switch worksheet views.

  a. Click the View tab on the Ribbon, then switch to Page Layout view.

  b. Add the header **Average Annual Weather Statistics** to the center header text box.

  c. Add your name to the right header box.

  d. Add the multi-line header **Potential Medical Research Locations** to the left header box.

  e. Delete the contents of the range A1:H1 and cell A17.

  f. Save your changes.

8. Choose print options.

  a. Use the Page Layout tab to change the orientation to Portrait.

  b. Turn off gridlines by deselecting both the Gridlines View and Gridlines Print check boxes (if necessary) in the Sheet Options group.

  c. Scale the worksheet so all the information fits on one page. (*Hint*: Click the Width list arrow in the Scale to Fit group, click 1 page, click the Height list arrow in the Scale to Fit group, then click 1 page.) Compare your screen to Figure A-20.

FIGURE A-20

  d. Preview the worksheet in Backstage view, then print the worksheet.

  e. Save your changes, submit your work to your instructor as directed, then close the workbook and exit Excel.

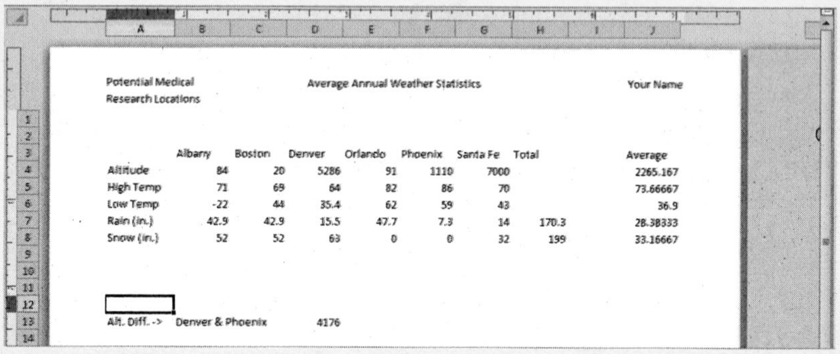

Independent Challenge 1

The Human Resources division of Allied Cardiology Associates has just notified you that they have hired two new physicians who will be relocating to your area. They would like you to create a workbook that contains real estate properties for their consideration. You've started a worksheet for this project that contains labels but no data.

  a. Open the file EMP A-3.xlsx from where you store your Data Files, then save it as **EMP A-Property Listings**.

  b. Enter the data shown in Table A-4 in columns A, C, D, and E (the property address information should spill into column B).

TABLE A-4

Property Address	Price	Bedrooms	Bathrooms
1507 Pinon Lane	425000	4	2.5
32 Zanzibar Way	325000	3	4
60 Pottery Lane	475500	2	2
902 Excelsior Drive	300000	4	3

Independent Challenge 1 (continued)

c. Use Page Layout view to create a header with the following components: the title **Property Listings** in the center and your name on the right.

d. Create formulas for totals in cells C6:E6.

e. Save your changes, then compare your worksheet to Figure A-21.

f. Submit your work to your instructor as directed.

g. Close the worksheet and exit Excel.

FIGURE A-21

Property Address	Price	Bedrooms	Bathrooms
1507 Pinon Lane	425000	4	2.5
32 Zanzibar Way	325000	3	4
60 Pottery Lane	475500	2	2
902 Excelsior Drive	300000	4	3
Total	1525500	13	11.5

Property Listings   Your Name

Independent Challenge 2

You are the General Manager for Top Flight Medical Supplies, Inc., a small wholesaler of medical supplies. Although the company is just 5 years old, it is expanding rapidly, and you are continually looking for ways to save time. You recently began using Excel to manage and maintain data on inventory and sales, which has greatly helped you to track information accurately and efficiently.

a. Start Excel.

b. Save a new workbook as **EMP A-Top Flight Medical Supplies** in the drive and folder where you store your Data Files.

c. Switch to an appropriate view, then add a header that contains your name in the left header text box and the title **Top Flight Medical Supplies** in the center header text box.

d. Using Figure A-22 as a guide, create labels for at least seven medical supply manufacturers and sales for the three months in Quarter 2. Include other labels as appropriate. The manufacturers should be in column A and the months should be in columns C, D, and E. A Total row should be beneath the data, and a Total column should be in column F.

FIGURE A-22

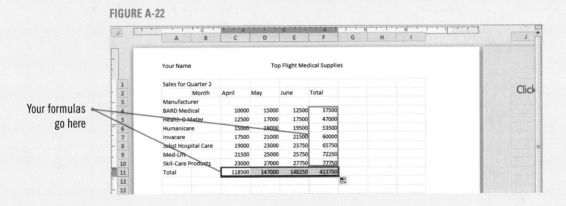

Your formulas go here

Your Name			Top Flight Medical Supplies		
Sales for Quarter 2					
Month	April	May	June	Total	
Manufacturer					
BARD Medical	10000	15000	12500	37500	
Health-O-Meter	12500	17000	17500	47000	
Humanicare	15000	19000	19500	53500	
Invacare	17500	21000	21500	60000	
Jobst Hospital Care	19000	23000	23750	65750	
Med-Lift	21500	25000	25750	72250	
Skil-Care Products	23000	27000	27750	77750	
Total	118500	147000	148250	413750	

Click

e. Enter values of your choice for the monthly sales for each manufacturer.

f. Add formulas in the Total column to calculate total quarterly sales for each manufacturer. Add formulas at the bottom of each column of values to calculate the total for that column. Remember that you can use the Sum button and the fill handle to save time.

g. Save your changes, preview the worksheet in Backstage view, then submit your work to your instructor as directed.

Independent Challenge 2 (continued)

Advanced Challenge Exercise

- Create a label two rows beneath the data in column A that says **15% increase**.
- Create a formula in each of the cells C13, D13, and E13 that calculates monthly sales plus a 15% increase.
- Display the formulas in the worksheet, then print a copy of the worksheet with formulas displayed.
- Save the workbook.

h. Close the workbook and exit Excel.

Independent Challenge 3

This Independent Challenge requires an Internet connection.

Some of the research staff at Great Plains Hospital prefer to use Celsius, rather than Fahrenheit temperatures, so you thought it would be helpful to create a worksheet that can be used to convert Fahrenheit temperatures. This will help employees who are unfamiliar with this type of temperature measurement.

a. Start Excel, then save a blank workbook as **EMP A-Temperature Conversions** in the drive and folder where you store your Data Files.

b. Create column headings using Figure A-23 as a guide. (*Hint:* You can widen column B by clicking cell B1, clicking the Format button in the Cells group on the Home tab, then clicking AutoFit Column Width.)

FIGURE A-23

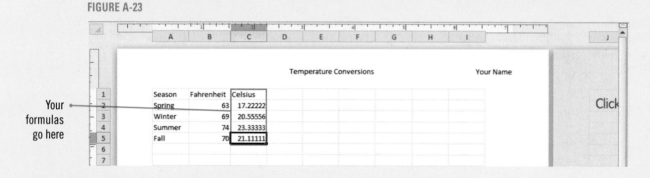

c. Create row labels for each of the seasons.

d. In the appropriate cells, enter what you determine to be a reasonable indoor temperature for each season.

e. Use your Web browser to find out the conversion rate for Fahrenheit to Celsius. (*Hint:* Use your favorite search engine to search on a term such as **temperature conversion formula**.)

f. In the appropriate cells, create a formula that calculates the conversion of the Fahrenheit temperature you entered into a Celsius temperature.

g. In Page Layout View, add your name and the title **Temperature Conversions** to the header.

h. Save your work, then submit your work to your instructor as directed.

i. Close the file, then exit Excel.

Real Life Independent Challenge

You've recently started working as a bookkeeper at the Candandaigua Clinic. You've set up a sample Excel worksheet to keep track of the many start-up expenses.

a. Start Excel, open the file EMP A-4.xlsx from the drive and folder where you store your Data Files, then save it as **EMP A-Candandaigua Clinic Checkbook**.

b. Type check numbers (using your choice of a starting number) in cells A5 through A9.

c. Create sample data for the date, item, and amount in cells B5 through D9.

d. Save your work.

Advanced Challenge Exercise

- Use Help to find out about creating a series of numbers.
- Delete the contents of cells A5:A9.
- Create a series of numbers in cells A5:A9.
- In cell C15, type a brief description of how you created the series.
- Save the workbook.

e. Create formulas in cells E5:E9 that calculate a running balance. (*Hint*: For the first check, the running balance equals the starting balance minus a check; for the subsequent checks, the running balance equals the previous balance value minus each check value.)

f. Create a formula in cell D10 that totals the amount of the checks.

g. Enter your name in cell C12, then compare your screen to Figure A-24.

h. Save your changes to the file, submit your work to your instructor, then exit Excel.

FIGURE A-24

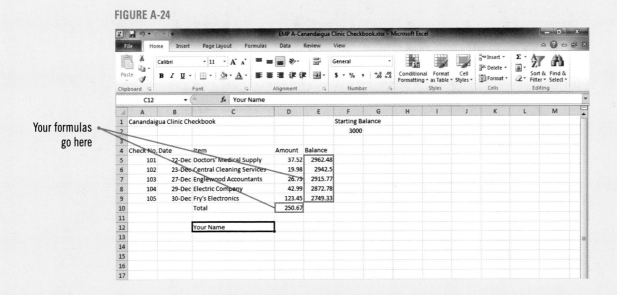

Visual Workshop

Open the file EMP A-5.xlsx from the drive and folder where you store your Data Files, then save it as **EMP A-Gold Coast Clinic Inventory Items**. Using the skills you learned in this unit, modify your worksheet so it matches Figure A-25. Enter formulas in cells D4 through D13 and in cells B14 and C14. Use the Sum button and fill handle to make entering your formulas easier. Add your name in the left header text box, print one copy of the worksheet with the formulas displayed, then turn off the formula display.

FIGURE A-25

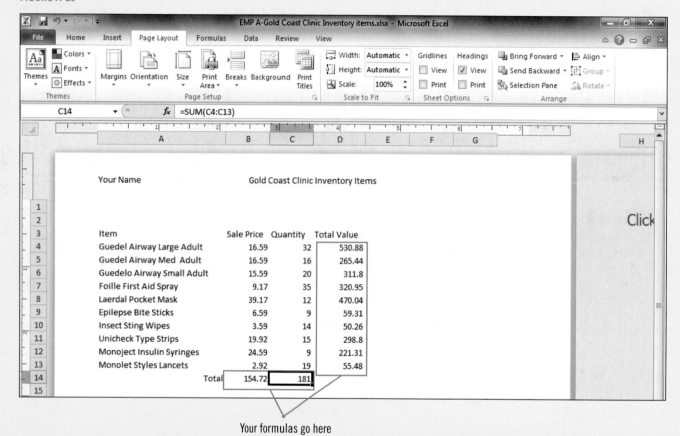

Your formulas go here

Working with Formulas and Functions

Files You Will Need:

EMP B-1.xlsx
EMP B-2.xlsx
EMP B-3.xlsx
EMP B-4.xlsx

Using your knowledge of Excel basics, you can develop your worksheets to include more complex formulas and functions. To work more efficiently, you can copy and move existing formulas into other cells instead of manually retyping the same information. When copying or moving, you can also control how cell references are handled so that your formulas always reference the intended cells. Tony Sanchez, R.N., office manager at Riverwalk Medical Clinic, needs to analyze departmental insurance reimbursements for the current year. He has asked you to prepare a worksheet that summarizes this reimbursement data and includes some statistical analysis. He would also like you to perform some what-if analysis, to see what quarterly revenues would look like with various projected increases.

OBJECTIVES

Create a complex formula

Insert a function

Type a function

Copy and move cell entries

Understand relative and absolute cell references

Copy formulas with relative cell references

Copy formulas with absolute cell references

Round a value with a function

©Jeffrey Coolidge/Photodisc/Getty Images

Creating a Complex Formula

A **complex formula** is one that uses more than one arithmetic operator. You might, for example, need to create a formula that uses addition and multiplication. In formulas containing more than one arithmetic operator, Excel uses the standard **order of precedence** rules to determine which operation to perform first. You can change the order of precedence in a formula by using parentheses around the part you want to calculate first. For example, the formula =4+2*5 equals 14, because the order of precedence dictates that multiplication is performed before addition. However, the formula =(4+2)*5 equals 30, because the parentheses cause 4+2 to be calculated first. ▰▰▰ You want to create a formula that calculates a 20% increase in insurance reimbursements.

STEPS

1. **Start Excel, open the file EMP B-1.xlsx from the drive and folder where you store your Data Files, then save it as EMP B-Insurance Reimbursement Analysis**

2. **Click cell B19, type =, click cell B17, then type +**

   In this first part of the formula, you are using a reference to the total insurance reimbursements for Quarter 1.

3. **Click cell B17, then type *.2**

   The second part of this formula adds a 20% increase (B17*.2) to the original value of the cell (the total insurance reimbursements for Quarter 1). Compare your worksheet to Figure B-1.

4. **Click the Enter button ☑ on the formula bar**

   The result, 410122.344, appears in cell B19.

5. **Press [Tab], type =, click cell C17, type +, click cell C17, type *.2, then click ☑**

   The result, 434969.712, appears in cell C19.

6. **Drag the fill handle from cell C19 to cell E19**

   The calculated values appear in the selected range, as shown in Figure B-2. Dragging the fill handle on a cell copies the cell's contents or continues a series of data (such as Quarter 1, Quarter 2, etc.) into adjacent cells. This option is called **Auto Fill**.

7. **Save your work**

Reviewing the order of precedence

When you work with formulas that contain more than one operator, the order of precedence is very important because it affects the final value. If a formula contains two or more operators, such as 4+.55/4000*25, Excel performs the calculations in a particular sequence based on the following rules: Operations inside parentheses are calculated before any other operations. Reference operators (such as ranges) are calculated first. Exponents are calculated next, then any multiplication and division—progressing from left to right.

Finally, addition and subtraction are calculated from left to right. In the example 4+.55/4000*25, Excel performs the arithmetic operations by first dividing 4000 into .55, then multiplying the result by 25, then adding 4. You can change the order of calculations by using parentheses. For example, in the formula (4+.55)/4000*25, Excel would first add 4 and .55, then divide that amount by 4000, then finally multiply by 25.

FIGURE B-1: Formula containing multiple arithmetic operators

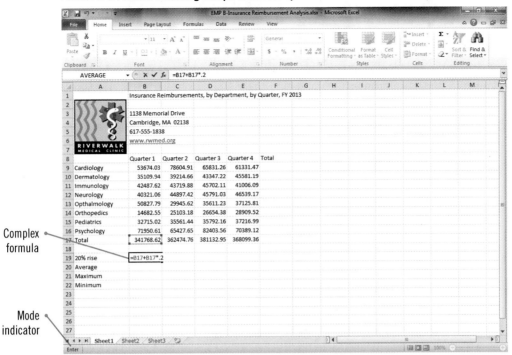

Complex formula

Mode indicator

FIGURE B-2: Complex formulas in worksheet

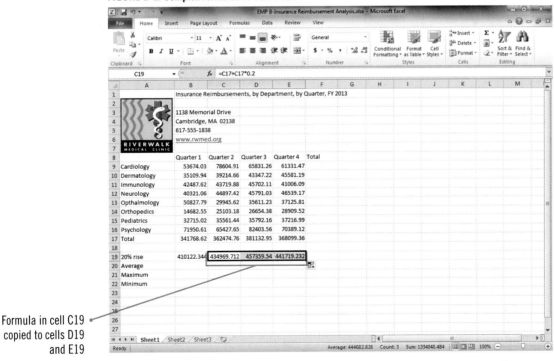

Formula in cell C19 copied to cells D19 and E19

Inserting a Function

Functions are predefined worksheet formulas that enable you to perform complex calculations easily. You can use the Insert Function button on the formula bar to choose a function from a dialog box. You can quickly insert the SUM function using the Sum button on the Ribbon, or you can click the Sum list arrow to enter other frequently used functions, such as AVERAGE. Functions are organized into categories, such as Financial, Date & Time, and Statistical, based on their purposes. You can insert a function on its own or as part of another formula. For example, you have used the SUM function on its own to add a range of cells. You could also use the SUM function within a formula that adds a range of cells and then multiplies the total by a decimal. If you use a function alone, it always begins with an equal sign (=) as the formula prefix. ░░░░░ You need to calculate the average reimbursements for the first quarter of the year, and decide to use a function to do so.

STEPS

1. **Click cell B20**

   This is the cell where you want to enter the calculation that averages reimbursements per department for the first quarter. You want to use the Insert Function dialog box to enter this function.

   QUICK TIP
   When using the Insert Function button or the Sum list arrow, it is not necessary to type the equal sign (=); Excel adds it as necessary.

2. **Click the Insert Function button 𝑓ₓ on the formula bar**

   An equal sign (=) is inserted in the active cell and in the formula bar, and the Insert Function dialog box opens, as shown in Figure B-3. In this dialog box, you specify the function you want to use by clicking it in the Select a function list. The Select a function list initially displays recently used functions. If you don't see the function you want, you can click the Or select a category list arrow to choose the desired category. If you're not sure which category to choose, you can type the function name or a description in the Search for a function field. The AVERAGE function is a statistical function, but you don't need to open the Statistical category because this function already appears in the Most Recently Used category.

   QUICK TIP
   To learn about a function, click it in the Select a function list. The arguments and format required for the function appear below the list.

3. **Click AVERAGE in the Select a function list if necessary, read the information that appears under the list, then click OK**

   The Function Arguments dialog box opens, in which you define the range of cells you want to average.

   QUICK TIP
   When selecting a range, remember to select all the cells between and including the two references in the range.

4. **Click the Collapse button 🔲 in the Number1 field of the Function Arguments dialog box, select the range B9:B16 in the worksheet, then click the Expand button 🔲 in the Function Arguments dialog box**

   Clicking the Collapse button minimizes the dialog box so you can select cells in the worksheet. When you click the Expand button, the dialog box is restored, as shown in Figure B-4. You can also begin dragging in the worksheet to automatically minimize the dialog box; after you select the desired range, the dialog box is restored.

5. **Click OK**

   The Function Arguments dialog box closes, and the calculated value is displayed in cell B20. The average reimbursement per department for Quarter 1 is 42721.0775.

6. **Click cell C20, click the Sum list arrow Σ ▾ in the Editing group on the Home tab, then click Average**

   A ScreenTip beneath cell C20 displays the arguments needed to complete the function. The text "number1" is shown in boldface type, telling you that the next step is to supply the first cell in the group you want to average. You want to average a range of cells.

7. **Select the range C9:C16 in the worksheet, then click the Enter button ✔ on the formula bar**

   The average reimbursements per department for the second quarter appears in cell C20.

8. **Drag the fill handle from cell C20 to cell E20**

   The formula in cell C20 is copied to the rest of the selected range, as shown in Figure B-5.

9. **Save your work**

FIGURE B-3: Insert Function dialog box

Search for a
function field

Select a
function
list; yours
may differ

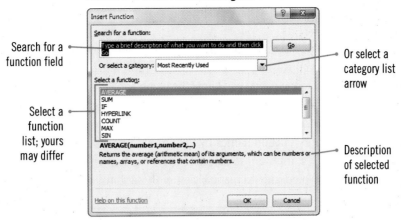

Or select a
category list
arrow

Description
of selected
function

FIGURE B-4: Expanded Function Arguments dialog box

Function in
formula bar

Insert
Function
button

Argument

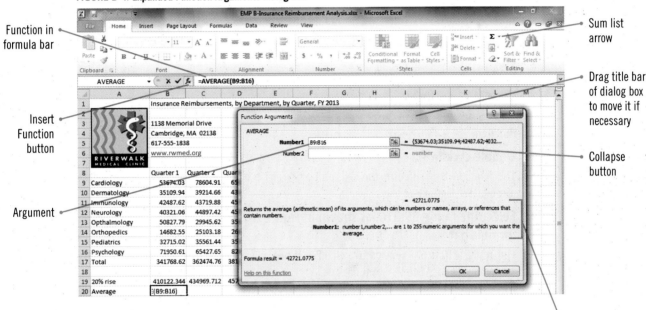

Sum list
arrow

Drag title bar
of dialog box
to move it if
necessary

Collapse
button

Description of function
and arguments

FIGURE B-5: Average functions used in worksheet

Completed
function
appears in
formula bar

Formula in
cell C20
copied to
cells D20
and E20

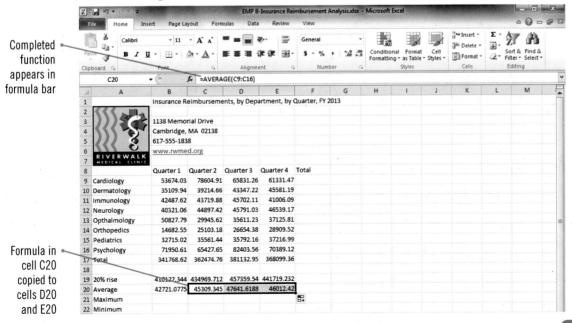

Typing a Function

In addition to using the Insert Function dialog box, the Sum button, or the Sum list arrow on the Ribbon to enter a function, you can manually type the function into a cell and then complete the arguments needed. This method requires that you know the name and initial characters of the function, but it can be faster than opening several dialog boxes. Experienced Excel users often prefer this method, but it is only an alternative, not better or more correct than any other method. Excel's Formula AutoComplete feature makes it easier to enter function names by typing, because it suggests functions depending on the first letters you type. You want to calculate the maximum and minimum quarterly reimbursements in your worksheet, and you decide to manually enter these statistical functions.

STEPS

1. **Click cell B21, type =, then type m**

   Because you are manually typing this function, it is necessary to begin with the equal sign (=). The Formula AutoComplete feature displays a list of function names beginning with "M" beneath cell B21. Once you type an equal sign in a cell, each letter you type acts as a trigger to activate the Formula AutoComplete feature. This feature minimizes the amount of typing you need to do to enter a function and reduces typing and syntax errors.

2. **Click MAX in the list**

   Clicking any function in the Formula AutoComplete list opens a ScreenTip next to the list that describes the function.

3. **Double-click MAX**

   The function is inserted in the cell, and a ScreenTip appears beneath the cell to help you complete the formula. See Figure B-6.

4. **Select the range B9:B16, as shown in Figure B-7, then click the Enter button ☑ on the formula bar**

   The result, 71950.61, appears in cell B21. When you completed the entry, the closing parenthesis was automatically added to the formula.

5. **Click cell B22, type =, type m, then double-click MIN in the list of function names**

   The MIN function appears in the cell.

6. **Select the range B9:B16, then press [Enter]**

   The result, 14682.55, appears in cell B22.

7. **Select the range B21:B22, then drag the fill handle from cell B22 to cell E22**

   The maximum and minimum values for all of the quarters appear in the selected range, as shown in Figure B-8.

8. **Save your work**

Using the COUNT and COUNTA functions

When you select a range, a count of cells in the range that are not blank appears in the status bar. For example, if you select the range A1:A5 and only cells A1 and A2 contain data, the status bar displays "Count: 2." To count nonblank cells more precisely, or to incorporate these calculations in a worksheet, you can use the COUNT and COUNTA functions. The COUNT function returns the number of cells in a range that contain numeric data, including numbers, dates, and formulas. The COUNTA function returns the number of cells in a range that contain any data at all, including numeric data, labels, and even a blank space. For example, the formula =COUNT(A1:A5) returns the number of cells in the range that contain numeric data, and the formula =COUNTA(A1:A5) returns the number of cells in the range that are not empty.

18					
19	20% rise	410122.344	434969.712	457359.54	441719.232
20	Average	42721.0775	45309.345	47641.6188	46012.42
21	Maximum	=MAX(			
22	Minimum	MAX(**number1**, [number2], ...)			
23					

FIGURE B-7: **Completing the MAX function**

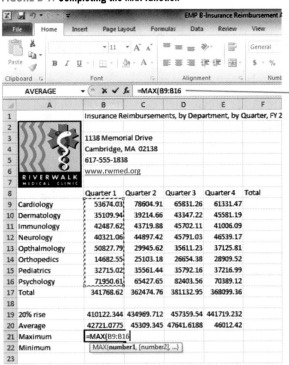

Closing parenthesis
will automatically
be added when you
accept the entry

FIGURE B-8: **Completed MAX and MIN functions**

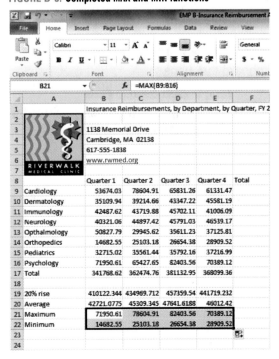

Copying and Moving Cell Entries

There are three ways you can copy or move cells and ranges (or the contents within them) from one location to another: the Cut, Copy, and Paste buttons on the Home tab on the Ribbon; the fill handle in the lower-right corner of the active cell or range; or the drag-and-drop feature. When you copy cells, the original data remains in the original location; when you cut or move cells, the original data is deleted from its original location. You can also cut, copy, and paste cells or ranges from one worksheet to another. ▓▓▓▓▓ In addition to the 20% rise in insurance reimbursements, you also want to show a 30% rise. Rather than retype this information, you copy and move the labels in these cells.

QUICK TIP
To cut or copy selected cell contents, activate the cell, then select the characters within the cell that you want to cut or copy.

1. **Select the range B8:E8, then click the Copy button 📋 in the Clipboard group on the Home tab**

   The selected range (B8:E8) is copied to the **Clipboard**, a temporary Windows storage area that holds the selections you copy or cut. A moving border surrounds the selected range until you press [Esc] or copy an additional item to the Clipboard.

2. **Click the dialog box launcher 🔲 in the Clipboard group**

   The Office Clipboard opens in the Clipboard task pane, as shown in Figure B-9. When you copy or cut an item, it is cut or copied both to the Clipboard provided by Windows and to the Office Clipboard. Unlike the Windows Clipboard, which holds just one item at a time, the Office Clipboard contains up to 24 of the most recently cut or copied items from any Office program. Your Clipboard task pane may contain more items than shown in the figure.

QUICK TIP
Once the Office Clipboard contains 24 items, the oldest existing item is automatically deleted each time you add an item.

3. **Click cell B25, then click the Paste button in the Clipboard group**

   A copy of the contents of range B8:E8 is pasted into the range B25:E25. When pasting an item from the Office Clipboard or Clipboard into a worksheet, you only need to specify the upper-left cell of the range where you want to paste the selection. Notice that the information you copied remains in the original range B8:E8; if you had cut instead of copied, the information would have been deleted from its original location once it was pasted.

4. **Press [Delete]**

   The selected cells are empty. You have decided to paste the cells in a different row. You can repeatedly paste an item from the Office Clipboard as many times as you like, as long as the item remains in the Office Clipboard.

QUICK TIP
You can also close the Office Clipboard pane by clicking the dialog box launcher in the Clipboard group.

5. **Click cell B24, click the first item in the Office Clipboard, then click the Close button ✖ on the Clipboard task pane**

   Cells B24:E24 contain the copied labels.

6. **Click cell A19, press and hold [Ctrl], point to any edge of the cell until the pointer changes to ▙⁺, drag cell A19 to cell A25, release the mouse button, then release [Ctrl]**

   The copy pointer ▙⁺ continues to appear as you drag, as shown in Figure B-10. When you release the mouse button, the contents of cell A19 are copied to cell A25.

7. **Click to the right of 2 in the formula bar, press [Backspace], type 3, then press [Enter]**

8. **Click cell B25, type =, click cell B17, type *1.3, click the Enter button ✔ on the formula bar, then save your work**

   This new formula calculates a 30% increase of the expenses for Quarter 1, though using a different method from what you previously used. Anything you multiply by 1.3 returns an amount that is 130% of the original amount, or a 30% increase. Compare your screen to Figure B-11.

FIGURE B-9: Copied data in Office Clipboard

Paste button

Copy button

Clipboard group dialog box launcher

Copied item in Office Clipboard

Clipboard task pane

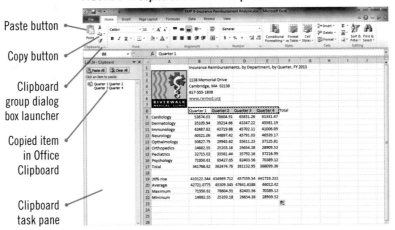

FIGURE B-10: Copying cell contents with drag-and-drop

Cell contents being copied

Plus (+) indicates copying in progress

Indicates new location of copy

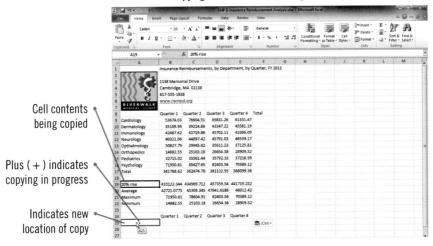

FIGURE B-11: Formula entered to calculate a 30% increase

Formula calculates a 30% increase

Inserting and deleting selected cells

As you add formulas to your workbook, you may need to insert or delete cells. When you do this, Excel automatically adjusts cell references to reflect their new locations. To insert cells, click the Insert list arrow in the Cells group on the Home tab, then click Insert Cells. The Insert dialog box opens, asking if you want to insert a cell and move the current active cell down or to the right of the new one. To delete one or more selected cells, click the Delete list arrow in the Cells group, click Delete Cells, and in the Delete dialog box, indicate which way you want to move the adjacent cells. When using this option, be careful not to disturb row or column alignment that may be necessary to maintain the accuracy of cell references in the worksheet. Click the Insert button or Delete button in the Cells group to insert or delete a single cell.

Understanding Relative and Absolute Cell References

As you work in Excel, you may want to reuse formulas in different parts of a worksheet to reduce the amount of data you have to retype. For example, you might want to include a what-if analysis in one part of a worksheet showing a set of sales projections if reimbursements increase by 10%. To include another analysis in another part of the worksheet showing projections if reimbursements increase by 50%, you can copy the formulas from one section to another and simply change the "1" to a "5". But when you copy formulas, it is important to make sure that they refer to the correct cells. To do this, you need to understand the difference between relative and absolute cell references. ▰▰▰▰ You plan to reuse formulas in different parts of your worksheets, so you want to understand relative and absolute cell references.

Consider the following when using relative and absolute cell references:

• **Use relative references when you want to preserve the relationship to the formula location**

When you create a formula that references another cell, Excel normally does not "record" the exact cell address for the cell being referenced in the formula. Instead, it looks at the relationship that cell has to the cell containing the formula. For example, in Figure B-12, cell F5 contains the formula: =SUM(B5:E5). When Excel retrieves values to calculate the formula in cell F5, it actually looks for "the four cells to the left of the formula," which in this case is cells B5:E5. This way, if you copy the cell to a new location, such as cell F6, the results will reflect the new formula location, and will automatically retrieve the values in cells B6, C6, D6, and E6. These are **relative cell references**, because Excel is recording the input cells *in relation to* or *relative to* the formula cell.

In most cases, you want to use relative cell references when copying or moving, so this is the Excel default. In Figure B-12, the formulas in F5:F12 and in B13:F13 contain relative cell references. They total the "four cells to the left of" or the "eight cells above" the formulas.

• **Use absolute cell references when you want to preserve the exact cell address in a formula**

There are times when you want Excel to retrieve formula information from a specific cell, and you don't want the cell address in the formula to change when you copy it to a new location. For example, you might have a price in a specific cell that you want to use in all formulas, regardless of their location. If you use relative cell referencing, the formula results would be incorrect, because Excel would use a different cell every time you copy the formula. Therefore you need to use an **absolute cell reference**, which is a reference that does not change when you copy the formula.

You create an absolute cell reference by placing a $ (dollar sign) in front of both the column letter and the row number of the cell address. You can either type the dollar sign when typing the cell address in a formula (for example, "=C12*$B$16"), or you can select a cell address on the formula bar and then press [F4] and the dollar signs are added automatically. Figure B-13 shows formulas containing both absolute and relative references. The formulas in cells B19 to E26 use absolute cell references to refer to a potential sales increase of 50%, shown in cell B16.

FIGURE B-12: Formulas containing relative references

Formula containing relative references

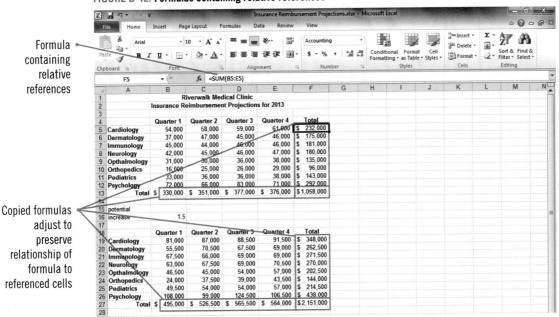

Copied formulas adjust to preserve relationship of formula to referenced cells

FIGURE B-13: Formulas containing absolute and relative references

Absolute references in copied formulas do not change

Cell referenced in absolute formulas

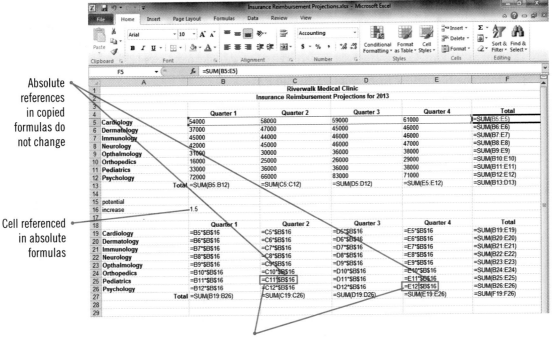

Relative references in copied formulas adjust to the new location

Using a mixed reference

Sometimes when you copy a formula, you want to change the row reference, but keep the column reference the same. This type of cell referencing combines elements of both absolute and relative referencing and is called a **mixed reference**. For example, when copied, a formula containing the mixed reference C$14 would change the column letter relative to its new location, but not the row number. In the mixed reference $C14, the column letter would not change, but the row number would be updated relative to its location. Like an absolute reference, a mixed reference can be created by pressing the [F4] function key with the cell reference selected. With each press of the [F4] key, you cycle through all the possible combinations of relative, absolute, and mixed references ($C$14, C$14, $C14, and C14).

Copying Formulas with Relative Cell References

Copying and moving a cell allows you to reuse a formula you've already created. Copying cells is usually faster than retyping the formulas in them and helps to prevent typing errors. If the cells you are copying contain relative cell references and you want to maintain the relative referencing, you don't need to make any changes to the cells before copying them. █████ You want to copy the formula in cell B25, which calculates the 30% increase in insurance reimbursements for Quarter 1, to cells C25 through E25. You also want to create formulas to calculate total reimbursements for each department.

STEPS

1. **Click cell B25 if necessary, then click the Copy button 📋 in the Clipboard group on the Home tab**

   The formula for calculating the 30% expense increase during Quarter 1 is copied to the Clipboard. Notice that the formula =B17*1.3 appears in the formula bar, and a moving border surrounds the active cell.

2. **Click cell C25, then click the Paste button** *(not the list arrow)* **in the Clipboard group**

   The formula from cell B25 is copied into cell C25, where the new result of 471217.188 appears. Notice in the formula bar that the cell references have changed, so that cell C17 is referenced in the formula. This formula contains a relative cell reference, which tells Excel to substitute new cell references within the copied formulas as necessary. This maintains the same relationship between the new cell containing the formula and the cell references within the formula. In this case, Excel adjusted the formula so that cell C17—the cell reference eight rows above C25—replaced cell B17, the cell reference nine rows above B25.

3. **Drag the fill handle from cell C25 to cell E25**

   A formula similar to the one in cell C25 now appears in cells D25 and E25. After you use the fill handle to copy cell contents, the **Auto Fill Options button** appears, as seen in Figure B-14. You can use the Auto Fill Options button to fill the cells with only specific elements of the copied cell if you wish.

4. **Click cell F9, click the Sum button Σ in the Editing group, then click the Enter button ✓ on the formula bar**

5. **Click 📋 in the Clipboard group, select the range F10:F11, then click the Paste button**

   See Figure B-15. After you click the Paste button, the **Paste Options button** appears, which you can use to paste only specific elements of the copied selection if you wish. The formula for calculating total expenses for tours in Britain appears in the formula bar. You would like totals to appear in cells F12:F16. The Fill button in the Editing group can be used to copy the formula into the remaining cells.

6. **Select the range F11:F16**

7. **Click the Fill button 📋▾ in the Editing group, then click Down**

   The formulas containing relative references are copied to each cell. Compare your worksheet to Figure B-16.

8. **Save your work**

Using Paste Preview

You can selectively copy formulas, values, or other choices using the Paste list arrow, and you can see how the pasted contents will look using the Paste Preview feature. When you click the Paste list arrow, a gallery of paste option icons opens. When you point to an icon, a preview of how the content will be pasted using that option is shown in the worksheet. Options include pasting values only, pasting values with number formatting, pasting formulas only, pasting formatting only, pasting transposed data so that column data appears in rows and row data appears in columns, and pasting with no borders (to remove any borders around pasted cells).

FIGURE B-14: Formula copied using the fill handle

		Quarter 1	Quarter 2	Quarter 3	Quarter 4
22	Minimum	14682.55	25103.18	26654.38	28909.52
23					
24		Quarter 1	Quarter 2	Quarter 3	Quarter 4
25	30% rise	444299.206	471217.188	495472.835	478529.168
26					
27					

Auto Fill Options button

FIGURE B-15: Formulas pasted in the range F10:F11

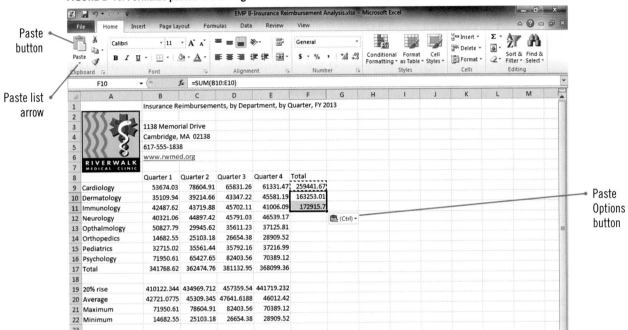

Paste button

Paste list arrow

Paste Options button

FIGURE B-16: Cells copied using Fill Down

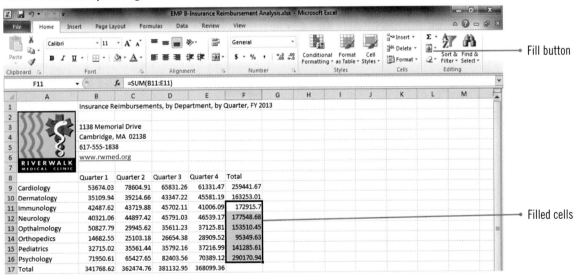

Fill button

Filled cells

Using Auto Fill Options

When you use the fill handle to copy cells, the Auto Fill Options button appears. Auto Fill options differ depending on what you are copying. If you had selected cells containing a series (such as "Monday" and "Tuesday") and then used the fill handle, you would see options for continuing the series (such as "Wednesday" and "Thursday") or for simply pasting the copied cells. Clicking the Auto Fill Options button opens a list that lets you choose from the following options: Copy Cells, Fill Series (if applicable), Fill Formatting Only, or Fill Without Formatting. Choosing Copy Cells means that the cell's contents and its formatting will be copied. The Fill Formatting Only option copies only the formatting attributes, but not cell contents. The Fill Without Formatting option copies the cell contents, but no formatting attributes. Copy Cells is the default option when using the fill handle to copy a cell, so if you want to copy the cell's contents and its formatting, you can ignore the Auto Fill Options button.

Copying Formulas with Absolute Cell References

When copying formulas, you might want one or more cell references in the formula to remain unchanged in relation to the formula. In such an instance, you need to apply an absolute cell reference before copying the formula to preserve the specific cell address when the formula is copied. You create an absolute reference by placing a dollar sign ($) before the column letter and row number of the address (for example, $A$1). ▨▨▨▨ You need to do some what-if analysis to see how various percentage increases might affect total reimbursements. You decide to add a column that calculates a possible increase in the total reimbursements, and then change the percentage to see various potential results.

STEPS

1. **Click cell G6, type Change, then press [Enter]**

2. **Type 1.1, then press [Enter]**
   You store the increase factor that will be used in the what-if analysis in this cell (G7). The value 1.1 can be used to calculate a 10% increase; anything you multiply by 1.1 returns an amount that is 110% of the original amount.

3. **Click cell H8, type What if?, then press [Enter]**

4. **In cell H9, type =, click cell F9, type *, click cell G7, then click the Enter button ☑ on the formula bar**
   The result, 285385.8, appears in cell H9. This value represents the total annual insurance reimbursements for the cardiology department if there is a 10% increase. You want to perform a what-if analysis for all the departments.

5. **Drag the fill handle from cell H9 to cell H16**
   The resulting values in the range H9:H16 are all zeros, which is *not* the result you wanted. Because you used relative cell addressing in cell H9, the copied formula adjusted so that the formula in cell H10 is =F10*G8. Because there is no value in cell G8, the result is 0, an error. You need to use an absolute reference in the formula to keep the formula from adjusting itself. That way, it will always reference cell G7.

6. **Click cell H9, press [F2] to change to Edit mode, then press [F4]**
   When you press [F2], the range finder outlines the arguments of the equation in blue and green. The insertion point appears next to the G7 cell reference in cell H9. When you press [F4], dollar signs are inserted in the G7 cell reference, making it an absolute reference. See Figure B-17.

7. **Click ☑, then drag the fill handle from cell H9 to cell H16**
   Because the formula correctly contains an absolute cell reference, the correct values for a 10% increase appear in cells H9:H16. You now want to see what a 20% increase in expenses looks like.

8. **Click cell G7, type 1.2, then click ☑**
   The values in the range H9:H16 change to reflect the 20% increase. Compare your worksheet to Figure B-18.

9. **Save your work**

FIGURE B-17: **Absolute reference created in formula**

Absolute cell reference in formula

Incorrect values from relative referencing in previously copied formulas

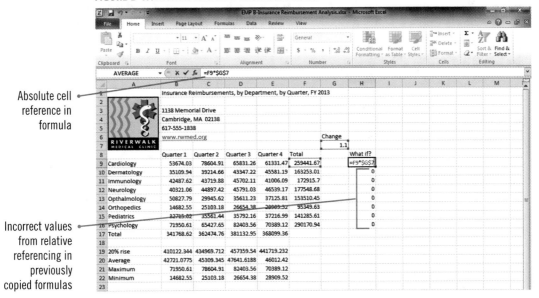

FIGURE B-18: **What-if analysis with modified change factor**

Modified change factor

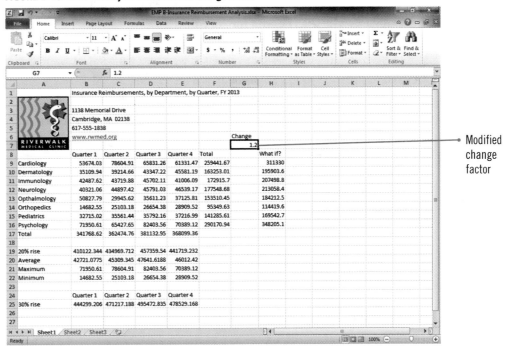

Using the fill handle for sequential text or values

Often, you need to fill cells with sequential text: months of the year, days of the week, years, or text plus a number (Quarter 1, Quarter 2,...). For example, you might want to create a worksheet that calculates data for every month of the year. Using the fill handle, you can quickly and easily create labels for the months of the year just by typing "January" in a cell. Drag the fill handle from the cell containing "January" until you have all the monthly labels you need. You can also easily fill cells with a date sequence by dragging the fill handle on a single cell containing a date. You can fill cells with a number sequence (such as 1, 2, 3,...) by dragging the fill handle on a selection of two or more cells that contain the sequence. To create a number sequence using the value in a single cell, press and hold [Ctrl] as you drag the fill handle of the cell. As you drag the fill handle, Excel automatically extends the existing sequence into the additional cells. (The content of the last filled cell appears in the ScreenTip.) To examine all the fill series options for the current selection, click the Fill button in the Editing group on the Home tab, then click Series to open the Series dialog box.

Rounding a Value with a Function

The more you explore features and tools in Excel, the more ways you'll find to simplify your work and convey information more efficiently. For example, cells containing financial data are often easier to read if they contain fewer decimal places than those that appear by default. You can round a value or formula result to a specific number of decimal places by using the ROUND function. In your worksheet, you'd like to round the cells showing the 20% rise in reimbursements to show fewer digits; after all, it's not important to show cents in the projections, only whole dollars. You want Excel to round the calculated value to the nearest integer. You decide to edit cell B19 so it includes the ROUND function, and then copy the edited formula into the other formulas in this row.

STEPS

1. **Click cell B19, then click to the right of = in the formula bar**

   You want to position the function at the beginning of the formula, before any values or arguments.

2. **Type RO**

   Formula AutoComplete displays a list of functions beginning with RO beneath the formula bar.

3. **Double-click ROUND in the functions list**

   The new function and an opening parenthesis are added to the formula, as shown in Figure B-19. A few additional modifications are needed to complete your edit of the formula. You need to indicate the number of decimal places to which the function should round numbers and you also need to add a closing parenthesis around the set of arguments that comes after the ROUND function.

4. **Press [END], type ,0), then click the Enter button ✔ on the formula bar**

   The comma separates the arguments within the formula, and 0 indicates that you don't want any decimal places to appear in the calculated value. When you complete the edit, the parentheses at either end of the formula briefly become bold, indicating that the formula has the correct number of open and closed parentheses and is balanced.

5. **Drag the fill handle from cell B19 to cell E19**

   The formula in cell B19 is copied to the range C19:E19. All the values are rounded to display no decimal places. Compare your worksheet to Figure B-20.

6. **Click cell A27, type your name, then click ✔ on the formula bar**

7. **Save your work, preview the worksheet in Backstage view, then submit your work to your Instructor as directed**

8. **Exit Excel**

FIGURE B-19: ROUND function added to an existing formula

ROUND function and opening parenthesis inserted in formula

Screentip indicates needed arguments

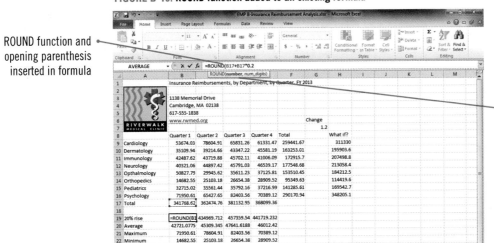

FIGURE B-20: Completed worksheet

Function surrounds existing formula

Calculated values with no decimals

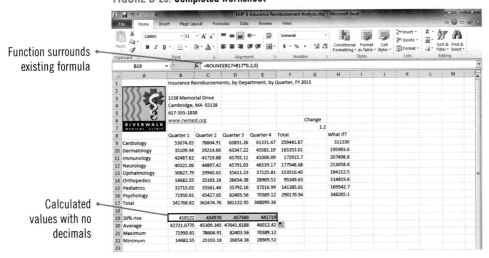

Creating a new workbook using a template

Excel **templates** are predesigned workbook files intended to save time when you create common documents such as balance sheets, budgets, or time cards. Templates contain labels, values, formulas, and formatting, so all you have to do is customize them with your own information. Excel comes with many templates, and you can also create your own or find additional templates on the Web. Unlike a typical workbook, which has the file extension .xlsx, a template has the extension .xltx. To create a workbook using a template, click the File tab, then click New on the navigation bar. The Available Templates pane in Backstage view lists templates installed on your computer and templates available through Office.com. The Blank Workbook template is selected by default and is used to create a blank workbook with no content or special formatting. A preview of the selected template appears to the right of the Available Templates pane. To select a template, click a category in the Available Templates pane, select the template you want in the category, then click Create (if you've selected an installed template) or Download (if you've selected an Office.com template). Figure B-21 shows a template selected in the Budgets category of Office.com templates. (Your list of templates may differ.) When you click Create or

Download, a new workbook is created based on the template; when you save the new file in the default format, it has the regular .xlsx extension. To save a workbook of your own as a template, open the Save As dialog box, click the Save as type list arrow, then change the file type to Excel Template.

FIGURE B-21: Budget template selected in Backstage view

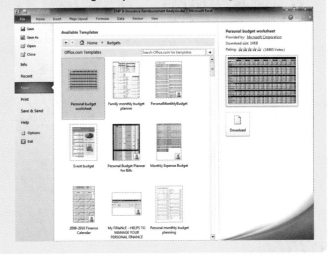

Practice

Concepts Review

For current SAM information, including versions and content details, visit SAM Central (http://www.cengage.com/samcentral). If you have a SAM user profile, you may have access to hands-on instruction, practice, and assessment of the skills covered in this unit. Since various versions of SAM are supported throughout the life of this text, check with your instructor for the correct instructions and URL/Web site for accessing assignments.

Label each element of the Excel worksheet window shown in Figure B-22.

FIGURE B-22

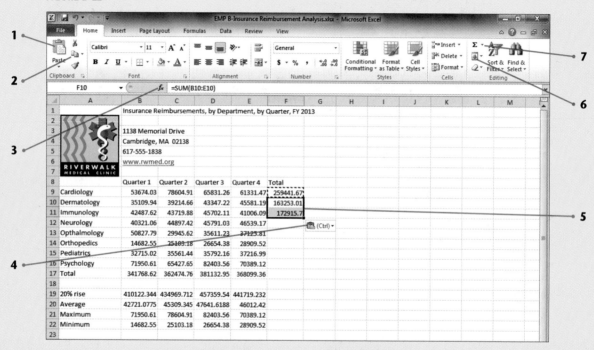

Match each term or button with the statement that best describes it.

8. Fill handle
9. Dialog box launcher
10. Drag-and-drop method
11. [Delete]
12. Formula AutoComplete

a. Clears the contents of selected cells
b. Item on the Ribbon that opens a dialog box or task pane
c. Lets you move or copy data from one cell to another without using the Clipboard
d. Displays an alphabetical list of functions from which you can choose
e. Lets you copy cell contents or continue a series of data into a range of selected cells

Select the best answer from the list of choices.

13. Which key do you press to copy while dragging and dropping selected cells?
    a. [Alt]
    b. [Ctrl]
    c. [F2]
    d. [Tab]

14. What type of cell reference is C$19?
    a. Relative
    b. Absolute
    c. Mixed
    d. Certain

15. What type of cell reference changes when it is copied?
    a. Circular
    b. Absolute
    c. Relative
    d. Specified

16. Which key do you press to convert a relative cell reference to an absolute cell reference?
    a. [F2]
    b. [F4]
    c. [F5]
    d. [F6]

17. You can use any of the following features to enter a function *except*:
    a. Insert Function button.
    b. Formula AutoComplete.
    c. Sum list arrow.
    d. Clipboard.

Skills Review

1. **Create a complex formula.**
   a. Open the file EMP B-2.xlsx from the drive and folder where you store your Data Files, then save it as **EMP B-Medical Supply Company Inventory**.
   b. In cell B11, create a complex formula that calculates a 30% decrease in the total number of cases of O_2 Masks.
   c. Use the fill handle to copy this formula into cell C11 through cell E11.
   d. Save your work.

2. **Insert a function.**
   a. Use the Sum list arrow to create a formula in cell B13 that averages the number of cases of O_2 Masks in each storage area.
   b. Use the Insert Function button to create a formula in cell B14 that calculates the maximum number of cases of O_2 Masks in a storage area.
   c. Use the Sum list arrow to create a formula in cell B15 that calculates the minimum number of cases of O_2 Masks in a storage area.
   d. Save your work.

3. **Type a function.**
   a. In cell C13, type a formula that includes a function to average the number of cases of O_2 Tubes in each storage area. (*Hint*: Use Formula AutoComplete to enter the function.)
   b. In cell C14, type a formula that includes a function to calculate the maximum number of cases of O_2 Tubes in a storage area.
   c. In cell C15, type a formula that includes a function to calculate the minimum number of cases of O_2 Tubes in a storage area.
   d. Save your work.

Skills Review (continued)

4. **Copy and move cell entries.**
   a. Select the range B3:F3.
   b. Copy the selection to the Clipboard.
   c. Open the Clipboard task pane, then paste the selection into cell B17.
   d. Close the Clipboard task pane, then select the range A4:A9.
   e. Use the drag-and-drop method to copy the selection to cell A18. (*Hint*: The results should fill the range A18:A23.)
   f. Save your work.

5. **Understand relative and absolute cell references.**
   a. Write a brief description of the difference between relative and absolute references.
   b. List at least three situations in which you think a business might use an absolute reference in its calculations. Examples can include calculations for different types of worksheets, such as time cards, invoices, and budgets.

6. **Copy formulas with relative cell references.**
   a. Calculate the total in cell F4.
   b. Use the Fill button to copy the formula in cell F4 down to cells F5:F8.
   c. Select the range C13:C15.
   d. Use the fill handle to copy these cells to the range D13:F15.
   e. Save your work.

7. **Copy formulas with absolute cell references.**
   a. In cell H1, enter the value **1.575**.
   b. In cell H4, create a formula that multiplies F4 and an absolute reference to cell H1.
   c. Use the fill handle to copy the formula in cell H4 to cells H5 and H6.
   d. Use the Copy and Paste buttons to copy the formula in cell H4 to cells H7 and H8.
   e. Change the amount in cell H1 to **2.3**.
   f. Save your work.

8. **Round a value with a function.**
   a. Click cell H4.
   b. Edit this formula to include the ROUND function showing one decimal place.
   c. Use the fill handle to copy the formula in cell H4 to the range H5:H8.
   d. Enter your name in cell A25, then compare your work to Figure B-23.
   e. Save your work, preview the worksheet in Backstage view, then submit your work to your instructor as directed.
   f. Close the workbook, then exit Excel.

FIGURE B-23

Your formulas
go here

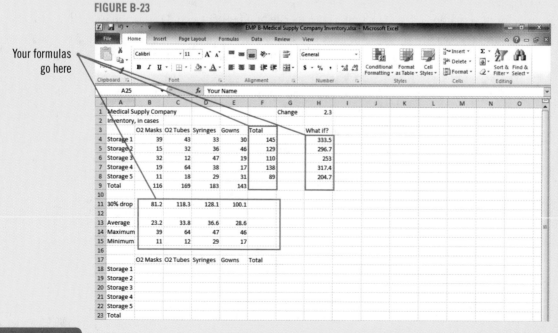

Working with Formulas and Functions

Independent Challenge 1

You keep the accounts for a local charity that wants to start a small clinic in an area that currently doesn't offer its residents any medical services. Before you begin, you need to evaluate what you think your monthly expenses will be. You've started a workbook, but need to complete the entries and add formulas.

a. Open the file EMP B-3.xlsx from the drive and folder where you store your Data Files, then save it as **EMP B-Estimated Clinic Expenses**.

b. Make up your own expense data, and enter it in cells B4:B10. (Monthly expenses are already included in the worksheet.)

c. Create a formula in cell C4 that calculates the annual rent.

d. Copy the formula in cell C4 to the range C5:C10.

e. Move the label in cell A15 to cell A14.

f. Create formulas in cells B11 and C11 that total the monthly and annual expenses.

g. Create a formula in cell C13 that calculates annual reimbursements.

h. Create a formula in cell B14 that determines whether the clinic will make a profit or loss, then copy the formula into cell C14.

i. Copy the labels in cells B3:C3 to cells E3:F3.

j. Type **Projection Increase** in cell G1, then type **.2** in cell I1.

k. Create a formula in cell E4 that calculates an increase in the monthly rent by the amount in cell I1. You will be copying this formula to other cells, so you'll need to use an absolute reference.

l. Create a formula in cell F4 that calculates the increased annual rent expense based on the calculation in cell E4.

m. Copy the formulas in cells E4:F4 into cells E5:F10 to calculate the remaining monthly and annual expenses.

n. Create a formula in cell E11 that calculates the total monthly expenses, then copy that formula to cell F11.

o. Copy the contents of cells B13:C13 into cells E13:F13.

p. Create formulas in cells E14 and F14 that calculate profit/loss based on the projected increase in monthly and annual reimbursements.

q. Change the projected increase to **.15**, then compare your work to the sample in Figure B-24.

r. Enter your name in a cell in the worksheet.

s. Save your work, preview the worksheet in Backstage view, submit your work to your instructor as directed, close the workbook, and exit Excel.

FIGURE B-24

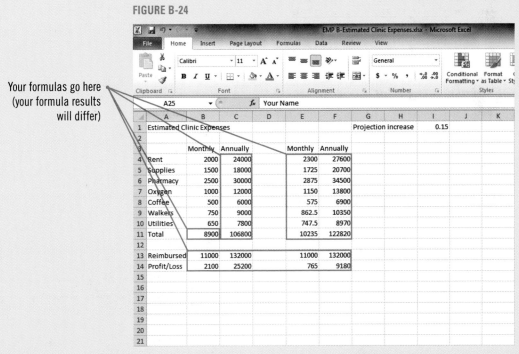

Independent Challenge 2

The Flight Nurse Training Academy is a small, growing flight nurse training center that has hired you to organize its accounting records using Excel. The owners want you to track the company's expenses. Before you were hired, one of the bookkeepers began entering last year's expenses in a workbook, but the analysis was never completed.

a. Start Excel, open the file EMP B-4.xlsx from the drive and folder where you store your Data Files, then save it as **EMP B-Flight Nurse Training Academy**. The worksheet includes labels for functions such as the average, maximum, and minimum amounts of each of the expenses in the worksheet.

b. Think about what information would be important for the bookkeeping staff to know.

c. Using the SUM function, create formulas for each expense in the Total column and each quarter in the Total row.

d. Create formulas for each expense and each quarter in the Average, Maximum, and Minimum columns and rows using the method of your choice.

e. Save your work, then compare your worksheet to the sample shown in Figure B-25.

FIGURE B-25

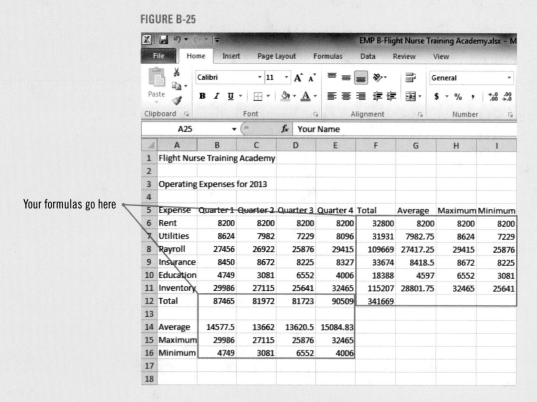

Your formulas go here

Advanced Challenge Exercise

- Create the label **Expense categories** in cell B19.
- In cell A19, create a formula using the COUNT function that determines the total number of expense categories listed per quarter.
- Save the workbook.

f. Enter your name in cell A25.

g. Preview the worksheet, then submit your work to your instructor as directed.

h. Close the workbook and exit Excel.

Independent Challenge 3

As the accounting manager of an independently-managed laboratory within a hospital, it is your responsibility to calculate accrued sales tax payments on a monthly basis and then submit the payments to the state government. You've decided to use an Excel workbook to make these calculations.

a. Start Excel, then save a new, blank workbook to the drive and folder where you store your Data Files as **EMP B-Sales Tax Calculations**.

b. Decide on the layout for all columns and rows. The worksheet will contain data for four labs, which you can name by department, or another method of your choice. For each lab, you will calculate total sales tax based on the local sales tax rate. You'll also calculate total tax owed by all four labs.

c. Make up sales data for all four labs.

d. Enter the rate to be used to calculate the sales tax, using your own local rate.

e. Create formulas to calculate the sales tax owed for each lab. If you don't know the local tax rate, use **6.65%**.

f. Create a formula to total all the owed sales tax, and reference the cell containing the total tax two rows down with descriptive text preceding it.

FIGURE B-26

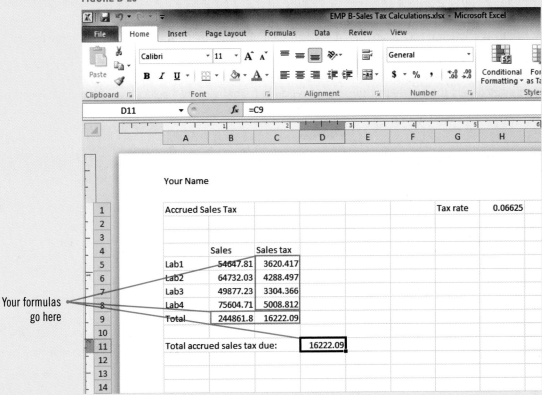

Your formulas go here

Advanced Challenge Exercise

- Use the ROUND function to eliminate any decimal places in the sales tax figures for each lab and the total due.
- Save the workbook.

g. Add your name to the header.

h. Save your work, preview the worksheet, compare your work to the sample shown in Figure B-26, and submit your work to your instructor as directed.

i. Close the workbook and exit Excel.

Real Life Independent Challenge

The doctors for whom you work are thinking of buying a residence and converting it into a private practice, and have asked you to help them with the process. As you begin the round of open houses and realtors' listings, you notice that there are many fees associated with buying a home. Some fees are based on a percentage of the purchase price, and others are a flat fee; overall, they seem to represent a substantial amount above the purchase prices you see listed. You've seen five houses so far that interest you; one is easily affordable, and the remaining four are all nice, but increasingly more expensive. Although the practice will be financing the house, the bottom line is still important to you, so you decide to create an Excel workbook to figure out the real cost of buying each one.

a. Find out the typical cost or percentage rate of at least three fees that are usually charged when buying a house and taking out a mortgage. (*Hint*: If you have access to the Internet you can research the topic of home buying on the Web, or you can ask friends about standard rates or percentages for items such as title insurance, credit reports, and inspection fees.)

b. Start Excel, then save a new, blank workbook to the drive and folder where you store your Data Files as **EMP B-Home Purchase Costs**.

c. Create labels and enter data for at least three houses. If you enter this information across the columns in your worksheet, you should have one column for each house, with the purchase price in the cell below each label. Be sure to enter a different purchase price for each house.

d. Create labels for the Fees column and for an Amount or Rate column. Enter the information for each of the fees you have researched.

e. In each house column, enter formulas that calculate the fee for each item. The formulas (and use of absolute or relative referencing) will vary depending on whether the charges are a flat fee or based on a percentage of the purchase price.

Working with Formulas and Functions

Real Life Independent Challenge (continued)

f. Total the fees for each house, then create formulas that add the total fees to the purchase price. A sample of what your workbook might look like is shown in Figure B-27.

g. Enter a title for the worksheet in the header.

h. Enter your name in the header, save your work, preview the worksheet, then submit your work to your instructor as directed.

i. Close the file and exit Excel.

FIGURE B-27

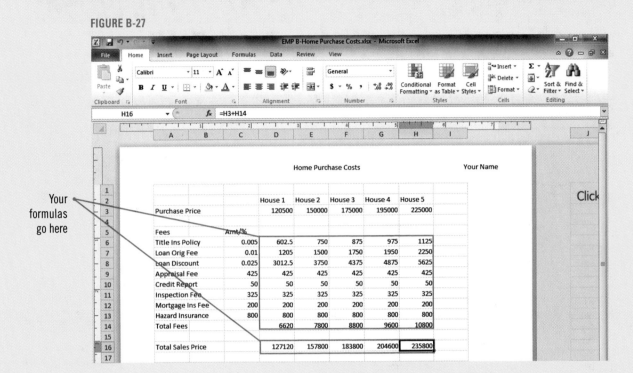

Visual Workshop

Create the worksheet shown in Figure B-28 using the skills you learned in this unit. Save the workbook as **EMP B-Health Insurance Cost Analysis** to the drive and folder where you store your Data Files. Enter your name in the header as shown, hide the gridlines, preview the worksheet, and then submit your work to your instructor as directed.

FIGURE B-28

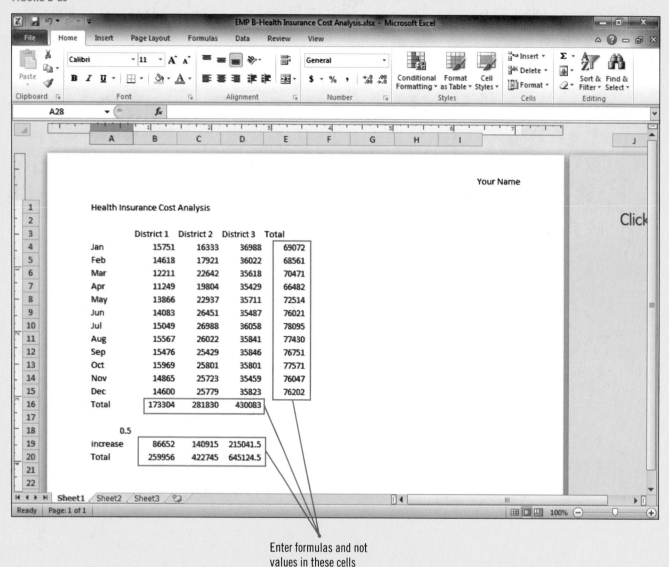

Enter formulas and not values in these cells

Working with Formulas and Functions

Formatting a Worksheet

Files You Will Need:

EMP C-1.xlsx
EMP C-2.xlsx
EMP C-3.xlsx
EMP C-4.xlsx
EMP C-5.xlsx

You can use formatting features to make a worksheet more attractive or easier to read, and to emphasize key data. You can apply different formatting attributes such as colors, font styles, and font sizes to the cell contents; you can adjust column width and row height; and you can insert or delete columns and rows. You can also apply conditional formatting so that cells meeting certain conditions are formatted differently from other cells. This makes it easy to emphasize selected information, such as sales that exceed or fall below a certain threshold.  The administrators at RMC have requested data on expenses incurred during the first quarter of this year. Tony Sanchez has created a worksheet listing this information. He asks you to format the worksheet to make it easier to read and to call attention to important data.

OBJECTIVES

Format values

Change font and font size

Change font styles and alignment

Adjust column width

Insert and delete rows and columns

Apply colors, patterns, and borders

Apply conditional formatting

Rename and move a worksheet

Check spelling

UNIT C
Excel 2010

Formatting Values

The **format** of a cell determines how the labels and values look—for example, whether the contents appear boldfaced, italicized, or with dollar signs and commas. Formatting changes only the appearance of a value or label; it does not alter the actual data in any way. To format a cell or range, first you select it, then you apply the formatting using the Ribbon, Mini toolbar, or a keyboard shortcut. You can apply formatting before or after you enter data in a cell or range. Tony has provided you with a worksheet that lists individual emergency room expenses, and you're ready to improve its appearance and readability. You decide to start by formatting some of the values so they are displayed as currency, percentages, and dates.

STEPS

1. **Start Excel, open the file EMP C-1.xlsx from the drive and folder where you store your Data Files, then save it as EMP C-RMC Emergency Room Expenses**
   This worksheet is difficult to interpret because all the information is crowded and looks the same. In column A, the contents appear cut off because there is too much data to fit given the current column width. You decide not to widen the column yet, because the other changes you plan to make might affect column width and row height. The first thing you want to do is format the data showing the cost of each ad.

2. **Select the range D11:D39, then click the Accounting Number Format button [$] in the Number group on the Home tab**
   The default **Accounting number format** adds dollar signs and two decimal places to the data, as shown in Figure C-1. Formatting this data in Accounting format makes it clear that its values are monetary values. Excel automatically resizes the column to display the new formatting. The Accounting and Currency number formats are both used for monetary values, but the Accounting format aligns currency symbols and decimal points of numbers in a column.

3. **Select the range F11:H39, then click the Comma Style button in the Number group**
   The values in columns F, G, and H display the Comma Style format, which does not include a dollar sign but can be useful for some types of accounting data.

4. **Select the range J11:J39, click the Number Format list arrow, click Percentage, then click the Increase Decimal button in the Number group three times**
   The Number Format list arrow lets you choose from popular number formats and shows an example of what the selected cell or cells would look like in each format (when multiple cells are selected, the example is based on the first cell in the range). Each time you click the Increase Decimal button, you add one decimal place; clicking the button twice would add two decimal places.

5. **Click the Decrease Decimal button in the Number group twice**
   Two decimal places are removed from the percentage values in column J. The data in the % of Total column is now formatted with a percent sign (%) and three decimal places.

6. **Select the range B11:B38, then click the dialog box launcher in the Number group**
   The Format Cells dialog box opens with the Date category already selected on the Number tab.

7. **Select the first 14-Mar-01 format in the Type list box as shown in Figure C-2, then click OK**
   The dates in column B appear in the 14-Mar-01 format. The second 14-Mar-01 format in the list displays all days in two digits (it adds a leading zero if the day is only a single-digit number), while the one you chose displays single-digit days without a leading zero.

8. **Select the range C11:C38, right-click the range, click Format Cells on the shortcut menu, click 14-Mar in the Type list box in the Format Cells dialog box, then click OK**
   Compare your worksheet to Figure C-3.

9. **Press [Ctrl][Home], then save your work**

QUICK TIP
You can use a different type of currency, such as Euros or British pounds, by clicking the Accounting Number Format list arrow, then clicking a different currency format.

QUICK TIP
Select any range of contiguous cells by clicking the upper-left cell of the range, pressing and holding [Shift], then clicking the lower-right cell of the range. Add a row to the selected range by continuing to hold down [Shift] and pressing ↓; add a column by pressing →.

QUICK TIP
Make sure you examine formatted data to confirm that you have applied the appropriate formatting; for example, dates should not have a currency format, and monetary values should not have a date format.

FIGURE C-1: **Accounting number format applied to range**

Number Format list arrow

Decrease Decimal button

Increase Decimal button

Comma Style button

Accounting Number Format button

Cells formatted with Accounting number format

Number group buttons change the appearance of a value

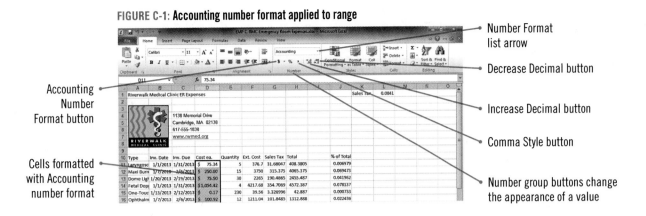

FIGURE C-2: **Format Cells dialog box**

Number categories

Date format types

Sample of selected type

This format looks similar to the one below it but displays single digit months and days with a preceding zero

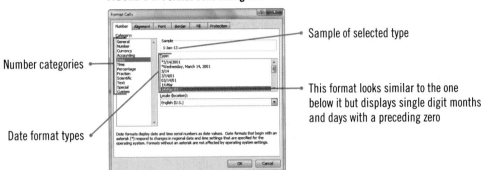

FIGURE C-3: **Worksheet with formatted values**

New format displays in the format box

Date formats appear without year

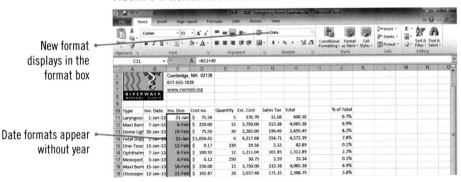

Formatting as a table

Excel includes 60 predefined **table styles** to make it easy to format selected worksheet cells as a table. You can apply table styles to any range of cells that you want to format quickly, or even to an entire worksheet, but they're especially useful for those ranges with labels in the left column and top row, and totals in the bottom row or right column. To apply a table style, select the data to be formatted or click anywhere within the intended range (Excel can automatically detect a range of cells filled with data), click the Format as Table button in the Styles group on the Home tab, then click a style in the gallery, as shown in Figure C-4. Table styles are organized in three categories: Light, Medium, and Dark. Once you click a style, Excel asks you to confirm the range selection, then applies the style. Once you have formatted a range as a table, you can use Live Preview to preview the table in other styles by pointing to any style in the Table Styles gallery.

FIGURE C-4: **Table Styles gallery**

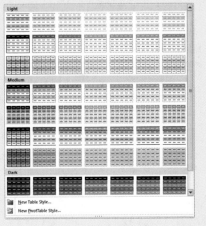

Changing Font and Font Size

A **font** is the name for a collection of characters (letters, numbers, symbols, and punctuation marks) with a similar, specific design. The **font size** is the physical size of the text, measured in units called points. A **point** is equal to $1/72$ of an inch. The default font and font size in Excel is 11-point Calibri. Table C-1 shows several fonts in different font sizes. You can change the font and font size of any cell or range using the Font and Font Size list arrows. The Font and Font Size list arrows appear on the Home tab on the Ribbon and on the Mini toolbar, which opens when you right-click a cell or range. *You want to change the font and font size of the labels and the worksheet title so that they stand out more from the data.*

STEPS

1. **Click cell A1, click the Font list arrow in the Font group on the Home tab, scroll down in the Font list to see an alphabetical listing of the fonts available on your computer, then click Times New Roman, as shown in Figure C-5**

   The font in cell A1 changes to Times New Roman. Notice that the font names on the list are displayed in the font they represent.

2. **Click the Font Size list arrow in the Font group, then click 20**

   The worksheet title appears in 20-point Times New Roman, and the Font and Font Size list boxes on the Home tab display the new font and font size information.

3. **Click the Increase Font Size button $\boxed{A^\cdot}$ in the Font group twice**

   The font size of the title increases to 24 point.

4. **Select the range A10:J10, right-click, then click the Font list arrow in the Font group on the Mini toolbar**

   The Mini toolbar includes the most commonly used formatting tools, so it's great for making quick formatting changes.

5. **Scroll down in the Font list and click Times New Roman, click the Font Size list arrow on the Mini toolbar, then click 14**

   The Mini toolbar closes when you move the pointer away from the selection. Compare your worksheet to Figure C-6. Notice that some of the column labels are now too wide to appear fully in the column. Excel does not automatically adjust column widths to accommodate cell formatting; you have to adjust column widths manually. You'll learn to do this in a later lesson.

6. **Save your work**

TABLE C-1: Examples of fonts and font sizes

font	12 point	24 point
Calibri	Excel	Excel
Playbill	Excel	Excel
Comic Sans MS	Excel	Excel
Times New Roman	Excel	Excel

FIGURE C-5: Font list in the Format Cells dialog box

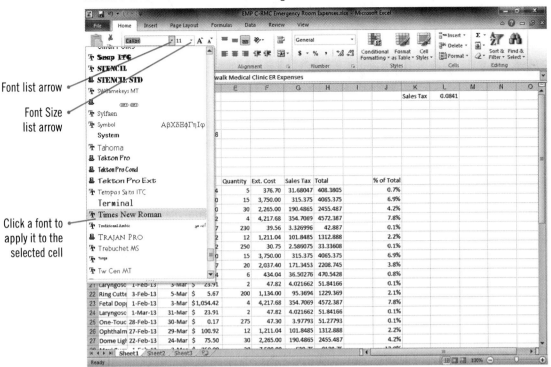

Font list arrow

Font Size list arrow

Click a font to apply it to the selected cell

FIGURE C-6: Worksheet with formatted title and column labels

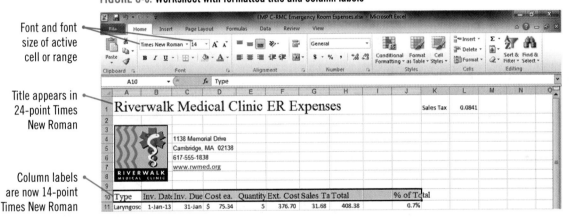

Font and font size of active cell or range

Title appears in 24-point Times New Roman

Column labels are now 14-point Times New Roman

Inserting and adjusting clip art and other images

You can illustrate your worksheets using clip art and other images. A **clip** is an individual media file, such as a graphic, sound, animation, or a movie. **Clip art** refers to images such as a corporate logo, a picture, or a photo. Microsoft Office comes with many clips available for your use. (The RMC files in this unit display the hospital's logo.) To add a clip to a worksheet, click the Clip Art button in the Illustrations group on the Insert tab. The Clip Art task pane opens. Here you can search for clips by typing one or more keywords (words related to your subject) in the Search for text box, then click Go. Clips that relate to your keywords appear in the Clip Art task pane, as shown in Figure C-7. (If you have a standard Office installation and an active Internet connection, click the Include Office.com content check box to see clips available through Office.com in addition to those on your computer.) When you click the image you want in the Clip Art task pane, the image is inserted at the location of the active cell. To add your own images to a worksheet, click the Insert tab on the Ribbon, then click the Picture button. Navigate to the file you want, then click Insert. To resize an image, drag any corner sizing handle. To move an image, point inside the clip until the pointer changes to ⁺⁺⁺, then drag it to a new location.

FIGURE C-7: Results of Clip Art search

Click to begin search

Type keyword(s) here

Formatting a Worksheet

Changing Font Styles and Alignment

Font styles are formats such as bold, italic, and underlining that you can apply to affect the way text and numbers look in a worksheet. You can also change the **alignment** of labels and values in cells to position them in relation to the cells' edges—such as left-aligned, right-aligned, or centered. You can apply font styles and alignment options using the Home tab, the Format Cells dialog box, or the Mini toolbar. See Table C-2 for a description of common font style and alignment buttons that are available on the Home tab and the Mini toolbar. Once you have formatted a cell the way you want it, you can "paint" or copy the cell's formats into other cells by using the Format Painter button in the Clipboard group on the Home tab. This is similar to using copy and paste, but instead of copying cell contents, it copies only the cell's formatting. You want to further enhance the worksheet's appearance by adding bold and underline formatting and centering some of the labels.

STEPS

1. **Press [Ctrl][Home], then click the Bold button** ▣ **in the Font group on the Home tab**
   The title in cell A1 appears in bold.

2. **Click cell A10, then click the Underline button** ▣ **in the Font group**
   The column label is now underlined, though this may be difficult to see with the cell selected.

3. **Click the Italic button** ▣ **in the Font group, then click** ▣
   The heading now appears in boldface, underlined, italic type. Notice that the Bold, Italic, and Underline buttons in the Font group are all selected.

4. **Click the Italic button** ▣ **to deselect it**
   The italic font style is removed from cell A3, but the bold and underline font styles remain.

5. **Click the Format Painter button** ▣ **in the Clipboard group, then select the range B10:J10**
   The formatting in cell A10 is copied to the rest of the column labels. To paint the formats on more than one selection, double-click the Format Painter button to keep it activated until you turn it off. You can turn off the Format Painter by pressing [Esc] or by clicking ▣. You decide the title would look better if it were centered over the data columns.

6. **Select the range A1:H1, then click the Merge & Center button** ▣ **in the Alignment group**
   The Merge & Center button creates one cell out of the eight cells across the row, then centers the text in that newly created, merged cell. The title "Riverwalk Medical Clinic ER Expenses" is centered across the eight columns you selected. To split a merged cell into its original components, select the merged cell, then click the Merge & Center button to deselect it. The merged and centered text might look awkward now, but you'll be changing the column widths shortly.

7. **Select the range A10:J10, right-click, then click the Center button** ▣ **on the Mini toolbar**
   Compare your screen to Figure C-8. Although they may be difficult to read, notice that all the headings are centered within their cells.

8. **Save your work**

FIGURE C-8: Worksheet with font styles and alignment applied

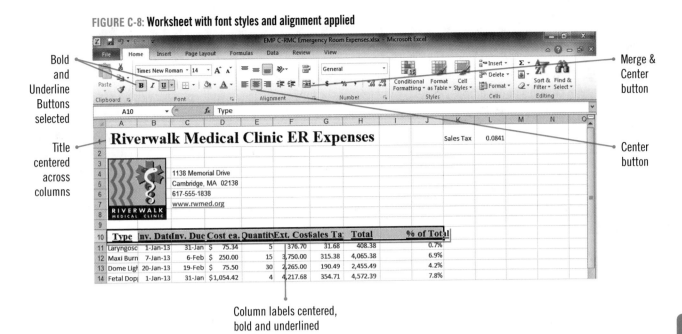

Bold and Underline Buttons selected

Title centered across columns

Merge & Center button

Center button

Column labels centered, bold and underlined

TABLE C-2: Common font style and alignment buttons

button	description	button	description
B	Bolds text	▤	Aligns text at the left edge of the cell
I	Italicizes text	▤	Centers text horizontally within the cell
<u>U</u>	Underlines text	▤	Aligns text at the right edge of the cell
▦	Centers text across columns, and combines two or more selected, adjacent cells into one cell		

Rotating and indenting cell entries

In addition to applying fonts and font styles, you can rotate or indent data within a cell to further change its appearance. You can rotate text within a cell by altering its alignment. To change alignment, select the cells you want to modify, then click the dialog box launcher ▣ in the Alignment group to open the Alignment tab of the Format Cells dialog box. Click a position in the Orientation box or type a number in the Degrees text box to rotate text from its default horizontal orientation, then click OK. You can indent cell contents using the Increase Indent button ▦ in the Alignment group, which moves cell contents to the right one space, or the Decrease Indent button ▦, which moves cell contents to the left one space.

Adjusting Column Width

As you format a worksheet, you might need to adjust the width of one or more columns to accommodate changes in the amount of text, the font size, or font style. The default column width is 8.43 characters, a little less than 1". With Excel, you can adjust the width of one or more columns by using the mouse, the Format button in the Cells group on the Home tab, or the shortcut menu. Using the mouse, you can drag or double-click the right edge of a column heading. The Format button and shortcut menu include commands for making more precise width adjustments. Table C-3 describes common column formatting commands. ⬛⬛ You have noticed that some of the labels in columns A through J don't fit in the cells. You want to adjust the widths of the columns so that the labels appear in their entirety.

STEPS

1. **Position the mouse pointer on the line between the column A and column B headings until it changes to ↔**

   See Figure C-9. The **column heading** is the box at the top of each column containing a letter. Before you can adjust column width using the mouse, you need to position the pointer on the right edge of the column heading for the column you want to adjust. The cell entry "Monoject Syringes" is the widest in the column.

2. **Click and drag the ↔ to the right until the column displays the "Monoject Syringes" cell entries fully (approximately 16.43 characters, 1.31", or 120 pixels)**

   As you change the column width, a ScreenTip is displayed listing the column width. In Normal view, the ScreenTip lists the width in characters and pixels; in Page Layout view, the ScreenTip lists the width in inches and pixels.

3. **Position the pointer on the line between columns B and C until it changes to ↔, then double-click**

   Double-clicking the right edge of a column heading activates the **AutoFit** feature, which automatically resizes the column to accommodate the widest entry in the column. Column B automatically widens to fit the widest entry, which is the column label "Inv. Date".

4. **Use AutoFit to resize columns D and J, and resize column C so it has a width of 10 characters**

5. **Select the range E12:H12**

   You can change the width of multiple columns at once, by first selecting either the column headings or at least one cell in each column.

6. **Click the Format button in the Cells group, then click Column Width**

   The Column Width dialog box opens. Column width measurement is based on the number of characters that will fit in the column when formatted in the Normal font and font size (in this case, 11 pt Calibri).

7. **Drag the dialog box by its title bar if its placement obscures your view of the worksheet, type 11 in the Column width text box, then click OK**

   The widths of columns E, F, G, and H change to reflect the new setting. See Figure C-10.

8. **Save your work**

TABLE C-3: Common column formatting commands

command	description	available using
Column Width	Sets the width to a specific number of characters	Format button; shortcut menu
AutoFit Column Width	Fits to the widest entry in a column	Format button; mouse
Hide & Unhide	Hides or displays hidden column(s)	Format button; shortcut menu
Default Width	Resets column to worksheet's default column width	Format button

FIGURE C-9: **Preparing to change the column width**

Resize pointer

Format button

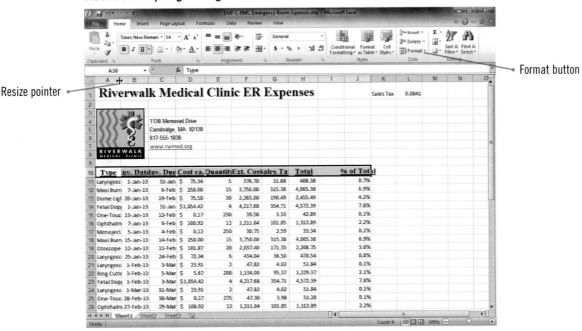

FIGURE C-10: **Worksheet with column widths adjusted**

Columns widened to display text

Columns widened to same width

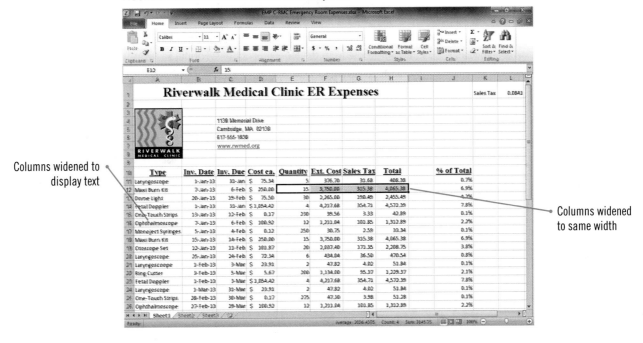

Changing row height

Changing row height is as easy as changing column width. Row height is calculated in points, the same units of measure used for fonts. The row height must exceed the size of the font you are using. Normally, you don't need to adjust row heights manually, because row heights adjust automatically to accommodate font size changes. If you format something in a row to be a larger point size, Excel adjusts the row to fit the largest point size in the row. However, you have just as many options for changing row height as you do

column width. Using the mouse, you can place the ✛ pointer on the line dividing a row heading from the heading below, and then drag to the desired height; double-clicking the line AutoFits the row height where necessary. You can also select one or more rows, then use the Row Height command on the shortcut menu, or click the Format button on the Home tab and click the Row Height or AutoFit Row Height command.

Inserting and Deleting Rows and Columns

As you modify a worksheet, you might find it necessary to insert or delete rows and columns to keep your worksheet current. For example, you might need to insert rows to accommodate new inventory products or remove a column of yearly totals that are no longer necessary. When you insert a new row, the row is inserted above the cell pointer and the contents of the worksheet shift down from the newly inserted row. When you insert a new column, the column is inserted to the left of the cell pointer and the contents of the worksheet shift to the right of the new column. To insert multiple rows, select the same number of row headings as you want to insert before using the Insert command. ███████ You want to improve the overall appearance of the worksheet by inserting a row between the last row of data and the totals. Also, you have learned that row 34 and column J need to be deleted from the worksheet.

STEPS

QUICK TIP

To insert a single row or column, right-click the row heading immediately below where you want the new row, or right-click the column heading to the right of where you want the new column, then click Insert on the short-cut menu.

1. **Right-click cell A39, then click Insert on the shortcut menu**

   The Insert dialog box opens. See Figure C-11. You can choose to insert a column or a row; insert a single cell and shift the cells in the active column to the right; or insert a single cell and shift the cells in the active row down. An additional row between the last row of data and the totals will visually separate the totals.

2. **Click the Entire row option button, then click OK**

   A blank row appears between the Otoscope Set data and the totals, and the formula result in cell E40 has not changed. The Insert Options button ⬚ appears beside cell A40. Pointing to the button displays a list arrow, which you can click and then choose from the following options: Format Same As Above (the default setting, already selected), Format Same As Below, or Clear Formatting.

QUICK TIP

If you inadvertently click the Delete list arrow instead of the button itself, click Delete Sheet Rows in the menu that opens.

3. **Click the row 34 heading**

   All of row 34 is selected, as shown in Figure C-12.

4. **Click the Delete button in the Cells group; *do not click the list arrow***

   Excel deletes row 34, and all rows below it shift up one row. You must use the Delete button or the Delete command on the shortcut menu to delete a row or column; pressing [Delete] on the keyboard removes only the *contents* of a selected row or column.

5. **Click the column J heading**

   The percentage information is calculated elsewhere and is no longer necessary in this worksheet.

QUICK TIP

After inserting or deleting rows or columns in a work-sheet, be sure to proof formulas that contain relative cell references.

6. **Click the Delete button in the Cells group**

   Excel deletes column J. The remaining columns to the right shift left one column.

7. **Save your work**

Hiding and unhiding columns and rows

When you don't want data in a column or row to be visible, but you don't want to delete it, you can hide the column or row. To hide a selected column, click the Format button in the Cells group on the Home tab, point to Hide & Unhide, then click Hide Columns. A hidden column is indicated by a dark black vertical line in its original position. This black line disappears when you click elsewhere in the worksheet. You can display a hidden column by selecting the columns on either side of the hidden column, clicking the Format button in the Cells group, pointing to Hide & Unhide, and then clicking Unhide Columns. (To hide or unhide one or more rows, substitute Hide Rows and Unhide Rows for the Hide Columns and Unhide Columns commands.)

FIGURE C-11: Insert dialog box

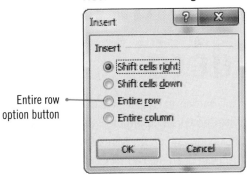

Entire row option button

FIGURE C-12: Worksheet with row 34 selected

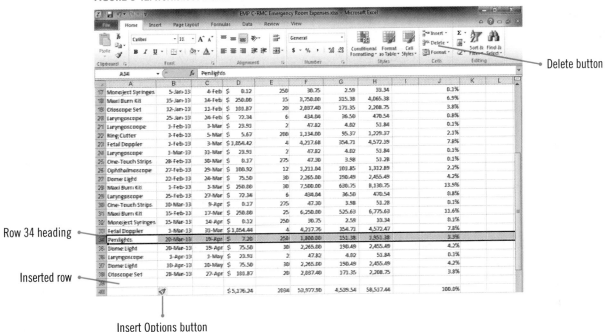

Delete button

Row 34 heading

Inserted row

Insert Options button

Adding and editing comments

Much of your work in Excel may be in collaboration with teammates with whom you share worksheets. You can share ideas with other worksheet users by adding comments within selected cells. To include a comment in a worksheet, click the cell where you want to place the comment, click the Review tab on the Ribbon, then click the New Comment button in the Comments group. You can type your comments in the resizable text box that opens containing the computer user's name. A small, red triangle appears in the upper-right corner of a cell containing a comment. If comments are not already displayed in a workbook, other users can point to the triangle to display the comment. To see all worksheet comments, as shown in Figure C-13, click the Show All Comments button in the Comments group. To edit a comment, click the cell containing the comment, then click the Edit Comment button in the Comments group. To delete a comment, click the cell containing the comment, then click the Delete button in the Comments group.

FIGURE C-13: Comments displayed in a worksheet

Applying Colors, Patterns, and Borders

You can use colors, patterns, and borders to enhance the overall appearance of a worksheet and make it easier to read. You can add these enhancements by using the Borders, Font Color, and Fill Color buttons in the Font group on the Home tab of the Ribbon and on the Mini toolbar, or by using the Fill tab and the Border tab in the Format Cells dialog box. You can open the Format Cells dialog box by clicking the dialog box launcher in the Font, Alignment, or Number group on the Home tab, or by right-clicking a selection, then clicking Format Cells on the shortcut menu. You can apply a color to the background of a cell or a range or to cell contents (such as letters and numbers), and you can apply a pattern to a cell or range. You can apply borders to all the cells in a worksheet or only to selected cells to call attention to selected information. To save time, you can also apply **cell styles**, predesigned combinations of formats. ▰▰▰ You want to add a pattern, a border, and color to the title of the worksheet to give the worksheet a more professional appearance.

1. **Select cell A1, click the Fill Color list arrow ⬛ ▾ in the Font group, then hover the pointer over the Turquoise, Accent 2 color (first row, sixth column from the left)**

   See Figure C-14. Live Preview shows you how the color will look *before* you apply it. (Remember that cell A1 spans columns A through H because the Merge & Center command was applied.)

2. **Click the Turquoise, Accent 2 color**

   The color is applied to the background (or fill) of this cell. When you change fill or font color, the color on the Fill Color or Font Color button changes to the last color you selected.

3. **Right-click cell A1, then click Format Cells on the shortcut menu**

   The Format Cells dialog box opens.

4. **Click the Fill tab, click the Pattern Style list arrow, click the 6.25% Gray style (first row, sixth column from the left), then click OK**

5. **Click the Borders list arrow ⬚ ▾ in the Font group, then click Thick Bottom Border**

   Unlike underlining, which is a text-formatting tool, borders extend to the width of the cell, and can appear at the bottom of the cell, at the top, on either side, or on any combination of the four sides. It can be difficult to see a border when the cell is selected.

6. **Select the range A10:H10, click the Font Color list arrow ⬛ ▾ in the Font group, then click the Blue, Accent 1 color (first Theme color row, fifth column from the left) on the palette**

   The new color is applied to the labels in the selected range.

7. **Select the range J1:K1, click the Cell Styles button in the Styles group, then click the Neutral cell style (first row, fourth column from the left) in the gallery**

   The font and color change in the range, as shown in Figure C-15.

8. **Save your work**

FIGURE C-14: **Live Preview of fill color**

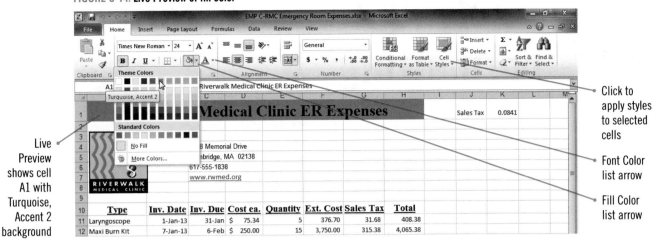

Live Preview shows cell A1 with Turquoise, Accent 2 background

Click to apply styles to selected cells

Font Color list arrow

Fill Color list arrow

FIGURE C-15: **Worksheet with color, patterns, border, and style applied**

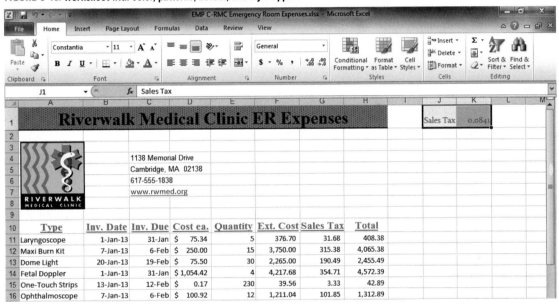

Working with themes and cell styles

Using themes and cell styles makes it easier to ensure that your worksheets are consistent. A **theme** is a predefined set of formats that gives your Excel worksheet a professional look. Formatting choices included in a theme are colors, fonts, and line and fill effects. To apply a theme, click the Themes button in the Themes group on the Page Layout tab to open the Themes gallery, as shown in Figure C-16, then click a theme in the gallery. **Cell styles** are sets of cell formats based on themes, so they are automatically updated if you change a theme. For example, if you apply the 20% - Accent1 cell style to cell A1 in a worksheet that has no theme applied, the fill color changes to light blue and the font changes to Constantia. If you change the theme of the worksheet to Metro, cell A1's fill color changes to light green and the font changes to Corbel, because these are the new theme's associated formats.

FIGURE C-16: **Themes gallery**

Formatting a Worksheet

Applying Conditional Formatting

So far, you've used formatting to change the appearance of different types of data, but you can also use formatting to highlight important aspects of the data itself. For example, you can apply formatting that changes the font color to red for any cells where ER costs exceed $4000 and to green where ER costs are below $2000. This is called **conditional formatting** because Excel automatically applies different formats to data if the data meets conditions you specify. The formatting is updated if you change data in the worksheet. You can also copy conditional formats the same way you copy other formats. ▓▓▓ Tony is concerned about emergency room costs exceeding the yearly budget. You decide to use conditional formatting to highlight certain trends and patterns in the data so that it's easy to spot the highest expenditures.

STEPS

1. **Select the range H11:H37, click the Conditional Formatting button in the Styles group on the Home tab, point to Data Bars, then point to the Light Blue Data Bar (second row, second from left)**

   Data bars are colored horizontal bars that visually illustrate differences between values in a range of cells. Live Preview shows how this formatting will appear in the worksheet, as shown in Figure C-17.

QUICK TIP
You can apply an Icon Set to a selected range by clicking the Conditional Formatting button in the Styles group, then pointing to Icon Sets; icons appear within the cells to illustrate differences in values.

2. **Point to the Green Data Bar (first row, second from left), then click it**

3. **Select the range F11:F37, click the Conditional Formatting button in the Styles group, then point to Highlight Cells Rules**

   The Highlight Cells Rules submenu displays choices for creating different formatting conditions. For example, you can create a rule for values that are greater than or less than a certain amount, or between two amounts.

4. **Click Between on the submenu**

   The Between dialog box opens, displaying input boxes you can use to define the condition and a default format (Light Red Fill with Dark Red Text) selected for cells that meet that condition. Depending on the condition you select in the Highlight Cells Rules submenu (such as "Greater Than" or "Less Than"), this dialog box displays different input boxes. You define the condition using the input boxes and then assign the formatting you want to use for cells that meet that condition. Values used in input boxes for a condition can be constants, formulas, cell references, or dates.

QUICK TIP
To define custom formatting for data that meets the condition, click Custom Format at the bottom of the with list, and then use the Format Cells dialog box to set the formatting to be applied.

5. **Type 2000 in the first text box, type 4000 in the second text box, click the with list arrow, click Light Red Fill, compare your settings to Figure C-18, then click OK**

   All cells with values between 2000 and 4000 in column F appear with a light red fill.

6. **Click cell F14, type 3975.55, then press [Enter]**

   When the value in cell F14 changes, the formatting also changes because the new value meets the condition you set. Compare your results to Figure C-19.

7. **Press [Ctrl][Home] to select cell A1, then save your work**

Managing conditional formatting rules

If you create a conditional formatting rule and then want to change the condition to reflect a different value or format, you don't need to create a new rule; instead, you can modify the rule using the Rules Manager. Select the cell(s) containing conditional formatting, click the Conditional Formatting button in the Styles group, then click Manage Rules. The Conditional Formatting Rules Manager dialog box opens. Select the rule you want to edit, click Edit Rule, and then modify the settings in the Edit the Rule Description area in the Edit Formatting Rule dialog box. To change the formatting for a rule, click the Format button in the Edit the Rule Description area, select the formatting styles you want the text to have, then click OK three times to close the Format Cells dialog box, the Edit Formatting Rule dialog box, and then the Conditional Formatting Rules Manager dialog box. The rule is modified, and the new conditional formatting is applied to the selected cells. To delete a rule, select the rule in the Conditional Formatting Rules Manager dialog box, then click the Delete Rule button.

FIGURE C-17: Previewing data bars in a range

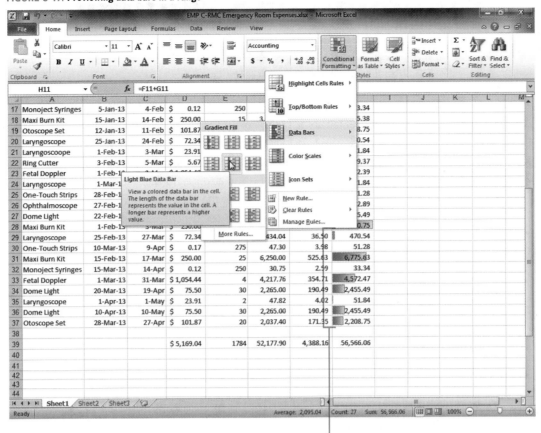

Live Preview shows data bars
displayed in selected range

FIGURE C-18: Between dialog box

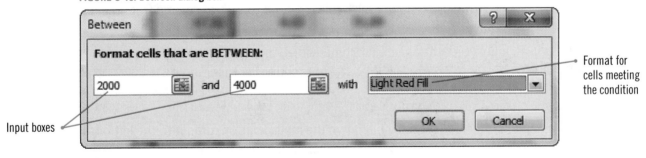

Format for
cells meeting
the condition

Input boxes

FIGURE C-19: Worksheet with conditional formatting

10	Type	Inv. Date	Inv. Due	Cost ea.	Quantity	Ext. Cost	Sales Tax	Total
11	Laryngoscope	1-Jan-13	31-Jan	$ 75.34	5	376.70	31.68	408.38
12	Maxi Burn Kit	7-Jan-13	6-Feb	$ 250.00	15	3,750.00	315.38	4,065.38
13	Dome Light	20-Jan-13	19-Feb	$ 75.50	30	2,265.00	190.49	2,455.49
14	Fetal Doppler	1-Jan-13	31-Jan	$ 1,054.42	4	3,975.55	334.34	4,309.89
15	One-Touch Strips	13-Jan-13	12-Feb	$ 0.17	230	39.56	3.33	42.89
16	Ophthalmoscope	7-Jan-13	6-Feb	$ 100.92	12	1,211.04	101.85	1,312.89
17	Monoject Syringes	5-Jan-13	4-Feb	$ 0.12	250	30.75	2.59	33.34
18	Maxi Burn Kit	15-Jan-13	14-Feb	$ 250.00	15	3,750.00	315.38	4,065.38
19	Otoscope Set	12-Jan-13	11-Feb	$ 101.87	20	2,037.40	171.35	2,208.75
20	Laryngoscope	25-Jan-13	24-Feb	$ 72.34	6	434.04	36.50	470.54
21	Laryngoscoope	1-Feb-13	3-Mar	$ 23.91	2	47.82	4.02	51.84
22	Ring Cutter	3-Feb-13	5-Mar	$ 5.67	200	1,134.00	95.37	1,229.37
23	Fetal Doppler	1-Feb-13	3-Mar	$ 1,054.42	4	4,217.68	354.71	4,572.39
24	Laryngoscope	1-Mar-13	31-Mar	$ 23.91	2	47.82	4.02	51.84
25	One-Touch Strips	28-Feb-13	30-Mar	$ 0.17	275	47.30	3.98	51.28
26	Ophthalmoscope	27-Feb-13	29-Mar	$ 100.92	12	1,211.04	101.85	1,312.89

Renaming and Moving a Worksheet

By default, an Excel workbook initially contains three worksheets, named Sheet1, Sheet2, and Sheet3. Each sheet name appears on a sheet tab at the bottom of the worksheet. When you open a new workbook, the first worksheet, Sheet1, is the active sheet. To move from sheet to sheet, you can click any sheet tab at the bottom of the worksheet window. The sheet tab scrolling buttons, located to the left of the sheet tabs, are useful when a workbook contains too many sheet tabs to display at once. To make it easier to identify the sheets in a workbook, you can rename each sheet and add color to the tabs. You can also organize them in a logical way. For instance, to better track performance goals, you could name each workbook sheet for an individual salesperson, and you could move the sheets so they appear in alphabetical order. ▰▰▰ In the current worksheet, Sheet1 contains information about actual ER expenses. Sheet2 contains an ER expense budget, and Sheet3 contains no data. You want to rename the two sheets in the workbook to reflect their contents, add color to a sheet tab to easily distinguish one from the other, and change their order.

STEPS

QUICK TIP

You can also rename a sheet by right-clicking the tab, clicking Rename on the shortcut menu, typing the new name, then pressing [Enter].

1. **Click the Sheet2 tab**

   Sheet2 becomes active, appearing in front of the Sheet1 tab; this is the worksheet that contains the budgeted emergency room expenses. See Figure C-20.

2. **Click the Sheet1 tab**

   Sheet1, which contains the actual emergency room expenses, becomes active again.

3. **Double-click the Sheet2 tab, type Budget, then press [Enter]**

   The new name for Sheet2 automatically replaces the default name on the tab. Worksheet names can have up to 31 characters, including spaces and punctuation.

QUICK TIP

To delete a sheet, click its tab, click the Delete list arrow in the Cells group, then click Delete Sheet. To insert a worksheet, click the Insert Worksheet button 🗐 to the right of the sheet tabs.

4. **Right-click the Budget tab, point to Tab Color on the shortcut menu, then click the Bright Green, Accent 4, Lighter 80% color (second row, third column from the right) as shown in Figure C-21**

5. **Double-click the Sheet1 tab, type Actual, then press [Enter]**

   Notice that the color of the Budget tab changes depending on whether it is the active tab; when the Actual tab is active, the color of the Budget tab changes to the green tab color you selected. You decide to rearrange the order of the sheets, so that the Budget tab is to the left of the Actual tab.

QUICK TIP

If you have more sheet tabs than are visible, you can move between sheets by using the tab scrolling buttons to the left of the sheet tabs: the First Worksheet button ⏮ ; the Last Worksheet button ⏭ ; the Previous Worksheet button ◀ ; and the Next Worksheet button ▶ .

6. **Click the Budget tab, hold down the mouse button, drag it to the left of the Actual tab, as shown in Figure C-22, then release the mouse button**

   As you drag, the pointer changes to ▯▯, the sheet relocation pointer, and a small, black triangle just above the tabs shows the position the moved sheet will be in when you release the mouse button. The first sheet in the workbook is now the Budget sheet. See Figure C-23.

7. **Click the Actual sheet tab, click the Page Layout button 🔲 on the status bar to open Page Layout view, enter your name in the left header text box, then click anywhere in the worksheet to deselect the header**

8. **Click the Page Layout tab on the Ribbon, click the Orientation button in the Page Setup group, then click Landscape**

9. **Press [Ctrl][Home], then save your work**

FIGURE C-20: **Sheet tabs in workbook**

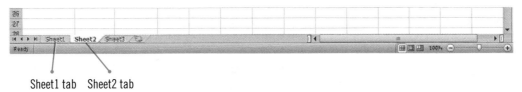

Sheet1 tab   Sheet2 tab

FIGURE C-21: **Tab Color palette**

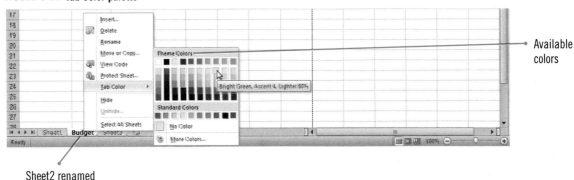

Available colors

Sheet2 renamed

FIGURE C-22: **Moving the Budget sheet**

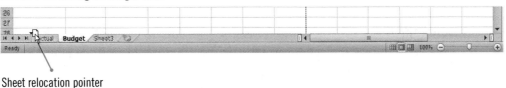

Sheet relocation pointer

FIGURE C-23: **Reordered sheets**

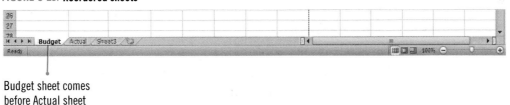

Budget sheet comes before Actual sheet

Copying worksheets

There are times when you may want to copy a worksheet. For example, a workbook might contain a sheet with Quarter 1 expenses, and you want to use that sheet as the basis for a sheet containing Quarter 2 expenses. To copy a sheet within the same workbook, press and hold [Ctrl], drag the sheet tab to the desired tab location, release the mouse button, then release [Ctrl]. A duplicate sheet appears with the same name as the copied sheet followed by "(2)" indicating it is a copy. You can then rename the sheet to a more meaningful name. To copy a sheet to a different workbook, both the source and destination workbooks must be open. Select the sheet to copy or move, right-click the sheet tab, then click Move or Copy in the shortcut menu. Complete the information in the Move or Copy dialog box. Be sure to click the Create a copy check box if you are copying rather than moving the worksheet. Carefully check your calculation results whenever you move or copy a worksheet.

Excel 2010

Checking Spelling

Excel includes a spell checker to help you ensure that the words in your worksheet are spelled correctly. The spell checker scans your worksheet, displays words it doesn't find in its built-in dictionary, and suggests replacements when they are available. To check all of the sheets in a multiple-sheet workbook, you need to display each sheet individually and run the spell checker for each one. Because the built-in dictionary cannot possibly include all the words that anyone needs, you can add words to the dictionary, such as your company name, an acronym, or an unusual technical term. Once you add a word or term, the spell checker no longer considers that word misspelled. Any words you've added to the dictionary using Word, Access, or PowerPoint are also available in Excel. ░░░░░ Before you distribute this workbook to Tony and the administrators, you check its spelling.

STEPS

QUICK TIP

The Spelling dialog box lists the name of the language currently being used in its title bar.

1. **Click the Review tab on the Ribbon, then click the Spelling button in the Proofing group**

   The Spelling: English (U.S.) dialog box opens, as shown in Figure C-24, with "Riverwalk" selected as the first misspelled word in the worksheet. For any word, you have the option to Ignore this case of the flagged word, Ignore All cases of the flagged word, Change the word to the selected suggestion, Change All instances of the flagged word to the selected suggestion, or add the flagged word to the dictionary using Add to Dictionary.

2. **Click Ignore All, then click Ignore All for the next two cases (Monoject and Otoscope)**

   Next, the spell checker finds the word "Laryngoscoope" and suggests "Laryngoscope" as an alternative.

3. **Verify that the word Laryngoscope is selected in the Suggestions list, then click Change**

   When no more incorrect words are found, Excel displays a message indicating that the spell check is complete.

4. **Click OK**

5. **Click the Home tab, click Find & Select in the Editing group, then click Replace**

   The Find and Replace dialog box opens. You can use this dialog box to replace a word or phrase. It might be a misspelling of a proper name that the spell checker didn't recognize as misspelled, or it could simply be a term that you want to change throughout the worksheet. Tony has just told you that each instance of "Maxi" in the worksheet should be changed to "ACE".

6. **Type Maxi in the Find what text box, press [Tab], then type ACE in the Replace with text box**

   Compare your dialog box to Figure C-25.

7. **Click Replace All, click OK to close the Microsoft Excel dialog box, then click Close to close the Find and Replace dialog box**

   Excel has made four replacements.

8. **Click the File tab, click Print on the navigation bar, click the No Scaling setting in the Settings section on the Print tab, then click Fit Sheet on One Page**

9. **Click the File tab to return to your worksheet, save your work, submit it to your instructor as directed, close the workbook, then exit Excel**

   The completed worksheet is shown in Figure C-26.

E-mailing a workbook

You can send an entire workbook from within Excel using your installed e-mail program, such as Microsoft Outlook. To send a workbook as an e-mail message attachment, open the workbook, click the File tab, then click Save & Send on the navigation bar. With the Send Using E-mail option selected in the Save & Send section in Backstage view, click Send as Attachment in the right pane. An e-mail message opens in your default e-mail program with the workbook automatically attached; the filename appears in the Attached field. Complete the To and optional Cc fields, include a message if you wish, then click Send.

FIGURE C-24: Spelling: English (U.S.) dialog box

Misspelled word →

Suggested replacements → for misspelled word

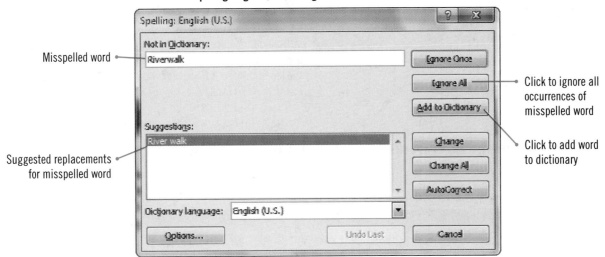

Click to ignore all occurrences of misspelled word

Click to add word to dictionary

FIGURE C-25: Find and Replace dialog box

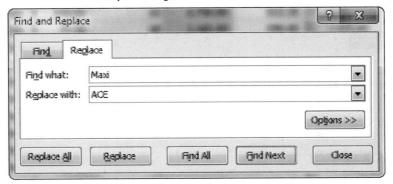

FIGURE C-26: Completed worksheet

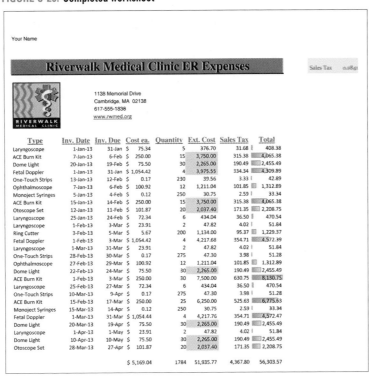

Your Name

Riverwalk Medical Clinic ER Expenses

Sales Tax   o.o8ç1

1138 Memorial Drive
Cambridge, MA 02138
617-555-1838
www.rwmed.org

Type	Inv. Date	Inv. Due	Cost ea.	Quantity	Ext. Cost	Sales Tax	Total
Laryngoscope	1-Jan-13	31-Jan	$ 75.34	5	376.70	31.68	408.38
ACE Burn Kit	7-Jan-13	6-Feb	$ 250.00	15	3,750.00	315.38	4,065.38
Dome Light	20-Jan-13	19-Feb	$ 75.50	30	2,265.00	190.49	2,455.49
Fetal Doppler	1-Jan-13	31-Jan	$ 1,054.42	4	3,975.55	334.34	4,309.89
One-Touch Strips	13-Jan-13	12-Feb	$ 0.17	230	39.56	3.33	42.89
Ophthalmoscope	7-Jan-13	6-Feb	$ 100.92	12	1,211.04	101.85	1,312.89
Monoject Syringes	5-Jan-13	4-Feb	$ 0.12	250	30.75	2.59	33.34
ACE Burn Kit	15-Jan-13	14-Feb	$ 250.00	15	3,750.00	315.38	4,065.38
Otoscope Set	12-Jan-13	11-Feb	$ 101.87	20	2,037.40	171.35	2,208.75
Laryngoscope	25-Jan-13	24-Feb	$ 72.34	6	434.04	36.50	470.54
Laryngoscope	1-Feb-13	3-Mar	$ 23.91	2	47.82	4.02	51.84
Ring Cutter	3-Feb-13	5-Mar	$ 5.67	200	1,134.00	95.37	1,229.37
Fetal Doppler	1-Feb-13	3-Mar	$ 1,054.42	4	4,217.68	354.71	4,572.39
Laryngoscope	1-Mar-13	31-Mar	$ 23.91	2	47.82	4.02	51.84
One-Touch Strips	28-Feb-13	30-Mar	$ 0.17	275	47.30	3.98	51.28
Ophthalmoscope	27-Feb-13	29-Mar	$ 100.92	12	1,211.04	101.85	1,312.89
Dome Light	22-Feb-13	24-Mar	$ 75.50	30	2,265.00	190.49	2,455.49
ACE Burn Kit	1-Feb-13	3-Mar	$ 250.00	30	7,500.00	630.75	8,130.75
Laryngoscope	25-Feb-13	27-Mar	$ 72.34	6	434.04	36.50	470.54
One-Touch Strips	10-Mar-13	9-Apr	$ 0.17	275	47.30	3.98	51.28
ACE Burn Kit	15-Feb-13	17-Mar	$ 250.00	25	6,250.00	525.63	6,775.63
Monoject Syringes	15-Mar-13	14-Apr	$ 0.12	250	30.75	2.59	33.34
Fetal Doppler	1-Mar-13	31-Mar	$ 1,054.44	4	4,217.76	354.71	4,572.47
Dome Light	20-Mar-13	19-Apr	$ 75.50	30	2,265.00	190.49	2,455.49
Laryngoscope	1-Apr-13	1-May	$ 23.91	2	47.82	4.02	51.84
Dome Light	10-Apr-13	10-May	$ 75.50	30	2,265.00	190.49	2,455.49
Otoscope Set	28-Mar-13	27-Apr	$ 101.87	20	2,037.40	171.35	2,208.75
			$ 5,169.04	1784	51,935.77	4,367.80	56,303.57

Practice

For current SAM information, including versions and content details, visit SAM Central (http://www.cengage.com/samcentral). If you have a SAM user profile, you may have access to hands-on instruction, practice, and assessment of the skills covered in this unit. Since various versions of SAM are supported throughout the life of this text, check with your instructor for the correct instructions and URL/Web site for accessing assignments.

Concepts Review

Label each element of the Excel worksheet window shown in Figure C-27.

FIGURE C-27

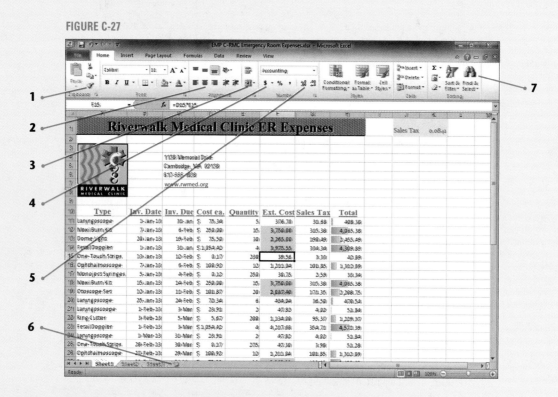

Match each command or button with the statement that best describes it.

8. **Conditional formatting**

9. [image button]

10. **Spelling button**

11. **[Ctrl][Home]**

12. [image button]

13. **$**

a. Centers cell contents over multiple cells

b. Adds dollar signs and two decimal places to selected data

c. Changes formatting of a cell that meets a certain rule

d. Displays background color options for a cell

e. Moves cell pointer to cell A1

f. Checks for apparent misspellings in a worksheet

Select the best answer from the list of choices.

14. Which of the following is an example of Accounting number format?

   a. 5555   **c.** 55.55%

   b. $5,555.55   **d.** 5,555.55

15. What feature is used to delete a conditional formatting rule?

   a. Rules Reminder   **c.** Condition Manager

   b. Conditional Formatting Rules Manager   **d.** Format Manager

16. Which button removes the italic font style from selected cells?

   a. *I*   **c.** ✔

   b. **B**   **d.** *I*

17. What is the name of the feature used to resize a column to accommodate its widest entry?

   a. AutoFormat   **c.** AutoResize

   b. AutoFit   **d.** AutoRefit

18. Which button increases the number of decimal places in selected cells?

   a. [button]   **c.** [button]

   b. [button]   **d.** [button]

19. Which button copies multiple formats from selected cells to other cells?

   a. [button]   **c.** [button]

   b. [button]   **d.** [button]

Excel 2010

Skills Review

1. Format values.

   a. Start Excel, open the file EMP C-2.xlsx from the drive and folder where you store your Data Files, then save it as **EMP C-Health Insurance Premiums**.

   b. Enter a formula in cell B10 that totals the number of employees.

   c. Create a formula in cell C5 that calculates the monthly insurance premium for the accounting department. (*Hint*: Make sure you use the correct type of cell reference in the formula. To calculate the department's monthly premium, multiply the number of employees by the monthly premium in cell B14.)

   d. Copy the formula in cell C5 to the range C6:C10.

   e. Format the range C5:C10 using Accounting number format.

   f. Change the format of the range C5:C9 to the Comma Style.

   g. Reduce the number of decimals in cell B14 to 0 using a button in the Number group on the Home tab.

   h. Save your work.

2. Change font and font sizes.

   a. Select the range of cells containing the column labels (in row 4).

   b. Change the font of the selection to Times New Roman.

   c. Increase the font size of the selection to 12 points.

   d. Increase the font size of the label in cell A1 to 14 points.

   e. Save your changes.

3. Change font styles and alignment.

   a. Apply the bold and italic font styles to the worksheet title in cell A1.

   b. Use the Merge & Center button to center the Health Insurance Premiums label over columns A through C.

   c. Apply the italic font style to the Health Insurance Premiums label.

   d. Add the bold font style to the labels in row 4.

   e. Use the Format Painter to copy the format in cell A4 to the range A5:A10.

   f. Apply the format in cell C10 to cell B14.

Skills Review (continued)

   g. Change the alignment of cell A10 to Align Right using a button in the Alignment group.

   h. Select the range of cells containing the column labels, then center them.

   i. Remove the italic font style from the Health Insurance Premiums label, then increase the font size to 14.

   j. Move the Health Insurance Premiums label to cell A3, then add the bold and underline font styles.

   k. Save your changes.

4. Adjust column width.

   a. Resize column C to a width of 10.71 characters.

   b. Use the AutoFit feature to resize columns A and B.

   c. Clear the contents of cell A13 (do not delete the cell).

   d. Change the text in cell A14 to **Monthly Insurance Premium**, then change the width of the column to 25 characters.

   e. Save your changes.

5. Insert and delete rows and columns.

   a. Insert a new row between rows 5 and 6.

   b. Add a new department, **Charity**, in the newly inserted row. Enter **6** as the number of employees in the department.

   c. Copy the formula in cell C7 to C6.

   d. Add the following comment to cell A6: **New Department**. Display the comment, then drag to move it out of the way, if necessary.

   e. Add a new column between the Department and Employees columns with the title **Family Coverage**, then resize the column using AutoFit.

   f. Delete the Legal row from the worksheet.

   g. Move the value in cell C14 to cell B14.

   h. Save your changes.

6. Apply colors, patterns, and borders.

   a. Add Outside Borders around the range A4:D10.

   b. Add a Bottom Double Border to cells C9 and D9 (above the calculated employee and premium totals).

   c. Apply the Aqua, Accent 5, Lighter 80% fill color to the labels in the Department column (do not include the Total label).

   d. Apply the Orange, Accent 6, Lighter 60% fill color to the range A4:D4.

   e. Change the color of the font in the range A4:D4 to Red, Accent 2, Darker 25%.

   f. Add a 12.5% Gray pattern style to cell A1.

   g. Format the range A14:B14 with a fill color of Dark Blue, Text 2, Lighter 40%, change the font color to White, Background 1, then apply the bold font style.

   h. Save your changes.

7. Apply conditional formatting.

   a. Select the range D5:D9, then create a conditional format that changes cell contents to green fill with dark green text if the value is between 150 and 275.

   b. Select the range C5:C9, then create a conditional format that changes cell contents to red text if the number of employees exceeds 10.

   c. Apply a blue gradient-filled data bar to the range C5:C9. (*Hint*: Click Blue Data Bar in the Gradient Fill section.)

   d. Use the Rules Manager to modify the conditional format in cells C5:C9 to display values greater than 10 in bold dark red text.

   e. Merge and center the title (cell A1) over columns A through D.

   f. Save your changes.

8. Rename and move a worksheet.

   a. Name the Sheet1 tab **Insurance Data**.

   b. Name the Sheet3 tab **Employee Data**.

   c. Change the Insurance Data tab color to Red, Accent 2, Lighter 40%.

   d. Change the Employee Data tab color to Aqua, Accent 5, Lighter 40%.

   e. Move the Employee Data sheet so it comes after (to the right of) the Insurance Data sheet.

   f. Make the Insurance Data sheet active, enter your name in cell A20, then save your work.

Skills Review (continued)

9. Check spelling.

a. Move the cell pointer to cell A1.

b. Use the Find & Select feature to replace the Accounting label in cell A5 with **Accounting/Legal**.

c. Check the spelling in the worksheet using the spell checker, and correct any spelling errors if necessary.

d. Save your changes, then compare your Insurance Data sheet to Figure C-28.

e. Preview the Insurance Data sheet in Backstage view, submit your work to your instructor as directed, then close the workbook and exit Excel.

FIGURE C-28

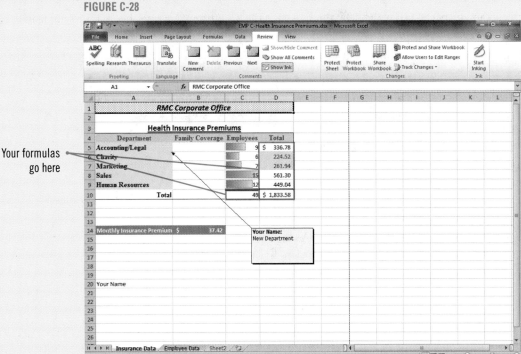

Independent Challenge 1

You run a wholesale medical supply distribution business, and one of your newest clients is Montebello, a small assisted living facility. Now that you've converted the facility's inventory records to Excel, the manager would like you to work on an analysis of the Montebello inventory. Although more items will be added later, the worksheet has enough items for you to begin your modifications.

a. Start Excel, open the file EMP C-3.xlsx from the drive and folder where you store your Data Files, then save it as **EMP C-Medical Supply Inventory**.

b. Create a formula in cell E4 that calculates the value of the items in stock based on the price paid per item in cell B4. Format the cell in the Comma Style.

c. In cell F4, calculate the sale price of the items in stock using an absolute reference to the markup value shown in cell H1.

d. Copy the formulas created above into the range E5:F14; first convert any necessary cell references to absolute so that the formulas work correctly.

e. Apply bold to the column labels, and italicize the inventory items in column A.

f. Make sure all columns are wide enough to display the data and labels.

g. Format the values in the Sale Price column as Accounting number format with two decimal places.

h. Format the values in the Price Paid column as Comma Style with two decimal places.

Independent Challenge 1 (continued)

i. Add a row under Thera-Band Assists for **Nail files**, price paid **$0.31**, sold individually (**each**), with **24** on hand. Copy the appropriate formulas to cells E5:F5.

j. Verify that all the data in the worksheet is visible and formulas are correct. Adjust any items as needed, and check the spelling of the entire worksheet.

k. Use conditional formatting to apply yellow fill with dark yellow text to items with a quantity of 25 or less on hand.

l. Use an icon set of your choosing in the range D4:D15 to illustrate the relative differences between values in the range.

m. Add an outside border around the data in the Item column (do not include the Item column label).

n. Delete the row containing the Pins entry.

o. Enter your name in an empty cell below the data, then save the file. Compare your worksheet to the sample in Figure C-29.

p. Preview the worksheet in Backstage view, submit your work to your instructor as directed, close the workbook, then exit Excel.

FIGURE C-29

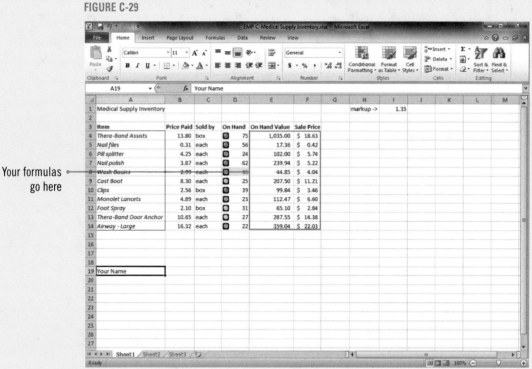

Your formulas go here

Independent Challenge 2

You are an administrative assistant with the Houston Association of Medical Clinics, and you are in charge of maintaining the membership list. You're currently planning a mailing campaign to members in certain regions of the city. You also want to create renewal letters for members whose membership expires soon. You decide to format the list to enhance the appearance of the worksheet and make your upcoming tasks easier to plan.

a. Start Excel, open the file EMP C-4.xlsx from the drive and folder where you store your Data Files, then save it as **EMP C-Houston Association of Medical Clinics**.

b. Remove any blank columns.

c. Create a conditional format in the Zip Code column so that entries greater than 77249 appear in light red fill with dark red text.

d. Make all columns wide enough to fit their data and labels.

e. Use formatting enhancements, such as fonts, font sizes, font styles, and fill colors, to make the worksheet more attractive.

f. Center the column labels.

Formatting a Worksheet

Independent Challenge 2 (continued)

g. Use conditional formatting so that entries for Year of Membership Expiration that are between 2014 and 2017 appear in green fill with bold black text. (*Hint*: Create a custom format for cells that meet the condition.)

h. Adjust any items as necessary, then check the spelling.

i. Change the name of the Sheet1 tab to one that reflects the sheet's contents, then add a tab color of your choice.

j. Enter your name in an empty cell, then save your work.

k. Preview the worksheet in Backstage view, make any final changes you think necessary, then submit your work to your instructor as directed. Compare your work to the sample shown in Figure C-30.

l. Close the workbook, then exit Excel.

FIGURE C-30

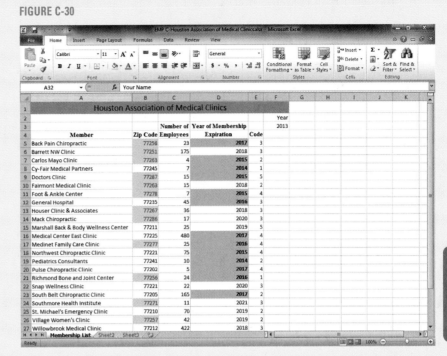

Independent Challenge 3

Emergent Health Care Systems is a Chicago-based healthcare provider that offers clinic and urgent-care services. As the finance manager for the company, one of your responsibilities is to analyze the monthly reports from the five district sales offices. Your boss, Joanne Bennington, has asked you to prepare a quarterly sales report for an upcoming meeting. Because several top executives will be attending this meeting, Joanne reminds you that the report must look professional. In particular, she asks you to emphasize the company's surge in profits during the last month and to highlight the fact that the Northeastern district continues to outpace the other districts.

a. Plan a worksheet that shows the company's revenue during the first quarter. Make sure you include the following:
- The number of patients seen (clients seen) and the associated revenues (revenue) for each of the five district sales offices. The five sales districts are Northeastern, Midwestern, Southeastern, Southern, and Western.
- Calculations that show month-by-month totals for January, February, and March, and a 3-month cumulative total.
- Calculations that show each district's share of sales (percent of Total Revenue).
- Labels that reflect the month-by-month data as well as the cumulative data.
- Formatting enhancements and data bars that emphasize the recent month's sales surge.

b. Ask yourself the following questions about the organization and formatting of the worksheet: What worksheet title and labels do you need, and where should they appear? How can you calculate the totals? What formulas can you copy to save time and keystrokes? Do any of these formulas need to use an absolute reference? How do you show dollar amounts? What information should be shown in bold? Do you need to use more than one font? Should you use more than one point size?

c. Start Excel, then save a new, blank workbook as **EMP C-Emergent Health Care Systems** to the drive and folder where you store your Data Files.

Independent Challenge 3 (continued)

d. Build the worksheet with your own number of clients seen and revenue data. Enter the titles and labels first, then enter the numbers and formulas. You can use the information in Table C-4 to get started.

TABLE C-4

Emergent Health Care Systems

1st Quarter Sales Report

| | Facilities | January | | February | | March | | Total | | Total % Revenue |
		Clients Seen	Revenue	Clients Seen	Revenue	Clients Seen	Revenue	Clients Seen	Revenue	
Northeastern										
Midwestern										
Southeastern										
Southern										
Western										

e. Add a row beneath the data containing the totals for each column.

f. Adjust the column widths as necessary.

g. Change the height of row 1 to 33 points.

h. Format labels and values to enhance the look of the worksheet, and change the font styles and alignment if necessary.

i. Resize columns and adjust the formatting as necessary.

j. Add data bars for the monthly Clients Seen columns.

k. Add a column that calculates a 25% increase in total revenue. Use an absolute cell reference in this calculation. (*Hint*: Make sure the current formatting is applied to the new information.)

Advanced Challenge Exercise

- Delete the contents of cells J4:K4 if necessary, then merge and center cell I4 over column I:K.
- Insert a clip art image related to healthcare in an appropriate location, adjusting its size and position as necessary.
- Save your work.

l. Enter your name in an empty cell.

m. Check the spelling in the workbook, change to a landscape orientation, save your work, then compare your work to Figure C-31.

n. Preview the worksheet in Backstage view, then submit your work to your instructor as directed.

o. Close the workbook file, then exit Excel.

FIGURE C-31

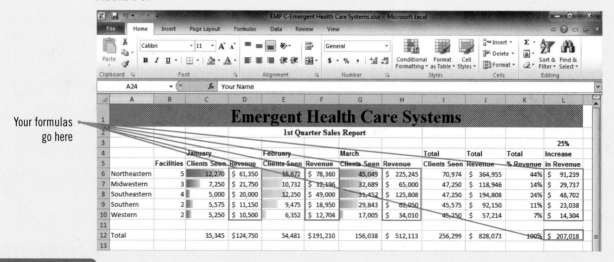

Your formulas go here

Formatting a Worksheet

Real Life Independent Challenge

This project requires an Internet connection.

You have been notified that your research grant to study the spread of airborne diseases has been approved. You plan to visit seven different countries over the course of 2 months, and you have budgeted an identical spending allowance in each country. You want to create a worksheet that calculates the amount of native currency you will have in each country based on the budgeted amount. You want the workbook to reflect the currency information for each country.

    a. Start Excel, then save a new, blank workbook as **EMP C-Research Grant Travel Budget** to the drive and folder where you store your Data Files.

    b. Add a title at the top of the worksheet.

    c. Think of seven countries you would like to visit, then enter column and row labels for your worksheet. (*Hint*: You may wish to include row labels for each country, plus column labels for the country, the $1 equivalent in native currency, the total amount of native currency you'll have in each country, and the name of each country's monetary unit.)

    d. Decide how much money you want to bring to each country (for example, $1,000), and enter that in the worksheet.

    e. Use your favorite search engine to find your own information sources on currency conversions for the countries you plan to visit.

    f. Enter the cash equivalent to $1 in U.S. dollars for each country on your list.

    g. Create an equation that calculates the amount of native currency you will have in each country, using an absolute cell reference in the formula.

    h. Format the entries in the column containing the native currency $1 equivalent as Number number format with three decimal places, and format the column containing the total native currency budget with two decimal places, using the correct currency number format for each country. (*Hint*: Use the Number tab in the Format cells dialog box; choose the appropriate currency number format from the Symbol list.)

    i. Create a conditional format that changes the font style and color of the calculated amount in the $1,000 US column to light red fill with dark red text if the amount exceeds **1000** units of the local currency.

    j. Merge and center the worksheet title over the column headings.

    k. Add any formatting you want to the column headings, and resize the columns as necessary.

    l. Add a background color to the title.

Advanced Challenge Exercise

    ■ Modify the conditional format in the $1,000 US column so that entries between 1500 and 3999 are displayed in red, boldface type; and entries above 4000 appear in blue, boldface type with a light red background.

    ■ Delete all the unused sheets in the workbook.

    ■ Save your work as **EMP C-Research Grant Travel Budget ACE** to the drive and folder where you store your Data Files.

    ■ If you have access to an e-mail account, e-mail this workbook to your instructor as an attachment.

    m. Enter your name in the header of the worksheet.

    n. Spell check the worksheet, save your changes, compare your work to Figure C-32, then preview the worksheet in Backstage view, and submit your work to your instructor as directed.

    o. Close the workbook and exit Excel.

FIGURE C-32

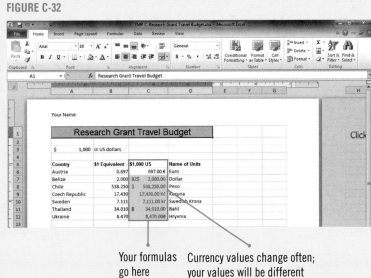

Your formulas go here

Currency values change often; your values will be different

Visual Workshop

Open the file EMP C-5.xlsx from the drive and folder where you store your Data Files, then save it as **EMP C-Tacoma General Hospital Administrative Staff**. Use the skills you learned in this unit to format the worksheet so it looks like the one shown in Figure C-33. Create a conditional format in the Level column so that entries greater than 3 appear in red text. Create an additional conditional format in the Review Cycle column so that any value equal to 3 appears in green bold text. Replace the Accounting department label with **Paralegal**. (*Hint:* The only additional font used in this exercise is 16-point Times New Roman in row 1.) Enter your name in cell A25, check the spelling in the worksheet, save your changes, then submit your work to your instructor as directed.

FIGURE C-33

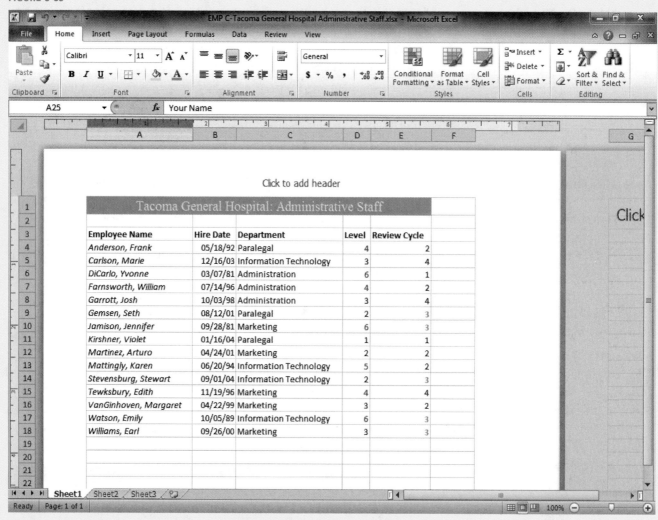

Working with Charts

Worksheets provide an effective layout for calculating and organizing data, but the grid layout is not always the best format for presenting your work to others. To display information so it's easier to interpret, you can create a chart. **Charts**, sometimes called graphs, present information in a graphic format, making it easier to see patterns, trends, and relationships. In this unit, you learn how to create a chart, how to edit the chart and change the chart type, how to add text annotations and arrows, and how to preview and print the chart. At the upcoming annual meeting, Tony Sanchez wants to emphasize a growth trend at Riverwalk Medical Clinic. He asks you to create a chart showing the increase in insurance reimbursements over the past four quarters.

OBJECTIVES

Plan a chart

Create a chart

Move and resize a chart

Change the chart design

Change the chart layout

Format a chart

Annotate and draw on a chart

Create a pie chart

Planning a Chart

Before creating a chart, you need to plan the information you want your chart to show and how you want it to look. Planning ahead helps you decide what type of chart to create and how to organize the data. Understanding the parts of a chart makes it easier to format and to change specific elements so that the chart best illustrates your data. ▰▰▰▰ In preparation for creating the chart for Tony's presentation, you identify your goals for the chart and plan its layout.

DETAILS

Use the following guidelines to plan the chart:

• **Determine the purpose of the chart, and identify the data relationships you want to communicate graphically**

You want to create a chart that shows quarterly insurance reimbursements throughout Riverwalk Medical Clinic. This worksheet data is shown in Figure D-1. In the first quarter, the Opthalmology department settled a dispute with a large insurance carrier, which resulted in greatly increased reimbursements starting in the third quarter. You also want the chart to illustrate whether the quarterly reimbursements for each department increased or decreased from quarter to quarter.

• **Determine the results you want to see, and decide which chart type is most appropriate**

Different chart types display data in distinctive ways. For example, a pie chart compares parts to the whole, so it's useful for showing what proportion of a budget amount was spent on print ads relative to what was spent on direct mail or radio commercials. A line chart, in contrast, is best for showing trends over time. To choose the best chart type for your data, you should first decide how you want your data displayed and interpreted. Table D-1 describes several different types of charts you can create in Excel and their corresponding buttons on the Insert tab on the Ribbon. Because you want to compare RMC reimbursements in multiple departments over a period of four quarters, you decide to use a column chart.

• **Identify the worksheet data you want the chart to illustrate**

Sometimes you use all the data in a worksheet to create a chart, while at other times you may need to select a range within the sheet. The worksheet from which you are creating your chart contains expense data for each of the past four quarters and the totals for the past year. You will need to use all the quarterly data contained in the worksheet except the quarterly totals.

• **Understand the elements of a chart**

The chart shown in Figure D-2 contains basic elements of a chart. In the figure, RMC departments are on the horizontal axis (also called the **x-axis**) and expense dollar amounts are on the vertical axis (also called the **y-axis**). The horizontal axis is also called the **category axis** because it often contains the names of data groups, such as locations, months, or years. The vertical axis is also called the **value axis** because it often contains numerical values that help you interpret the size of chart elements. (3-D charts also contain a **z-axis**, for comparing data across both categories and values.) The area inside the horizontal and vertical axes is the **plot area**. The **tick marks**, on the vertical axis, and **gridlines** (extending across the plot area) create a scale of measure for each value. Each value in a cell you select for your chart is a **data point**. In any chart, a **data marker** visually represents each data point, which in this case is a column. A collection of related data points is a **data series**. In this chart, there are four data series (Quarter 1, Quarter 2, Quarter 3, and Quarter 4). Each is made up of column data markers of a different color, so a **legend** is included to make it easy to identify them.

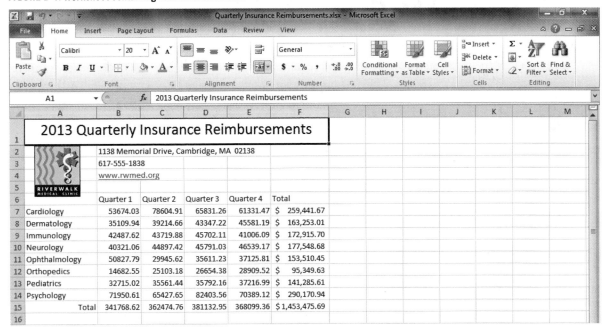

FIGURE D-2: Chart elements

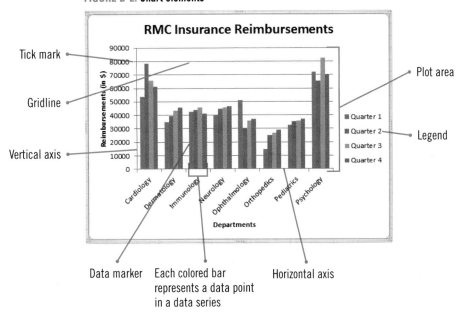

TABLE D-1: Common chart types

type	button	description
Column		Compares data using columns; the Excel default; sometimes referred to as a bar chart in other spreadsheet programs
Line		Compares trends over even time intervals; looks similar to an area chart, but does not emphasize total
Pie		Compares sizes of pieces as part of a whole; used for a single series of numbers
Bar		Compares data using horizontal bars; sometimes referred to as a horizontal bar chart in other spreadsheet programs
Area		Shows how individual volume changes over time in relation to total volume
Scatter		Compares trends over uneven time or measurement intervals; used in scientific and engineering disciplines for trend spotting and extrapolation

Creating a Chart

To create a chart in Excel, you first select the range in a worksheet containing the data you want to chart. Once you've selected a range, you can use buttons on the Insert tab on the Ribbon to create a chart based on the data in the range. ▨▨▨▨ Using the worksheet containing the quarterly reimbursement data, you create a chart that shows how the reimbursements for each department varied across the quarters.

STEPS

QUICK TIP
When charting data for a particular time period, make sure all series are for the same time period.

1. **Start Excel, open the file EMP D-1.xlsx from the drive and folder where you store your Data Files, then save it as EMP D-Quarterly Insurance Reimbursements**

   You want the chart to include the quarterly insurance reimbursement figures, as well as quarter and department labels. You don't include the Total column and row because the figures in these cells would skew the chart.

2. **Select the range A6:E14, then click the Insert tab on the Ribbon**

   The Insert tab contains groups for inserting various types of objects, including charts. The Charts group includes buttons for each major chart type, plus an Other Charts button for additional chart types, such as stock charts for charting stock market data.

QUICK TIP
To base a chart on data in nonadjacent ranges, press and hold [Ctrl] while selecting each range, then use the Insert tab to create the chart.

3. **Click the Column button in the Charts group, then click Clustered Column under 2-D Column in the Column chart gallery, as shown in Figure D-3**

   The chart is inserted in the center of the worksheet, and three contextual Chart Tools tabs appear on the Ribbon: Design, Layout, and Format. On the Design tab, which is currently in front, you can quickly change the chart type, chart layout, and chart style, and you can swap how the columns and rows of data in the worksheet are represented in the chart. Currently, the departments are charted along the horizontal x-axis, with the quarterly reimbursement dollar amounts charted along the y-axis. This lets you easily compare the quarterly reimbursements for each department.

4. **Click the Switch Row/Column button in the Data group on the Chart Tools Design tab**

   The quarters are now charted along the x-axis. The expense amounts per department are charted along the y-axis, as indicated by the updated legend. See Figure D-4.

5. **Click the Undo button 🔁 on the Quick Access toolbar**

   The chart returns to its original design.

6. **Click the Chart Tools Layout tab, click the Chart Title button in the Labels group, then click Above Chart**

   A title placeholder appears above the chart.

QUICK TIP
You can also triple-click to select the chart title text.

7. **Click anywhere in the Chart Title text box, press [Ctrl][A] to select the text, type Quarterly Insurance Reimbursements, then click anywhere in the chart to deselect the title**

   Adding a title helps identify the chart. The border around the chart and the chart's **sizing handles**, the small series of dots at the corners and sides of the chart's border, indicate that the chart is selected. See Figure D-5. Your chart might be in a different location on the worksheet and may look slightly different; you will move and resize it in the next lesson. Any time a chart is selected, as it is now, a blue border surrounds the worksheet data range on which the chart is based, a purple border surrounds the cells containing the category axis labels, and a green border surrounds the cells containing the data series labels. This chart is known as an **embedded chart** because it is inserted directly in the current worksheet and doesn't exist in a separate file. Embedding a chart in the current sheet is the default selection when creating a chart, but you can also embed a chart on a different sheet in the workbook, or on a newly created chart sheet. A **chart sheet** is a sheet in a workbook that contains only a chart that is linked to the workbook data.

8. **Save your work**

FIGURE D-3: Column chart gallery

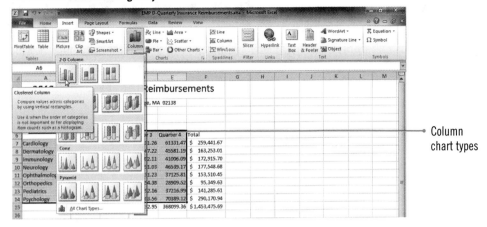

Column chart types

FIGURE D-4: Clustered Column chart with different presentation of data

Undo button

Switch Row/Column button

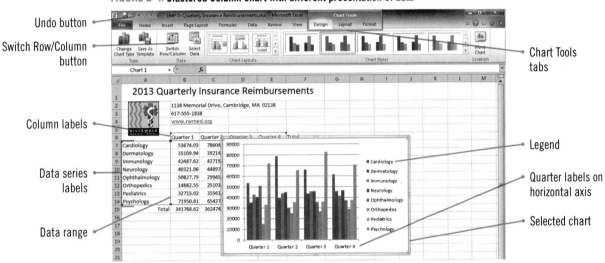

Chart Tools tabs

Column labels

Data series labels

Data range

Legend

Quarter labels on horizontal axis

Selected chart

FIGURE D-5: Chart with rows and columns restored and title added

Chart title

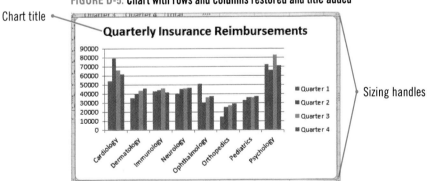

Sizing handles

Creating sparklines

You can quickly create a miniature chart called a **sparkline** that serves as a visual indicator of data trends. To do this, select a range of data, click the Insert tab, then click the Line, Column, or Win/Loss button in the Sparklines group. In the Create Sparklines dialog box that opens, enter the cell in which you want the sparkline to appear, then click OK. Figure D-6 shows four sparklines created in four different cells. Any changes to data in the range are reflected in the sparkline. To delete a selected sparkline from a cell, click the Clear button in the Group group on the Sparkline Tools Design tab.

FIGURE D-6: Sparklines in cells

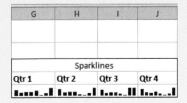

Moving and Resizing a Chart

A chart is an **object**, or an independent element on a worksheet, and is not located in a specific cell or range. You can select an object by clicking it; sizing handles around the object indicate it is selected. (When a chart is selected in Excel, the Name box, which normally tells you the address of the active cell, tells you the chart number.) You can move a selected chart anywhere on a worksheet without affecting formulas or data in the worksheet. However, any data changed in the worksheet is automatically updated in the chart. You can even move a chart to a different sheet in the workbook, and it will still reflect the original data. You can resize a chart to improve its appearance by dragging its sizing handles. A chart contains chart objects, such as a title and legend, which you can also move and resize. You can reposition chart objects to pre-defined locations using commands on the Layout tab, or you can freely move any chart object by dragging it or by cutting and pasting it to a new location. When you point to a chart object, the name of the object appears as a ScreenTip. ▨▨▨▨ You want to resize the chart, position it below the worksheet data, and move the legend.

STEPS

QUICK TIP
To delete a selected chart, press [Delete].

1. **Make sure the chart is still selected, then position the pointer over the chart**

   The pointer shape ⛶ indicates that you can move the chart. For a table of commonly used object pointers, refer to Table D-2.

TROUBLE
If you do not drag a blank area on the chart, you might inadvertently move a chart element instead of the whole chart; if this happens, undo the action and try again.

2. **Position ⛶ on a blank area near the upper-left edge of the chart, press and hold the left mouse button, drag the chart until its upper-left corner is at the upper-left corner of cell A18, then release the mouse button**

   As you drag the chart, you can see an outline representing the chart's perimeter. The chart appears in the new location.

3. **Position the pointer on the right-middle sizing handle until it changes to ⟷, then drag the right border of the chart to the right edge of column F**

   The chart is widened. See Figure D-7.

QUICK TIP
To resize a selected chart to an exact specification, click the Chart Tools Format tab, then enter the desired height and width in the Size group.

4. **Position the pointer over the upper-middle sizing handle until it changes to ↕, then drag the top border of the chart to the top edge of row 17**

5. **Scroll down if necessary so row 32 is visible, position the pointer over the lower-middle sizing handle until it changes to ↕, then drag the bottom border of the chart to the bottom border of row 30**

   You can move any object on a chart. You want to align the top of the legend with the top of the plot area.

QUICK TIP
You can move a legend to the right, top, left, or bottom of a chart by clicking the Legend button in the Labels group on the Chart Tools Layout tab, then clicking a location option.

6. **Click the legend to select it, press and hold [Shift], drag the legend up using ⛶ so the dotted outline is approximately 1/4" above the top of the plot area, then release [Shift]**

   When you click the legend, sizing handles appear around it and "Legend" appears as a ScreenTip when the pointer hovers over the object. As you drag, a dotted outline of the legend border appears. Pressing and holding the [Shift] key holds the horizontal position of the legend as you move it vertically. Although the sizing handles on objects within a chart look different from the sizing handles that surround a chart, they function the same way.

7. **Click cell A14, type Psychiatry, click the Enter button ✓ on the formula bar, use AutoFit to resize column A, then press [Ctrl][Home]**

   The axis label changes to reflect the updated cell contents, as shown in Figure D-8. Changing any data in the worksheet modifies corresponding text or values in the chart. Because the chart is no longer selected, the Chart Tools tabs no longer appear on the Ribbon.

8. **Save your work**

Working with Charts

FIGURE D-7: **Moved and resized chart**

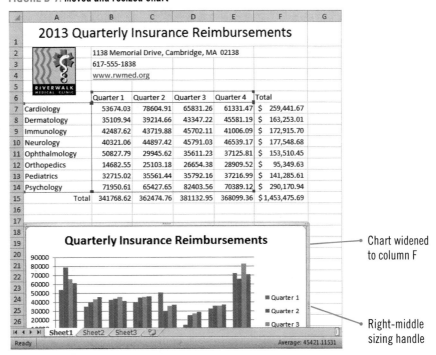

Chart widened
to column F

Right-middle
sizing handle

FIGURE D-8: **Worksheet with modified legend and label**

Modified
text

Plot
area

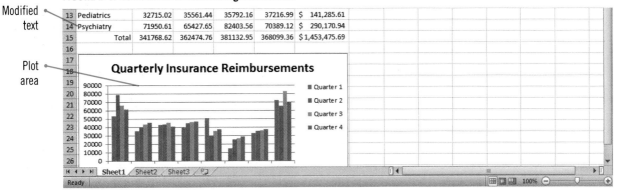

TABLE D-2: **Common object pointers**

name	pointer	use	name	pointer	use
Diagonal resizing	⤢ or ⤡	Change chart shape from corners	I-beam	I	Edit object text
Draw	+	Draw an object	Move	↖↗	Move object
Horizontal resizing	⟺	Change object width	Vertical resizing	↕	Change object height

Moving an embedded chart to a sheet

Suppose you have created an embedded chart that you decide would look better on a chart sheet or in a different worksheet. You can make this change without recreating the entire chart. To do so, first select the chart, click the Chart Tools Design tab, then click the Move Chart button in the Location group. The Move Chart dialog box opens. To move the chart to its own chart sheet, click the New sheet option button, type a name for the new sheet if desired, then click OK. If the chart is already on its own sheet, click the Object in option button, select the worksheet to where you want to move it, then click OK.

Changing the Chart Design

Once you've created a chart, it's easy to modify the design using the Chart Tools Design tab. You can change the chart type, modify the data range and column/row configuration, apply a different chart style, and change the layout of objects in the chart. The layouts in the Chart Layouts group on the Chart Tools Design tab offer preconfigured arrangements of objects in your chart, such as its legend, title, or gridlines; choosing one of these layouts is an alternative to manually changing how objects are arranged in a chart. ▧▧▧▧▧ You look over your worksheet and realize the data for Pediatrics and Psychiatry in Quarter 2 is incorrect. After you correct this data, you want to see how the corrected data looks using different chart layouts and types.

STEPS

1. **Click cell C13, type 39462.01, press [Enter], type 62947.18, then press [Enter]**
    In the chart, the Quarter 2 data markers for Pediatrics and Psychiatry reflect the adjusted reimbursements. See Figure D-9.

QUICK TIP
You can see more layout choices by clicking the More button ⯆ in the Chart Layouts group.

2. **Select the chart by clicking a blank area within the chart border, click the Chart Tools Design tab on the Ribbon, then click Layout 3 in the Chart Layouts group**
    The legend moves to the bottom of the chart. You prefer the original layout.

3. **Click the Undo button ▨ on the Quick Access toolbar, then click the Change Chart Type button in the Type group**
    The Change Chart Type dialog box opens, as shown in Figure D-10. The left pane of the dialog box lists the available categories, and the right pane shows the individual chart types. An orange border surrounds the currently selected chart type.

4. **Click Bar in the left pane of the Change Chart Type dialog box, confirm that the Clustered Bar chart type is selected in the right pane, then click OK**
    The column chart changes to a clustered bar chart. See Figure D-11. You look at the bar chart, then decide to see how the data looks in a three-dimensional column chart.

5. **Click the Change Chart Type button in the Type group, click Column in the left pane of the Change Chart Type dialog box, click 3-D Clustered Column (fourth from the left in the first row) in the right pane, then click OK**
    A three-dimensional column chart appears. You notice that the three-dimensional column format gives you a sense of volume, but it is more crowded than the two-dimensional column format.

QUICK TIP
If you plan to print a chart on a black-and-white printer, you may wish to apply a black-and-white chart style to your chart so you can see how the output will look as you work.

6. **Click the Change Chart Type button in the Type group, click Clustered Column (first from the left in the first row) in the right pane of the Change Chart Type dialog box, then click OK**

7. **Click the Style 3 chart style in the Chart Styles group**
    The columns change to shades of blue. You prefer the previous chart style's color scheme.

8. **Click ▨ on the Quick Access toolbar, then save your work**

Creating a combination chart

A **combination chart** is two charts in one; a column chart with a line chart, for example. This type of chart (which cannot be used with all data) is helpful when charting dissimilar but related data. For example, you can create a combination chart based on home price and home size data, showing home prices in a column chart, and related home sizes in a line chart. In such a combination chart, a **secondary axis** (such as a vertical axis on the right side of the chart) would supply the scale for the home sizes. To create a combination chart, you can apply a chart type to a data series in an existing chart. Select the chart data

series that you want plotted on a secondary axis, then click Format Selection in the Current Selection group on the Chart Tools Layout tab or Format tab to open the Format Data Series dialog box. In the dialog box, click Series Options if necessary, click the Secondary Axis option button under Plot Series On, then click Close. Click the Chart Tools Layout tab if necessary, click the Axes button in the Axes group, then click the type of secondary axis you want and where you want it to appear. To finish, click the Change Chart Type button in the Type group on the Design tab, then select a chart type for the data series.

FIGURE D-9: **Worksheet with modified data**

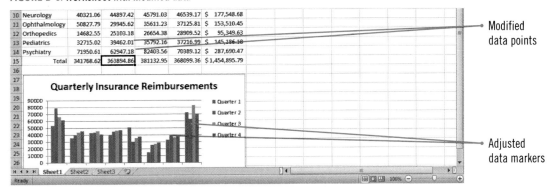

Modified data points

Adjusted data markers

FIGURE D-10: **Change Chart Type dialog box**

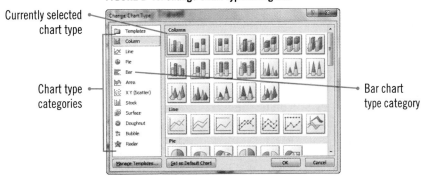

Currently selected chart type

Chart type categories

Bar chart type category

FIGURE D-11: **Column chart changed to bar chart**

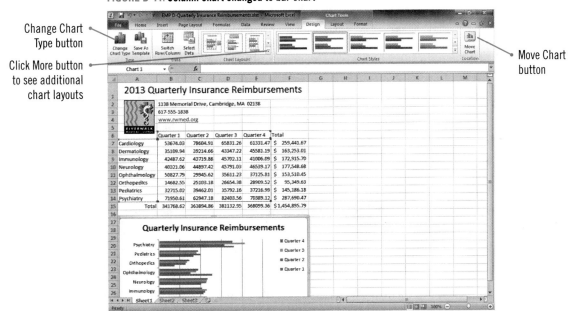

Change Chart Type button

Click More button to see additional chart layouts

Move Chart button

Working with a 3-D chart

Excel includes two kinds of 3-D chart types. In a true 3-D chart, a third axis, called the **z-axis**, lets you compare data points across both categories and values. The z-axis runs along the depth of the chart, so it appears to advance from the back of the chart. To create a true 3-D chart, look for chart types that begin with "3-D," such as 3-D Column. Charts that are formatted in 3-D, but are not true 3-D, contain only two axes but their graphics give the illusion of three-dimensionality. To create a chart that is only formatted in 3-D, look for chart types that end with "in 3-D." In any 3-D chart, data series

can sometimes obscure other columns or bars in the same chart, but you can rotate the chart to obtain a better view. Right-click the chart, then click 3-D Rotation. The Format Chart Area dialog box opens with the 3-D Rotation category active. The 3-D Rotation options let you change the orientation and perspective of the chart area, plot area, walls, and floor. The 3-D Format category lets you apply three-dimensional effects to selected chart objects. (Not all 3-D Rotation and 3-D Format options are available on all charts.)

Changing the Chart Layout

While the Chart Tools Design tab contains preconfigured chart layouts you can apply to a chart, the Chart Tools Layout tab makes it easy to add, remove, and modify individual chart objects such as a chart title or legend. Using buttons on this tab, you can also add shapes, pictures, and additional text to a chart, add and modify labels, change the display of axes, modify the fill behind the plot area, create titles for the horizontal and vertical axes, and eliminate or change the look of gridlines. You can format the text in a chart object using the Home tab or the Mini toolbar, just as you would the text in a worksheet. 🔳🔳 You want to change the layout of the chart by creating titles for the horizontal and vertical axes. To improve the chart's appearance, you'll add a drop shadow to the chart title.

STEPS

1. **With the chart still selected, click the** Chart Tools Layout tab **on the Ribbon, click the** Gridlines button **in the Axes group, point to** Primary Horizontal Gridlines, **then click** None

   The gridlines that extend from the value axis tick marks across the chart's plot area are removed from the chart, as shown in Figure D-12.

2. **Click the** Gridlines button **in the Axes group, point to** Primary Horizontal Gridlines, **then click** Major & Minor Gridlines

   Both major and minor gridlines now appear in the chart. **Major gridlines** represent the values at the value axis tick marks, and **minor gridlines** represent the values between the tick marks.

   > **QUICK TIP**
   > You can move any title to a new position by clicking one of its edges, then dragging it.

3. **Click the** Axis Titles button **in the Labels group, point to** Primary Horizontal Axis Title, **click** Title Below Axis, **triple-click the** axis title, **then type** Departments

   Descriptive text on the category axis helps readers understand the chart.

4. **Click the** Axis Titles button **in the Labels group, point to** Primary Vertical Axis Title, **then click** Rotated Title

   A placeholder for the vertical axis title is added to the left of the vertical axis.

   > **QUICK TIP**
   > You can also edit text in a chart or axis title by positioning the pointer over the selected title until it changes to I, clicking the title, then editing the text.

5. **Scroll down so the entire chart is displayed, triple-click the** vertical axis title, **then type** Revenue (in $)

   The text "Expenses (in $)" appears to the left of the vertical axis, as shown in Figure D-13.

6. **Right-click the** horizontal axis labels ("Cardiology", "Dermatology", etc.), **click the** Font list arrow **on the Mini toolbar, click** Times New Roman, **click the** Font Size list arrow **on the Mini toolbar, then click** 8

   The font of the horizontal axis labels changes to Times New Roman, and the font size decreases, making more of the plot area visible.

   > **QUICK TIP**
   > You can also apply a border to a selected chart object by clicking the Shape Outline list arrow on the Chart Tools Format tab, and then selecting from the available options.

7. **Right-click the** vertical axis labels, **click the** Font list arrow **on the Mini toolbar, click** Times New Roman, **click the** Font Size list arrow **on the Mini toolbar, then click** 8

8. **Right-click the** chart title ("Quarterly Insurance Reimbursements"), **click** Format Chart Title **on the shortcut menu, click** Border Color **in the left pane of the Format Chart Title dialog box, then click the** Solid line option button **in the right pane**

   A solid border will appear around the chart title with the default blue color.

   > **QUICK TIP**
   > You can also apply a shadow to a selected chart object by clicking the Shape Effects button on the Chart Tools Format tab, pointing to Shadow, and then clicking a shadow effect.

9. **Click** Shadow **in the left pane of the Format Chart Title dialog box, click the** Presets list arrow, **click** Offset Diagonal Bottom Right **in the Outer group (first row, first from the left), click** Close, **then save your work**

   A blue border with a drop shadow surrounds the title. Compare your work to Figure D-14.

FIGURE D-12: Gridlines removed from chart

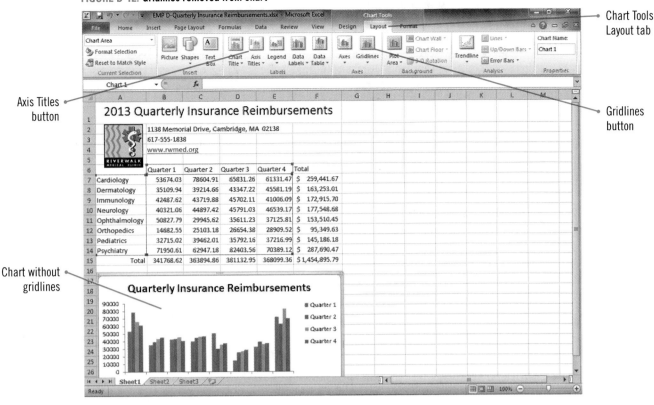

Chart Tools Layout tab

Axis Titles button

Gridlines button

Chart without gridlines

FIGURE D-13: Axis titles added to chart

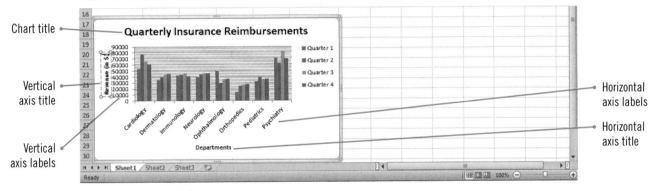

Chart title

Vertical axis title

Vertical axis labels

Horizontal axis labels

Horizontal axis title

FIGURE D-14: Enhanced chart

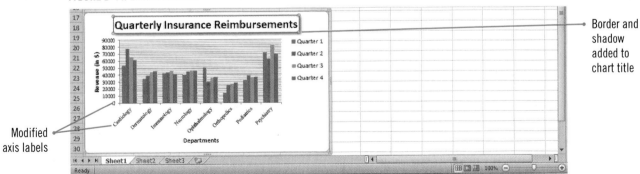

Border and shadow added to chart title

Modified axis labels

Adding data labels to a chart

There are times when your audience might benefit by seeing data labels on a chart. These labels appear next to the data markers in the chart and can indicate the series name, category name, and/or the value of one or more data points. Once your chart is selected, you can add this information to your chart by clicking the Data Labels button in the Labels group on the Chart Tools Layout tab, and then clicking a display option for the data labels. Once you have added the data labels, you can format them or delete individual data labels. To delete a data label, select it and then press [Delete].

Formatting a Chart

Formatting a chart can make it easier to read and understand. Many formatting enhancements can be made using the Chart Tools Format tab. You can change the fill color for a specific data series, or you can apply a shape style to a title or a data series using the Shape Styles group. Shape styles make it possible to apply multiple formats, such as an outline, fill color, and text color, all with a single click. You can also apply different fill colors, outlines, and effects to chart objects using arrows and buttons in the Shape Styles group. ▨▧ You want to use a different color for one data series in the chart and apply a shape style to another to enhance the look of the chart.

STEPS

1. **With the chart selected, click the Chart Tools Format tab on the Ribbon, then click any column in the Quarter 4 data series**

   The Chart Tools Format tab opens, and handles appear on each column in the Quarter 4 data series, indicating that the entire series is selected.

2. **Click the Shape Fill list arrow in the Shape Styles group on the Chart Tools Format tab**

3. **Click Orange, Accent 6 (first row, 10th from the left) as shown in Figure D-15**

   All the columns for the series become orange, and the legend changes to match the new color. You can also change the color of selected objects by applying a shape style.

4. **Click any column in the Quarter 3 data series**

   Handles appear on each column in the Quarter 3 data series.

5. **Click the More button ▾ on the Shape Styles gallery, then hover the pointer over the Moderate Effect – Olive Green, Accent 3 shape style (fifth row, fourth from the left) in the gallery, as shown in Figure D-16**

   Live Preview shows the data series in the chart with the shape style applied.

QUICK TIP

To apply a WordArt style to a text object (such as the chart title), select the object, then click a style in the WordArt Styles group on the Chart Tools Format tab.

6. **Click the Subtle Effect – Olive Green, Accent 3 shape style (fourth row, fourth from the left) in the gallery**

   The style for the data series changes, as shown in Figure D-17.

7. **Save your work**

Changing alignment and angle in axis labels and titles

The buttons on the Chart Tools Layout tab provide a few options for positioning axis labels and titles, but you can customize their position and rotation to exact specifications using the Format Axis dialog box or Format Axis Title dialog box. With a chart selected, right-click the axis text you want to modify, then click Format Axis or Format Axis Title on the shortcut menu. In the dialog box that opens, click Alignment, then select the appropriate Text layout option. You can also create a custom angle by clicking the Custom angle up and down arrows. When you have made the desired changes, click Close.

FIGURE D-15: New shape fill applied to data series

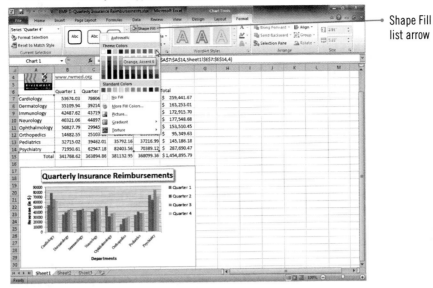

Shape Fill list arrow

FIGURE D-16: Live Preview of new style applied to data series

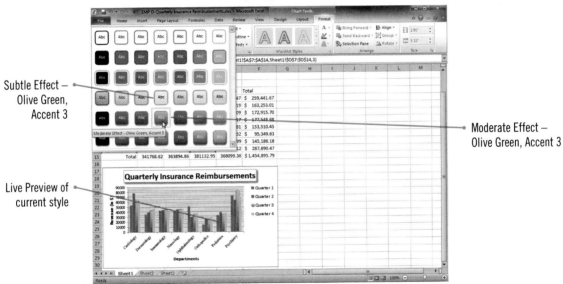

Subtle Effect — Olive Green, Accent 3

Moderate Effect — Olive Green, Accent 3

Live Preview of current style

FIGURE D-17: Style of data series changed

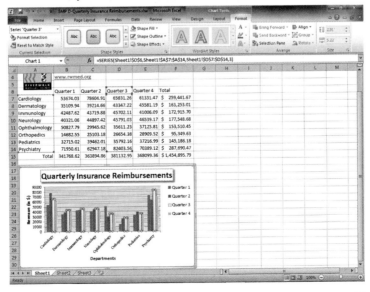

Annotating and Drawing on a Chart

You can use text annotations and graphics to point out critical information in a chart. **Text annotations** are labels that further describe your data. You can also draw lines and arrows that point to the exact locations you want to emphasize. Shapes such as arrows and boxes can be added from the Illustrations group on the Insert tab or from the Insert group on the Chart Tools Layout group on the Ribbon. These groups are also used to insert pictures and clip art into worksheets and charts. ▰▰▰▰ You want to call attention to the Orthopedics revenue increases, so you decide to add a text annotation and an arrow to this information in the chart.

STEPS

1. **Make sure the chart is selected, click the Chart Tools Layout tab, click the Text Box button in the Insert group, then move the pointer over the worksheet**
   The pointer changes to ↓, indicating that you will insert a text box where you next click.

2. **Click to the right of the chart (anywhere *outside* the chart boundary)**
   A text box is added to the worksheet, and the Drawing Tools Format tab appears on the Ribbon so that you can format the new object. First you need to type the text.

3. **Type Great improvement**
   The text appears in a selected text box on the worksheet, and the chart is no longer selected, as shown in Figure D-18. Your text box may be in a different location; this is not important, because you'll move the annotation in the next step.

4. **Point to an edge of the text box so that the pointer changes to ⁺⁺ₖ, drag the text box into the chart beneath the chart title, as shown in Figure D-19, then release the mouse button**
   The text box is a text annotation for the chart. You also want to add a simple arrow shape in the chart.

5. **Click the chart to select it, click the Chart Tools Layout tab, click the Shapes button in the Insert group, click the Arrow shape in the Lines category, then move the pointer over the text box on the chart**
   The pointer changes to ╂, and the status bar displays "Click and drag to insert an AutoShape." When ╂ is over the text box, red handles appear around the text in the text box. A red handle can act as an anchor for the arrow.

6. **Position ╂ on the red handle to the right of the "t" in the word "improvement" (in the text box), press and hold the left mouse button, drag the line to the Quarter 1 column for the Orthopedics series, then release the mouse button**
   An arrow points to the Quarter 1 expense for Orthopedics, and the Drawing Tools Format tab displays options for working with the new arrow object. You can resize, format, or delete it just like any other object in a chart.

7. **Click the Shape Outline list arrow in the Shape Styles group, click the Automatic color, click the Shape Outline list arrow again, point to Weight, then click 1½ pt**
   Compare your finished chart to Figure D-20.

8. **Save your work**

FIGURE D-18: Text box added

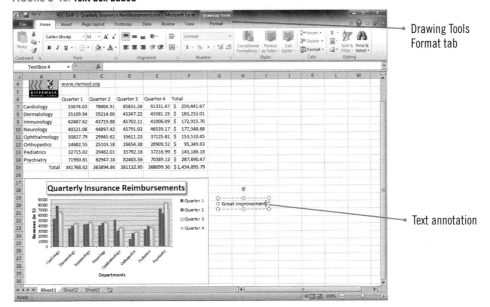

Drawing Tools Format tab

Text annotation

FIGURE D-19: Text annotation on the chart

Text annotation

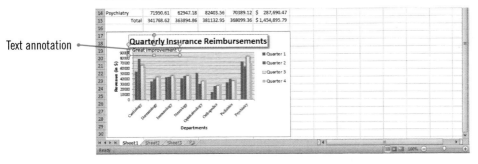

FIGURE D-20: Arrow shape added to chart

Arrow drawn and formatted

Adding SmartArt graphics

In addition to charts, annotations, and drawn objects, you can create a variety of diagrams using SmartArt graphics. **SmartArt graphics** are available in List, Process, Cycle, Hierarchy, Relationship, Matrix, and Pyramid categories. To insert SmartArt, click the SmartArt button in the Illustrations group on the Insert tab to open the Choose a SmartArt Graphic dialog box. Click a SmartArt category in the left pane, then click the layout for the graphic in the center pane. The right pane shows a sample of the selected SmartArt layout, as shown in Figure D-21. The SmartArt graphic appears in the worksheet as an embedded object with sizing handles. Click the Text Pane button on the SmartArt Tools Design tab to open a text pane next to the graphic; you can enter text into the graphic using the text pane or by typing directly in the shapes in the diagram.

FIGURE D-21: Choose a SmartArt Graphic dialog box

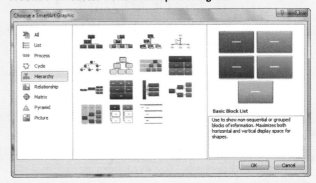

Creating a Pie Chart

You can create multiple charts based on the same worksheet data. While a column chart may illustrate certain important aspects of your worksheet data, you may find you want to create an additional chart to emphasize a different point. Depending on the type of chart you create, you have additional options for calling attention to trends and patterns. For example, if you create a pie chart, you can emphasize one data point by **exploding**, or pulling that slice away from, the pie chart. When you're ready to print a chart, you can preview it just as you do a worksheet to check the output before committing it to paper. You can print a chart by itself or as part of the worksheet. ▓▓▓▓ At an upcoming meeting, Tony plans to discuss the total reimbursement revenue and which departments need improvement. You want to create a pie chart he can use to illustrate total revenue. Finally, you want to fit the worksheet and the charts onto one worksheet page.

STEPS

1. **Select the range A7:A14, press and hold [Ctrl], select the range F7:F14, release [Ctrl], click the Insert tab, click the Pie button in the Charts group, then click Pie in 3-D in the Pie chart gallery**

   The new chart appears in the center of the worksheet. You can move the chart and quickly format it using a chart layout.

2. **Drag the chart so its upper-left corner is at the upper-left corner of cell G1, then click Layout 2 in the Chart Layouts group**

   The chart is repositioned on the page, and its layout changes so that a chart title is added and the legend appears just below the chart title.

3. **Select the chart title text, then type Reimbursements, by Department**

4. **Click the slice for the Orthopedics data point, click it again so it is the only slice selected, right-click it, then click Format Data Point**

   The Format Data Point dialog box opens, as shown in Figure D-22. You can use the Point Explosion slider to control the distance a pie slice moves away from the pie, or you can type a value in the Point Explosion text box.

5. **Double-click 0 in the Point Explosion text box, type 40, then click Close**

   Compare your chart to Figure D-23. You decide to preview the chart and data before you print.

6. **Click cell A1, switch to Page Layout view, type your name in the left header text box, then click cell A1**

   You decide the chart and data would fit better on the page if they were printed in landscape orientation.

7. **Click the Page Layout tab, click the Orientation button in the Page Setup group, then click Landscape**

8. **Click the File tab, click Print on the navigation bar, click the No Scaling setting in the Settings section on the Print tab, then click Fit Sheet on One Page**

   The data and chart are positioned horizontally on a single page, as shown in Figure D-24. The printer you have selected may affect the appearance of your preview screen.

9. **Save and close the workbook, submit your work to your instructor as directed, then exit Excel**

Previewing a chart

To print or preview just a chart, select the chart (or make the chart sheet active), click the File tab, then click Print on the navigation bar. To reposition a chart by changing the page's margins, click the Show Margins button ▥ in the lower-right corner of the Print tab to display the margins in the preview. You can drag the margin lines to the exact settings you want; as the margins change, the size and placement of the chart on the page changes too.

FIGURE D-22: **Format Data Point dialog box**

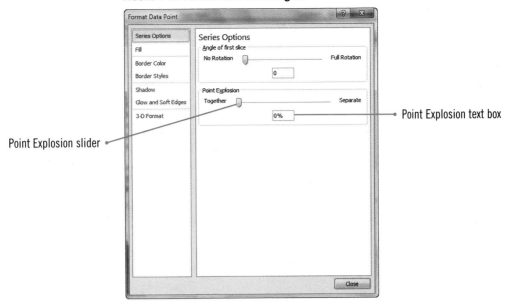

Point Explosion slider

Point Explosion text box

FIGURE D-23: **Exploded pie slice**

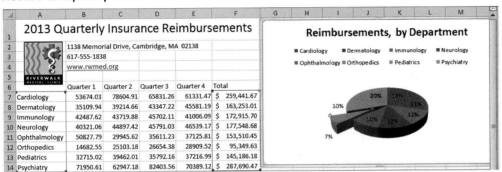

FIGURE D-24: **Preview of worksheet with charts in Backstage view**

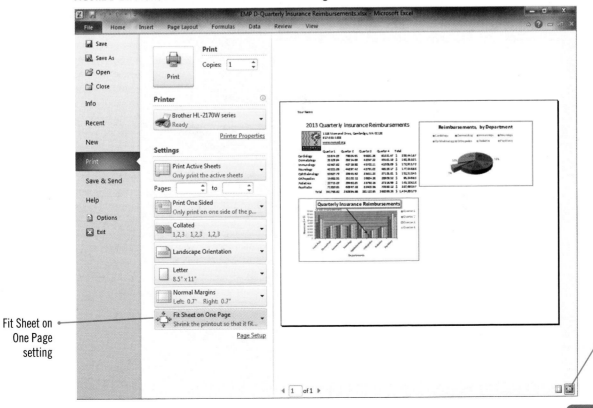

Fit Sheet on One Page setting

Show Margins button

Practice

For current SAM information, including versions and content details, visit SAM Central (http://www.cengage.com/samcentral). If you have a SAM user profile, you may have access to hands-on instruction, practice, and assessment of the skills covered in this unit. Since various versions of SAM are supported throughout the life of this text, check with your instructor for the correct instructions and URL/Web site for accessing assignments.

Concepts Review

Label each element of the Excel chart shown in Figure D-25.

FIGURE D-25

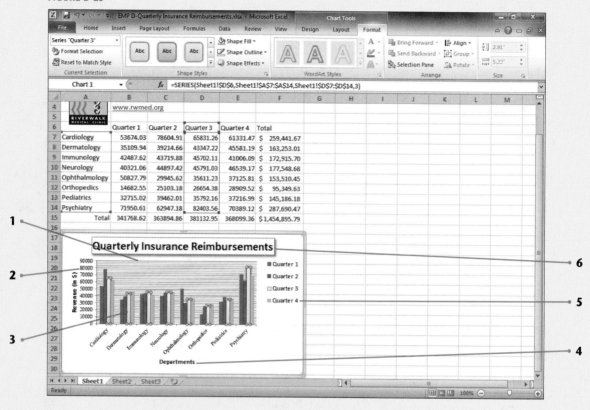

Match each chart type with the statement that best describes it.

7. Column
8. Line
9. Combination
10. Pie
11. Area

a. Displays a column and line chart using different scales of measurement
b. Compares trends over even time intervals
c. Compares data using columns
d. Compares data as parts of a whole
e. Shows how volume changes over time

Select the best answer from the list of choices.

12. **Which pointer do you use to resize a chart?**
    - **a.** ✛
    - **b.** I
    - **c.** ↕
    - **d.** ✛

13. **The object in a chart that identifies the colors used for each data series is a(n):**
    - **a.** Data marker.
    - **b.** Data point.
    - **c.** Organizer.
    - **d.** Legend.

14. **Which tab appears only when a chart is selected?**
    - **a.** Insert
    - **b.** Chart Tools Format
    - **c.** Review
    - **d.** Page Layout

15. **How do you move an embedded chart to a chart sheet?**
    - **a.** Click a button on the Chart Tools Design tab.
    - **b.** Drag the chart to the sheet tab.
    - **c.** Delete the chart, switch to a different sheet, then create a new chart.
    - **d.** Use the Copy and Paste buttons on the Ribbon.

16. **Which tab on the Ribbon do you use to create a chart?**
    - **a.** Design
    - **b.** Insert
    - **c.** Page Layout
    - **d.** Format

17. **A collection of related data points in a chart is called a:**
    - **a.** Data series.
    - **b.** Data tick.
    - **c.** Cell address.
    - **d.** Value title.

Skills Review

1. **Plan a chart.**
    - **a.** Start Excel, open the Data File EMP D-2.xlsx from the drive and folder where you store your Data Files, then save it as **EMP D-Departmental Software Usage**.
    - **b.** Describe the type of chart you would use to plot this data.
    - **c.** What chart type would you use to compare the number of Excel users in each department?

2. **Create a chart.**
    - **a.** In the worksheet, select the range containing all the data and headings.
    - **b.** Click the Insert tab.
    - **c.** Create a Clustered Column chart, then add the chart title **Software Usage, by Department** above the chart.
    - **d.** Save your work.

3. **Move and resize a chart.**
    - **a.** Make sure the chart is still selected.
    - **b.** Move the chart beneath the worksheet data.
    - **c.** Widen the chart so it extends to the right edge of column H.
    - **d.** Use the Chart Tools Layout tab to move the legend below the charted data. (*Hint*: Click the Legend button, then click Show Legend at Bottom.)
    - **e.** Resize the chart so its bottom edge is at the top of row 25.
    - **f.** Save your work.

4. **Change the chart design.**
    - **a.** Change the value in cell B3 to **15**. Observe the change in the chart.
    - **b.** Select the chart.
    - **c.** Use the Chart Layouts group on the Chart Tools Design tab to apply the Layout 7 layout to the chart, then undo the change.
    - **d.** Use the Change Chart Type button on the Chart Tools Design tab to change the chart to a Clustered Bar chart.
    - **e.** Change the chart to a 3-D Clustered Column chart, then change it back to a Clustered Column chart.
    - **f.** Save your work.

Skills Review (continued)

5. **Change the chart layout.**

   a. Use the Chart Tools Layout tab to turn off the major horizontal gridlines in the chart.

   b. Change the font used in the horizontal and vertical axes labels to Times New Roman.

   c. Turn on the major gridlines for both the horizontal and vertical axes.

   d. Change the chart title's font to Times New Roman if necessary, with a font size of 20.

   e. Insert **Departments** as the horizontal axis title.

   f. Insert **Number of Users** as the vertical axis title.

   g. Change the font size of the horizontal and vertical axis titles to 10 and the font to Times New Roman, if necessary.

   h. Change "Personnel" in the worksheet column heading to **Human Resources**, then AutoFit column E.

   i. Change the font size of the legend to 14.

   j. Add a solid line border in the default color and an Offset Diagonal Bottom Right shadow to the chart title.

   k. Save your work.

6. **Format a chart.**

   a. Make sure the chart is selected, then select the Chart Tools Format tab, if necessary.

   b. Change the shape fill of the Excel data series to Dark Blue, Text 2.

   c. Change the shape style of the Excel data series to Subtle Effect Orange, Accent 6.

   d. Save your work.

7. **Annotate and draw on a chart.**

   a. Make sure the chart is selected, then create the text annotation **Needs more users**.

   b. Position the text annotation so the word "Needs" is just below the word "Software" in the chart title.

   c. Select the chart, then use the Chart Tools Layout tab to create a 1½ pt weight arrow that points from the bottom center of the text box to the Excel users in the Neurology department.

   d. Deselect the chart.

   e. Save your work.

8. **Create a pie chart.**

   a. Select the range A1:F2, then create a Pie in 3-D chart.

   b. Drag the 3-D pie chart beneath the existing chart.

   c. Change the chart title to **Excel Users**.

   d. Apply the Style 42 chart style to the chart.

   e. Explode the Human Resources slice from the pie chart at **25%**, then make cell A1 active.

   f. In Page Layout view, enter your name in the left section of the worksheet header.

   g. Preview the worksheet and charts in Backstage view, make sure all the contents fit on one page, then submit your work to your instructor as directed. When printed, the worksheet should look like Figure D-26.

   h. Save your work, close the workbook, then exit Excel.

FIGURE D-26

The position of your annotation may vary.

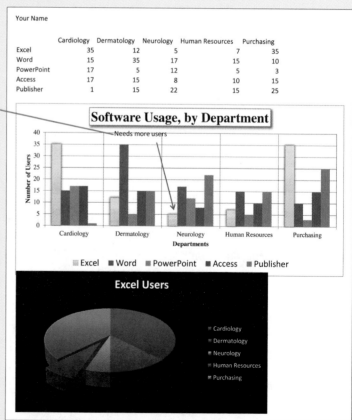

	Cardiology	Dermatology	Neurology	Human Resources	Purchasing
Excel	35	12	5	7	35
Word	15	35	17	15	10
PowerPoint	17	5	12	5	3
Access	17	15	8	10	15
Publisher	1	15	22	15	25

Independent Challenge 1

You are the operations manager for the Springfield Medical Research Group in Massachusetts. Each year the group applies to various state and federal agencies for matching funds. For this year's funding proposal, you need to create charts to document the number of grants in previous years.

a. Start Excel, open the file EMP D-3.xlsx from the drive and folder where you store your Data Files, then save it as **EMP D-Springfield Medical Research Group**.

b. Take some time to plan your charts. Which type of chart or charts might best illustrate the information you need to display? What kind of chart enhancements do you want to use? Will a 3-D effect make your chart easier to understand?

c. Create a Clustered Column chart for the data.

d. Change at least one of the colors used in a data series.

e. Make the appropriate modifications to the chart to make it visually attractive and easier to read and understand. Include a legend to the right of the chart, and add chart titles and horizontal and vertical axis titles using the text shown in Table D-3.

TABLE D-3

title	text
Chart title	Number of Research Grants
Vertical axis title	Numbers of Grants
Horizontal axis title	Departments

f. Create at least two additional charts for the same data to show how different chart types display the same data. Reposition each new chart so that all charts are visible in the worksheet. One of the additional charts should be a pie chart; the other is up to you.

g. Modify each new chart as necessary to improve its appearance and effectiveness. A sample worksheet containing three charts based on the worksheet data is shown in Figure D-27.

h. Change the data in cell E3 from 2 to 5.

i. Enter your name in the worksheet header.

j. Save your work. Before printing, preview the worksheet in Backstage view, then adjust any settings as necessary so that all the worksheet data and charts print on a single page.

k. Submit your work to your instructor as directed.

l. Close the workbook, then exit Excel.

FIGURE D-27

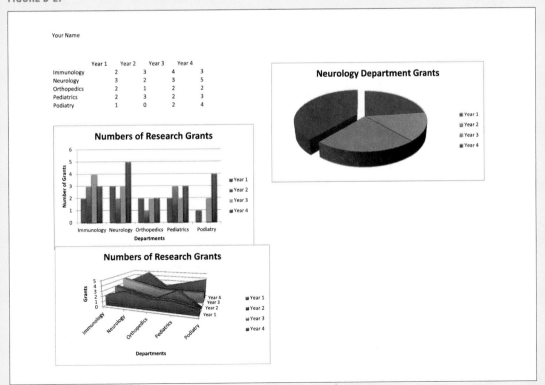

Independent Challenge 2

You work at Pinnacle Medical Consultants, a locally owned medical consortium. One of your responsibilities is to manage the company's revenues and expenses using Excel. Another is to convince the current staff that Excel can help them make daily operating decisions more easily and efficiently. To do this, you've decided to create charts using the previous year's operating expenses including rent, utilities, and payroll. The manager will use these charts at the next monthly meeting.

a. Start Excel, open the Data File EMP D-4.xlsx from the drive and folder where you store your Data Files, then save it as **EMP D-Pinnacle Medical Consultants**.

b. Decide which data in the worksheet should be charted. What chart types are best suited for the information you need to show? What kinds of chart enhancements are necessary?

c. Create a 3-D Clustered Column chart in the worksheet showing the expense data for all four quarters. (*Hint*: The expense categories should appear on the x-axis. Do not include the totals.)

d. Change the vertical axis labels (Expenses data) so that no decimals are displayed. (*Hint*: Right-click the axis labels you want to modify, click Format Axis, click the Number category in the Format Axis dialog box, change the number of decimal places, then click Close.)

e. Using the worksheet data, create two charts on this worksheet: one that analyzes expenses and one that analyzes revenues. (*Hint*: Move each chart to a new location on the worksheet, then deselect it before creating the next one.)

f. In one chart of the expense data, add data labels, then add chart titles as you see fit.

g. Make any necessary formatting changes to make the charts look more attractive, then enter your name in a worksheet cell.

h. Save your work.

i. Preview each chart in Backstage view, and adjust any items as needed. Fit the worksheet to a single page, then submit your work to your instructor as directed. A sample of a printed worksheet is shown in Figure D-28.

j. Close the workbook, then exit Excel.

FIGURE D-28

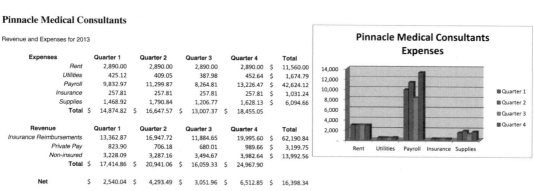

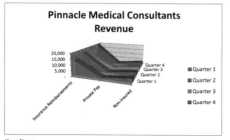

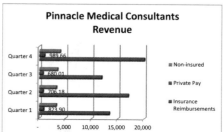

Independent Challenge 3

You are reviewing expenses for the Bethesda Medical Hospital's operating room. The board of directors wants to examine the expenses incurred recently and has asked you to prepare charts that can be used in this evaluation. In particular, you want to see how dollar amounts compare among the different expenses, and you also want to see how expenses compare with each other proportionally to the total budget.

a. Start Excel, open the Data File EMP D-5.xlsx from the drive and folder where you store your Data Files, then save it as **EMP D-OR Expenses**.

b. Identify three types of charts that seem best suited to illustrate the data in the range A16:B24. What kinds of chart enhancements are necessary?

c. Create at least two different types of charts that show the distribution of operating room expenses. (*Hint*: Move each chart to a new location on the same worksheet.) One of the charts should be a 3-D pie chart.

d. In at least one of the charts, add annotated text and arrows highlighting important data, such as the largest expense.

e. Change the color of at least one data series in at least one of the charts.

f. Add chart titles and category and value axis titles where appropriate. Format the titles with a font of your choice. Apply a shadow to the chart title in at least one chart.

g. Add your name to a section of the header, then save your work.

h. Preview the worksheet in Backstage view. Adjust any items as needed. Be sure the charts are all visible on one page. Compare your work to the sample in Figure D-29.

FIGURE D-29

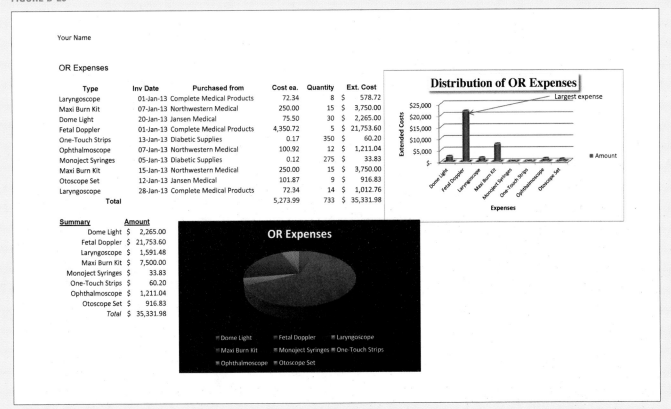

Independent Challenge 3 (continued)

Advanced Challenge Exercise

- Explode a slice from the 3-D pie chart.
- Add a data label to the exploded pie slice.
- Change the number format of the data label in the pie chart so no decimals are displayed.
- Save your work, then preview it in Backstage view.

i. Submit your work to your instructor as directed, close the workbook, then exit Excel.

Real Life Independent Challenge

This project requires an Internet connection.

You are so indispensable in your role as financial manager at the Good Health Clinic that the company wants to move you and your family to its new location, which you get to choose. You have a good idea where you'd like to live, and you decide to use the Web to find out more about houses that are currently available.

a. Start Excel, then save a new, blank workbook as **EMP D-My Dream House** to the drive and folder where you save your Data Files.

b. Decide on where you would like to live, and use your favorite search engine to find information sources on homes for sale in that area. (*Hint*: Try using realtor.com or other realtor-sponsored sites.)

c. Determine a price range and features within the home. Find data for at least five homes that meet your location and price requirements, and enter them in the worksheet. See Table D-4 below for a suggested data layout.

TABLE D-4

suggested data layout					
Location					
Price range					
	House 1	House 2	House 3	House 4	House 5
Asking price					
Bedrooms					
Bathrooms					
Year built					
Size (in sq. ft.)					

Real Life Independent Challenge (continued)

d. Format the data so it looks attractive and professional.

e. Create any type of column chart using only the House and Asking Price data. Place it on the same worksheet as the data. Include a descriptive title.

f. Change the colors in the chart using the chart style of your choice.

g. Enter your name in a section of the header.

h. Save the workbook. Preview the worksheet in Backstage view and make adjustments if necessary to fit all of the information on one page. See Figure D-30 for an example of what your worksheet might look like.

i. Submit your work to your instructor as directed.

Advanced Challenge Exercise

- Change the chart type to a Clustered Column chart.
- Change the data used for the chart to include the size data in cells A9:F9.
- Create a combination chart that plots the asking price on one axis and the size of the home on the other axis. (*Hint:* Use Help to get tips on how to chart with a secondary axis.)

j. Close the workbook, then exit Excel.

FIGURE D-30

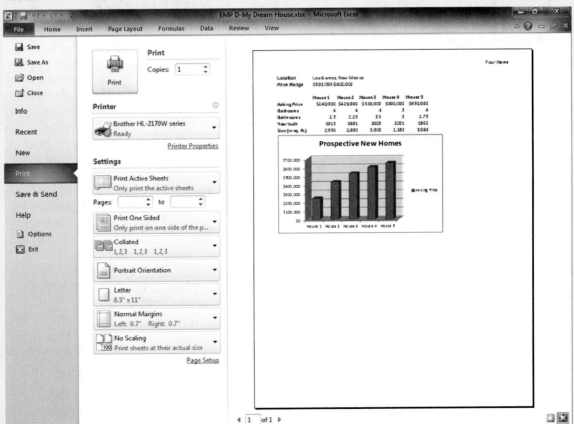

Visual Workshop

Open the Data File EMP D-6.xlsx from the drive and folder where you store your Data Files, then save it as
EMP D-Projected Diagnostics Laboratory Revenue. Format the worksheet data so it looks like Figure D-31, then create and modify two charts to match the ones shown in the figure. You will need to make formatting, layout, and design changes once you create the charts. (Hint: The shadow used in the 3-D pie chart title is made using the Outer Offset Diagonal Bottom Right shadow.) Enter your name in the left text box of the header, then save and preview the worksheet. Submit your work to your instructor as directed, then close the workbook and exit Excel.

FIGURE D-31

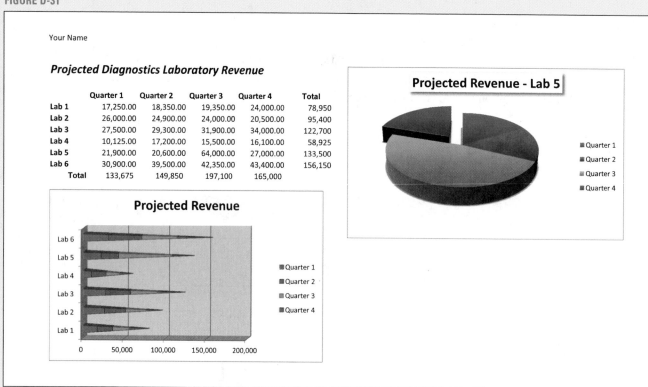

Analyzing Data Using Formulas

**Files You
Will Need:**

EMP E-1.xlsx

EMP E-2.xlsx

EMP E-3.xlsx

EMP E-4.xlsx

EMP E-5.xlsx

EMP E-6.xlsx

EMP E-7.xlsx

As you have learned, formulas and functions help you to analyze worksheet data. As you learn how to use different types of formulas and functions, you will discover more valuable uses for Excel. In this unit, you will gain a deeper understanding of Excel formulas and learn how to use several Excel functions. RMC is considering the acquisition of a local medical imaging company to assist with their growing demand for diagnostic tests. The imaging company, NE Imaging, has three facilities. Tony Sanchez, RMC's office manager, will use Excel formulas and functions to analyze insurance reimbursement data for the imaging company's facilities and to consolidate reimbursement data from several worksheets. Because RMC is considering adding its own imaging center, Tony asks you to estimate the loan costs for a new imaging facility and to compare the reimbursement data for the facilities RMC may acquire.

OBJECTIVES

Format data using text functions

Sum a data range based on conditions

Consolidate data using a formula

Check formulas for errors

Construct formulas using named ranges

Build a logical formula with the IF function

Build a logical formula with the AND function

Calculate payments with the PMT function

Formatting Data Using Text Functions

Often, you need to import data into Excel from an outside source, such as another program or the Internet. Sometimes you need to reformat this data to make it understandable and attractive. Instead of handling these tasks manually in each cell, you can save time by using Excel text functions to perform these tasks automatically for a range of cell data. The Convert Text to Columns feature breaks data fields in one column into separate columns. The text function PROPER capitalizes the first letter in a string of text as well as any text following a space. You can use the CONCATENATE function to join two or more strings into one text string. ▓▓▓▓▓ Tony has received the technicians' data from the Human Resources Department of the imaging company. He asks you to use text formulas to format the data into a more useful layout.

STEPS

1. **Start Excel, open the file EMP E-1.xlsx from the drive and folder where you store your Data Files, then save it as EMP E-Imaging Data**

2. **On the Technicians sheet, select the range A4:A15, click the Data tab, then click the Text to Columns button in the Data Tools group**

   The Convert Text to Columns Wizard opens, as shown in Figure E-1. The data fields on your worksheet are separated by commas, which will act as delimiters. A **delimiter** is a separator, such as a space, comma, or semicolon that should separate your data. Excel separates your data into columns at the delimiter.

3. **If necessary, click the Delimited option button to select it, click Next, in the Delimiters area of the dialog box click the Comma check box to select it if necessary, click any other selected check boxes to deselect them, then click Next**

   You instructed Excel to separate your data at the comma delimiter.

4. **Click the Text option button in the Column data format area, click the second column with the city data to select it in the Data preview area, click the Text option button again in the Column data format area, observe the column headings and data in the Data preview area, then click Finish**

   The data are separated into three columns of text. You want to format the letters in the names and cities to the correct cases.

QUICK TIP

You can move the Function Arguments dialog box if it overlaps a cell or range that you need to click. You can also click the Collapse Dialog box button ▒▒, select the cell or range, then click the Expand Dialog box button ▒▒ to return to the Function Arguments dialog box.

5. **Click cell D4, click the Formulas tab, click the Text button in the Function Library group, click PROPER, with the insertion point in the Text text box click cell A4, then click OK**

   The name is copied from cell A4 to cell D4 with the correct uppercase letters for proper names. The remaining names and the cities are still in lowercase letters.

6. **Drag the fill handle to copy the formula in cell D4 to cell E4, then copy the formulas in cells D4:E4 into the range D5:E15**

   You want to format the years data to be more descriptive.

QUICK TIP

Excel automatically inserts quotation marks to enclose the space and the Years text.

7. **Click cell F4, click the Text button in the Function Library group, click CONCATENATE, with the insertion point in the Text1 text box click cell C4, press [Tab], with the insertion point in the Text2 text box press [Spacebar], type Years, then click OK**

8. **Copy the formula in cell F4 into the range F5:F15, compare your work to Figure E-2, click the Insert tab, click the Header & Footer button in the Text group, click the Go to Footer button in the Navigation group, enter your name in the center text box, click on the worksheet, scroll up and click cell A1, then click the Normal button ▦ in the status bar**

9. **Save your file, then preview the worksheet**

FIGURE E-1: **Convert Text to Columns dialog box**

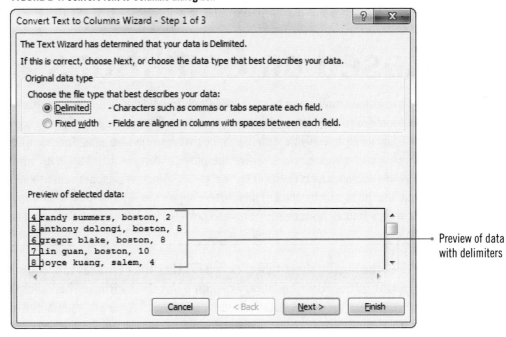

Preview of data with delimiters

FIGURE E-2: **Worksheet with data formatted in columns**

	A	B	C	D	E	F	G	H	I
1				NE Imaging Technicians					
2									
3				Name	Location	Years of Service			
4	randy summers	boston	2	Randy Summers	Boston	2 Years			
5	anthony dolongi	boston	5	Anthony Dolongi	Boston	5 Years			
6	gregor blake	boston	8	Gregor Blake	Boston	8 Years			
7	lin guan	boston	10	Lin Guan	Boston	10 Years			
8	joyce kuang	salem	4	Joyce Kuang	Salem	4 Years			
9	garrin cunha	salem	7	Garrin Cunha	Salem	7 Years			
10	cathy jaques	salem	5	Cathy Jaques	Salem	5 Years			
11	alyssa maztta	salem	4	Alyssa Maztta	Salem	4 Years			
12	april radka	newton	6	April Radka	Newton	6 Years			
13	jose costello	newton	7	Jose Costello	Newton	7 Years			
14	joyce haddad	newton	4	Joyce Haddad	Newton	4 Years			
15	sandra zenny	newton	7	Sandra Zenny	Newton	7 Years			
16									
17									

Using text functions

Other useful text functions include UPPER, LOWER, and SUBSTITUTE. The UPPER function converts text to all uppercase letters, the LOWER function converts text to all lowercase letters, and SUBSTITUTE replaces text in a text string. For example, if cell A1 contains the text string "Today is Wednesday", then =LOWER(A1) would produce "today is wednesday"; =UPPER(A1) would produce "TODAY IS WEDNESDAY"; and =SUBSTITUTE(A1, "Wednesday", "Tuesday") would result in "Today is Tuesday".

If you want to copy and paste data that you have formatted using text functions, you need to select Values Only from the Paste Options drop-down list to paste the cell values rather than the text formulas.

Summing a Data Range Based on Conditions

You have learned how to use the SUM, COUNT, and AVERAGE functions for data ranges. You can also use Excel functions to sum, count, and average data in a range based on criteria, or conditions, you set. The SUMIF function totals only the cells in a range that meet given criteria. For example, you can total the values in a column of reimbursements where the provider name equals Joe Smith (the criterion). Similarly, the COUNTIF function counts cells and the AVERAGEIF function averages cells in a range based on a specified condition. The format for the SUMIF function appears in Figure E-3. ▆▆▟▟▟ Tony asks you to analyze the Boston site's January reimbursement data to provide him with information about each procedure.

STEPS

1. **Click the Boston sheet tab, click cell F7, click the Formulas tab, click the More Functions button in the Function Library group, point to Statistical, then click COUNTIF**

   The Function Arguments dialog box opens, as shown in Figure E-4. You want to count the number of times PET appears in the Procedure column. The formula you use will say, in effect, "Examine the range I specify, then count the number of cells in that range that contain "PET." You will specify absolute addresses for the range so you can copy the formula.

2. **With the insertion point in the Range text box, select the range A6:A25, press [F4], press [Tab], with the insertion point in the Criteria text box, click cell E7, then click OK**

   Your formula asks Excel to search the range A6:A25, and where it finds the value shown in cell E7 (that is, when it finds the value "PET"), add one to the total count. The number of PET procedures, 4, appears in cell F7. You want to calculate the total revenue for the PET procedures.

QUICK TIP
You can also sum, count, and average ranges with multiple criteria using the functions SUMIFS, COUNTIFS, and AVERAGEIFS.

3. **Click cell G7, click the Math & Trig button in the Function Library group, scroll down the list of functions, then click SUMIF**

   The Function Arguments dialog box opens. You want to enter two ranges and a criterion; the first range is the one where you want Excel to search for the criteria entered. The second range contains the corresponding cells that Excel will total when it finds the criterion you specify in the first range.

4. **With the insertion point in the Range text box, select the range A6:A25, press [F4], press [Tab], with the insertion point in the Criteria text box, click cell E7, press [Tab], with the insertion point in the Sum_range text box, select the range B6:B25, press [F4], then click OK**

   Your formula asks Excel to search the range A6:A25, and where it finds the value shown in cell E7 (that is, when it finds the value "PET"), add the corresponding amounts from column B. The reimbursement amount for the PET procedures, $10,900, appears in cell G7. You want to calculate the average price paid for the PET procedures.

5. **Click cell H7, click the More Functions button in the Function Library group, point to Statistical, then click AVERAGEIF**

6. **With the insertion point in the Range text box, select the range A6:A25, press [F4], press [Tab], with the insertion point in the Criteria text box, click cell E7, press [Tab], with the insertion point in the Average_range text box, select the range B6:B25, press [F4], then click OK**

   The average price paid for PET procedures, $2,725, appears in cell H7.

TROUBLE
Follow the same steps that you used to add a footer to the Technicians worksheet in the previous lesson.

7. **Select the range F7:H7, then drag the fill handle to fill the range F8:H10**

   Compare your results with those in Figure E-5.

8. **Add your name to the center of the footer, save the workbook, then preview the worksheet**

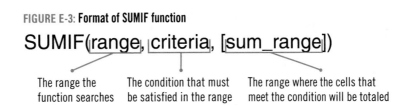

SUMIF(range, criteria, [sum_range])

The range the
function searches

The condition that must
be satisfied in the range

The range where the cells that
meet the condition will be totaled

FIGURE E-4: **COUNTIF function in the Function Arguments dialog box**

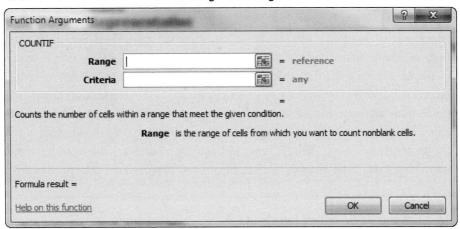

FIGURE E-5: **Worksheet with conditional statistics**

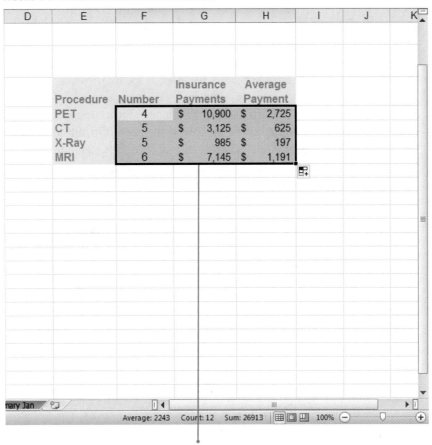

Conditional statistics

Excel 2010

Consolidating Data Using a Formula

When you want to summarize similar data that exists in different sheets or workbooks, you can **consolidate**, or combine and display, the data in one sheet. For example, you might have entered insurance payments for different facilities on separate sheets that you want to consolidate on one summary sheet, showing total insurance payments for all facilities. Or, you may have quarterly insurance data on separate sheets that you want to total for yearly payments on a summary sheet. The best way to consolidate data is to use cell references to the various sheets on a consolidation, or summary, sheet. Because they reference other sheets that are usually behind the summary sheet, such references effectively create another dimension in the workbook and are called **3-D references**, as shown in Figure E-6. You can reference, or **link** to, data in other sheets and in other workbooks. Linking to a worksheet or workbook is better than retyping calculated results from another worksheet or workbook because the data values that the calculated totals depend on might change. If you reference the values, any changes to the original values are automatically reflected in the consolidation sheet. ██████ Tony asks you to prepare a January reimbursement summary sheet comparing the total NE Imaging reimbursements for the procedures performed in the month.

STEPS

1. **Click the NE Summary Jan sheet tab**

   Because the NE Summary Jan sheet (which is the consolidation sheet) will contain the reference to the data in the other sheets, the cell pointer must reside there when you begin entering the reference.

2. **Click cell B7, click the Formulas tab, click the AutoSum button in the Function Library group, click the Boston sheet tab, press and hold [Shift] and click the Newton sheet tab, scroll up if necessary and click cell F7, then click the Enter button ✔ on the formula bar**

   The NE Summary Jan sheet becomes active, and the formula bar reads =SUM(Boston:Newton!F7), as shown in Figure E-7. "Boston:Newton" references the Boston, Salem, and Newton sheets. The exclamation point (!) is an **external reference indicator**, meaning that the cells referenced are outside the active sheet; F7 is the actual cell reference you want to total in the external sheets. The result, 13, appears in cell B7 of the NE Summary Jan sheet; it is the sum of the number of PET procedures performed and referenced in cell F7 of the Boston, Salem, and Newton sheets. Because the Insurance Payments data is in the column to the right of the Number column on the Boston, Salem, and Newton sheets, you can copy the number summary formula, with its relative addresses, into the cell that holds the insurance payment information.

3. **Drag the fill handle to copy the formula in cell B7 to cell C7, click the Auto Fill options list arrow 📑▾, then click the Fill Without Formatting option button**

   The result, $39,579, appears in cell C7 of the NE Summary Jan sheet, showing the sum of the PET insurance payments referenced in cell G7 of the Boston, Salem, and Newton sheets.

4. **In the NE Summary Jan sheet, with the range B7:C7 selected, drag the fill handle to fill the range B8:C10**

   You can test a consolidation reference by changing one cell value on which the formula is based and seeing if the formula result changes.

5. **Click the Newton sheet tab, edit cell A6 to read PET, then click the NE Summary Jan sheet tab**

   The number of PET procedures performed is automatically updated to 14, and the insurance payments amount is increased to $40,079, as shown in Figure E-8.

▶ 6. **Save the workbook, then preview the worksheet**

QUICK TIP
You can preview your worksheet with the worksheet gridlines and column and row headings for printing at a later time. Click the Print check boxes under Gridlines and Headings in the Sheet Options group of the Page Layout tab.

FIGURE E-6: Consolidating data from three worksheets

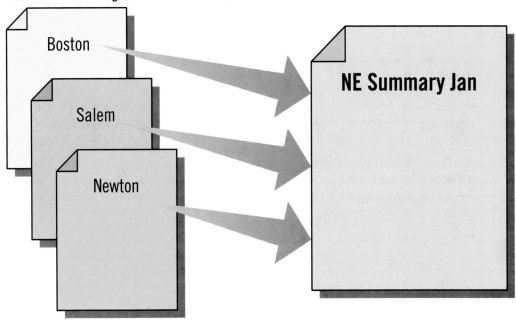

FIGURE E-7: Worksheet showing total PET procedures performed

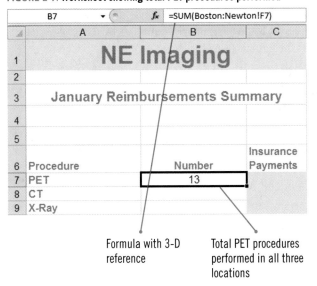

B7 · fx =SUM(Boston:Newton!F7)

	A	B	C
1	NE Imaging		
2			
3	January Reimbursements Summary		
4			
5			
6	Procedure	Number	Insurance Payments
7	PET	13	
8	CT		
9	X-Ray		

Formula with 3-D reference

Total PET procedures performed in all three locations

FIGURE E-8: NE Summary Jan worksheet with updated totals

	A	B	C	D
1	NE Imaging			
2				
3	January Reimbursements Summary			
4				
5				
6	Procedure	Number	Insurance Payments	
7	PET	14	$ 40,079	
8	CT	13	$ 7,960	
9	X-Ray	16	$ 3,085	
10	MRI	17	$ 20,266	
11	Total			
12				
13	Procedure Payments as a Percentage			
14	PET			
15	CT			
16	X-Ray			
17	MRI			
18				
19				
20				

Updated totals

Linking data between workbooks

Just as you can link data between cells in a worksheet and between sheets in a workbook, you can link workbooks so that changes made in referenced cells in one workbook are reflected in the consolidation sheet in the other workbook. To link a single cell between workbooks, open both workbooks, select the cell to receive the linked data, type the equal sign (=), select the cell in the other workbook containing the data to be linked, then press [Enter]. Excel automatically inserts the name of the referenced workbook in the cell reference. For example, if the linked data is contained in cell C7 of the Sales worksheet in the Product workbook, the cell entry reads =[Product.xlsx]Sales!$C$7. To perform calculations, enter formulas on the consolidation sheet using cells in the supporting sheets.

Checking Formulas for Errors

When formulas result in errors, Excel displays an error value based on the error type. See Table E-1 for a description of the error types and error codes that might appear in worksheets. One way to check formulas in a worksheet for errors is to display the formulas on the worksheet rather than the formula results. You can also check for errors when entering formulas by using the IFERROR function. The IFERROR function simplifies the error-checking process for your worksheets. This function displays a message or value that you specify, rather than the one automatically generated by Excel, if there is an error in a formula. ▰▰▰▰ Tony asks you to use formulas to compare the reimbursement amounts for January. You will use the IFERROR function to help catch formula errors.

STEPS

1. **Click cell B11, click the Formulas tab, click the AutoSum button in the Function Library group, then click the Enter button ✔ on the formula bar**

   The number of procedures performed, 60, appears in cell B11.

2. **Drag the fill handle to copy the formula in cell B11 into cell C11, click the Auto Fill options list arrow ▦▾, then click the Fill Without Formatting option button**

   The insurance payment total of $71,390 appears in cell C11. You decide to enter a formula to calculate the percentage of payments the PET procedures represent by dividing the PET payments by the total payments. To help with error checking, you decide to enter the formula using the IFERROR function.

3. **Click cell B14, click the Logical button in the Function Library group, click IFERROR, with the insertion point in the Value text box, click cell C7, type /, click cell C11, press [Tab], in the Value_if_error text box, type ERROR, then click OK**

   The PET procedure payments percentage of 56.14% appears in cell B14. You want to be sure that your error message will be displayed properly, so you decide to test it by intentionally creating an error. You copy and paste the formula—which has a relative address in the denominator, where an absolute address should be used.

4. **Drag the fill handle to copy the formula in cell B14 into the range B15:B17**

   The ERROR value appears in cells B15:B17, as shown in Figure E-9. The errors are a result of the relative address for C11 in the denominator of the copied formula. Changing the relative address of C11 in the copied formula to an absolute address of $C$11 will correct the errors.

5. **Double-click cell B14, select C11 in the formula, press [F4], then click ✔ on the formula bar**

   The formula now contains an absolute reference to cell C11.

6. **Copy the corrected formula in cell B14 into the range B15:B17**

   The procedure payments percentages now appear in all four cells, without error messages, as shown in Figure E-10. You want to check all of your worksheet formulas by displaying them on the worksheet.

7. **Click the Show Formulas button in the Formula Auditing group**

   The formulas appear in columns B and C. You want to display the formula results again. The Show Formulas button works as a toggle, turning the feature on and off with each click.

8. **Click the Show Formulas button in the Formula Auditing group**

   The formula results appear on the worksheet.

9. **Add your name to the center section of the footer, save the workbook, preview the worksheet, close the workbook, then submit the workbook to your instructor**

Analyzing Data Using Formulas

FIGURE E-9: Worksheet with error codes

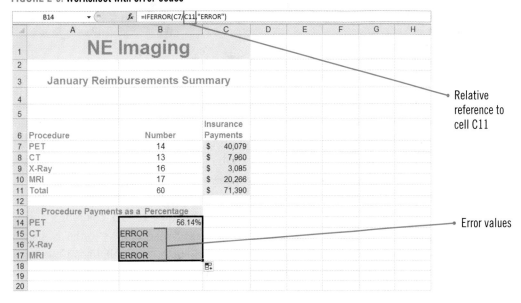

Relative reference to cell C11

Error values

FIGURE E-10: Worksheet with procedure percentages

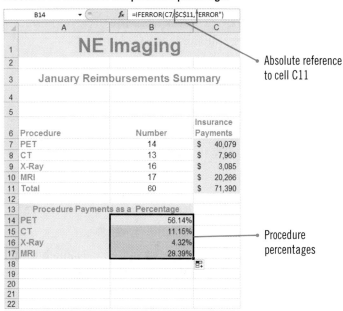

Absolute reference to cell C11

Procedure percentages

TABLE E-1: Understanding error values

error value	cause of error	error value	cause of error
#DIV/0!	A number is divided by 0	#NAME?	Formula contains text error
#NA	A value in a formula is not available	#NULL!	Invalid intersection of areas
#NUM!	Invalid use of a number in a formula	#REF!	Invalid cell reference
#VALUE!	Wrong type of formula argument or operand	#####	Column is not wide enough to display data

Correcting circular references

A cell with a circular reference contains a formula that refers to its own cell location. If you accidentally enter a formula with a circular reference, a warning box opens, alerting you to the problem. Click OK to open a Help window explaining how to find the circular reference. In simple formulas, a circular reference is easy to spot. To correct it, edit the formula to remove any reference to the cell where the formula is located.

Constructing Formulas Using Named Ranges

To make your worksheet easier to follow, you can assign names to cells and ranges. You can also use names in formulas to make them easier to build and to reduce formula errors. For example, the formula "revenue-cost" is easier to understand than the formula "A5-A8". Cell and range names can use uppercase or lowercase letters as well as digits, but cannot have spaces. After you name a cell or range, you can define its **scope**, or the worksheets where you will be able to use it. When defining a name's scope, you can limit its use to a worksheet or make it available to the entire workbook. If you move a named cell or range, its name moves with it, and if you add or remove rows or columns to the worksheet the ranges are adjusted to their new position in the worksheet. When used in formulas, names become absolute cell references by default. 🔧 As part of the analysis of the NE Imaging company, you are given their patient accounts to review. Tony asks you to calculate the number of days since each patient statement was created. You will use range names to construct the formula.

STEPS

QUICK TIP

You can create range names by selecting a cell or range, typing a name in the Name Box, then pressing [Enter]. By default, its scope will be the workbook.

1. **Open the file EMP E-2.xlsx from the drive and folder where you store your Data Files, then save it as EMP E-Patient Accounts**

2. **Click cell B4, click the Formulas tab if necessary, click the Define Name button in the Defined Names group**

   The New Name dialog box opens, as shown in Figure E-11. You can give a name to a cell that contains a date to make it easier to build formulas that perform date calculations.

QUICK TIP

Because names cannot contain spaces, underscores are often used between words to replace spaces.

3. **Type current_date in the Name text box, click the Scope list arrow, click Accounts, then click OK**

   The name assigned to cell B4, current_date, appears in the Name Box. Because its scope is the Accounts worksheet, the range name current_date will appear on the name list only on that worksheet. You can also name ranges that contain dates.

4. **Select the range B7:B13, click the Define Name button in the Defined Names group, enter statement_date in the Name text box, click the Scope list arrow, click Accounts, then click OK**

   Now you can use the named cell and named range in a formula. The formula =current_date-statement_date is easier to understand than =$B$4-B7.

QUICK TIP

Named cells and ranges can be used as a navigational tool in a worksheet by selecting the name in the Name Box. The named cell or range becomes active.

5. **Click cell C7, type =, click the Use in Formula button in the Defined Names group, click current_date, type –, click the Use in Formula button, click statement_date, then click the Enter button ✓ on the formula bar**

   The age of the first statement, 40, appears in cell C7. This patient's statement was created 40 days ago. You can use the same formula to calculate the age of the other statements.

6. **Drag the fill handle to copy the formula in cell C7 into the range C8:C13, then compare your formula results with those in Figure E-12**

7. **Save the workbook**

Consolidating data using named ranges

You can consolidate data using named cells and ranges. For example, you might have entered team sales figures using the names team1, team2, and team3 on different sheets that you want to consolidate on one summary sheet. As you enter the summary formula you can click the Formulas tab, click the Use in Formula button in the Defined Names group, and select the cell or range name.

Enter cell or range name here

FIGURE E-12: **Worksheet with statement ages**

Name box

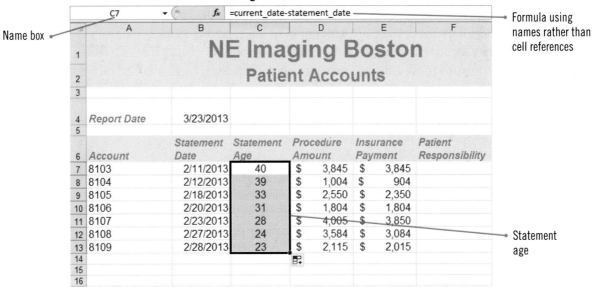

Formula using names rather than cell references

Statement age

Managing workbook names

You can use the Name Manager to create, delete, and edit names in a workbook. Click the Name Manager button in the Defined Names group on the Formulas tab to open the Name Manager dialog box, as shown in Figure E-13. Click the New button to create a new

named cell or range, click Edit to change a highlighted cell name, and click Delete to remove a highlighted name. Click Filter to see options for displaying specific criteria for displaying names.

FIGURE E-13: **Name Manager dialog box**

Click to create new name

Click to change name

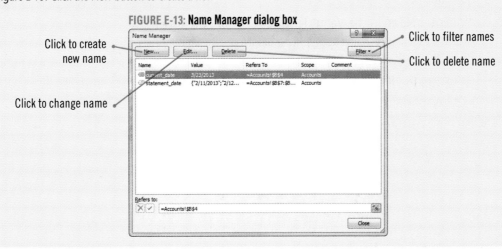

Click to filter names

Click to delete name

Building a Logical Formula with the IF Function

You can build a logical formula using an IF function. A **logical formula** makes calculations based on criteria that you create, called **stated conditions**. For example, you can build a formula to calculate bonuses based on a person's performance rating. If a person is rated a 5 (the stated condition) on a scale of 1 to 5, with 5 being the highest rating, he or she receives an additional 10% of his or her salary as a bonus; otherwise, there is no bonus. A condition that can be answered with a true or false response is called a **logical test**. The IF function has three parts, separated by commas: a condition or logical test, an action to take if the logical test or condition is true, and an action to take if the logical test or condition is false. Another way of expressing this is: IF(test_cond,do_this,else_this). Translated into an Excel IF function, the formula to calculate bonuses might look like this: IF(Rating=5,Salary*0.10,0). In other words, if the rating equals 5, multiply the salary by 0.10 (the decimal equivalent of 10%), then place the result in the selected cell; if the rating does not equal 5, place a 0 in the cell. When entering the logical test portion of an IF statement, you typically use some combination of the comparison operators listed in Table E-2. Tony asks you to use an IF function to calculate the amount for which the patient is responsible on each account.

STEPS

1. **Click cell F7, on the Formulas tab, click the Logical button in the Function Library group, then click IF**

   The Function Arguments dialog box opens. You want the function to calculate the patient's responsibility as follows: If the procedure amount is greater than the insurance payment, calculate the amount the patient must pay (procedure amount – insurance payment), and place the result in cell F7; otherwise, place the text "None" in the cell.

2. **With the insertion point in the Logical_test text box, click cell D7, type >, click cell E7, then press [Tab]**

   The symbol (>) represents "greater than." So far, the formula reads "If the procedure amount is greater than the insurance payment,". The next part of the function tells Excel the action to take if the procedure amount exceeds the insurance payment.

3. **With the insertion point in the Value_if_true text box, click cell D7, type –, click cell E7, then press [Tab]**

   This part of the formula tells the program what you want it to do if the logical test is true. Continuing the translation of the formula, this part means "Subtract the insurance payment from the procedure amount." The last part of the formula tells Excel the action to take if the logical test is false (that is, if the procedure amount does not exceed the insurance payment).

4. **Enter None in the Value_if_false text box, then click OK**

   The function is complete, and the result, None (the amount for which the patient is responsible), appears in cell F7, as shown in Figure E-14.

5. **Drag the fill handle to copy the formula in cell F7 into the range F8:F13**

   Compare your results with Figure E-15.

6. **Save the workbook**

	F7			f_x	=IF(D7>E7,D7-E7,"None")	
	A	B	C	D	E	F	G

NE Imaging Boston
Patient Accounts

4	Report Date	3/23/2013					
6	Account	Statement Date	Statement Age	Procedure Amount	Insurance Payment	Patient Responsibility	Account Past Due
7	8103	2/11/2013	40	$ 3,845	$ 3,845	None	
8	8104	2/12/2013	39	$ 1,004	$ 904		
9	8105	2/18/2013	33	$ 2,550	$ 2,350		
10	8106	2/20/2013	31	$ 1,804	$ 1,804		
11	8107	2/23/2013	28	$ 4,005	$ 3,850		
12	8108	2/27/2013	24	$ 3,584	$ 3,084		
13	8109	2/28/2013	23	$ 2,115	$ 2,015		

IF function   Amount patient owes

FIGURE E-15: **Worksheet showing patient responsibility**

	F7			f_x	=IF(D7>E7,D7-E7,"None")	
	A	B	C	D	E	F	G

NE Imaging Boston
Patient Accounts

4	Report Date	3/23/2013					
6	Account	Statement Date	Statement Age	Procedure Amount	Insurance Payment	Patient Responsibility	Account Past Due
7	8103	2/11/2013	40	$ 3,845	$ 3,845	None	
8	8104	2/12/2013	39	$ 1,004	$ 904	$ 100	
9	8105	2/18/2013	33	$ 2,550	$ 2,350	$ 200	
10	8106	2/20/2013	31	$ 1,804	$ 1,804	None	
11	8107	2/23/2013	28	$ 4,005	$ 3,850	$ 155	
12	8108	2/27/2013	24	$ 3,584	$ 3,084	$ 500	
13	8109	2/28/2013	23	$ 2,115	$ 2,015	$ 100	

Amount patients owe

TABLE E-2: **Comparison operators**

operator	meaning	operator	meaning
<	Less than	<=	Less than or equal to
>	Greater than	>=	Greater than or equal to
=	Equal to	<>	Not equal to

Building a Logical Formula with the AND Function

You can also build a logical function using the AND function. The AND function evaluates all of its arguments and **returns**, or displays, TRUE if every logical test in the formula is true. The AND function returns a value of FALSE if one or more of its logical tests is false. The AND function arguments can include text, numbers, or cell references. ▓▓▓▓▓ Tony wants you to analyze the imaging company's account data to find accounts that are past due. You will use the AND function to check for accounts that have balances that are over 30 days old.

STEPS

1. **Click cell G7, click the Logical button in the Function Library group, then click AND**

   The Function Arguments dialog box opens. You want the function to evaluate the past due status as follows: The patient must have a balance and the statement must be over 30 days old.

TROUBLE

If you get a formula error, check to be sure that you typed the quotation marks around None.

2. **With the insertion point in the Logical1 text box, click cell F7, type < >, type "None", then press [Tab]**

   The symbol (<>) represents "not equal to." So far, the formula reads "If the patient responsibility is not equal to None,"—in other words, if it is a number. The next logical test checks the statement age.

3. **With the insertion point in the Logical2 text box, click cell C7, type >30, then click OK**

   The function is complete, and the result, FALSE, appears in cell G7, as shown in Figure E-16.

4. **Drag the fill handle to copy the formula in cell G7 into the range G8:G13**

   Compare your results with Figure E-17.

5. **Add your name to the center of the footer, save the workbook, then preview the worksheet**

TABLE E-3: Examples of AND, OR, and NOT functions with cell values A1=10 and B1=20

function	formula	result
AND	=AND(A1>5,B1>25)	FALSE
OR	=OR(A1>5,B1>25)	TRUE
NOT	=NOT(A1=0)	TRUE

Using the OR and NOT logical functions

The OR logical function has the same syntax as the AND function, but rather than returning TRUE if every argument is true, the OR function will return TRUE if any of its arguments are true. It will only return FALSE if all of its arguments are false. The NOT logical function reverses the value of its argument. For example NOT(TRUE) reverses its argument of TRUE and returns FALSE. This can be used in a worksheet to ensure that a cell is not equal to a particular value. See Table E-3 for examples of the AND, OR, and NOT functions.

FIGURE E-16: Worksheet with AND function

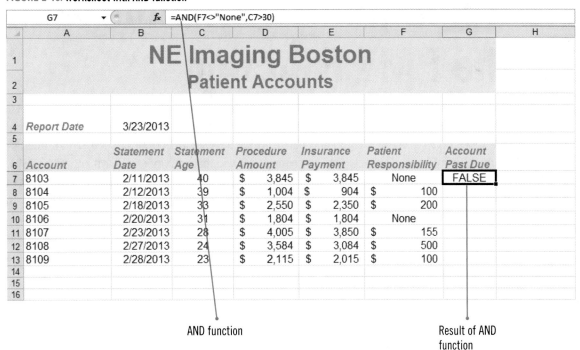

AND function

Result of AND function

FIGURE E-17: Worksheet with accounts past due evaluated

Inserting an equation into a worksheet

If your worksheet contains formulas, you might want to place an equation on the worksheet to document how you arrived at your results. First create a text box to hold the equation: Click the Insert tab, click the Text box button in the Text group, then click on the worksheet location where you want the equation to appear. To place the equation in the text box, click the Insert tab again, then click the Equation button in the Symbols group. When you see "Type equation here," you can build an equation by clicking the mathematical symbols in the Structures group of the Equation Tools Design tab. For example, if you wanted to enter a fraction of 2/7, you click the Fraction button, choose the first option, click the top box, enter 2,

press [Tab], enter 7, then click outside of the fraction. To insert the symbol x^2 into a text box, click the Script list arrow in the Structures group of the Equation Tools Design tab, click the first option, click in the lower-left box and enter "x", press [Tab], enter 2 in the upper-right box, then click to the right of the boxes to exit the symbol. You can also add built-in equations to a text box: On the Equation Tools Design tab, click the Equation list arrow in the Tools group, then select the equation. Built-in equations include the equation for the area of a circle, the binomial theorem, Pythagorean theorem, and the quadratic equation.

Calculating Payments with the PMT Function

PMT is a financial function that calculates the periodic payment amount for money borrowed. For example, if you want to borrow money to buy a car, and you know the principal amount, interest rate, and loan term, the PMT function can calculate your monthly payment. Say you want to borrow $20,000 at 6.5% interest and pay off the loan in 5 years. The Excel PMT function can tell you that your monthly payment will be $391.32. The main parts of the PMT function are PMT(rate, nper, pv). See Figure E-18 for an illustration of a PMT function that calculates the monthly payment in the car loan example. ⬛⬛⬛⬛ After reviewing the reimbursement and patient data for the NE Imaging company, the management of RMC has decided to expand its own clinic rather than acquire the new company. Tony has obtained quotes from three different lenders on borrowing $800,000 to begin the expansion. He obtained loan quotes from a commercial bank, a venture capitalist, and an investment banker. He wants you to summarize the information using the Excel PMT function.

STEPS

1. **Click the Loan sheet tab, click cell F5, click the Formulas tab, click the Financial button in the Function Library group, scroll down the list of functions, then click PMT**

2. **With the insertion point in the Rate text box, click cell D5 on the worksheet, type /12, then press [Tab]**

   You must divide the annual interest by 12 because you are calculating monthly, not annual, payments. You need to be consistent about the units you use for rate and nper. If you express nper as the number of monthly payments, then you must express the interest rate as a monthly rate.

3. **With the insertion point in the Nper text box, click cell E5; click the Pv text box, click cell B5, then click OK**

   The payment of ($6,990.87) in cell F5 appears in red, indicating that it is a negative amount. Excel displays the result of a PMT function as a negative value to reflect the negative cash flow the loan represents to the borrower. To show the monthly payment as a positive number, you can place a minus sign in front of the Pv cell reference in the function.

4. **Double-click cell F5 and edit it so it reads =PMT(D5/12,E5,-B5), then click the Enter button on the formula bar**

   A positive value of $6,990.87 now appears in cell F5, as shown in Figure E-19. You can use the same formula to generate the monthly payments for the other loans.

5. **With cell F5 selected, drag the fill handle to fill the range F6:F7**

   A monthly payment of $8,982.41 for the venture capitalist loan appears in cell F6. A monthly payment of $15,447.65 for the investment banker loan appears in cell F7. The loans with shorter terms have much higher monthly payments. But you will not know the entire financial picture until you calculate the total payments and total interest for each lender.

6. **Click cell G5, type =, click cell E5, type *, click cell F5, then press [Tab], in cell H5 type =, click cell G5, type –, click cell B5, then click ✓**

7. **Copy the formulas in cells G5:H5 into the range G6:H7, then click cell A1**

   You can experiment with different interest rates, loan amounts, or terms for any one of the lenders; the PMT function generates a new set of values automatically.

8. **Add your name to the center section of the footer, save the workbook, preview the worksheet, then submit the workbook to your instructor**

   Your worksheet appears as shown in Figure E-20.

9. **Close the workbook and exit Excel**

FIGURE E-18: Example of PMT function for car loan

$$PMT(0.065/12, 60, 20000) = \$391.32$$

Interest rate per month (rate) — Number of monthly payments — Present value of loan amount (pv) — Monthly payment calculated

FIGURE E-19: PMT function calculating monthly loan payment

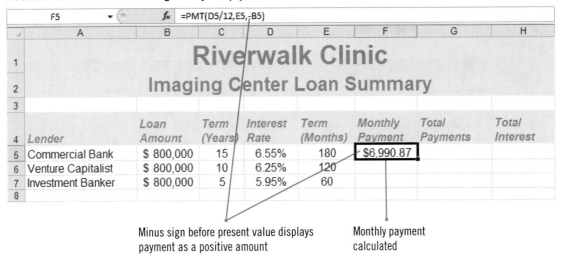

	F5			f_x	=PMT(D5/12,E5,-B5)		
	A	B	C	D	E	F	G	H

Riverwalk Clinic
Imaging Center Loan Summary

Lender	Loan Amount	Term (Years)	Interest Rate	Term (Months)	Monthly Payment	Total Payments	Total Interest
Commercial Bank	$ 800,000	15	6.55%	180	$6,990.87		
Venture Capitalist	$ 800,000	10	6.25%	120			
Investment Banker	$ 800,000	5	5.95%	60			

Minus sign before present value displays payment as a positive amount

Monthly payment calculated

FIGURE E-20: Completed worksheet

Riverwalk Clinic
Imaging Center Loan Summary

Lender	Loan Amount	Term (Years)	Interest Rate	Term (Months)	Monthly Payment	Total Payments	Total Interest
Commercial Bank	$ 800,000	15	6.55%	180	$6,990.87	$ 1,258,356.10	$ 458,356.10
Venture Capitalist	$ 800,000	10	6.25%	120	$8,982.41	$ 1,077,888.93	$ 277,888.93
Investment Banker	$ 800,000	5	5.95%	60	$15,447.65	$ 926,858.91	$ 126,858.91

Copied formula calculates total payments and interest for remaining two loan options

Calculating future value with the FV function

You can use the FV (Future Value) function to determine the amount of money a given monthly investment will amount to, at a given interest rate, after a given number of payment periods. The syntax is similar to that of the PMT function: FV(rate,nper,pmt,pv,type). The rate is the interest paid by the financial institution, the nper is the number of periods, and the pmt is the amount that you deposit. For example, suppose you want to invest $1,000 every month for the next 12 months into an account that pays 2% a year, and you want to know how much you will have at the end of 12 months (that is, its future value). You enter the function FV(.02/12,12,-1000), and Excel returns the value $12,110.61 as the future value of your investment. As with the PMT function, the units for the rate and nper must be consistent.

Practice

Concepts Review

For current SAM information, including versions and content details, visit SAM Central (http://www.cengage.com/samcentral). If you have a SAM user profile, you may have access to hands-on instruction, practice, and assessment of the skills covered in this unit. Since various versions of SAM are supported throughout the life of this text, check with your instructor for the correct instructions and URL/Web site for accessing assignments.

FIGURE E-21

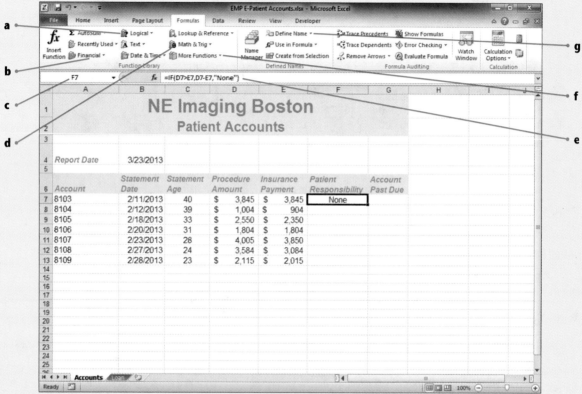

1. Which element do you click to name a cell or range?
2. Which element do you click to add a statistical function to a worksheet?
3. Which element points to a logical formula?
4. Which element points to the area where the name of a selected cell or range appears?
5. Which element do you click to insert a PMT function into a worksheet?
6. Which element do you click to add a SUMIF function to a worksheet?
7. Which element do you click to add an IF function to a worksheet?

Match each term with the statement that best describes it.

8. FV
9. PV
10. SUMIF
11. PROPER
12. test_cond

a. Function used to change the first letter of a string to uppercase
b. Function used to determine the future amount of an investment
c. Part of the PMT function that represents the loan amount
d. Part of the IF function in which the conditions are stated
e. Function used to conditionally total cells

Select the best answer from the list of choices.

13. When you enter the rate and nper arguments in a PMT function, you must:

a. Multiply both units by 12.

b. Be consistent in the units used.

c. Divide both values by 12.

d. Always use annual units.

14. To express conditions such as less than or equal to, you can use a:

a. Comparison operator.

b. Text formula.

c. PMT function.

d. Statistical function.

Skills Review

1. Format data using text functions.

a. Start Excel, open the file EMP E-3.xlsx from the drive and folder where you store your Data Files, then save it as **EMP E-Reviews**.

b. On the Managers worksheet, select the range A2:A9 and, using the Text to Columns button on the Data tab, separate the names into two text columns. (*Hint*: The delimiter is a space.)

c. In cell D2, enter the text formula to convert the first letter of the department in cell C2 to uppercase, then copy the formula in cell D2 into the range D3:D9.

d. In cell E2, enter the text formula to convert all letters of the department in cell C2 to uppercase, then copy the formula in cell E2 into the range E3:E9.

e. In cell F2, use the text formula to convert all letters of the department in cell C2 to lowercase, then copy the formula in cell F2 into the range F3:F9.

f. In cell G2, use the text formula to substitute "Medical Records" for "mr" if that text exists in cell F2. (*Hint*: In the Function Arguments dialog box, Text is F2, Old_text is "mr", and New_text is "Medical Records".) Copy the formula in cell G2 into the range G3:G9 to change the other cells containing "mr" to "Medical Records". (The clinic and ultrasound entries will not change because the formula searches for the text "mr".)

g. Save your work, then enter your name in the worksheet footer. Compare your screen to Figure E-22.

h. Display the formulas in the worksheet.

i. Redisplay the formula results.

FIGURE E-22

	A	B	C	D	E	F	G	H
1	**Name**		**Department**	**PROPER**	**UPPER**	**LOWER**	**SUBSTITUTE**	
2	Pete	Kayce	mR	Mr	MR	mr	Medical Records	
3	Samantha	Story	Clinic	Clinic	CLINIC	clinic	clinic	
4	Kim	Hanson	mR	Mr	MR	mr	Medical Records	
5	Albert	Ny	Clinic	Clinic	CLINIC	clinic	clinic	
6	Reggie	Delgado	ultrasound	Ultrasound	ULTRASOUND	ultrasound	ultrasound	
7	Harry	DePaul	ultrasound	Ultrasound	ULTRASOUND	ultrasound	ultrasound	
8	Mel	Abbott	clinic	Clinic	CLINIC	clinic	clinic	
9	Jody	Wallace	mR	Mr	MR	mr	Medical Records	
10								

2. Sum a data range based on conditions.

a. Make the Clinic sheet active.

b. In cell B20, use the COUNTIF function to count the number of employees with a rating of 5.

c. In cell B21, use the AVERAGEIF function to average the salaries of those with a rating of 5.

d. In cell B22, enter the SUMIF function that totals the salaries of employees with a rating of 5.

e. Format cells B21 and B22 with the Number format using commas and no decimals. Save your work, then compare your formula results to Figure E-23.

FIGURE E-23

	A	B
17		
18	**Department Statistics**	
19	**Rating of 5**	
20	Number	4
21	Average Salary	29,600
22	Total Salary	118,400
23		

3. Consolidate data using a formula.

a. Make the Summary sheet active.

b. In cell B4, use the AutoSum function to total cell F15 on the Clinic and Ultrasound sheets.

c. Format cell B4 with the Accounting number format.

d. Enter your name in the worksheet footer, then save your work. Compare your screen to Figure E-24.

e. Display the formula in the worksheet, then redisplay the formula results in the worksheet.

FIGURE E-24

	A	B
1	**Payroll Summary**	
2		
3		Salary
4	TOTAL	$ 565,787.00
5		

4. Check formulas for errors.

a. Make the Clinic sheet active.

b. In cell I6, use the IFERROR function to display "ERROR" in the event that the formula F6/F15 results in a formula error. (*Note*: This formula will generate an intentional error after the next step, which you will correct in a moment.)

Skills Review (continued)

   c. Copy the formula in cell I6 into the range I7:I14.

   d. Correct the formula in cell I6 by making the denominator, F15, an absolute address.

   e. Copy the new formula in cell I6 into the range I7:I14.

   f. Format the range I6:I14 as a percentage with two decimal places.

   g. Save your work.

5. Construct formulas using named ranges.

   a. On the Clinic sheet, name the range C6:C14 **review_date**, and limit the scope of the name to the Clinic worksheet.

   b. In cell E6, enter the formula **=review_date+183**, using the Use in Formula button to enter the cell name.

   c. Copy the formula in cell E6 into the range E7:E14.

   d. Use the Name Manager to add a comment of **Date of last review** to the review_date name. (*Hint*: In the Name Manager dialog box, click the review_date name, then click Edit to enter the comment.) Save your work.

6. Build a logical formula with the IF function.

   a. In cell G6, use the Function Arguments dialog box to enter the formula **=IF(D6=5,F6*0.05,0)**.

   b. Copy the formula in cell G6 into the range G7:G14.

   c. In cell G15, use AutoSum to total the range G6:G14.

   d. Format the range G6:G15 with the Currency number format, using the $ symbol and no decimal places.

   e. Save your work.

7. Build a logical formula with the AND function.

   a. In cell H6, use the Function Arguments dialog box to enter the formula **=AND(G6>0,B6>5)**.

   b. Copy the formula in cell H6 into the range H7:H14.

   c. Enter your name in the worksheet footer, save your work, then compare your worksheet to Figure E-25.

   d. Make the Ultrasound sheet active.

   e. In cell H6, indicate if the employee needs more development hours to reach the minimum of 5. Use the Function Arguments dialog box for the NOT function to enter **B6>5** in the Logical text box. Copy the formula in cell H6 into the range H7:H14.

   f. In cell I6, indicate if the employee needs to enroll in a quality class, as indicated by a rating less than 5 or having fewer than 5 development hours. Use the Function Arguments dialog box for the OR function to enter **D6<5** in the Logical1 text box and **B6<5** in the Logical2 text box. Copy the formula in cell I6 into the range I7:I14.

   g. Enter your name in the worksheet footer, save your work, then compare your screen to Figure E-26.

8. Calculate payments with the PMT function.

   a. Make the Loan sheet active.

   b. In cell B9, determine the monthly payment using the loan information shown: Use the Function Arguments dialog box to enter the formula **=PMT(B5/12,B6,-B4)**.

   c. In cell B10, enter a formula that multiplies the number of payments by the monthly payment.

   d. In cell B11, enter the formula that subtracts the loan amount from the total payment amount, then compare your screen to Figure E-27.

FIGURE E-25

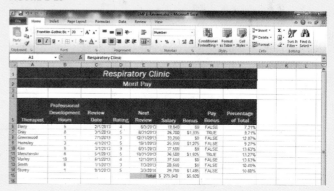

FIGURE E-26

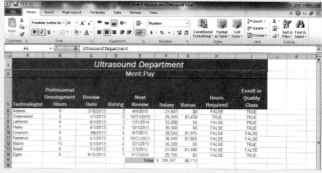

FIGURE E-27

Facilities

Analyzing Data Using Formulas

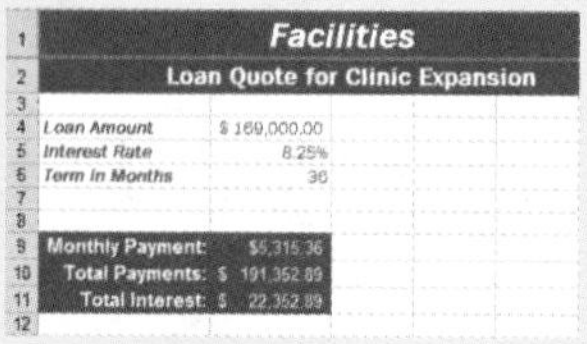

Skills Review (continued)

    e. Enter your name in the worksheet footer, save the workbook, then submit your workbook to your instructor.

    f. Close the workbook, then exit Excel.

Independent Challenge 1

As the accounting manager of a travel health clinic, you are reviewing the patient account information and prioritizing the over-due invoices for your collections service. You will analyze the invoices and use logical functions to emphasize priority accounts.

    a. Start Excel, open the file EMP E-4.xlsx from the drive and folder where you store your Data Files, then save it as **EMP E-Accounts**.

    b. Name the range B7:B13 **invoice_date**, and give the name a scope of the accounts worksheet.

    c. Name the cell B4 **current_date**, and give the name a scope of the accounts worksheet.

    d. Enter a formula using the named range invoice_date in cell E7 that calculates the invoice due date by adding 30 to the invoice date.

    e. Copy the formula in cell E7 to the range E8:E13.

    f. In cell F7, enter a formula using the named range invoice_date and the named cell current_date that calculates the invoice age by subtracting the invoice date from the current date.

    g. Copy the formula in cell F7 to the range F8:F13.

    h. In cell G7, enter an IF function that calculates the number of days an invoice is overdue, assuming that an invoice must be paid in 30 days. (*Hint*: The Logical_test should check to see if the age of the invoice is greater than 30, the Value_if_true should calculate the current date minus the invoice due date, and the Value_if_false should be 0.) Copy the IF function into the range G8:G13.

    i. In cell H7, enter an AND function to prioritize the overdue invoices that are more than $100 for collection services. (*Hint*: The Logical1 condition should check to see if the number of days overdue is more than 0, and the Logical2 condition should check if the amount is more than 100.) Copy the AND function into the range H8:H13.

    j. Enter your name in the worksheet footer, save the workbook, preview the worksheet, then submit the workbook to your instructor.

Advanced Challenge Exercise

    ■ Use the "Refers to:" text box in the Name Manager dialog box to verify that the names in the worksheet refer to the correct ranges.

    ■ Use the Filter button in the Name Manager dialog box to verify that your names are scoped to the worksheet and not the workbook.

    ■ Use the Filter button in the Name Manager dialog box to verify that your names are defined, free of errors, and not part of a table. If necessary, clear the Filter.

    k. Close the workbook, then exit Excel.

Independent Challenge 2

The management of the biomedical supply company at which you work is interested in expanding their business. In an effort to decide on which areas to focus the expansion resources, they ask you to analyze the first-quarter sales records. You are inter-ested in what percent of annual sales each category represents. You will use a formula on a summary worksheet to summarize the sales for January, February, and March, and to calculate the overall first-quarter percentage of the sales categories.

    a. Start Excel, open the file EMP E-5.xlsx from the drive and folder where you store your Data Files, then save it as **EMP E-Products**.

    b. In cell B10 of the Jan, Feb, and Mar sheets, enter the formulas to calculate the sales totals for the month.

Independent Challenge 2 (continued)

c. For each month, in cell C5, create a formula calculating the percent of sales for the Diagnostic sales category. Use a function to display **INCORRECT** if there is a mistake in the formula. Verify that the percent appears with two decimal places. Copy this formula as necessary to complete the % of sales for all sales categories on all sheets. If any cells display INCORRECT, fix the formulas in those cells.

d. In column B of the Summary sheet, use formulas to total the sales categories for the Jan, Feb, and Mar worksheets.

e. Enter the formula to calculate the first quarter sales total in cell B10 using the sales totals on the Jan, Feb, and Mar worksheets. Calculate the percent of each sales category on the Summary sheet. Use a function to display **MISCALCULATION** if there is a mistake in the formula. Copy this formula as necessary. If any cells display MISCALCULATION, fix the formulas in those cells.

f. Enter your name in the Summary worksheet footer.

g. On the Products sheet, separate the product list in cell A1 into separate columns of text data. (*Hint*: The products are delimited with commas.) Widen the columns as necessary. Use the second row to display the products with the first letter of each word in uppercase, as shown in Figure E-28.

h. Enter your name in the Products worksheet footer, save the workbook, preview the worksheet, then submit the workbook to your instructor.

FIGURE E-28

	A	B	C	D	E	F
1	diagnostic	treatment	clinical	accessories	laboratory	
2	Diagnostic	Treatment	Clinical	Accessories	Laboratory	
3						

Advanced Challenge Exercise

- Add a new sheet to the workbook and name it **Equations**.
- Use the built-in equations to enter the Pythagorean theorem in a text box on the worksheet. (*Hint*: Click the Equation list arrow in the Tools group of the Equation Tools Design tab and click Pythagorean Theorem. Also, see the Clues to Use "Inserting an equation into a worksheet" for more information about adding equations.)
- In a new text box, build the Pythagorean theorem below the built-in equation using the mathematical symbols. (*Hint*: To insert a^2 into a text box, click the Script list arrow in the Structures group of the Equation Tools Design tab, click the first option, click in the lower-left box and enter **a**, press [Tab], enter **2** in the upper-right box, then click to the right of the boxes to exit the symbol.)
- Enter your name in the Equations worksheet footer, save the workbook, preview the worksheet, then submit the workbook to your instructor.

i. Close the workbook, then exit Excel.

Independent Challenge 3

The physical therapy clinic at which you work needs to update its equipment. It is your responsibility to research options for a $30,000 equipment loan. You check three loan sources: the Small Business Administration (SBA), your local bank, and a consortium of investors. The SBA will lend you the money at 6.5% interest, but you have to pay it off in 3 years. The local bank offers you the loan at 7.75% interest over 4 years. The consortium offers you an 8% loan, but they require you to pay it back in 2 years. To analyze all three loan options, you decide to build a loan summary worksheet. Using the loan terms provided, build a worksheet summarizing your options.

a. Start Excel, open a new workbook, then save it as **EMP E-Loan**.

b. Using Figure E-29 as a guide, enter labels and worksheet data for the three loan sources in columns A through D. (*Hint*: The worksheet in the figure uses the

FIGURE E-29

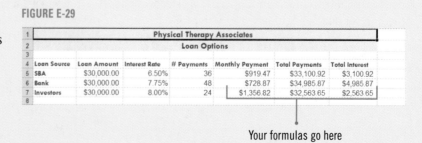

Your formulas go here

Independent Challenge 3 (continued)

Median theme with Ice Blue, Accent 1, Lighter 80%, as the fill color in the first two rows. Rows 1, 2 and 4 are bolded. The labels in column A are also bolded. The worksheet text color is Ice Blue, Accent 1, Darker 50%. The font size is 14 for the first two rows and 12 for the other rows.)

c. Enter the monthly payment formula for your first loan source (making sure to show the payment as a positive amount), copy the formula as appropriate, then name the range containing the monthly payment formulas **Monthly_Payment** with a scope of the workbook.

d. Name the cell range containing the number of payments **Number_Payments** with the scope of the workbook.

e. Enter the formula for total payments for your first loan source using the named ranges Monthly_Payment and Number_Payments, then copy the formula as necessary.

f. Name the cell range containing the formulas for Total payments **Total_Payments**. Name the cell range containing the loan amounts **Loan_Amount**. Each name should have the workbook as its scope.

g. Enter the formula for total interest for your first loan source using the named ranges Total_Payments and Loan_Amount, then copy the formula as necessary.

h. Enter your name in the worksheet footer.

i. Save the workbook, preview the worksheet and change it to landscape orientation, then submit the workbook to your instructor.

Advanced Challenge Exercise

- Turn on the print gridlines option for the sheet, then turn on printing of row and column headings.
- Display the worksheet formulas, save the workbook and submit it to your instructor.

j. Close the workbook then exit Excel.

Real Life Independent Challenge

You manage a diabetes health program at your clinic. A fitness program is part of this initiative and the patients are required to document their daily aerobic activities and summarize their weekly exercise. To better communicate with and help your patients, you decide to participate in the fitness program with them. As part of the exercise log, you record your aerobic activity along with the number of minutes spent working out. If you do more than one activity in a day, for example, if you bike and walk, record each as a separate event. Along with each activity, you record the location where you exercise. For example, you may walk in the gym or outdoors. You will use the log to analyze the amount of time that you spend on each type of exercise.

a. Start Excel, open the file EMP E-6.xlsx from the drive and folder where you store your Data Files, then save it as **EMP E-Exercise Log**.

b. Use the structure of the worksheet to record your aerobic exercise activities. Change the data in columns A, B, C, D, and F to reflect your activities, locations, and times. If you do not have any data to enter, use the provided worksheet data.

c. Use a SUMIF function in the column G cells to calculate the total minutes spent on each activity.

d. Enter an AVERAGEIF function in the column H cells to average the number of minutes spent on each activity.

e. Enter a COUNTIF function in the column I cells to calculate the number of times each activity was performed. (*Hint*: The Range of cells to count is $B$2:$B$12 and the criteria is in cell F3.)

f. Format the Average Minutes column as number with two decimal places.

Advanced Challenge Exercise

- Enter one of your activities with a specific location, such as Walk Outdoors, in a column F cell, then enter the SUMIFS function in the adjacent column G cell that calculates the total number of minutes spent on that activity in the specific location.
- Enter the AVERAGEIFS function in the corresponding column H cell that calculates the average number of minutes spent on the activity in the specified location.
- Enter the COUNTIFS function in the corresponding column I cell that calculates the number of days spent on the activity in the specific location.

g. Enter your name in the worksheet footer, save the workbook, preview the worksheet, then submit it to your instructor.

h. Close the workbook, then exit Excel.

Visual Workshop

Open the file EMP E-7.xlsx from the drive and folder where you store your Data Files, then save it as **EMP E-Discount**. Create the worksheet shown in Figure E-30 using the data in columns B, C, and D along with the following criteria:

- A person is eligible for a health insurance discount if:

    - The person is under 40.

    AND

    - The person does not smoke.

- If a person is eligible for a discount, the discount amount is calculated as 5% of the monthly premium. Otherwise the discount amount is 0.

Enter your name in the worksheet footer, save the workbook, preview the worksheet, then submit the worksheet to your instructor.

(*Hint*: Use an AND formula to determine if a person is eligible for a discount, and use an IF formula to check eligibility and to calculate the discount amount.)

FIGURE E-30

	A	B	C	D	E	F
1	Health Insurance Discount Program Summary					
2						
3	Last Name	Monthly Premium	Age	Smoke	Eligible	Discount
4	Allen	$160	35	Yes	FALSE	$0.00
5	Gray	$182	64	No	FALSE	$0.00
6	Greenwood	$142	30	Yes	FALSE	$0.00
7	Hanson	$135	27	No	TRUE	$6.75
8	Kerns	$175	59	No	FALSE	$0.00
9	Maloney	$118	24	No	TRUE	$5.90
10	Martin	$197	67	Yes	FALSE	$0.00
11	Smith	$119	25	Yes	FALSE	$0.00
12	Storey	$127	30	No	TRUE	$6.35
13						

Analyzing Data Using Formulas

Managing Workbook Data

Files You Will Need:

EMP F-1.xlsx
EMP F-2.xlsx
EMP F-3.gif
EMP F-4.xlsx
EMP F-5.xlsx
EMP F-6.xlsx
EMP F-7.gif
EMP F-Classifications
 .xlsx
EMP F-Contact
 Information.xlsx
EMP F-Dermatology
 Revenue.xlsx
EMP F-Equipment
 .xlsx
EMP F-Logo.gif
EMP F-Op
 Elective.xlsx

As you analyze data using Excel, you will find that your worksheets and workbooks become more complex. In this unit, you will learn several Excel features to help you manage workbook data. In addition, you will want to share workbooks with coworkers, but you need to ensure that they can view your data while preventing unwarranted changes. You will learn how to save workbooks in different formats and how to prepare workbooks for distribution. Tony Sanchez, the office manager at RMC, asks for your help in analyzing yearly revenue data for the clinic's procedures. When the analysis is complete, he will distribute the workbook for the vice presidents to review.

OBJECTIVES

View and arrange worksheets

Protect worksheets and workbooks

Save custom views of a worksheet

Add a worksheet background

Prepare a workbook for distribution

Insert hyperlinks

Save a workbook for distribution

Group worksheets

Viewing and Arranging Worksheets

As you work with workbooks made up of multiple worksheets, you might need to compare data in the various sheets. To do this, you can view each worksheet in its own workbook window, called an **instance**, and display the windows in an arrangement that makes it easy to compare data. When you work with worksheets in separate windows, you are working with different views of the same workbook; the data itself remains in one file. Tony asks you to compare the monthly revenue totals for elective and acute procedures. Because the revenue totals are on different worksheets, you want to arrange the worksheets side by side in separate windows.

STEPS

1. **Start Excel, open the file EMP F-1.xlsx from the drive and folder where you store your Data Files, then save it as EMP F-Revenue**

2. **With the Elective sheet active, click the View tab, then click the New Window button in the Window group**

   There are now two instances of the EMP F-Revenue workbook open. You can see them when you place the mouse pointer over the Excel icon on the task bar: EMP F-Revenue.xlsx:1 and EMP F-Revenue.xlsx:2. The EMP F-Revenue.xlsx:2 window is active—you can see its name on the title bar.

3. **Click the Acute sheet tab, click the Switch Windows button in the Window group, then click EMP F-Revenue.xlsx:1**

   The EMP F-Revenue.xlsx:1 instance is active. The Elective sheet is active in the EMP F-Revenue.xlsx:1 workbook, and the Acute sheet is active in the EMP F-Revenue.xlsx:2 workbook.

4. **Click the Arrange All button in the Window group**

   The Arrange Windows dialog box, shown in Figure F-1, lets you choose how to display the instances. You want to view the workbooks next to each other.

5. **Click the Vertical option button to select it, then click OK**

   The windows are arranged next to each other, as shown in Figure F-2. You can activate a workbook by clicking one of its cells. You can also view only one of the workbooks by hiding the one you do not wish to see.

6. **Scroll horizontally to view the data in the EMP F-Revenue.xlsx:1 workbook, click anywhere in the EMP F-Revenue.xlsx:2 workbook, scroll horizontally to view the data in the EMP F-Revenue.xlsx:2 workbook, then click the Hide button in the Window group**

   When you hide the second instance, only the EMP F-Revenue.xlsx:1 workbook is visible.

7. **Click the Unhide button in the Window group; click EMP F-Revenue.xlsx:2, if necessary, in the Unhide dialog box; then click OK**

   The EMP F-Revenue.xlsx:2 book reappears.

8. **Close the EMP F-Revenue.xlsx:2 instance, then maximize the Elective worksheet in the EMP F-Revenue.xlsx workbook**

   Closing the EMP F-Revenue.xlsx:2 instance leaves only the first instance open. Its name in the title bar returns to EMP F-Revenue.xlsx.

QUICK TIP

You can use the View Side by Side button in the Window group to arrange the windows in their previous configuration. The Synchronous Scrolling button below the View Side by Side button is active by default, allowing you to scroll through the arranged worksheets simultaneously.

QUICK TIP

You can also hide a worksheet by right-clicking its sheet tab and clicking Hide on the shortcut menu. To display the hidden sheet, right-click any sheet tab, click Unhide, in the Unhide dialog box, select the sheet, then click OK.

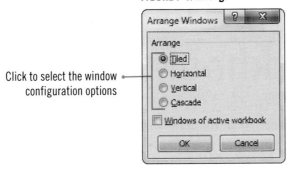

FIGURE F-2: Windows displayed vertically

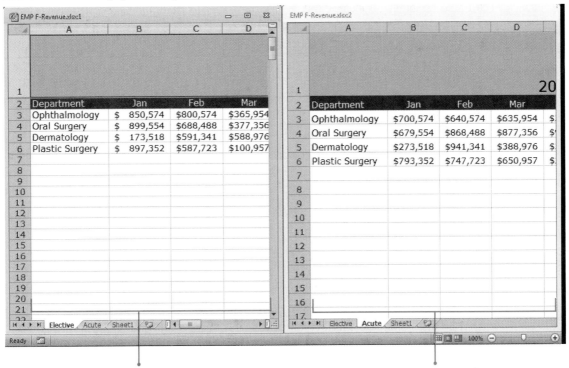

EMP F-Revenue.xlsx:1   EMP F-Revenue.xlsx:2

Splitting the worksheet into multiple panes

Excel lets you split the worksheet area into vertical and/or horizontal panes, so that you can click inside any one pane and scroll to locate information in that pane while the other panes remain in place, as shown in Figure F-3. To split a worksheet area into multiple panes, drag a split box (the small box at the top of the vertical scroll bar or

at the right end of the horizontal scroll bar) in the direction you want the split to appear. To remove the split, move the pointer over the split until the pointer changes to a double-headed arrow, then double-click.

FIGURE F-3: Worksheet split into two horizontal and two vertical panes

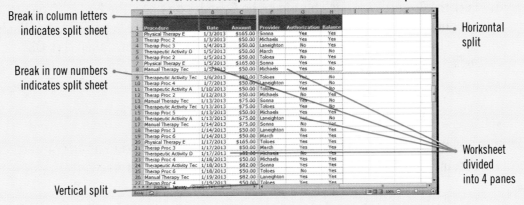

Break in column letters
indicates split sheet

Break in row numbers
indicates split sheet

Horizontal
split

Worksheet
divided
into 4 panes

Vertical split

Protecting Worksheets and Workbooks

To protect sensitive information, Excel lets you **lock** one or more cells so that other people can view the values and formulas in those cells, but not change it. Excel locks all cells by default, but this locking does not take effect until you activate the protection feature. A common worksheet protection strategy is to unlock cells in which data will be changed, sometimes called the **data entry area**, and to lock cells in which the data should not be changed. Then, when you protect the worksheet, the unlocked areas can still be changed. ⬛⬛⬛ Because the elective revenue figures for January through March have been finalized, Tony asks you to protect that area of the worksheet so the figures can not be altered.

STEPS

1. **On the Elective sheet, select the range E3:M6, click the** Home tab, **click the** Format button **in the Cells group, click** Format Cells, **then in the Format Cells dialog box click the** Protection tab

   The Locked check box in the Protection tab is already checked, as shown in Figure F-4. All the cells in a new workbook start out locked. The protection feature is inactive by default. Because the April through December revenue figures have not yet been confirmed as final and may need to be changed, you do not want those cells to be locked when the protection feature is activated. You decide to unlock the cell range and protect the worksheet.

2. **Click the** Locked check box **to deselect it, click** OK, **click the** Review tab, **then click the** Protect Sheet button **in the Changes group**

   The Protect Sheet dialog box opens, as shown in Figure F-5. In the "Allow users of this worksheet to" list, you can select the actions that you want your worksheet users to be able to perform. The default options protect the worksheet while allowing users to select locked or unlocked cells only. You choose not to use a password.

3. **Verify that** Protect worksheet and contents of locked cells **is checked, that the password text box is blank, and that** Select locked cells **and** Select unlocked cells **are checked, then click** OK

   You are ready to test the new worksheet protection.

4. **In cell B3, type 1 to confirm that locked cells cannot be changed, click** OK, **click cell F3, type 1, notice that Excel lets you begin the entry, press [Esc] to cancel the entry, then save your work**

   When you try to change a locked cell, a dialog box, shown in Figure F-6, reminds you of the protected cell's read-only status. **Read-only format** means that users can view but not change the data. Because you unlocked the cells in columns E through M before you protected the worksheet, you can change these cells. You decide to protect the workbook from these changes to the workbook's structure, but decide not to require a password.

5. **Click the** Protect Workbook button **in the Changes group, in the Protect Structure and Windows dialog box, make sure the** Structure check box **is selected, click the** Windows check box **to select it, verify that the password text box is blank, then click** OK

   You are ready to test the new workbook protection.

6. **Right-click the** Elective sheet tab

   The Insert, Delete, Rename, Move or Copy, Tab Color, Hide, and Unhide menu options are not available because the sheet is protected. You decide to remove the workbook and worksheet protections.

7. **Click the** Protect Workbook button **in the Changes group to turn off the protection, then click the** Unprotect Sheet button **to remove the worksheet protection**

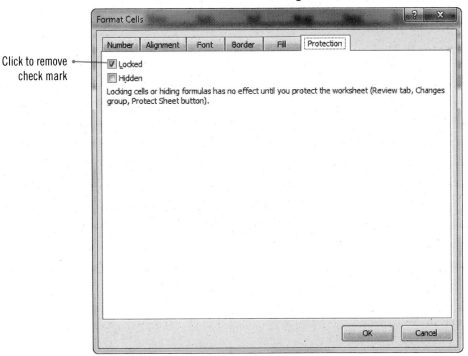

Click to remove
check mark

FIGURE F-5: **Protect Sheet dialog box**

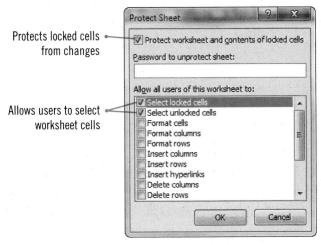

Protects locked cells
from changes

Allows users to select
worksheet cells

FIGURE F-6: **Reminder of protected cell's read-only status**

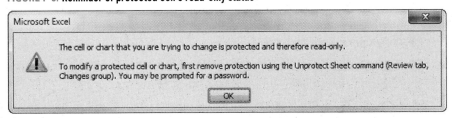

Freezing rows and columns

As the rows and columns of a worksheet fill up with data, you might need to scroll through the worksheet to add, delete, change, and view information. You can temporarily freeze columns and rows so you can keep column or row labels in view as you scroll. **Panes** are the columns and rows that **freeze**, or remain in place, while you scroll through your worksheet. To freeze panes, click the first cell in the area you want to scroll, click the View tab, click the Freeze Panes button in the Window group, then click Freeze Panes. Excel freezes the columns to the left and the rows above the selected cell. You can also select Freeze Top Row or Freeze First Column to freeze the top row or left worksheet column.

Saving Custom Views of a Worksheet

A **view** is a set of display and/or print settings that you can name and save, then access at a later time. By using the Excel Custom Views feature, you can create several different views of a worksheet without having to create separate sheets. For example, if you often hide columns in a worksheet, you can create two views, one that displays all of the columns and another with the columns hidden. You set the worksheet display first, then name the view. Because Tony wants to generate a revenue report from the final revenue data for January through March, he asks you to save the first-quarter revenue data as a custom view. You begin by creating a view showing all of the worksheet data.

STEPS

1. **With the Elective sheet active, click the View tab, then click the Custom Views button in the Workbook Views group**

    The Custom Views dialog box opens. Any previously defined views for the active worksheet appear in the Views box. No views are defined for the Elective worksheet. You decide to add a named view for the current view, which shows all the worksheet columns. That way, you can easily return to it from any other views you create.

2. **Click Add**

    The Add View dialog box opens, as shown in Figure F-7. Here, you enter a name for the view and decide whether to include print settings and hidden rows, columns, and filter settings. You want to include the selected options.

    > **QUICK TIP**
    > To delete views from the active worksheet, select the view in the Custom Views dialog box, then click Delete.

3. **In the Name box, type Year Revenue, then click OK**

    You have created a view called Year Revenue that shows all the worksheet columns. You want to set up another view that will hide the April through December columns.

4. **Drag across the column headings to select columns E through M, right-click the selected area, then click Hide on the shortcut menu**

    You are ready to create a custom view of the January through March revenue data.

5. **Click cell A1, click the Custom Views button in the Workbook Views group, click Add, in the Name box type First Quarter, then click OK**

    You are ready to test the two custom views.

    > **TROUBLE**
    > If you receive the message "Some view settings could not be applied", turn off worksheet protection by clicking the Unprotect Sheet button in the Changes group of the Review tab.

6. **Click the Custom Views button in the Workbook Views group, click Year Revenue in the Views list, then click Show**

    The Year Revenue custom view displays all of the months' revenue data. Now you are ready to test the First Quarter custom view.

7. **Click the Custom Views button in the Workbook Views group, then with First Quarter in the Custom Views dialog box selected, click Show**

    Only the January through March revenue figures appear on the screen, as shown in Figure F-8.

8. **Return to the Year Revenue view, then save your work**

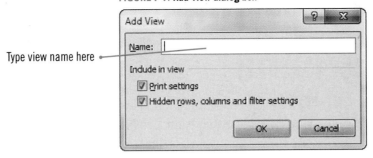

Type view name here →

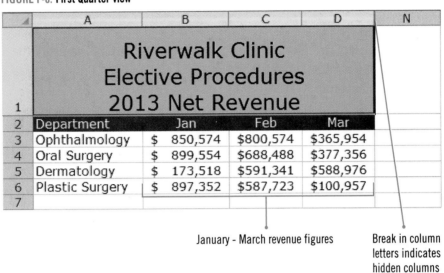

January - March revenue figures

Break in column letters indicates hidden columns

Excel 2010

Using Page Break Preview

The vertical and horizontal dashed lines in the Normal view of worksheets represent page breaks. Excel automatically inserts a page break when your worksheet data doesn't fit on one page. These page breaks are **dynamic**, which means they adjust automatically when you insert or delete rows and columns and when you change column widths or row heights. Everything to the left of the first vertical dashed line and above the first horizontal dashed line is printed on the first page. You can manually add or remove page breaks by clicking the Page Layout tab, clicking the Breaks button in the Page Setup group, then clicking the appropriate command. You can also view and change page breaks manually by clicking the View tab, then clicking the Page Break Preview button in the Workbook Views group, or by clicking the Page Break Preview button 🔲 on the status bar, then clicking OK. You can drag the blue page break lines to the desired location, as shown in Figure F-9. Some cells may temporarily display ##### while you are in Page Break Preview. If you drag a page break to the right to include more data on a page, Excel shrinks the type to fit the data on that page. To exit Page Break Preview, click the Normal button in the Workbook Views group.

FIGURE F-9: **Page Break Preview window**

Drag blue page break lines to change page breaks →

Adding a Worksheet Background

In addition to using a theme's font colors and fills, you can make your Excel data more attractive on the screen by adding a picture to the worksheet background. Companies often use their logo as a worksheet background. A worksheet background will be displayed on the screen but will not print with the worksheet. If you want to add a worksheet background that appears on printouts, you can add a **watermark**, a translucent background design that prints behind your data. To add a watermark, you add the image to the worksheet header or footer. Tony asks you to add the RMC logo to the printed background of the Elective worksheet. But first he wants to see it as a nonprinting background.

STEPS

1. **With the Elective sheet active, click the Page Layout tab, then click the Background button in the Page Setup group**
   The Sheet Background dialog box opens.

2. **Navigate to the drive and folder where you store your Data Files, click EMP F-Logo.gif, then click Insert**
   The RMC logo appears behind the worksheet data. It appears multiple times because the graphic is **tiled**, or repeated, to fill the background.

3. **Click the File tab, click Print, view the preview of the Elective worksheet, then click the Page Layout tab**
   Because the logo is only for display purposes, it will not print with the worksheet, so is not visible in the Print preview. You want the logo to print with the worksheet, so you decide to remove the background and add the logo to the worksheet header.

4. **Click the Delete Background button in the Page Setup group, click the Insert tab, then click the Header & Footer button in the Text group**
   The Header & Footer Tools Design tab appears, as shown in Figure F-10. The Header & Footer group buttons add preformatted headers and footers to a worksheet. The Header & Footer Elements buttons let you add page numbers, the date, the time, the file location, names, and pictures to the header or footer. The Navigation group buttons move the insertion point from the header to the footer and back. You want to add a picture to the header.

5. **With the insertion point in the center section of the header, click the Picture button in the Header & Footer Elements group, navigate to the drive and folder where you store your Data Files, click EMP F-Logo.gif, then click Insert**
   A code representing a picture, "&[Picture]", appears in the center of the header.

6. **Click cell A1, then click the Normal button ⊞ on the Status Bar**
   You want to scale the worksheet data to print on one page.

QUICK TIP
You can also scale the worksheet to fit on one page by clicking the File tab, clicking Print, clicking the No Scaling list arrow, then clicking Fit Sheet on One Page.

7. **Click the Page Layout tab, click the Width list arrow in the Scale to Fit group, click 1 page, click the Height list arrow in the Scale to Fit group, click 1 page, then preview the worksheet**
   Your worksheet should look like Figure F-11.

8. **Click the Home tab, then save the workbook**

Click these
buttons to
customize
the header
and footer

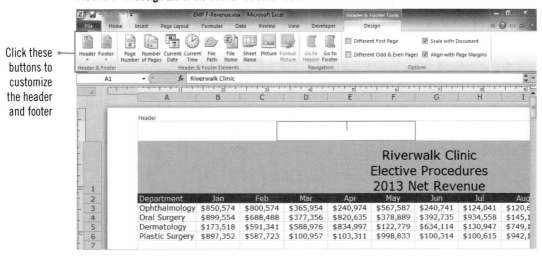

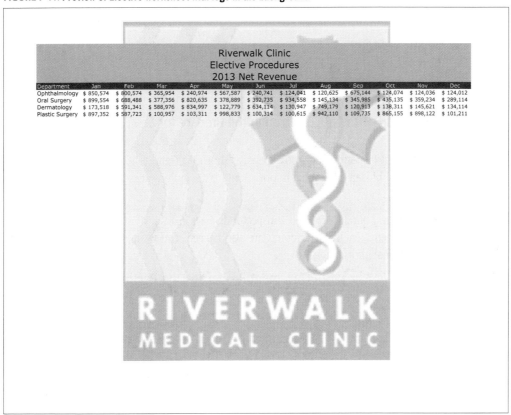

Clipping Screens in Excel

You can paste an image of an open file into an Excel workbook or another Office document. This pastes the screenshot into your document as an image that you can move, copy, or edit. To insert a screenshot, click the Insert tab, click the Screenshot button in the Illustrations group, then click on one of the available windows in the gallery. This pastes a screen shot of the window you clicked into the current Excel document. You can also click the Screen Clipping button in the gallery to select and paste an area from an open window.

After you paste an image on your worksheet, you can also cut or copy and paste in another program or in an e-mail. In addition to pasting screenshots from other windows into Excel, you can use the Screenshot feature to paste Excel screens into other programs such as Word, PowerPoint, and Outlook. This is helpful if you are having a problem with an Excel worksheet and want to e-mail your screen image to a Help Desk.

Excel 2010

Preparing a Workbook for Distribution

If you are collaborating with others and want to share a workbook with them, you might want to remove sensitive information before distributing the file. Sensitive information can include headers, footers, or hidden elements. You can use Backstage view in Excel to open the Document Inspector, which finds hidden data and personal information in your workbooks and helps you remove it. On the other hand, you might want to add helpful information, called **properties**, to a file to help others identify, understand, and locate it. Properties might include keywords, the author's name, a title, the status, and comments. **Keywords** are terms users can search for that will help them locate your workbook. Properties are a form of **metadata**, information that describes data and is used in Microsoft Windows document searches. You enter properties in the Document Properties Panel. In addition, to ensure that others do not make unauthorized changes to your workbook, you can mark a file as final. This makes it a read-only file, which others can open but not change. ▄▄▄▄ Tony wants you to protect the workbook and prepare it for distribution.

STEPS

1. **Click the File tab**

   Backstage view opens, with the Info tab in front. It shows you a preview of your printed worksheet and information about your file. This information includes who has permission to open, copy, or change your workbook. It also includes tools you can use to check for security issues.

2. **Click the Check for Issues button in the Prepare for Sharing area, then click Inspect Document**

   The Document Inspector dialog box opens, as shown in Figure F-12. It lists items from which you can have Excel evaluate hidden or personal information. All the options are selected by default.

3. **Click Inspect**

   After inspecting your document, the inspector displays its results. Areas with personal information have a "!" in front of them. Headers and footers are also flagged. You want to keep the file's header and footer and remove personal information.

QUICK TIP

You can view a file's summary information by clicking the File Tab and reviewing the information on the right side of the information area.

4. **Click Remove All next to Document Properties and Personal Information, then click Close**

   You decide to add keywords to help the vice presidents find the worksheet. The search words "Elective" or "Acute" would be good keywords for this workbook.

5. **Click the Properties list arrow on the right side of Backstage view, then click Show Document Panel**

   The Document Properties Panel appears at the top of the worksheet, as shown in Figure F-13. You decide to add a title, status, keywords, and comments.

QUICK TIP

If you have access to an Information Rights Management server, you can use the Information Rights Management (IRM) feature to specify access permissions to your files. You can also access this service through Windows Live ID.

6. **In the Title text box type Revenue, in the Keywords text box type Elective Acute Revenue, in the Status text box type DRAFT, then in the Comments text box type The first-quarter figures are final., then click the Close button on the Document Properties Panel**

   You are ready to mark the workbook as final.

7. **Click the File tab, click the Protect Workbook button in the Permissions area, click Mark as Final, click OK, then click OK again**

   "[Read-Only]" appears in the title bar indicating the workbook is saved as a read-only file.

8. **Click the Home tab, click cell B3, type 1 to confirm that the cell cannot be changed, then click the Edit Anyway button above the formula bar**

   Marking a workbook as final is not a strong form of workbook protection because a workbook recipient can remove this Final status. Removing the read-only status makes it editable again.

FIGURE F-12: **Document Inspector dialog box**

Items you can inspect for personal information →

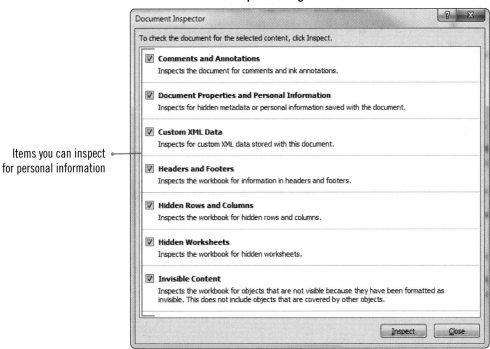

FIGURE F-13: **Document Properties panel**

Add file information in text boxes →

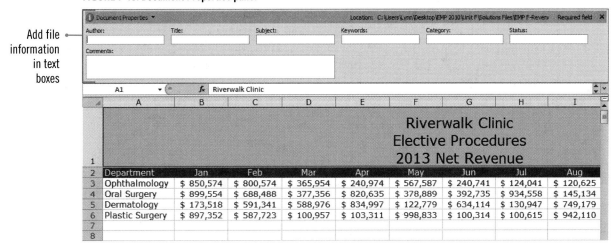

Sharing a workbook

You can make an Excel file a **shared workbook** so that several users can open and modify it at the same time. Click the Review tab, click the Share Workbook button in the Changes group, then on the Editing tab of the Share Workbook dialog box click "Allow changes by more than one user at the same time. This also allows workbook merging.", then click OK. If you get an error that the workbook cannot be shared because privacy is enabled, click the File tab, click Options in the left section, click the Trust Center category on the left side of the dialog box, click Trust Center Settings, click Privacy Options in the list on the left, click the "Remove personal information from file properties on save" check box to deselect it, then click OK twice. When you share workbooks, it is often helpful to **track** modifications, or identify who made which changes. You can track all changes to a workbook by clicking the Track Changes button in the Changes group, and then clicking Highlight Changes. To view all changes that have been tracked in a workbook, click the Review tab, click the Track Changes button in the Changes group, click Highlight Changes, select the When check box in the Highlight Changes dialog box, click the When text box list arrow, then select All in the list. To resolve the tracked changes in a workbook, click the Track Changes button, then click Accept/Reject Changes. The changes are displayed one by one. You can accept the change or, if you disagree with any of the changes, you can reject them.

Inserting Hyperlinks

As you manage the content and appearance of your workbooks, you might want the workbook user to view information that exists in another location. It might be nonessential information or data that is too detailed to place in the workbook itself. In these cases, you can create a hyperlink. A **hyperlink** is an object (a filename, word, phrase, or graphic) in a worksheet that, when you click it, displays, or "jumps to," another location, called the **target**. The target can also be a worksheet, another document, or a site on the World Wide Web. For example, in a worksheet that lists customer invoices, at each customer's name, you might create a hyperlink to an Excel file containing payment terms for each customer. 🔲🔳 Tony wants vice presidents who view the Revenue workbook to be able to view a breakdown of the revenue totals for each elective ophthalmology procedure. He asks you to create a hyperlink at the Ophthalmology heading so that users can click the hyperlink to view the revenue for each elective procedure in the ophthalmology department.

STEPS

1. **Click cell A3 on the Elective worksheet**

2. **Click the Insert tab, then click the Hyperlink button in the Links group**

   The Insert Hyperlink dialog box opens, as shown in Figure F-14. The icons under "Link to" on the left side of the dialog box let you select the type of location to where you want the link jump: an existing file or Web page, a place in the same document, a new document, or an e-mail address. Because you want the link to display an already-existing document, the selected first icon, Existing File or Web Page, is correct, so you won't have to change it.

3. **Click the Look in list arrow, navigate to the location where you store your Data Files if necessary, then click EMP F-Op Elective.xlsx in the file list**

   The filename you selected appears in the Address text box. This is the document users will see when they click the hyperlink. You can also specify the ScreenTip that users see when they hold the pointer over the hyperlink.

4. **Click the ScreenTip button, type Revenue by Procedure, click OK, then click OK again**

   Cell A3 now contains underlined green text, indicating that it is a hyperlink. The color of a hyperlink depends on the worksheet theme colors. You need to change the text color of the hyperlink text so it is easier to see on the worksheet. After you create a hyperlink, you should check it to make sure that it jumps to the correct destination.

5. **Click the Home tab, click the Font Color list arrow [A▾] in the Font group, click Dark Green, Accent 4 color (third color from the right in the Theme Colors), move the pointer over the Ophthalmology text, view the ScreenTip, then click once**

   After you click, the EMP F-Op Elective workbook opens, displaying ophthalmology elective procedures, as shown in Figure F-15.

6. **Close the EMP F-Op Elective workbook, click Don't Save, then save the EMP F-Revenue workbook**

Returning to your document

After you click a hyperlink and view the destination document, you will often want to return to your original document that contains the hyperlink. To do this, you can add the Back button to the Quick Access toolbar. However, the Back button does not appear in the Quick Access toolbar by default; you need to customize the toolbar. (If you are using a computer in a lab, check with your system administrator to see if you have permission to do this.) To customize the Quick Access toolbar, click the Customize Quick Access Toolbar arrow, click More Commands, click the Choose Commands from list arrow, select All Commands, scroll down, click the Back button, click Add, then click OK.

FIGURE F-14: Insert Hyperlink dialog box

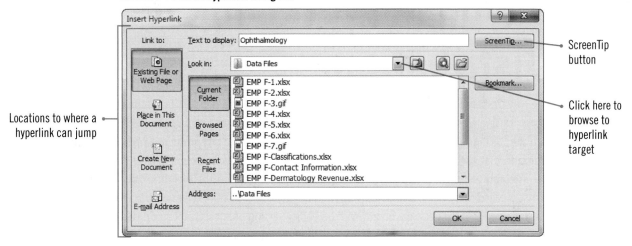

Locations to where a hyperlink can jump

ScreenTip button

Click here to browse to hyperlink target

FIGURE F-15: Target document

	A	B	C
1	**Ophthalmology**		
2	**Elective Procedures**		
3	**Procedure**	**2013 Revenue**	
4	CK	$88,812	
5	Lasik	$1,713,456	
6	PRK	$597,425	
7	LTK	$1,213,456	
8	Intacs	$1,205,187	
9			
10			
11			
12			
13			
14			
15			
16			
17			
18			
19			
20			
21			
22			
23			
24			
25			
26			
27			

Sheet1 / Sheet2 / Sheet3

Ready

Using research tools

You can access resources online and locally on your computer using the Research task pane. To open the Research task pane, click the Review tab, then click the Research button in the Proofing group. The Search for text box in the Research pane lets you specify a research topic. The Research pane has a drop-down list of the resources available to search for your topic. You can use this list to access resources such as a thesaurus, a dictionary, financial Web sites, and research Web sites. You can also quickly access the thesaurus in the Research task pane using the Thesaurus button on the Review tab in the Proofing group.

Saving a Workbook for Distribution

One way to share Excel data is to place, or **publish**, the data on a network or on the Web so that others can access it using their Web browsers. To publish an Excel document to an **intranet** (a company's internal Web site) or the Web, you can save it in an HTML format. **HTML (Hypertext Markup Language)**, is the coding format used for all Web documents. You can also save your Excel file as a **single-file Web page** that integrates all of the worksheets and graphical elements from the workbook into a single file. This file format is called MHTML, also known as MHT. In addition to distributing files on the Web, you might need to distribute your files to people working with an earlier version of Excel. You can do this by saving your files as Excel 97-2003 workbooks. See Table F-1 for a list of the most popular formats. 🖱️ Tony asks you to create a workbook version that managers running an earlier Excel version can use. He also asks you to save the EMP F-Revenue workbook in MHT format so he can publish it on the RMC intranet.

1. **Click the File tab, click Save As, click the Save as type list arrow in the Save As dialog box, click Excel 97-2003 Workbook (*.xls), navigate to the drive and folder where you store your Data Files if necessary, then click Save**

   The Compatibility Checker dialog box opens. It alerts you to the features that will be lost or converted by saving in the earlier format. Some Excel 2010 features are not available in earlier versions of Excel.

2. **Click Continue, close the workbook, then reopen the EMP F-Revenue.xls workbook**

   "[Compatibility Mode]" appears in the title bar, as shown in Figure F-16. Compatibility mode prevents you from including Excel features in your workbook that are not supported in Excel 97-2003 workbooks. To exit compatibility mode, you need to save your file in one of the Excel 2010 formats and reopen the file.

3. **Click the File tab, click Save As, click the Save as type list arrow in the Save As dialog box, click Excel Workbook (*.xlsx); if necessary, navigate to the drive and folder where you store your Data Files, click Save, then click Yes when you are asked if you want to replace the existing file**

   "[Compatibility Mode]" remains displayed in the title bar. You decide to close the file and reopen it to exit compatibility mode.

4. **Close the workbook, then reopen the EMP F-Revenue.xlsx workbook**

   The title bar no longer displays "[Compatibility mode]". You still need to save the file for Web distribution.

5. **Click the File tab, click Save As, in the Save As dialog box navigate to the drive and folder where you store your Data Files if necessary, change the filename to revenue, then click the Save as type list arrow and click Single File Web Page (*.mht, *.mhtml)**

   The Save as type list box indicates that the workbook is to be saved as a Single File Web Page, which is in MHTML or MHT format. To avoid problems when publishing your pages to a Web server, it is best to use lowercase characters, omit special characters and spaces, and limit your filename to eight characters with an additional three-character extension.

6. **Click Save, then click Yes**

   The dialog box indicated that some features may not be retained in the Web page file. Excel saves the workbook as an MHT file in the location you specified. The MHT file is open on your screen. See Figure F-17. It's a good idea to open an MHT file in your browser to see how it will look to viewers.

7. **Close the revenue.mht file in Excel, start your browser, open the revenue.mht file by double-clicking it in the folder where you store your Data Files, click the Acute sheet tab, then close your browser window**

Managing Workbook Data

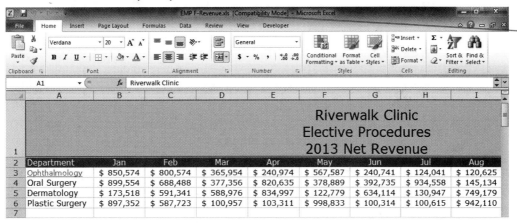

File is marked as using compatibility mode

Web file with new name

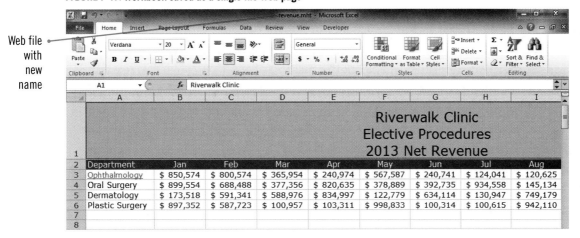

TABLE F-1: Workbook formats

type of file	file extension(s)	used for
Macro-enabled workbook	.xlsm	Files that contain macros
Excel 97 – 2003 workbook	.xls	Working with people using older versions of Excel
Single file Web page	.mht, .mhtml	Web sites with multiple pages and graphics
Web page	.htm, .html	Simple single-page Web sites
Excel template	.xltx	Excel files that will be reused with small changes
Excel macro-enabled template	.xltm	Excel files that will be used again and contain macros
Portable document format	.pdf	Files with formatting that needs to be preserved
XML paper specification	.xps	Files with formatting that needs to be preserved and files that need to be shared
OpenDocument spreadsheet	.ods	Files created with OpenOffice

Understanding Excel file formats

The default file format for Excel 2010 files is the Office Open XML format, which supports all Excel features. This has been the default file format of Office files since Microsoft Office 2007. This format stores Excel files in small XML components that are zipped for compression making the files smaller. The most often used format, .xlsx, does not support macros. **Macros**, programmed instructions that perform tasks, can be a security risk. If your worksheet contains macros, you need to save it with an extension of .xlsm so the macros can function in the workbook. If you use a workbook's text and formats repeatedly, you might want to save it as a template with the extension .xltx. If your template contains macros, you need to save it with the .xltm extension.

Excel 2010

Grouping Worksheets

You can group worksheets to work on them as a collection. When you enter data into one worksheet, that data is also automatically entered into all of the worksheets in the group. This is useful for data that is common to every sheet of a workbook, such as headers and footers, or for column headings that will apply to all monthly worksheets in a yearly summary. Grouping worksheets can also be used to print multiple worksheets at one time. ▰▰▰▰▰ Tony asks you to add the text "Riverwalk" to the footer of both the Elective and Acute worksheets. You will also add 1-inch margins to the top of both worksheets.

STEPS

1. **Open the EMP F-Revenue.xlsx file from the drive and folder where you store your Data Files**

QUICK TIP

You can group non-contiguous worksheets by pressing and holding [Ctrl] while clicking the sheet tabs that you want to group.

2. **With the Elective sheet active, press and hold [Shift], click the Acute sheet, then release [Shift]**
   Both sheet tabs are selected, and the title bar now contains "[Group]", indicating that the worksheets are grouped together. Now any changes you make to the Elective sheet will also be made to the Acute sheet.

3. **Click the Insert tab, then click the Header & Footer button in the Text group**

4. **On the Header & Footer Tools Design tab, click the Go to Footer button in the Navigation group, type Riverwalk in the center section of the footer, enter your name in the left section of the footer, click cell A1, then click the Normal button ▦ on the Status Bar**
   You decide to check the footers in Print Preview.

5. **With the worksheets still grouped, click the File tab, click Print, preview the first page, then click the Next Page button ▶ to preview the second page**
   Because the worksheets are grouped, both pages contain the footer with "Riverwalk" and your name. The worksheets would look better with a wider top margin.

6. **Click the Normal Margins list arrow, click Custom Margins, in the Top text box on the Margins tab of the Page Setup dialog box type 1, then click OK**
   You decide to ungroup the worksheets.

7. **Click the Home tab, right-click the Elective worksheet sheet tab, then click Ungroup Sheets**

8. **Save and close the workbook, exit Excel, then submit the workbook to your instructor**

9. **The completed worksheets are shown in Figures F-18 and F-19**

Adding a digital signature to a workbook

You can digitally sign a workbook to establish its validity and prevent it from being changed. You can obtain a valid certificate from a certificate authority to authenticate the workbook or you can create your own digital signature. To add a signature line in a workbook, click the Insert tab, click the Signature Line button in the Text group, then click OK. In the Signature Setup dialog box, enter information about the signer of the worksheet and then click OK. To add a signature, double-click the signature line, click OK; if prompted, in the Get a Digital ID dialog box, click the Create your own digital ID option button, then click OK. Click Create, in the Sign dialog box, click Select Image next to the sign box, browse to the location where your signature is saved, click Sign, then click OK. To add the certificate authenticating the workbook, click the File tab, click the Protect Workbook button, click Add a Digital Signature, then click OK. In the Sign dialog box click Sign, then click OK. The workbook will be saved as read-only, and it will not be able to be changed by other users.

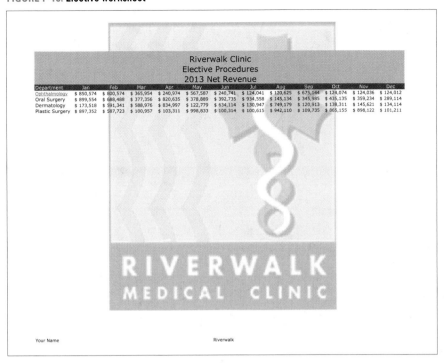

Riverwalk Clinic
Elective Procedures
2013 Net Revenue

Department	Jan	Feb	Mar	Apr	May	Jun	Jul	Aug	Sep	Oct	Nov	Dec
Ophthalmology	$ 850,574	$ 800,574	$ 365,954	$ 240,974	$ 567,587	$ 240,741	$ 124,041	$ 120,625	$ 675,144	$ 124,074	$ 124,036	$ 124,012
Oral Surgery	$ 899,554	$ 688,488	$ 377,356	$ 820,635	$ 378,889	$ 392,735	$ 934,558	$ 145,134	$ 345,985	$ 435,135	$ 359,234	$ 289,114
Dermatology	$ 173,518	$ 591,341	$ 588,976	$ 834,997	$ 122,779	$ 634,114	$ 130,947	$ 749,179	$ 120,913	$ 138,311	$ 145,621	$ 134,114
Plastic Surgery	$ 897,352	$ 587,723	$ 100,957	$ 103,311	$ 998,833	$ 100,314	$ 100,615	$ 942,110	$ 109,735	$ 865,155	$ 898,122	$ 101,211

Your Name   Riverwalk

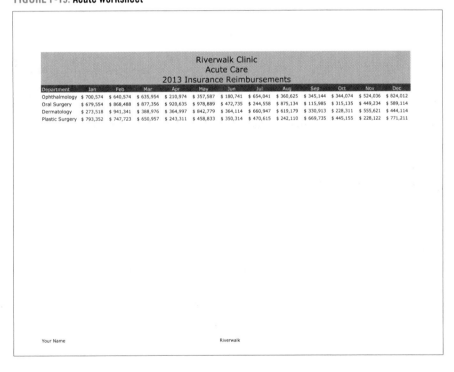

Riverwalk Clinic
Acute Care
2013 Insurance Reimbursements

Department	Jan	Feb	Mar	Apr	May	Jun	Jul	Aug	Sep	Oct	Nov	Dec
Ophthalmology	$ 700,574	$ 640,574	$ 635,954	$ 210,974	$ 357,587	$ 180,741	$ 654,041	$ 360,625	$ 345,144	$ 344,074	$ 524,036	$ 824,012
Oral Surgery	$ 679,554	$ 868,488	$ 877,356	$ 920,635	$ 978,889	$ 472,735	$ 244,558	$ 875,134	$ 115,985	$ 315,135	$ 449,234	$ 589,114
Dermatology	$ 273,518	$ 941,341	$ 388,976	$ 364,997	$ 842,779	$ 364,114	$ 660,947	$ 619,179	$ 330,913	$ 228,311	$ 555,621	$ 444,114
Plastic Surgery	$ 793,352	$ 747,723	$ 650,957	$ 243,311	$ 458,833	$ 350,314	$ 470,615	$ 242,110	$ 669,735	$ 445,155	$ 228,122	$ 771,211

Your Name   Riverwalk

Creating a workspace

If you work with several workbooks at a time in a particular arrangement on the screen, you can group them so that you can open them in one step by creating a workspace. A **workspace** is a file with an .xlw extension. Then, instead of opening each workbook individually, you can open the workspace. To create a workspace, open the workbooks you wish to group, then position and size them as you would like them to appear. Click the View tab, click the Save Workspace button in the Window group, type a name for the workspace file, navigate to the location where you want to store it, then click Save. The workspace file does not contain the workbooks themselves, however. You still have to save any changes you make to the original workbook files. If you work at another computer, you need to have the workspace file and all of the workbook files that are part of the workspace.

Practice

Concepts Review

For current SAM information, including versions and content details, visit SAM Central (http://www.cengage.com/samcentral). If you have a SAM user profile, you may have access to hands-on instruction, practice, and assessment of the skills covered in this unit. Since various versions of SAM are supported throughout the life of this text, check with your instructor for the correct instructions and URL/Web site for accessing assignments.

FIGURE F-20

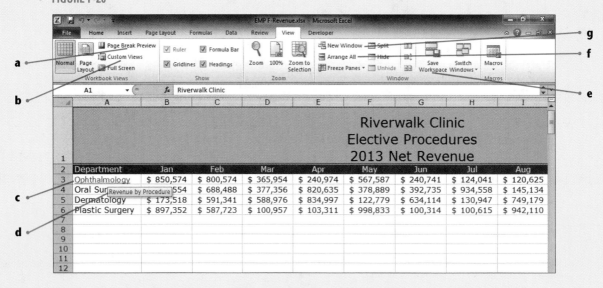

1. **Which element do you click to view and change the way worksheet data is distributed on printed pages?**
2. **Which element do you click to group workbooks so that they open together as a unit?**
3. **Which element do you click to name and save a set of display and/or print settings?**
4. **Which element do you click to open the active worksheet in a new window?**
5. **Which element points to a hyperlink?**
6. **Which element points to a ScreenTip for a hyperlink?**
7. **Which element do you click to organize windows in a specific configuration?**

Match each term with the statement that best describes it.

8. **Dynamic page breaks**
9. **HTML**
10. **Watermark**
11. **Hyperlink**
12. **Data entry area**

a. Web page format
b. Portion of a worksheet that can be changed
c. Translucent background design on a printed worksheet
d. An object that when clicked displays another worksheet or a Web page
e. Adjusted automatically when rows and columns are inserted or deleted

Select the best answer from the list of choices.

13. **You can establish the validity of a workbook by adding a:**
    a. Template.
    c. Custom View.
    b. Digital signature.
    d. Keyword.

14. **So that they can be opened together rather than individually, you can group several workbooks in a:**
    a. Workspace.
    c. Workgroup.
    b. Consolidated workbook.
    d. Work unit.

Skills Review

1. **View and arrange worksheets.**
    a. Start Excel, open the file EMP F-2.xlsx from the drive and folder where you store your Data Files, then save it as **EMP F-Sports Medicine Budget**.
    b. Activate the 2013 sheet if necessary, then open the 2014 sheet in a new window.
    c. Activate the 2013 sheet in the EMP F-Sports Medicine Budget.xlsx:1 workbook. Activate the 2014 sheet in the EMP F-Sports Medicine Budget.xlsx:2 workbook.
    d. View the EMP F-Sports Medicine Budget.xlsx:1 and EMP F-Sports Medicine Budget.xlsx:2 workbooks tiled horizontally. View the workbooks in a vertical arrangement.
    e. Hide the EMP F-Sports Medicine Budget.xlsx:2 instance, then unhide the instance. Close the EMP F-Sports Medicine Budget.xlsx:2 instance, and maximize the EMP F-Sports Medicine Budget.xlsx workbook.
    f. Split the 2013 sheet into two horizontal panes. (*Hint*: Drag the Horizontal split box.) Remove the split by double-clicking it, then save your work.

2. **Protect worksheets and workbooks.**
    a. On the 2013 sheet, unlock the expense data in the range C9:F16.
    b. Protect the sheet without using a password.
    c. To make sure the other cells are locked, attempt to make an entry in cell D4 and verify that you receive an error message.
    d. Change the first-quarter mortgage expense in cell C9 to 5500.
    e. Protect the workbook's structure and windows without applying a password. Right-click the 2013 and 2014 sheet tabs to verify that you cannot insert, delete, rename, move, copy, hide, or unhide the sheets, or change their tab color.
    f. Unprotect the workbook. Unprotect the 2013 worksheet.
    g. Save the workbook.

3. **Save custom views of a worksheet.**
    a. Using the 2013 sheet, create a custom view of the entire worksheet called **Entire 2013 Budget**.
    b. Hide rows 8 through 19, then create a new view called **Income** showing only the income data.
    c. Use the Custom Views dialog box to display all of the data on the 2013 worksheet.
    d. Use the Custom Views dialog box to display only the income data on the 2013 worksheet.
    e. Use the Custom Views dialog box to return to the Entire 2013 Budget view.
    f. Save the workbook.

4. **Add a worksheet background.**
    a. Use EMP F-3.gif as a worksheet background for the 2013 sheet, then delete it.
    b. Add EMP F-3.gif to the 2013 header, then preview the sheet to verify that the background will print.
    c. Add your name to the left section of the 2013 worksheet footer, then save the workbook.

5. **Prepare a workbook for distribution.**
    a. Inspect the workbook and remove any properties, personal data, and header and footer information.
    b. Use the Document Properties Panel to add a title of **Quarterly Budget** and the keywords **sports** and **medicine**.
    c. Mark the workbook as final and verify that "[Read-Only]" is in the title bar.
    d. Remove the final status, then save the workbook.

6. **Insert hyperlinks.**
    a. On the 2013 worksheet, make cell B11 a hyperlink to the file **EMP F-Equipment.xlsx** in your Data Files folder.
    b. Test the link and verify that Sheet1 of the target file displays equipment details.

Skills Review (continued)

c. Return to the EMP F-Sports Medicine Budget.xlsx workbook, edit the hyperlink in cell B11, adding a ScreenTip that reads **Equipment Details**, then verify that the ScreenTip appears.

d. On the 2014 worksheet, enter the text **Based on 2013 budget** in cell A22.

e. Make the text in cell A22 a hyperlink to cell A1 in the 2013 worksheet. (*Hint*: Use the Place in This Document button and note the cell reference in the Type the cell reference text box.)

f. Test the hyperlink. Remove the hyperlink in cell A22 of the 2014 worksheet, then save the workbook.

7. **Save a workbook for distribution.**

a. Save the EMP F-Sports Medicine Budget.xlsx workbook as a single file Web page with the name **sports.mht**. Close the sports.mht file that is open in Excel, then open the sports.mht file in your Web browser. (The Information bar at the top of the Web page notifies you about blocked content. Your Web page doesn't contain any scripts that need to run so you can ignore the Information bar.) Close your browser window, and reopen EMP F-Sports Medicine Budget.xlsx.

b. Save the EMP F-Sports Medicine Budget.xlsx workbook with the 2013 sheet active as a PDF file. Close the file EMP F-Sports Medicine Budget.pdf.

c. Save the EMP F-Sports Medicine Budget workbook as an Excel 97-2003 workbook, and review the results of the Compatibility Checker.

d. Close the EMP F-Sports Medicine Budget.xls file, and reopen the EMP F-Sports Medicine Budget.xlsx file.

e. Save the workbook as a macro-enabled template in the drive and folder where you store your Data Files. (*Hint*: Select the type Excel Macro-Enabled Template (*.xltm) in the Save as type list.)

f. Close the template file, then reopen the EMP F-Sports Medicine Budget.xlsx file.

8. **Grouping worksheets.**

a. Group the 2013 and 2014 worksheets, then add your name to the center footer section of the worksheets.

b. Save the workbook, preview both sheets, comparing your worksheets to Figure F-21, then ungroup the sheets.

c. Submit your EMP F-Sports Medicine Budget.xlsx workbook to your instructor, close all open files, and exit Excel.

FIGURE F-21

Sports Medicine Clinic 2013 Quarterly Budget						
Income	Description	1st QTR	2nd QTR	3rd QTR	4th QTR	TOTAL	% OF TOTAL
	Payments	$ 950,000	$ 870,000	$ 850,000	$ 910,000	$ 3,580,000	53.21%
	Reimbursements	$ 750,000	$ 780,000	$ 570,000	$ 680,000	$ 2,780,000	41.32%
	Fees	$ 91,000	$ 91,000	$ 87,000	$ 99,000	$ 368,000	5.47%
	TOTAL	$ 1,791,000	$ 1,741,000	$ 1,507,000	$ 1,689,000	$ 6,728,000	100.00%
Expenses							
	Mortgage	$ 5,500	$ 4,300	$ 4,300	$ 4,300	$ 18,400	0.80%
	Payroll	$ 550,000	$ 575,000	$ 550,000	$ 580,000	$ 2,255,000	97.55%
	Equipment	$ 5,150	$ 5,150	$ 5,150	$ 5,150	$ 20,600	0.89%
	Utilities	$ 880	$ 770	$ 680	$ 880	$ 3,210	0.14%
	Supplies	$ 890	$ 790	$ 890	$ 990	$ 3,560	0.15%
	Insurance	$ 1,580	$ 1,580	$ 1,580			
	Events	$ 970	$ 500	$ 970			
	Advertising	$ 430	$ 230	$ 230			
	TOTAL	$ 565,400	$ 588,320	$ 563,800			
Cash Flow		$ 1,225,600	$ 1,152,680	$ 943,200			

Sports Medicine Clinic 2014 Quarterly Budget						
Income	Description	1st QTR	2nd QTR	3rd QTR	4th QTR	TOTAL	% OF TOTAL
	Payments	$ 850,000	$ 1,070,000	$ 850,000	$ 810,000	$ 3,580,000	50.61%
	Reimbursements	$ 780,000	$ 780,000	$ 670,000	$ 780,000	$ 3,010,000	42.55%
	Fees	$ 197,000	$ 101,000	$ 87,000	$ 99,000	$ 484,000	6.84%
	TOTAL	$ 1,827,000	$ 1,951,000	$ 1,607,000	$ 1,689,000	$ 7,074,000	100.00%
Expenses							
	Mortgage	$ 4,500	$ 4,300	$ 4,300	$ 4,300	$ 17,400	0.72%
	Payroll	$ 650,000	$ 575,000	$ 550,000	$ 580,000	$ 2,355,000	97.68%
	Equipment	$ 5,150	$ 5,150	$ 5,150	$ 5,150	$ 20,600	0.85%
	Utilities	$ 980	$ 770	$ 680	$ 880	$ 3,310	0.14%
	Supplies	$ 790	$ 790	$ 890	$ 990	$ 3,460	0.14%
	Insurance	$ 1,680	$ 1,580	$ 1,580	$ 1,580	$ 6,420	0.27%
	Events	$ 1,070	$ 500	$ 970	$ 1,070	$ 3,610	0.15%
	Advertising	$ 530	$ 230	$ 230	$ 230	$ 1,220	0.05%
	TOTAL	$ 664,700	$ 588,320	$ 563,800	$ 594,200	$ 2,411,020	100.00%
Cash Flow		$ 1,162,300	$ 1,362,680	$ 1,043,200	$ 1,094,800	$ 4,662,980	

Based on 2013 Budget

Your Name

Your Name

Independent Challenge 1

As the manager of Mercy Hospital's four pharmacies, you are organizing your first-quarter sales in an Excel worksheet. Because the sheet for the month of January includes the same type of information you need for February and March, you decide to enter the headings for all of the first-quarter months at the same time. You use a separate worksheet for each month and create data for 3 months.

a. Start Excel, then save the workbook as **EMP F-Pharmacy Sales.xlsx** in the drive and folder where you store your Data Files.

b. Name the first sheet **January**, name the second sheet **February**, and name the third sheet **March**.

c. Group the worksheets.

d. With the worksheets grouped, add the title **Mercy Hospital** centered across cells A1 and B1. Enter the label **Pharmacy Reimbursements** in cell B2. Enter campus labels in column A beginning in cell A3 and ending in cell A6. Use the following labels in the range A3:A6: **East Campus**, **West Campus**, **North Campus**, and **South Campus**. Add the label **Total** in cell A7.

e. Enter the formula to sum the Amount column in cell B7. Ungroup the worksheets, and enter your own data for each of the reimbursement categories in the January, February, and March sheets.

f. Display each worksheet in its own window, then arrange the three sheets vertically.

g. Hide the window displaying the March sheet. Unhide the March sheet window.

h. Split the March window into two panes: the upper pane displaying rows 1 through 4, and the lower pane displaying rows 5 through 7. Scroll through the data in each pane, then remove the split.

i. Close the windows displaying EMP F-Pharmacy Sales.xlsx:2 and EMP F-Pharmacy Sales.xlsx:3, then maximize the EMP F-Pharmacy Sales.xlsx workbook.

j. Add the keywords **pharmacy sales** to your workbook, using the Document Properties Panel.

k. Group the worksheets again.

l. Add headers to all three worksheets that include your name in the left section and the sheet name in the center section.

m. With the worksheets still grouped, format the worksheets appropriately.

n. Ungroup the worksheets, then mark the workbook status as final. Close the workbook, reopen the workbook, and enable editing.

o. Save the workbook, submit the workbook to your instructor, then exit Excel.

Independent Challenge 2

As the payroll manager at a respiratory medical center, you decide to organize the weekly timecard data using Excel worksheets. You use a separate worksheet for each week and track the hours for employees with different job classifications. A hyperlink in the worksheet provides pay rates for each classification, and custom views limit the information that is displayed.

a. Start Excel, open the file EMP F-4.xlsx from the drive and folder where you store your Data Files, then save it as **EMP F-Timesheets**.

b. Compare the data in the workbook by arranging the Week 1, Week 2, and Week 3 sheets horizontally.

c. Maximize the Week 1 window. Unlock the hours data in the Week 1 sheet and protect the worksheet. Verify that the employee names, numbers, and classifications cannot be changed. Verify that the total hours data can be changed, but do not change the data.

d. Unprotect the Week 1 sheet, and create a custom view called **Complete Worksheet** that displays all the data.

e. Hide column E and create a custom view of the data in the range A1:D22. Name the view **Employee Classifications**. Display each view, then return to the Complete Worksheet view.

f. Add a page break between columns D and E so that the Total Hours data prints on a second page. Preview the worksheet, then remove the page break. (*Hint*: Use the Breaks button on the Page Layout tab.)

Independent Challenge 2 (continued)

g. Add a hyperlink to the Classification heading in cell D1 that links to the file EMP F-Classifications.xlsx. Add a ScreenTip that reads **Pay rates**, then test the hyperlink. Compare your screen to Figure F-22.

FIGURE F-22

	A	B
1	**Respiratory Therapist**	
2	Classifications	Pay Rate
3	Assistant	$30
4	Associate	$35
5	Senior	$40

h. Save the EMP F-Classifications workbook as an Excel 97-2003 workbook, reviewing the Compatibility Checker information. Close the EMP F-Classifications.xls file.

i. Group the three worksheets in the EMP F-Timesheets.xlsx workbook, and add your name to the center footer section.

j. Save the workbook, then preview the grouped worksheets.

k. Ungroup the worksheets, and add 2-inch top and left margins to the Week 1 worksheet.

l. Hide the Week 2 and Week 3 worksheets, inspect the file and remove all document properties, personal information, and hidden worksheets. Do not remove header and footer information.

m. Add the keyword **hours** to the workbook, save the workbook, then mark it as final.

Advanced Challenge Exercise

- Remove the final status from the workbook.
- If you have access to an Information Rights Management server, restrict the permissions to the workbook by granting only yourself permission to change the workbook.
- If you have a valid certificate authority, add a digital signature to the workbook.
- Delete the hours data in the worksheet, and save the workbook as an Excel template.

n. Submit the workbook to your instructor, close the workbook, and exit Excel.

Independent Challenge 3

One of your responsibilities as the office manager at Bay View Medical Center is to keep track of payments and insurance reimbursements. You decide to create a spreadsheet to record revenue, placing each month's data on its own sheet. You create custom views that will focus on the departments at the center. A hyperlink will provide additional procedure information.

a. Start Excel, open the file EMP F-5.xlsx from the drive and folder where you store your Data Files, then save it as **EMP F-Bay View**.

b. Arrange the sheets for the 3 months horizontally to compare revenue, then close the extra workbook windows and maximize the remaining window.

c. Create a custom view of the entire January worksheet named **All Revenue**. Hide the Cancer Care, Wellness, and Laboratory revenue, and create a custom view displaying only the Surgery revenue. Call the view **Surgery**.

d. Display the All Revenue view, group the worksheets, and create a total for the total costs in cell D28 on each month's sheet.

e. With the sheets grouped, add the sheet name to the center section of each sheet's header and your name to the center section of each sheet's footer.

f. Ungroup the sheets and use the Compatibility Checker to view the features that are unsupported in earlier Excel formats.

g. Add a hyperlink in cell A4 of the January sheet that opens the file EMP F-Dermatology Revenue.xlsx. Add a ScreenTip of **Procedure Information**. Test the link, viewing the ScreenTip, then return to the EMP F-Bay View.xlsx workbook without closing the EMP F-Dermatology Revenue.xlsx workbook. Save the EMP F-Bay View.xlsx workbook.

h. Create a workspace that includes the workbooks EMP F-Bay View.xlsx and EMP F-Dermatology Revenue.xlsx in the tiled layout. Name the workspace **EMP F-Bay View Revenue**. (*Hint*: Save Workspace is a button on the View tab in the Window group.)

i. Hide the EMP F-Dermatology Revenue.xlsx workbook, then unhide it.

j. Close the EMP F-Dermatology Revenue.xlsx file, and maximize the EMP F-Bay View.xlsx worksheet.

k. Save the EMP F-Bay View workbook as a macro-enabled workbook. Close the workbook, submit the workbook to your instructor, then exit Excel.

Real Life Independent Challenge

Excel can be a useful tool in tracking expenses for traveling to conferences. Whether you are planning to attend a medical conference now or will be in the future, you can use Excel to enter and organize your expenses. After your data is entered, you create custom views of the data, add a hyperlink and keywords, and save the file in an earlier version of Excel.

a. Start Excel, save the new workbook as **EMP F-Conference Expenses** in the drive and folder where you store your Data Files.

b. Enter the label **Conference Activity** in cell A1 and **Expenses** in cell A2. Center each label across columns A and B. Enter the labels **Category** in cell A4 and **Amount** in cell B4. Enter your expenses in column A. Examples of expenses might be **Air**, **Cab**, **Hotel**, **Conference fees**, **Shipping fees**, and **Meals**. Add the corresponding expense amounts in column B.

c. Add a hyperlink to cell A1 that links to a Web page with information about a medical conference. If necessary, adjust the formatting for cell A1 so the label is visible in the cell. (*Hint*: In the Insert Hyperlink dialog box, click the Existing File or Web Page button, and enter the address of the Web page in the Address text box.)

d. Create a custom view called **Expenses** that displays all of the budget information. Create a custom view named **Categories** that displays only the Column A data. Check each view, then display the Expenses view.

e. Using the Document Panel, add your name in the Author text box, add **conference** in the Subject text box, and add the keywords **expenses** and **conference**.

f. Add a footer that includes your name on the left side of the printout. Preview the worksheet.

g. Unlock the expense amounts in the worksheet. Protect the worksheet without using a password.

h. Remove the worksheet protection, then save the workbook.

i. Save the workbook in Excel 97-2003 format, then close the EMP F-Conference Expenses.xls file.

Advanced Challenge Exercise

- Open the EMP F-Conference Expenses.xlsx file and verify the worksheet is not protected.
- Enable the workbook to be changed by multiple people simultaneously.
- Save and close the workbook.

j. Submit the workbook to your instructor. Exit Excel.

Visual Workshop

Start Excel, open the file EMP F-6.xlsx from the drive and folder where you store your Data Files, then save it as **EMP F-Blood Pressure Study**. Make your worksheet look like the one shown in Figure F-23. The text in cell A3 is a hyperlink to the EMP F-Contact Information workbook, and it has been formatted in the standard color of green. The worksheet background is the Data File EMP F-7.gif. Enter your name in the footer, preview the worksheet, then submit the worksheet to your instructor.

FIGURE F-23

	A	B	C	D	E	F	G	H
1			Lakeside Clinic					
2			Blood Pressure Study					
3	Patient Number	Group	Supervising Physician	Begin Date	End Date			
4	1022	Experimental	Murphy	1/3/2013	4/4/2013			
5	1561	Control	Janes	1/3/2013	4/4/2013			
6	1987	Control	Carlo	1/3/2013	4/4/2013			
7	1471	Control	Carlo	1/3/2013	4/4/2013			
8	1132	Experimental	Murphy	1/3/2013	4/4/2013			
9	1462	Experimental	Murphy	1/3/2013	4/4/2013			
10	1024	Experimental	Janes	1/10/2013	4/11/2013			
11	1563	Control	Janes	1/10/2013	4/11/2013			
12	1988	Control	Carlo	1/10/2013	4/11/2013			
13	1478	Experimental	Murphy	1/10/2013	4/11/2013			
14	1133	Experimental	Janes	1/10/2013	4/11/2013			
15	1469	Control	Murphy	1/17/2013	4/18/2013			
16	1887	Control	Murphy	1/18/2013	4/18/2013			
17	1964	Control	Carlo	1/19/2013	4/18/2013			
18	1756	Experimental	Carlo	1/20/2013	4/18/2013			
19								
20								
21								
22								
23								
24								

Managing Data Using Tables

In addition to using Excel spreadsheet features, you can analyze and manipulate data in a table structure. An Excel **table** is an organized collection of rows and columns of similarly structured worksheet data. For example, a table might contain customer information, with a different customer in each row, with columns holding address, phone, and sales data for each customer. You can use a table to work with data independently of other data on your worksheet. A table lets you easily change the order of information while keeping all row information together and it extends formatting and formulas as you add data. You can also use a table to show and perform calculations on only the type of data you need, making it easier to understand large lists of data. In this unit, you'll learn how to plan and create a table; add, change, find, and delete table information; and then sort table data, perform table calculations, and print a table. Tony Sanchez asks you to help him build and manage a table of physical therapy procedure information for January.

OBJECTIVES

Plan a table
Create and format a table
Add table data
Find and replace table data
Delete table data
Sort table data
Use formulas in a table
Print a table

Planning a Table

Tables are a convenient way to understand and manage large amounts of information. When planning a table, consider what information you want your table to contain and how you want to work with the data, now and in the future. As you plan a table, you should understand its most important components. A table is organized into rows called records. A **record** is a table row that contains data about an object, person, or other item. Records are composed of fields. **Fields** are columns in the table; each field describes a characteristic of the record, such as a customer's last name or street address. Each field has a **field name**, which is a column label, such as "Address," that describes its contents. Tables usually have a **header row** as the first row that contains the field names. To plan your table, use the steps below. Tony asks you to compile a table of the January physical therapy procedures. Before entering the procedure data into an Excel worksheet, you plan the table contents.

DETAILS

As you plan your table, use the following guidelines:

- **Identify the purpose of the table**

   The purpose of the table determines the kind of information the table should contain. You want to use the procedure information table to find all dates for a particular procedure and to display the procedures in order of date.

- **Plan the structure of the table**

   In designing your table's structure, determine the fields (the table columns) you need to achieve the table's purpose. You have worked with the physical therapy and finance departments to determine the type of information they record about each procedure. Figure G-1 shows a layout sketch for the table. Each row will contain one procedure record. The columns represent fields that contain pieces of financial information you will enter for each procedure, such as the name, date, and amount.

- **Plan your row and column structure**

   You can create a table from any contiguous range of cells on your worksheet. Plan and design your table so that all rows have similar types of information in the same column. A table should not have any blank rows or columns. Instead of using blank rows to separate table headings from data, use a table style, which will use formatting to make column labels stand out from your table data. Figure G-2 shows a table, populated with data, that has been formatted using a table style.

- **Document the table design**

   In addition to your table sketch, you should make a list of the field names to document the type of data and any special number formatting required for each field. Field names should be as short as possible while still accurately describing the column information. When naming fields it is important to use text rather than numbers because Excel could interpret numbers as parts of formulas. Your field names should be unique and not easily confused with cell addresses, such as the name D2. You want your procedure information table to contain eight field names, each one corresponding to the financial details of the procedures. Table G-1 shows the documentation of the field names in your table.

January PT Procedures

Procedure	Date	Amount	Adjustment	Insurance Payment	Provider	Patient ID	Balance

Header row will contain field names

Each procedure will be placed in a table row

FIGURE G-2: **Formatted table with data**

	Procedure	Date	Amount	Adjustment	Insurance Payment	Provider	Patient ID	Balance
2	Therap Proc 2	1/21/2013	$55.00	$10.12	$0.00	March	1125	Yes
3	Therap Proc 2	1/12/2013	$55.00	$12.73	$0.00	Michaels	1126	Yes
4	Therap Proc 5	1/21/2013	$55.00	$8.22	$8.00	Toloes	1127	Yes
5	Therapeutic Activity B	1/21/2013	$55.00	$14.93	$10.00	Appleton	1128	Yes
6	Therap Proc 5	1/21/2013	$55.00	$17.00	$0.00	Appleton	1129	Yes
7	Therap Proc 6	1/14/2013	$55.00	$17.00	$24.14	March	1130	Yes
8	Therap Proc 4	1/20/2013	$55.00	$17.86	$24.14	Michaels	1131	Yes
9	Therap Proc 2	1/3/2013	$55.00	$18.77	$24.14	Michaels	1132	Yes
10	Therapeutic Activity Tec	1/6/2013	$55.00	$20.15	$30.07	Toloes	1133	Yes
11	Therap Proc 4	1/7/2013	$55.00	$22.00	$30.07	Laneighton	1134	Yes
12	Therap Proc 3	1/4/2013	$55.00	$23.00	$0.00	Appleton	1135	Yes
13	Therap Proc 1	1/21/2013	$55.00	$23.00	$8.00	Michaels	1136	Yes
14	Therapeutic Activity B	1/21/2013	$55.00	$23.00	$15.00	Toloes	1137	Yes
15	Manual Therapy Tec	1/31/2013	$55.00	$23.00	$32.00	Sonna	1138	No
16	Therapeutic Activity D	1/5/2013	$55.00	$23.00	$32.00	March	1139	No
17	Therap Proc 2	1/5/2013	$55.00	$24.93	$0.00	Laneighton	1140	Yes
18	Therap Proc 3	1/14/2013	$55.00	$24.93	$0.00	Appleton	1141	Yes
19	Therap Proc 3	1/21/2013	$55.00	$24.93	$0.00	March	1142	Yes
20	Therap Proc 1	1/20/2013	$55.00	$24.93	$24.14	Appleton	1143	Yes
21	Therap Proc 3	1/17/2013	$55.00	$24.93	$24.14	March	1144	Yes
22	Therap Proc 3	1/19/2013	$55.00	$24.93	$24.14	Sonna	1145	Yes
23	Therap Proc 4	1/19/2013	$55.00	$24.93	$24.14	Toloes	1146	Yes

Excel 2010

TABLE G-1: **Table documentation**

field name	type of data	description of data
Procedure	Text	Name of procedure
Date	Date	Date of procedure
Amount	Currency with 2 decimal places	Procedure cost
Adjustment	Currency with 2 decimal places	Price adjustment for the procedure
Insurance Payment	Currency with 2 decimal places	Amount received from the insurance company
Provider	Text	Person performing the procedure
Patient ID	Number with 0 decimal places	Patient ID number
Balance	Text	Yes: Balance due from patient No: No balance due

Creating and Formatting a Table

Once you have planned the table structure, the sequence of fields, and appropriate data types, you are ready to create the table in Excel. After you create a table, a Table Tools Design tab appears, containing a gallery of table styles. **Table styles** allow you to easily add formatting to your table by using preset formatting combinations of fill color, borders, type style, and type color. ░░░░░ Tony asks you to build a table with the January PT procedure data. You begin by entering the field names. Then you enter the procedure data that corresponds to each field name, create the table, and format the data using a table style.

STEPS

1. **Start Excel, open the file EMP G-1.xlsx from the drive and folder where you store your Data Files, then save it as EMP G-PT Procedures**

TROUBLE
Don't worry if your field names are wider than the cells; you will fix this later.

2. **Beginning in cell A1 of the Practice sheet, enter each field name shown in Figure G-3 in a separate column**
   Field names are usually in the first row of the table.

QUICK TIP
Do not insert extra spaces at the beginning of a cell because it can affect sorting and finding data in a table.

3. **Enter the information from Figure G-4 in the rows immediately below the field names, leaving no blank rows**
   The data appears in columns organized by field name.

4. **Select the range A1:H4, click the Format button in the Cells group, click AutoFit Column Width, then click cell A1**
   Resizing the column widths this way is faster than double-clicking the column divider lines.

QUICK TIP
You can also create a table using the shortcut key combination [Ctrl] + T.

5. **With cell A1 selected, click the Insert tab, click the Table button in the Tables group, in the Create Table dialog box verify that your table data is in the range $A$1:$H$4, and make sure My table has headers is checked as shown in Figure G-5, then click OK**
   The data range is now defined as a table. **Filter list arrows**, which let you display portions of your data, now appear next to each column header. When you create a table, Excel automatically applies a table style. The default table style has a dark blue header row and alternating gray and white data rows. The Table Tools Design tab appears, and the Table Styles group displays a gallery of table formatting options. You decide to choose a different table style from the gallery.

6. **Click the Table Styles More button ⊽, scroll to view all of the table styles, then move the mouse pointer over several styles without clicking**
   The Table Styles gallery on the Table Tools Design tab has three style categories: Light, Medium, and Dark. Each category has numerous design types; for example, in some of the designs, the header row and total row are darker and the rows alternate colors. The available table designs use the current workbook theme colors so the table coordinates with your existing workbook content. If you select a different workbook theme and color scheme in the Themes group on the Page Layout tab, the Table Styles gallery uses those colors. As you point to each table style, Live Preview shows you what your table will look like with the style applied. However, you only see a preview of each style; you need to click a style to apply it.

7. **Click the Table Style Medium 21 to apply it to your table, then click cell A1**
   Compare your table to Figure G-6.

FIGURE G-3: Field names entered in row 1

	A	B	C	D	E	F	G	H
1	Procedure	Date	Amount	Adjustment	Insurance Payment	Provider	Patient ID	Balance
2								

FIGURE G-4: Three records entered in the worksheet

	A	B	C	D	E	F	G	H
1	Procedure	Date	Amount	Adjustment	Insurance Payment	Provider	Patient ID	Balance
2	Therap Proc 2	1/21/2013	$55.00	$10.12	$0.00	March	1125	Yes
3	Therap Proc 2	1/12/2013	$55.00	$12.73	$0.00	Michaels	1126	Yes
4	Therap Proc 5	1/21/2013	$55.00	$8.22	$8.00	Toloes	1127	Yes
5								

FIGURE G-5: Insert Table dialog box

Table range

Verify that this box is checked

FIGURE G-6: Formatted table with three records

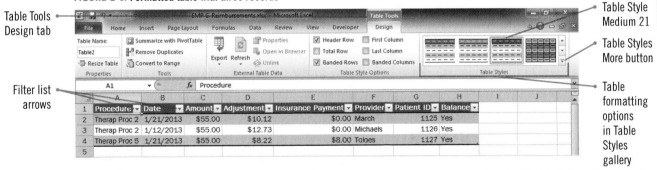

Table Tools Design tab

Filter list arrows

Table Style Medium 21

Table Styles More button

Table formatting options in Table Styles gallery

Changing table style options

You can change a table's appearance by using the check boxes in the Table Styles Options group on the Table Tools Design tab. For example, you can turn on or turn off the following options: **banding**, which creates different formatting for adjacent rows and columns; special formatting for first and last columns; Total Row, which calculates totals for each column; and Header Row, which displays or hides the header row. Use these options to modify a table's appearance either before or after applying a table style. For example, if your table has banded rows, you can select the Banded Columns check box to change the table to be displayed with banded columns. Also, you may want to deselect the Header Row check box to hide a table's header row if a table will be included in a presentation. Figure G-7 shows the available table style options.

You can also create your own table style by clicking the Table Styles More button, then at the bottom of the Table Styles Gallery, clicking New Table Style. In the New Table Quick Style dialog box, name the style in the Name text box, click a table element, then format selected table elements by clicking Format. You can also set a custom style as the default style for your tables by checking the Set as default table quick style for this document check box. You can click Clear at the bottom of the Table Styles gallery if you want to clear a table style.

FIGURE G-7: Table Styles Options

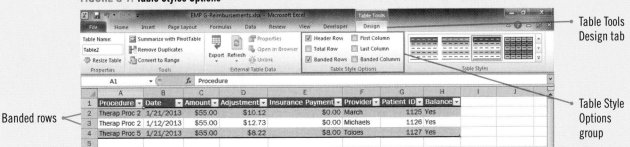

Banded rows

Table Tools Design tab

Table Style Options group

Adding Table Data

You can add records to a table by typing data directly below the last row of the table. After you press [Enter], the new row becomes part of the table and the table formatting extends to the new data. When the active cell is the last cell of a table, you can add a new row by pressing [Tab]. You can also insert rows in any table location. If you decide you need additional data fields, you can add new columns to a table. You can also expand a table by dragging the sizing handle in a table's lower-right corner; drag down to add rows and drag to the right to add columns. ▆▆▆▆ After entering all of the January PT procedure data, Tony is informed that two additional procedures need to be added to the table. He also wants the table to display the amount due for each procedure and whether authorization is required for the procedure.

STEPS

1. **Click the January sheet tab**

   The sheet containing the January PT procedure data becomes active.

2. **Scroll down to the last table row, click cell A65 in the table, enter the data in the range A65:G65 for the new procedure shown in Figure G-8, then press [Enter]**

   Cell H65 displays "Yes" because the formula in column H is extended into the new row of data. As you scroll down, the table headers are visible at the top of the table as long as the active cell is inside the table. The new procedure is part of the table. You want to enter a record about a new procedure above row 6.

3. **Scroll up to and click the inside left edge of cell A6 to select the table row data, click the Insert list arrow in the Cells group, then click Insert Table Rows Above**

   Clicking the left edge of the first cell in a table row selects the entire table row, rather than the entire worksheet row. A new blank row 6 is available to enter the new record.

4. **Click cell A6, then enter the procedure shown in Figure G-9**

   The new procedure is part of the table. You want to add a new field that displays the amount a patient owes to the clinic.

5. **Click cell I1, enter the field name Amount Due, press [Enter], then resize column I to display the field name**

   The new field becomes part of the table, and the header formatting extends to the new field. The AutoCorrect menu allows you to undo or stop the automatic table expansion, but in this case you decide to leave this feature on. You want to add another new field to the table to display procedures that require authorization, but this time you will add the new field by resizing the table.

QUICK TIP

You can also resize a table by clicking the Table Tools Design tab, clicking the Resize Table button in the Properties group, selecting the new data range for the table, then clicking OK.

6. **Scroll down until cell I66 is visible, drag the sizing handle in the table's lower-right corner one column to the right to add column J to the table, as shown in Figure G-10**

   The table range is now A1:J66, and the new field name is Column1.

7. **Scroll up to and click cell J1, enter Authorization Required, press [Enter], then resize column J to display the field name**

8. **Click the Insert tab, click the Header & Footer button in the Text group, enter your name in the center header text box, click cell A1, click the Normal button ▦ in the status bar, then save the workbook**

FIGURE G-8: **New record in row 65**

	A	B	C	D	E	F	G	H	I
61	Physical Therapy E	1/3/2013	$165.00	$83.24	$65.41	Sonna	1184	Yes	
62	Physical Therapy E	1/5/2013	$165.00	$83.24	$65.41	Sonna	1185	Yes	
63	Physical Therapy E	1/5/2013	$165.00	$83.24	$65.41	Sonna	1186	Yes	
64	Physical Therapy E	1/27/2013	$165.00	$88.33	$65.41	March	1187	Yes	
65	Therap Proc 2	1/5/2013	$52.00	$10.00	$30.00	Michaels	1188	Yes	
66									
67									

New record
in row 65

FIGURE G-9: **New record in row 6**

	A	B	C	D	E	F	G	H
					Insurance			
1	Procedure	Date	Amount	Adjustment	Payment	Provider	Patient ID	Balance
2	Therap Proc 2	1/21/2013	$55.00	$10.12	$0.00	March	1125	Yes
3	Therap Proc 2	1/12/2013	$55.00	$12.73	$0.00	Michaels	1126	Yes
4	Therap Proc 5	1/21/2013	$55.00	$8.22	$8.00	Toloes	1127	Yes
5	Therapeutic Activity B	1/21/2013	$55.00	$14.93	$10.00	Appleton	1128	Yes
6	Therap Proc 4	1/14/2013	$57.00	$12.00	$32.00	Toloes	1189	Yes
7	Therap Proc 5	1/21/2013	$55.00	$17.00	$0.00	Appleton	1129	Yes
8	Therap Proc 6	1/14/2013	$55.00	$17.00	$24.14	March	1130	Yes
9	Therap Proc 4	1/20/2013	$55.00	$17.86	$24.14	Michaels	1131	Yes
10	Therap Proc 2	1/3/2013	$55.00	$18.77	$24.14	Michaels	1132	Yes
11	Therapeutic Activity Tec	1/6/2013	$55.00	$20.15	$30.07	Toloes	1133	Yes
12	Therap Proc 4	1/7/2013	$55.00	$22.00	$30.07	Laneighton	1134	Yes

New record
in row 6

FIGURE G-10: **Resizing a table using the resizing handles**

I1 = fx Amount Due

	Date	Amount	Adjustment	Insurance Pay	Provider	Patient ID	Balance	Amount Due	J
53	1/20/2013	$82.00	$40.00	$30.00	Michaels	1175	Yes		
54	1/18/2013	$82.00	$40.00	$30.00	Sonna	1176	Yes		
55	1/27/2013	$75.00	$46.52	$22.78	Toloes	1177	Yes		
56	1/28/2013	$75.00	$46.52	$22.78	Toloes	1178	Yes		
57	1/27/2013	$75.00	$46.52	$22.78	Appleton	1179	Yes		
58	1/28/2013	$75.00	$46.52	$22.78	Sonna	1180	Yes		
59	1/27/2013	$75.00	$46.52	$22.78	Sonna	1181	Yes		
60	1/20/2013	$165.00	$83.24	$0.00	March	1182	Yes		
61	1/21/2013	$165.00	$83.24	$0.00	Michaels	1183	Yes		
62	1/3/2013	$165.00	$83.24	$65.41	Sonna	1184	Yes		
63	1/5/2013	$165.00	$83.24	$65.41	Sonna	1185	Yes		
64	1/5/2013	$165.00	$83.24	$65.41	Sonna	1186	Yes		
65	1/27/2013	$165.00	$88.33	$65.41	March	1187	Yes		
66	1/5/2013	$52.00	$10.00	$30.00	Michaels	1188	Yes		
67									

Drag
sizing
handle
to add
column J

Selecting table elements

When working with tables you often need to select rows, columns, and even the entire table. Clicking to the right of a row number, inside column A, selects the entire table row. You can select a table column by clicking the top edge of the header. Be careful not to click a column letter or row number, however, because this selects the entire worksheet row or column. You can select the table data by clicking the upper-left corner of the first table cell. When selecting a column or a table, the first click selects only the data in the column or table. If you click a second time, you add the headers to the selection.

Finding and Replacing Table Data

From time to time, you need to locate specific records in your table. You can use the Excel Find feature to search your table for the information you need. You can also use the Replace feature to locate and replace existing entries or portions of entries with information you specify. If you don't know the exact spelling of the text for which you are searching, you can use wildcards to help locate the records. **Wildcards** are special symbols that substitute for unknown characters. ████████ Tony needs to update the table in response to a memo from the Human Resources Department that Ms. Laneighton is now Mrs. Crowley. He asks you to replace "Laneighton" with "Crowley" in all of the provider names. He also wants to know how many Physical Therapy E procedures were performed in January. You begin by searching for records with the text "Physical Therapy E".

1. **Click cell A1 if necessary, click the Home tab, click the Find & Select button in the Editing group, then click Find**

   The Find and Replace dialog box opens, as shown in Figure G-11. In this dialog box, you enter criteria that specify the records you want to find in the Find what text box. You want to search for records whose Procedure field contains the label "Physical Therapy E".

2. **Type Physical Therapy E in the Find what text box, then click Find Next**

   A47 is the active cell because it is the first instance of Physical Therapy E in the table.

3. **Click Find Next and examine the record for each Physical Therapy E procedure found until no more matching cells are found in the table and the active cell is A47 again, then click Close**

   There are eight Physical Therapy E procedures.

4. **Return to cell A1, click the Find & Select button in the Editing group, then click Replace**

   The Find and Replace dialog box opens with the Replace tab selected and "Physical Therapy E" in the Find what text box, as shown in Figure G-12. You will search for entries containing "Laneighton" and replace them with "Crowley". To save time, you will use the (*) wildcard to help you locate the records containing Laneighton.

5. **Delete the text in the Find what text box, type La* in the Find what text box, click the Replace with text box, then type Crowley**

   The asterisk (*) wildcard stands for one or more characters, meaning that the search text "La*" will find words such as "Lake", "Lane", and "Lately". Because you notice that there are other table entries containing the text "la" with a lowercase "l" (in the Balance column heading), you need to make sure that only capitalized instances of the letter "L" are replaced.

6. **Click Options, click the Match case check box to select it, click Options, then click Find Next**

   Excel moves the cell pointer to the cell containing the first occurrence of "Laneighton".

7. **Click Replace All, click OK, then click Close**

   The dialog box closes. Excel made three replacements, in cells F12, F18, and F35. The Balance field heading remains unchanged.

8. **Save the workbook**

FIGURE G-11: Find and Replace dialog box

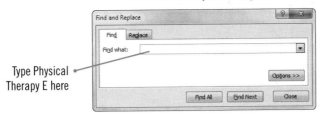

Type Physical Therapy E here

FIGURE G-12: The Replace tab in the Find and Replace dialog box

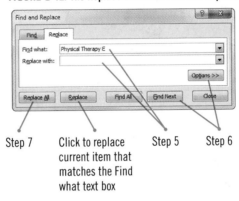

Step 7   Click to replace   Step 5   Step 6
         current item that
         matches the Find
         what text box

Using Find and Select features

You can also use the Find feature to navigate to a specific place in a workbook by clicking the Find & Select button in the Editing group, clicking Go To, typing a cell address, then clicking OK. Clicking the Find & Select button also allows you to find comments and conditional formatting in a worksheet. You can use the Go to Special dialog box to select cells that contain different types of formulas or objects. Some Go to Special commands also appear on the Find & Select menu. Using this menu, you can also change the mouse pointer shape to the Select Objects pointer so you can quickly select drawing objects when necessary. To return to the standard Excel pointer, press [Esc].

Deleting Table Data

To keep a table up to date, you need to be able to periodically remove records. You may even need to remove fields if the information stored in a field becomes unnecessary. You can delete table data using the Delete button in the Cells group or by dragging the sizing handle at the table's lower-right corner. You can also easily delete duplicate records from a table. ▓▓▓▓ The Physical Therapy Department informs you that the record for the Manual Therapy Tec procedure on 1/31/2013 is an error and needs to be deleted from the table. You will also remove any duplicate records from the table. Because the authorization requirements are difficult to keep up with, Tony asks you to delete the field for authorization information.

STEPS

1. **Click the left edge of cell A16 to select the table row data, click the Delete button list arrow in the Cells group, then click Delete Table Rows**

   The procedure is deleted, and the Therapeutic Activity D procedure moves up to row 16, as shown in Figure G-13. You can also delete a table row or a column using the Resize Table button in the Properties group of the Table Tools Design tab, or by right-clicking the row or column, pointing to Delete on the shortcut menu, then clicking Table Columns or Table Rows. You decide to check the table for duplicate records.

QUICK TIP

You can also remove duplicates from worksheet data by clicking the Data tab, then clicking the Remove Duplicates button in the Data Tools group.

2. **Click the Table Tools Design tab, then click the Remove Duplicates button in the Tools group**

   The Remove Duplicates dialog box opens, as shown in Figure G-14. You need to select the columns that will be used to evaluate duplicates. Because you don't want to delete procedures with the same provider but different dates, you will look for duplicate data in all of the columns.

3. **Make sure the "My data has headers" check box is checked and that all the columns headers are checked, then click OK**

   One duplicate record is found and removed, leaving 63 records of data and a total of 64 rows in the table, including the header row. You want to remove the last column, which contains space for authorization information.

4. **Click OK, scroll down until cell J64 is visible, drag the sizing handle of the table's lower-right corner one column to the left to remove column J from the table**

   The table range is now A1:I64, and the Authorization Required field no longer appears in the table.

5. **Delete the contents of cell J1, return to cell A1, then save the workbook**

FIGURE G-13: Table with row deleted

	Procedure	Date	Amount	Adjustment	Insurance Payment	Provider	Patient ID	Balance
2	Therap Proc 2	1/21/2013	$55.00	$10.12	$0.00	March	1125	Yes
3	Therap Proc 2	1/12/2013	$55.00	$12.73	$0.00	Michaels	1126	Yes
4	Therap Proc 5	1/21/2013	$55.00	$8.22	$8.00	Toloes	1127	Yes
5	Therapeutic Activity B	1/21/2013	$55.00	$14.93	$10.00	Appleton	1128	Yes
6	Therap Proc 4	1/14/2013	$57.00	$12.00	$32.00	Toloes	1189	Yes
7	Therap Proc 5	1/21/2013	$55.00	$17.00	$0.00	Appleton	1129	Yes
8	Therap Proc 6	1/14/2013	$55.00	$17.00	$24.14	March	1130	Yes
9	Therap Proc 4	1/20/2013	$55.00	$17.86	$24.14	Michaels	1131	Yes
10	Therap Proc 2	1/3/2013	$55.00	$18.77	$24.14	Michaels	1132	Yes
11	Therapeutic Activity Tec	1/6/2013	$55.00	$20.15	$30.07	Toloes	1133	Yes
12	Therap Proc 4	1/7/2013	$55.00	$22.00	$30.07	Crowley	1134	Yes
13	Therap Proc 3	1/4/2013	$55.00	$23.00	$0.00	Appleton	1135	Yes
14	Therap Proc 1	1/21/2013	$55.00	$23.00	$8.00	Michaels	1136	Yes
15	Therapeutic Activity B	1/21/2013	$55.00	$23.00	$15.00	Toloes	1137	Yes
16	Therapeutic Activity D	1/5/2013	$55.00	$23.00	$32.00	March	1139	No
17	Therap Proc 2	1/5/2013	$55.00	$24.93	$0.00	Crowley	1140	Yes
18	Therap Proc 3	1/14/2013	$55.00	$24.93	$0.00	Appleton	1141	Yes
19	Therap Proc 3	1/21/2013	$55.00	$24.93	$0.00	March	1142	Yes
20	Therap Proc 1	1/20/2013	$55.00	$24.93	$24.14	Appleton	1143	Yes
21	Therap Proc 3	1/17/2013	$55.00	$24.93	$24.14	March	1144	Yes
22	Therap Proc 3	1/19/2013	$55.00	$24.93	$24.14	Sonna	1145	Yes
23	Therap Proc 4	1/19/2013	$55.00	$24.93	$24.14	Toloes	1146	Yes
24	Therap Proc 5	1/13/2013	$55.00	$24.93	$24.14	Michaels	1147	Yes

Row is deleted and procedures move up one row

FIGURE G-14: Remove Duplicates dialog box

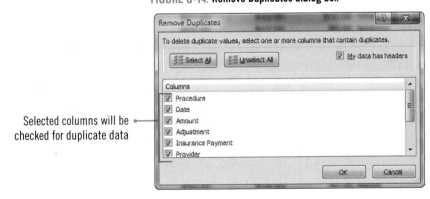

Selected columns will be checked for duplicate data

Sorting Table Data

Usually, you enter table records in the order in which you receive information, rather than in alphabetical or numerical order. When you add records to a table, you usually enter them at the end of the table. You can change the order of the records any time using the Excel **sort** feature. Because the data is structured as a table, Excel changes the order of the records while keeping each record, or row of information, together. You can sort a table in ascending or descending order on one field using the filter list arrows next to the field name. In **ascending order**, the lowest value (the beginning of the alphabet or the earliest date) appears at the top of the table. In a field containing labels and numbers, numbers appear first in the sorted list. In **descending order**, the highest value (the end of the alphabet or the latest date) appears at the top of the table. In a field containing labels and numbers, labels appear first. Table G-2 provides examples of ascending and descending sorts. ██████ Tony wants the procedure data sorted by date, displaying procedures that were performed the earliest in the month at the top of the table.

STEPS

1. **Click the Date filter list arrow, then click Sort Oldest to Newest**

   Excel rearranges the records in ascending order by date, as shown in Figure G-15. The Date filter list arrow has an upward pointing arrow indicating the ascending sort in the field. You can also sort the table on one field using the Sort & Filter button.

2. **Click the Home tab, click any cell in the Amount column, click the Sort & Filter button in the Editing group, then click Sort Largest to Smallest**

   Excel sorts the table, placing those records with the higher amount at the top. The Amount filter list arrow now has a downward pointing arrow next to the filter list arrow, indicating the descending sort order. You can also rearrange the table data using a **multilevel sort**. This type of sort rearranges the table data using more than one field, where each field is a different level, based on its importance in the sort. If you use two sort levels, the data is sorted by the first field, and the second field is sorted within each grouping of the first field. Since you have many groups of procedures with different dates, you want to use a multilevel sort to arrange the table data by procedures and then by dates within each procedure.

3. **Click the Sort & Filter button in the Editing group, then click Custom Sort**

   The Sort dialog box opens, as shown in Figure G-16.

4. **Click the Sort by list arrow, click Procedure, click the Order list arrow, click A to Z, click Add Level, click the Then by list arrow, click Date, click the second Order list arrow, click Oldest to Newest if necessary, then click OK**

   Figure G-17 shows the table sorted alphabetically in ascending order (A–Z) by Procedure, and within each procedure grouping, in ascending order by the Date.

5. **Save the workbook**

Sorting a table using conditional formatting

If conditional formats have been applied to a table, you can sort the table using conditional formatting to arrange the rows. For example, if cells are conditionally formatted with color, you can sort a field on Cell Color, using the color with the order of On Top or On Bottom in the Sort dialog box.

FIGURE G-15: Table sorted by date

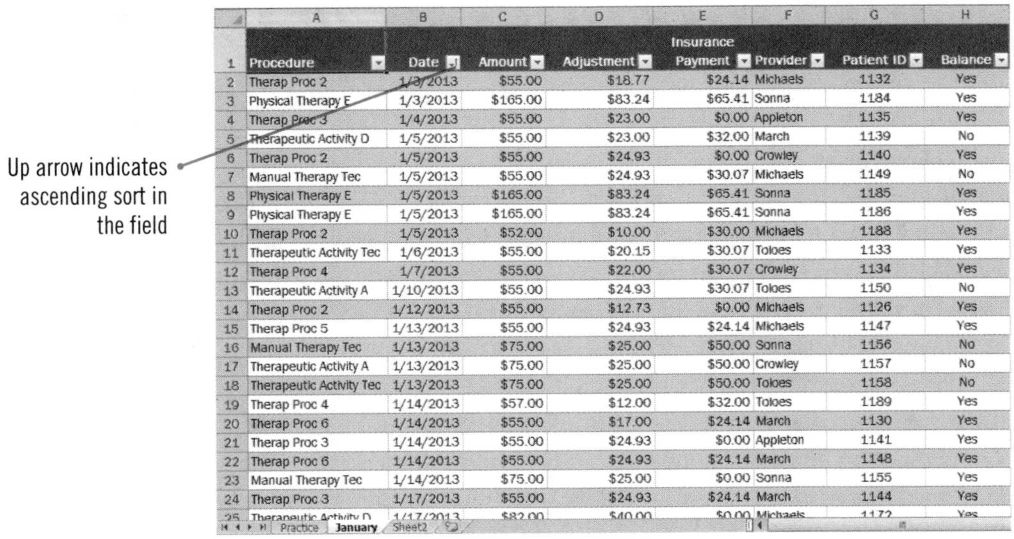

Up arrow indicates ascending sort in the field

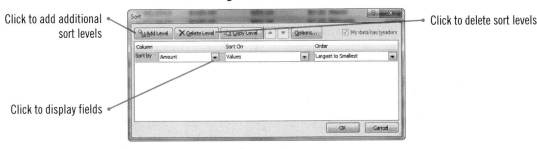

FIGURE G-16: Sort dialog box

Click to add additional sort levels

Click to delete sort levels

Click to display fields

FIGURE G-17: Table sorted using two levels

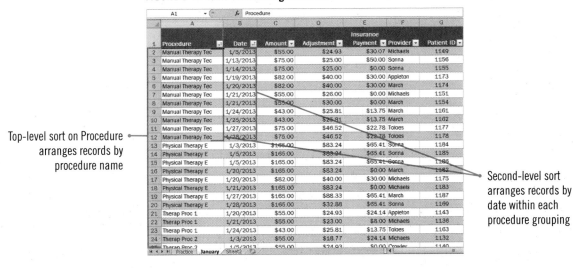

Top-level sort on Procedure arranges records by procedure name

Second-level sort arranges records by date within each procedure grouping

TABLE G-2: Sort order options and examples

option	alphabetic	numeric	date	alphanumeric
Ascending	A, B, C	7, 8, 9	1/1, 2/1, 3/1	12A, 99B, DX8, QT7
Descending	C, B, A	9, 8, 7	3/1, 2/1, 1/1	QT7, DX8, 99B, 12A

Specifying a custom sort order

You can identify a custom sort order for the field selected in the Sort by box. Click the Order list arrow in the Sort dialog box, click Custom List, then click the desired custom order. Commonly used custom sort orders are days of the week (Sun, Mon, Tues, Wed, etc.) and months (Jan, Feb, Mar, etc.); alphabetic sorts do not sort these items properly.

Using Formulas in a Table

Many tables are large, making it difficult to know from viewing them what the "story" the table tells. The Excel table calculation features help you summarize table data so you can see important trends. After you enter a single formula into a table cell, the **calculated columns** feature fills in the remaining cells with the formula's results. The column continues to fill with the formula results as you enter rows in the table. This makes it easy to update your formulas because you only need to edit the formula once, and the change will fill in to the other column cells. The **structured reference** feature allows your formulas to refer to table columns by names that are automatically generated when you create the table. These names automatically adjust as you add or delete table fields. An example of a table reference is =[Sales]–[Costs], where Sales and Costs are field names in the table. Tables also have a specific area at the bottom called the **table total row** for calculations using the data in the table columns. The cells in this row contain a dropdown list of functions that can be used for the column calculation. The table total row adapts to any changes in the table size. 🎞️🎞️ Tony wants you to use a formula to calculate the amount due for each procedure. You will also add summary information to the bottom of the table.

STEPS

1. **Click cell I2, then type =[**

   A list of the table field names appears, as shown in Figure G-18. Structured referencing allows you to use the names that Excel created when you defined your table to reference fields in a formula. You can choose a field by clicking it and pressing [TAB] or by double-clicking the field name.

2. **Click Amount, press [Tab], then type]**

   Excel begins the formula, placing Amount in the cell in blue and framing the Amount data in a blue border.

3. **Type -[, double-click Adjustment, type], type -[, double-click Insurance Payment, then type]**

   Excel places Adjustment in the cell in green and outlines the Adjustment data in a green border. The Insurance Payment data displays in purple.

4. **Press [Enter]**

   The formula result, $0.00, is displayed in cell I2. The table column also fills with the formula displaying the amount due for each procedure.

QUICK TIP

You can undo the calculated column results by clicking Undo Calculated Column in the AutoCorrect Options list. You can turn off the Calculated Columns feature by clicking Stop Automatically Creating Calculated Columns in the AutoCorrect Options list.

5. **Click the AutoCorrect Options list arrow 📄 ▾**

   Because the calculated columns option saves time, you decide to leave the feature on. You want to display the amount due for all of the procedures.

6. **Click any cell inside the table if necessary, click the Table Tools Design tab, then click the Total Row check box in the Table Style Options group to select it**

   A total row appears at the bottom of the table, and the total amount due, $1,108.56, is displayed in cell I65. You can select other formulas in the total row.

7. **Click cell C65, then click the cell list arrow on the right side of the cell**

   The list of available functions appears, as shown in Figure G-19. You want to find the average procedure amount.

8. **Click Average, then save your workbook**

   The average procedure amount, $70.84, appears in cell C65.

FIGURE G-18: **Table field names**

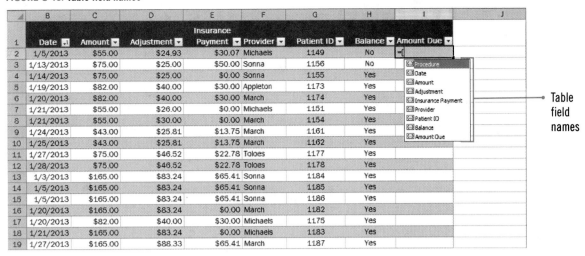

	Date	Amount	Adjustment	Insurance Payment	Provider	Patient ID	Balance	Amount Due	
2	1/5/2013	$55.00	$24.93	$30.07	Michaels	1149	No	=(	
3	1/13/2013	$75.00	$25.00	$50.00	Sonna	1156	No		
4	1/14/2013	$75.00	$25.00	$0.00	Sonna	1155	Yes		
5	1/19/2013	$82.00	$40.00	$30.00	Appleton	1173	Yes		
6	1/20/2013	$82.00	$40.00	$30.00	March	1174	Yes		
7	1/21/2013	$55.00	$26.00	$0.00	Michaels	1151	Yes		
8	1/21/2013	$55.00	$30.00	$0.00	March	1154	Yes		
9	1/24/2013	$43.00	$25.81	$13.75	March	1161	Yes		
10	1/25/2013	$43.00	$25.81	$13.75	March	1162	Yes		
11	1/27/2013	$75.00	$46.52	$22.78	Toloes	1177	Yes		
12	1/28/2013	$75.00	$46.52	$22.78	Toloes	1178	Yes		
13	1/3/2013	$165.00	$83.24	$65.41	Sonna	1184	Yes		
14	1/5/2013	$165.00	$83.24	$65.41	Sonna	1185	Yes		
15	1/5/2013	$165.00	$83.24	$65.41	Sonna	1186	Yes		
16	1/20/2013	$165.00	$83.24	$0.00	March	1182	Yes		
17	1/20/2013	$82.00	$40.00	$30.00	Michaels	1175	Yes		
18	1/21/2013	$165.00	$83.24	$0.00	Michaels	1183	Yes		
19	1/27/2013	$165.00	$88.33	$65.41	March	1187	Yes		

Table field names

Drop-down list: Procedure, Date, Amount, Adjustment, Insurance Payment, Provider, Patient ID, Balance, Amount Due

FIGURE G-19: **Functions in the Total Row**

	Date	Amount	Adjustment	Insurance Payi	Provider	Patient ID	Balance	Amount Due
50	1/27/2013	$75.00	$46.52	$22.78	Sonna	1181	Yes	$5.70
51	1/10/2013	$55.00	$24.93	$30.07	Toloes	1150	No	$0.00
52	1/13/2013	$75.00	$25.00	$50.00	Crowley	1157	No	$0.00
53	1/24/2013	$43.00	$25.81	$13.75	Michaels	1167	Yes	$3.44
54	1/21/2013	$55.00	$14.93	$10.00	Appleton	1128	Yes	$30.07
55	1/21/2013	$55.00	$23.00	$15.00	Toloes	1137	Yes	$17.00
56	1/21/2013	$50.00	$32.24	$0.00	Michaels	1168	Yes	$17.76
57	1/5/2013	$55.00	$23.00	$32.00	March	1139	No	$0.00
58	1/17/2013	$82.00	$40.00	$0.00	Michaels	1172	Yes	$42.00
59	1/20/2013	$82.00	$32.99	$0.00	March	1170	Yes	$49.01
60	1/6/2013	$55.00	$20.15	$30.07	Toloes	1133	Yes	$4.78
61	1/13/2013	$75.00	$25.00	$50.00	Toloes	1158	No	$0.00
62	1/18/2013	$82.00	$40.00	$30.00	Sonna	1176	Yes	$12.00
63	1/20/2013	$55.00	$27.00	$24.14	Toloes	1152	Yes	$3.86
64	1/26/2013	$43.00	$25.81	$0.00	Sonna	1160	Yes	$17.19
65								$1,108.56
66								
67								

Drop-down list: None, Average, Count, Count Numbers, Max, Min, Sum, StdDev, Var, More Functions...

Functions available in the Total Row

Using structured references

When you create a table from worksheet data, Excel creates a default table name such as Table1. This table name appears in structured references. Structured references make it easier to work with formulas that use table data. You can reference the entire table, columns in the table, or specific data. Structured references are especially helpful to use in formulas because they automatically adjust as data ranges change in a table, so you don't need to edit formulas.

Printing a Table

You can determine the way a table will print using the Page Layout tab. Because tables often have more rows than can fit on a page, you can define the first row of the table (containing the field names) as the **print title**, which prints at the top of every page. Most tables do not have any descriptive information above the field names on the worksheet, so to augment the field name information, you can use headers and footers to add identifying text, such as the table title or the report date. ▰▰▰▰▰ Tony asks you for a printout of the procedure information. You begin by previewing the table.

STEPS

1. **Click the File tab, click Print, then view the table preview**
   Below the table you see 1 of 4.

2. **In the Preview window, click the Next Page button ▶ in the Preview area to view the second page, then click ▶ two times to view pages three and four**
   The third and fourth pages only contain one column, so you will scale the table to place all columns on one page. Because the records on page 2 appear without column headings, you want to set up the first row of the table, which contains the field names, as a repeating print title.

3. **Click the Page Layout tab, click the Width list arrow in the Scale to Fit group, then click 1 page**

4. **Click the Print Titles button in the Page Setup group, click inside the Rows to repeat at top text box under Print titles, scroll up to row 1 if necessary, click any cell in row 1 on the table, then compare your Page Setup dialog box to Figure G-20**
   When you select row 1 as a print title, Excel automatically inserts an absolute reference to the row that will repeat at the top of each page.

5. **Click the Print Preview button in the Page Setup dialog box, then click ▶ in the preview window to view the second page**
   Setting up a print title to repeat row 1 causes the field names to appear at the top of each printed page. The printout would be more informative with a header to identify the table information.

6. **Click the Insert tab, click the Header & Footer button in the Text group, click the left header section text box, then type January PT Procedures**

7. **Select the left header section information, click the Home tab, click the Increase Font Size button A˄ in the Font group twice to change the font size to 14, click the Bold button B in the Font group, click any cell in the table, then click the Normal button ▦ in the status bar**

8. **Save the table, preview it, close the workbook, exit Excel, then submit the workbook to your instructor**
   Compare your table with Figure G-21.

FIGURE G-20: Page Setup dialog box

Print title is set to row 1 →

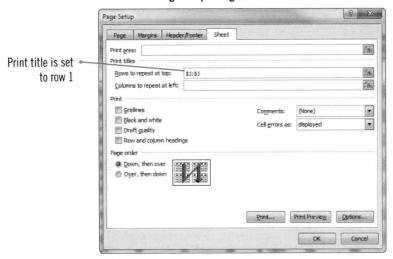

FIGURE G-21: Completed table

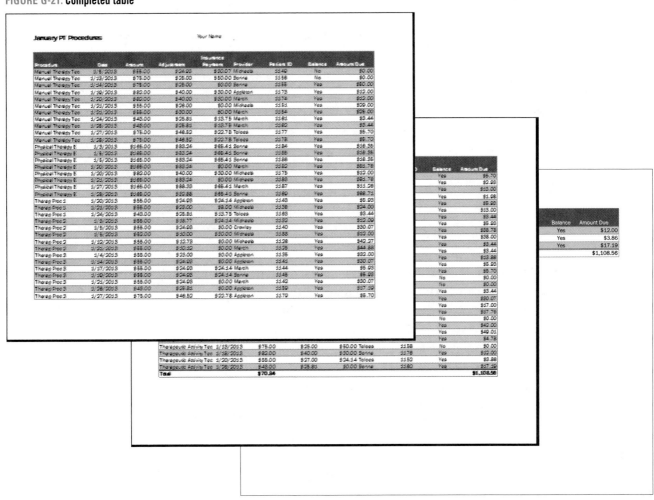

Setting a print area

Sometimes you will want to print only part of a worksheet. To do this, select any worksheet range, click the File tab, click Print, click the Print Active Sheets list arrow, then click Print Selection. If you want to print a selected area repeatedly, it's best to define a **print area**, the area of the worksheet that previews and prints when you use the Print command in Backstage view. To set a print area, select the range of data on the worksheet that you want to print, click the Page Layout tab, click the Print Area button in the Page Setup group, then click Set Print Area. You can add to the print area by selecting a range, clicking the Print Area button, then clicking Add to Print Area. A print area can consist of one contiguous range of cells, or multiple areas in different parts of a worksheet.

Practice

Concepts Review

For current SAM information, including versions and content details, visit SAM Central (http://www.cengage.com/samcentral). If you have a SAM user profile, you may have access to hands-on instruction, practice, and assessment of the skills covered in this unit. Since various versions of SAM are supported throughout the life of this text, check with your instructor for the correct instructions and URL/Web site for accessing assignments.

FIGURE G-22

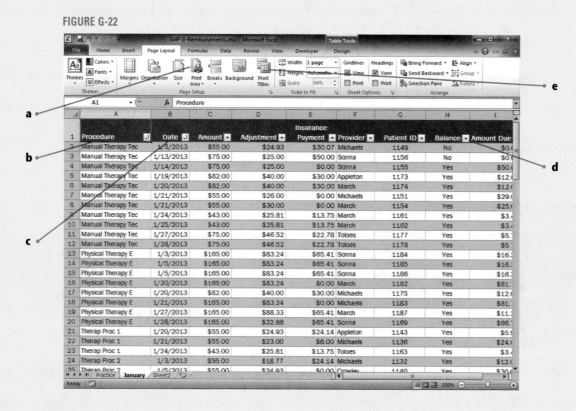

1. Which element do you click to set a range in a table that will print using Quick Print?
2. Which element do you click to print field names at the top of every page?
3. Which element do you click to sort field data on a worksheet?
4. Which element points to a second-level sort field?
5. Which element points to a top-level sort field?

Match each term with the statement that best describes it.

6. **Sort**   a. Organized collection of related information in Excel
7. **Field**   b. Arrange records in a particular sequence
8. **Table**   c. Column in an Excel table
9. **Record**   d. First row of a table containing field names
10. **Header row**   e. Row in an Excel table

Managing Data Using Tables

Select the best answer from the list of choices.

11. **Which of the following Excel sorting options do you use to sort a table of employee names in order from Z to A?**
    a. Ascending
    b. Absolute
    c. Descending
    d. Alphabetic

12. **Which of the following series appears in descending order?**
    a. 8, 6, 4, C, B, A
    b. 4, 5, 6, A, B, C
    c. C, B, A, 6, 5, 4
    d. 8, 7, 6, 5, 6, 7

13. **You can easily add formatting to a table by using:**
    a. Print titles.
    b. Table styles.
    c. Print areas.
    d. Calculated columns.

14. **When printing a table on multiple pages, you can define a print title to:**
    a. Include the sheet name in table reports.
    b. Include appropriate fields in the printout.
    c. Exclude from the printout all rows under the first row.
    d. Include field names at the top of each printed page.

Skills Review

1. **Create and format a table.**
    a. Start Excel, open the file EMP G-2.xlsx from the drive and folder where you store your data files, then save it as **EMP G-Employees**.
    b. Using the Practice sheet, enter the field names in the first row and the first two records in rows two and three, as shown in Table G-3. Create a table using the data you entered.

TABLE G-3

Last Name	First Name	Years Employed	Department	Full/Part Time	Training Completed
Lane	Sarah	4	Phlebotomy Tech	F	Y
Magnum	Darrin	3	X-Ray Tech	P	N

    c. On the Staff sheet, create a table with a header row. Adjust the column widths, if necessary, to display the field names.
    d. Apply a table style of Light 12 to the table, and adjust the column widths if necessary.
    e. Enter your name in the center section of the worksheet footer, then save the workbook.

2. **Add table data.**
    a. Add a new record in row seven for **Hank Worthen**, a 5-year employee as an X-Ray Tech. Hank works full time and has completed training. Adjust the height of the new row to match the other table rows.
    b. Insert a table row above Jay Kelly's record, and add a new record for **Stacy Atkins**. Stacy works full time, has worked at the clinic for 2 years as a Phlebotomy Tech, and has not completed training.
    c. Insert a new data field in cell G1 with a label **Weeks Vacation**. Widen the column to fit the label.
    d. Add a new column to the table by dragging the table's sizing handle, and give the new field a label of **Employee #**. Widen the column to fit the label.
    e. Save the file.

3. **Find and replace table data.**
    a. Return to cell A1.
    b. Open the Find and Replace dialog box and if necessary uncheck the Match Case option. Find the first record that contains the text **X-Ray Tech**.
    c. Find the second and third records that contain the text **X-Ray Tech**.
    d. Replace all **Tech** text in the table with **Technician**, widen Column D to fit the new data, then save the file.

Skills Review (continued)

4. Delete table data.

   a. Go to cell A1.

   b. Delete the record for Sally Lee.

   c. Use the Remove Duplicates button to confirm that the table does not have any duplicate records.

   d. Delete the Employee # table column, then delete its column header, if necessary.

   e. Save the file.

5. Sort table data.

   a. Sort the table by years employed in largest to smallest order.

   b. Sort the table by last name in A to Z order.

   c. Perform a multilevel sort: Sort the table first by Full/Part Time in A to Z order and then by last name in A to Z order.

   d. Check the table to make sure the records appear in the correct order.

   e. Save the file.

6. Use formulas in a table.

   a. In cell G2, enter the formula that calculates an employee's vacation time; base the formula on the clinic's policy that employees working at the clinic less than 3 years have 2 weeks of vacation. At 3 years of employment and longer, an employee has 3 weeks of vacation time. Use the table's field names where appropriate. (*Hint*: The formula is: =IF([Years Employed]<3,2,3.)

   b. Check the table to make sure the formula filled into the cells in column G and that the correct vacation time is calculated for all cells in the column.

   c. Add a Total Row to display the total number of vacation weeks.

   d. Change the function in the Total Row to display the average number of vacation weeks.

   e. Compare your table to Figure G-23, then save the workbook.

FIGURE G-23

	A	B	C	D	E	F	G	H
1	Last Name	First Name	Years Employed	Position	Full/Part Time	Training Completed	Weeks Vacation	
2	Atkins	Stacy	2	Phlebotomy Technician	F	N	2	
3	Guan	Joyce	1	Phlebotomy Technician	F	N	2	
4	Kelly	Jay	1	Phlebotomy Technician	F	Y	2	
5	Worthen	Hank	5	X-Ray Technician	F	Y	3	
6	Murray	Donato	3	X-Ray Technician	P	N	3	
7	Rand	Mimi	1	X-Ray Technician	P	Y	2	
8	Total						2.333333333	
9								
10								

7. Print a table.

   a. Add a header that reads **Employees** in the center section, then format the header in bold with a font size of 16.

   b. Add column A as a print title that repeats at the left of each printed page.

   c. Preview your table to check that the last names appear on both pages.

   d. Change the page orientation to landscape, save the workbook.

   e. Submit your worksheet to your instructor. Close the workbook, then exit Excel.

Managing Data Using Tables

Independent Challenge 1

You are working on a marketing initiative at a community health clinic. You decide to organize the results of an advertising survey using an Excel worksheet. You will create a table using the data, and analyze the survey results to help focus the clinic's advertising expenses in the most successful areas.

a. Start Excel, open the file EMP G-3.xlsx from the drive and folder where you store your Data Files, then save it as **EMP G-Survey Results**.

b. Create a table from the worksheet data, and apply Table Style Light 16. Widen the columns as necessary to display the table data.

c. Add the two records shown in Table G-4 to the table:

TABLE G-4

Last Name	First Name	Street Address	City	State	Zip	Area Code	Ad Source
Ross	Cathy	92 Arrow St.	Seattle	WA	98101	206	TV
Jones	Sarah	402 9th St.	Seattle	WA	98001	206	Newspaper

d. Find the record for Mary Riley, then delete it.

e. Click cell A1 and replace all instances of **TV** with **Cable TV**. Compare your table to Figure G-24.

FIGURE G-24

	A	B	C	D	E	F	G	H	I	J	K
1	Last Name	First Name	Street Address	City	State	Zip	Area Code	Ad Source			
2	Kelly	Karen	19 North St.	San Francisco	CA	94177	415	Newspaper			
3	Johnson	Mel	Hamilton Park St.	San Francisco	CA	94107	415	Newspaper			
4	Markette	Kathy	1 Spring St.	San Luis	CA	94018	510	Radio			
5	Worthen	Sally	2120 Central St.	San Francisco	CA	93772	415	Retail Website			
6	Herbert	Greg	1192 Dome St.	San Diego	CA	93303	619	Newspaper			
7	Chavez	Jane	11 Northern St.	San Diego	CA	92208	619	Cable TV			
8	Chelly	Yvonne	900 Sola St.	San Diego	CA	92106	619	Retail Website			
9	Smith	Carolyn	921 Lopez St.	San Diego	CA	92104	619	Newspaper			
10	Oren	Scott	72 Yankee St.	Brookfield	CT	06830	203	Health Website			
11	Warner	Salvatore	100 Westside St.	Chicago	IL	60620	312	Newspaper			
12	Roberts	Bob	56 Water St.	Chicago	IL	60618	771	Retail Website			
13	Miller	Hope	111 Stratton St.	Chicago	IL	60614	773	Newspaper			
14	Duran	Maria	Galvin St.	Chicago	IL	60614	773	Health Website			
15	Roberts	Bob	56 Water St.	Chicago	IL	60614	312	Newspaper			
16	Graham	Shelley	989 26th St.	Chicago	IL	60611	773	Education Website			
17	Kelly	Janie	9 First St.	San Francisco	CA	94177	415	Newspaper			
18	Kim	Janie	9 First St.	San Francisco	CA	94177	415	Health Website			
19	Williams	Tasha	1 Spring St.	Reading	MA	03882	413	Newspaper			
20	Juarez	Manuel	544 Cameo St.	Belmont	MA	02483	617	Newspaper			
21	Masters	Latrice	88 Las Puntas Rd.	Boston	MA	02205	617	Education Website			
22	Kooper	Peter	671 Main St	Cambridge	MA	02138	617	Cable TV			
23	Kelly	Shawn	22 Kendall St.	Cambridge	MA	02138	617	Education Website			
24	Rodriguez	Virginia	123 Main St.	Boston	MA	02007	617	Radio			
25	Frei	Carol	123 Elm St.	Salem	MA	01970	978	Newspaper			
26	Stevens	Crystal	14 Waterford St.	Salem	MA	01970	508	Radio			
27	Ichikawa	Pam	232 Shore Rd.	Boston	MA	01801	617	Newspaper			
28	Paxton	Gail	100 Main St.	Woburn	MA	01801	508	Newspaper			
29	Spencer	Robin	293 Serenity Dr.	Concord	MA	01742	508	Radio			
30	Lopez	Luis	1212 City St.	Kansas City	MO	64105	816	Cable TV			
31	Nelson	Michael	229 Rally Rd.	Kansas City	MO	64105	816	Education Website			
32	Lee	Ginny	3 Way St.	Kansas City	MO	64102	816	Radio			

f. Remove duplicate records where all fields are identical.

g. Sort the list by Last Name in A to Z order.

h. Sort the list again by Area Code in Smallest to Largest order.

i. Sort the table first by State in A to Z order, then within the state, by Zip in Smallest to Largest order.

j. Enter your name in the center section of the worksheet footer.

k. Add a centered header that reads **Survey Data** in bold with a font size of 16.

l. Add print titles to repeat the first row at the top of printed pages.

m. Save the workbook, then preview it.

Advanced Challenge Exercise

- Create a print area that prints only the first six columns of the table.
- Print the print area.
- Clear the print area.

n. Save the workbook, close the workbook, submit the workbook to your instructor, then exit Excel.

Independent Challenge 2

You manage an orthopedic supply firm that sells products to physicians' offices. You sell four categories of products: Brace, Support, Insert, and Guard. The physicians' offices generally purchase items in quantities of 10 or more to have on hand when treating their patients. You decide to plan and build a table of sales information with eight records.

a. Prepare a plan for a table that states your goal, outlines the data you need, and identifies the table elements.

b. Sketch a sample table on a piece of paper, indicating how the table should be built. Create a table documenting the table design including the field names, type of data, and description of the data.

c. Start Excel, create a new workbook, then save it as **EMP G-Ortho Products** in the drive and folder where you store your Data Files. Enter the field names from Table G-6 in the designated cells.

d. Enter eight data records using your own data. The physician's practice name will be entered in the Customer column with the office contact in the adjacent Contact column. The categories are Brace, Support, Insert, and Guard.

e. Create a table using the data in the range A1:E9. Adjust the column widths as necessary.

f. Apply the Table Style Light 18 to the table.

g. Add a field named **Total** in cell F1.

h. Enter a formula to calculate the total (Quantity*Cost) in cell F2. Check that the formula was filled down in the column.

i. Format the Cost and Total columns using the Accounting number format with two decimal places and the dollar symbol ($). Adjust the column widths as necessary.

j. Add a new record to your table in row 10. Add another record above row 4.

k. Sort the table in ascending order by Category.

l. Enter your name in the worksheet footer, then save the workbook.

m. Preview the worksheet, then submit your worksheet to your instructor.

n. Close the workbook, then exit Excel.

TABLE G-6

cell	field name
A1	Customer
B1	Contact
C1	Category
D1	Quantity
E1	Cost

Independent Challenge 3

You are the project manager at a local firm that offers medical seminars. You are managing your accounts using an Excel worksheet and have decided that a table will provide additional features to help you keep track of the accounts. You will use the table sorting features and table formulas to analyze your account data.

a. Start Excel, open the file EMP G-4.xlsx from the drive and folder where you store your Data Files, then save it as **EMP G-Accounts**.

b. Create a table with the worksheet data, and apply Table Style Light 10. Adjust the column widths as necessary.

c. Sort the table on the Budget field using the Smallest to Largest order.

d. Sort the table using two fields, by Contact in A to Z order, then by Budget in Smallest to Largest order. Compare your table to Figure G-25.

FIGURE G-25

	A	B	C	D	E	F	G
1	Seminar	Date	Code	Budget	Expenses	Contact	
2	Electronic Medical Records	3/3/2013	AA1	$100,000	$30,000	Cathy Brown	
3	Health Care Corporate Compliance	3/14/2013	C43	$200,000	$170,000	Cathy Brown	
4	Electronic Medical Records	3/11/2013	V13	$390,000	$400,000	Cathy Brown	
5	Confidentiality of Medical Records	3/18/2013	C21	$450,000	$400,000	Cathy Brown	
6	Electronic Medical Records	3/23/2013	C43	$100,000	$150,000	Jill Saunders	
7	Confidentiality of Medical Records	3/21/2013	V53	$200,000	$210,000	Jill Saunders	
8	HIPAA Compliance	3/16/2013	V51	$300,000	$320,000	Jill Saunders	
9	HIPAA Compliance	3/1/2013	AA5	$500,000	$430,210	Jill Saunders	
10	Health Care Corporate Compliance	3/7/2013	A3A	$200,000	$210,000	Kim Jess	
11	HIPAA Compliance	3/9/2013	B12	$810,000	$700,000	Kim Jess	
12							

Independent Challenge 3 (continued)

e. Add the new field label **Balance** in cell G1, and adjust the column width as necessary.

f. Enter a formula in cell G2 that uses structured references to table fields to calculate the balance on an account as the Budget minus the Expenses. Format the Balance column using the Currency format with no decimal places and the dollar symbol ($).

g. Add a new record for a conference named **Confidentiality of Medical Records** with a date of **3/2/2013**, a code of **AB2**, a budget of **$300,000**, expenses of **$150,000**, and a contact of **Cathy Brown**.

h. Verify that the formula accurately calculated the balance for the new record.

i. Replace all of the Jill Saunders data with **Jill Jones**.

j. Enter your name in the center section of the worksheet footer, add a center section header of **Accounts** using formatting of your choice, change the page orientation to landscape, then save the workbook.

Advanced Challenge Exercise

- Sort the table on the Balance field using the Smallest to Largest order.
- Use conditional formatting to format the cells of the table containing negative balances with a light red fill with dark red text.
- Sort the table using the Balance field with the order of no cell color on top.
- Format the table to emphasize the Balance column, and turn off the banded rows. (*Hint*: Use the Table Style Options on the Table Tools Design tab.)
- Compare your table with Figure G-26. Save the workbook.

FIGURE G-26

	A	B	C	D	E	F	G	H
1	Seminar	Date	Code	Budget	Expenses	Contact	Balance	
2	Health Care Corporate Compliance	3/14/2013	C43	$200,000	$170,000	Cathy Brown	$30,000	
3	Confidentiality of Medical Records	3/18/2013	C21	$450,000	$400,000	Cathy Brown	$50,000	
4	HIPAA Compliance	3/1/2013	AA5	$500,000	$430,210	Jill Jones	$69,790	
5	Electronic Medical Records	3/3/2013	AA1	$100,000	$30,000	Cathy Brown	$70,000	
6	HIPAA Compliance	3/9/2013	B12	$810,000	$700,000	Kim Jess	$110,000	
7	Confidentiality of Medical Records	3/2/2013	AB2	$300,000	$150,000	Cathy Brown	$150,000	
8	Electronic Medical Records	3/23/2013	C43	$100,000	$150,000	Jill Jones	-$50,000	
9	HIPAA Compliance	3/16/2013	V51	$300,000	$320,000	Jill Jones	-$20,000	
10	Electronic Medical Records	3/11/2013	V13	$390,000	$400,000	Cathy Brown	-$10,000	
11	Confidentiality of Medical Records	3/21/2013	V53	$200,000	$210,000	Jill Jones	-$10,000	
12	Health Care Corporate Compliance	3/7/2013	A3A	$200,000	$210,000	Kim Jess	-$10,000	
13								
14								
15								

k. Submit the worksheet to your instructor, close the workbook, then exit Excel.

Real Life Independent Challenge

You have decided to organize your medical expenses for your health care savings account. These expenses may also be used for tax deduction purposes. You will use a table in Excel. You can add records to your table as you incur future medical expenses.

a. Using the fields Item, Provider, Date, and Amount, prepare a diagram of your table structure.

b. Document the table design by detailing the type of data that will be in each field and a description of the data. For example, in the Item field you may have copayment, deductible, aspirin, or other medical expenses.

c. Start Excel, create a new workbook, then save it as **EMP G-Health Expenses** in the drive and folder where you store your Data Files.

d. Enter the field names into the worksheet, enter the records for seven of your health expenses, then save the workbook.

e. Create a table that contains your health expense information. Resize the columns as necessary.

f. Choose a Table Style, and apply it to your table.

g. Add a new field with a label of **Comments**. Enter information in the new table column providing additional information about the expense.

h. Add a record to the table for another health expense.

i. Sort the records by the Date field using Oldest to Newest.

j. Add a Total row to your table, and verify that the Sum function accurately calculated the total in the Amount column.

k. Enter your name in the worksheet footer, then save the workbook.

l. Submit the worksheet to your instructor, close the workbook, then exit Excel.

Visual Workshop

Start Excel, open the file EMP G-5.xlsx from the drive and folder where you store your Data Files, then save it as **EMP G-Cardiology**. Create the table and sort the data as shown in Figure G-27. (*Hint*: The table is formatted using Table Style Medium 7.) Add a worksheet header with the file name in the center section that is formatted in bold with a size of 14. Enter your name in the center section of the worksheet footer. Save the workbook, preview the table, close the workbook, submit the worksheet to your instructor, then exit Excel. (*Hint*: If your table includes Filter list arrows that need to be removed, you can click Filter on the Data tab.)

FIGURE G-27

	A	B	C	D	E
1	Order Number	Order date	Amount	Shipping	Sales Rep
2	1134	4/30/2013	$ 200,000	Air	Ellie Cranson
3	1465	11/15/2013	$ 210,000	Air	Ellie Cranson
4	7733	3/15/2013	$ 230,000	Air	Ellie Cranson
5	2889	2/15/2013	$ 300,000	Air	Ellie Cranson
6	1532	10/10/2013	$ 450,000	Air	Ellie Cranson
7	9345	1/15/2013	$ 100,000	Ground	Gene Coburn
8	5623	2/1/2013	$ 130,000	Air	Gene Coburn
9	1112	9/30/2013	$ 300,000	Ground	Gene Coburn
10	2156	6/1/2013	$ 500,000	Ground	Gene Coburn
11	2134	7/10/2013	$ 390,000	Ground	Neil Boxer
12	2144	12/15/2013	$ 810,000	Ground	Neil Boxer

Analyzing Table Data

Excel tables let you manipulate and analyze data in many ways. One way is to filter a table so that it displays only the rows that meet certain criteria. In this unit, you will display selected records using the AutoFilter feature, create a custom filter, and filter a table using an Advanced Filter. In addition, you will learn to insert automatic subtotals, use lookup functions to locate table entries, and apply database functions to summarize table data that meet specific criteria. You'll also learn how to restrict entries in a column by using data validation. RMC's office manager, Tony Sanchez, asks you to display information from a table of the first quarter January Physical Therapy procedures to help the therapists with patient inquiries. He also asks you to prepare summaries of the insurance reimbursements for a meeting with the clinic managers.

OBJECTIVES

Filter a table

Create a custom filter

Filter a table with the Advanced Filter

Extract table data

Look up values in a table

Summarize table data

Validate table data

Create subtotals

Filtering a Table

An Excel table lets you easily manipulate large amounts of data to view only the data you want, using a feature called **AutoFilter**. When you create a table, arrows automatically appear next to each column header. These arrows are called **filter list arrows**, **AutoFilter list arrows**, or **list arrows**, and you can use them to **filter** a table to display only the records that meet criteria you specify, temporarily hiding records that do not meet those criteria. For example, you can use the filter list arrow next to the Procedure field header to display only records that contain Physical Therapy E in the Procedure field. Once you filter data, you can copy, chart, and print the displayed records. You can easily clear a filter to redisplay all the records. Tony asks you to display only the records for the Therapeutic Activity B procedures. He also asks for information about the provider adjustments that have the most amount due and the procedures that were scheduled in February.

STEPS

1. **Start Excel, open the file** EMP H-1.xlsx **from the drive and folder where you save your Data Files, then save it as** EMP H-Procedures

2. **Click the** Procedure list arrow
   Sort options appear at the top of the menu, advanced filtering options appear in the middle, and at the bottom is a list of the procedure data from column A, as shown in Figure H-1. Because you want to display data for only the Therapeutic Activity B procedures, your **search criterion** (the text for which you are searching) is Therapeutic Activity B. You can select one of the Procedure data options in the menu, which acts as your search criterion.

QUICK TIP
You can also filter the table to display only the Therapeutic Activity B procedures information by clicking the Procedure list arrow, entering "Therapeutic Activity B" in the Search text box on the menu options below Text Filters, then clicking OK.

3. ▶ **In the list of procedures for the Procedure field, click** Select All **to clear the checks from the procedures, scroll down the list of procedures, click** Therapeutic Activity B, **then click** OK
   Only those records containing "Therapeutic Activity B" in the Procedure field appear, as shown in Figure H-2. The row numbers for the matching records change to blue, and the list arrow for the filtered field has a filter icon. Both indicate that there is a filter in effect and that some of the records are temporarily hidden.

4. **Move the pointer over the** Procedure list arrow
   The ScreenTip Procedure: Equals "Therapeutic Activity B" describes the filter for the field, meaning that only the Therapeutic Activity B records appear. You decide to remove the filter to redisplay all of the table data.

5. **Click the** Procedure list arrow, **then click** Clear Filter From "Procedure"
   You have cleared the Therapeutic Activity B filter, and all the records reappear. You want to display the procedure records that have the highest amount due to the clinic, those in the top five percent.

QUICK TIP
You can also filter or sort a table by the color of the cells if conditional formatting has been applied.

6. ▶ **Click the** Amount Due list arrow, **point to** Number Filters, **click** Top 10, **select** 10 **in the middle box, type** 5, **click the** Items list arrow, **click** Percent, **then click** OK
   Excel displays the records for the top five percent in the Amount Due field, as shown in Figure H-3. You decide to clear the filter to redisplay all the records.

7. **On the Home tab, click the** Sort & Filter button **in the Editing group, then click** Clear
   You can clear a filter using either the AutoFilter menu command or the Sort and Filter menu on the Home tab. You have cleared the filter and all the records reappear. The Sort and Filter button is convenient for clearing multiple filters at once. You want to find all of the procedures that were scheduled in February.

8. **Click the** Date list arrow, **point to** Date Filters, **point to** All Dates in the Period, **then click** February
   Excel displays the records for only the 15 procedures that were scheduled in February. You decide to clear the filter and display all of the records.

QUICK TIP
You can also clear a filter by clicking the Clear button in the Sort & Filter group on the Data tab.

9. ▶ **Click the** Sort & Filter button **in the Editing group, click** Clear, **then save the workbook**

FIGURE H-1: Worksheet showing filter options

Procedure Filter list arrow

Sort options

Advanced filtering options

List of procedures

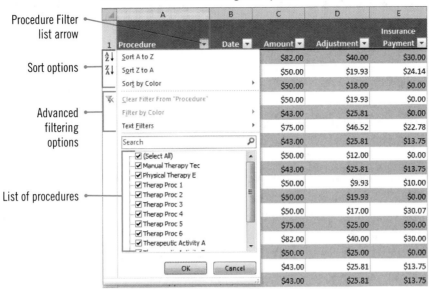

FIGURE H-2: Table filtered to show Therapeutic Activity B procedures

List arrow changed to filter icon

Matching row numbers are blue and sequence indicates that not all rows appear

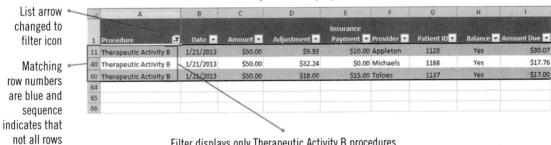

Filter displays only Therapeutic Activity B procedures

	A	B	C	D	E	F	G	H	I
					Insurance				
1	Procedure	Date	Amount	Adjustment	Payment	Provider	Patient ID	Balance	Amount Due
11	Therapeutic Activity B	1/21/2013	$50.00	$9.93	$10.00	Appleton	1128	Yes	$30.07
40	Therapeutic Activity B	1/21/2013	$50.00	$32.24	$0.00	Michaels	1168	Yes	$17.76
60	Therapeutic Activity B	1/21/2013	$50.00	$18.00	$15.00	Toloes	1137	Yes	$17.00

FIGURE H-3: Table filtered with top 5% of Amount Due

	A	B	C	D	E	F	G	H	I
					Insurance				
1	Procedure	Date	Amount	Adjustment	Payment	Provider	Patient ID	Balance	Amount Due
19	Physical Therapy E	1/20/2013	$165.00	$83.24	$0.00	March	1182	Yes	$81.76
31	Physical Therapy E	1/8/2013	$165.00	$83.24	$0.00	Michaels	1183	Yes	$81.76
47	Physical Therapy E	3/28/2013	$165.00	$32.88	$65.41	Sonna	1169	Yes	$66.71

Table filtered with top 5% in this field

Analyzing Table Data

Creating a Custom Filter

While AutoFilter lists can display records that are equal to certain amounts, you will often need more detailed filters. You can use more complex filters with the help of options in the Custom AutoFilter dialog box. For example, your criteria can contain comparison operators such as "greater than" or "less than" that let you display values above or below a certain amount. You can also use **logical conditions** like And and Or to narrow a search even further. You can have Excel display records that meet a criterion in a field *and* another criterion in that same field. This is often used to find records between two values. For example, by specifying an And logical condition, you can display records for customers with incomes between $40,000 *and* $70,000. You can also have Excel display records that meet either criterion in a field by specifying an Or condition. The Or condition is used to find records that satisfy either of two values. For example, in a table of book data you can use the Or condition to find records that contain either Beginning *or* Introduction in the title name. Tony wants to locate manual and physical procedure records for patients at the RMC Physical Therapy clinic. He also wants to find procedures scheduled between January 15, 2013, and January 31, 2013. He asks you to create custom filters to find the procedures satisfying these criteria.

STEPS

1. **Click the** Procedure list arrow, **point to** Text Filters, **then click** Contains

   The Custom AutoFilter dialog box opens. You enter your criteria in the text boxes. The left text box on the first line currently displays "contains." You want to display procedures that contain the word "manual" in their names.

2. **Type** manual **in the right text box on the first line**

   You want to see entries that contain either manual or physical.

   QUICK TIP
   When specifying criteria in the Custom Filter dialog box, you can use the (?) wildcard to represent any single character and the (*) wildcard to represent any series of characters.

3. **Click the** Or option button **to select it, click the** left text box list arrow **on the second line, scroll to and select** contains, **then type** physical **in the right text box on the second line**

   Your completed Custom AutoFilter dialog box should match Figure H-4.

4. **Click** OK

   The dialog box closes, and only those records having "manual" or "physical" in the Procedure field appear in the worksheet. You want to find all procedures scheduled between January 15, 2013 and January 31, 2013.

5. **Click the** Procedure list arrow, **click** Clear Filter From "Procedure", **click the** Date list arrow, **point to** Date Filters, **then click** Custom Filter

   The Custom AutoFilter dialog box opens. The word "equals" appears in the left text box on the first line. You want to find the dates that are between January 15, 2013 and January 31, 2013 (that is, after January 15 *and* before January 31).

6. **Click the** left text box list arrow **on the first line, click** is after, **then type** 1/15/2013 **in the right text box on the first line**

   The And condition is selected, which is correct.

7. **Click the** left text box list arrow **on the second line, select** is before, **type** 1/31/2013 **in the right text box on the second line, then click** OK

   The records displayed have dates between January 15, 2013, and January 31, 2013. Compare your records to those shown in Figure H-5.

8. **Click the** Date list arrow, **then click** Clear Filter From "Date"

   You have cleared the filter, and all the procedure records reappear.

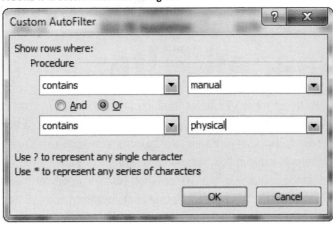

FIGURE H-4: **Custom AutoFilter dialog box**

FIGURE H-5: **Results of custom filter**

	A	B	C	D	E	F	G	H	I
1	Procedure	Date	Amount	Adjustment	Insurance Payment	Provider	Patient ID	Balance	Amount Due
2	Manual Therapy Tec	1/19/2013	$82.00	$40.00	$30.00	Appleton	1173	Yes	$12.00
3	Therap Proc 1	1/20/2013	$50.00	$19.93	$24.14	Appleton	1143	Yes	$5.93
9	Therap Proc 5	1/21/2013	$50.00	$12.00	$0.00	Appleton	1129	Yes	$38.00
11	Therapeutic Activity B	1/21/2013	$50.00	$9.93	$10.00	Appleton	1128	Yes	$30.07
15	Manual Therapy Tec	1/20/2013	$82.00	$40.00	$30.00	March	1174	Yes	$12.00
19	Physical Therapy E	1/20/2013	$165.00	$83.24	$0.00	March	1182	Yes	$81.76
20	Physical Therapy E	1/27/2013	$165.00	$88.33	$65.41	March	1187	Yes	$11.26
21	Therap Proc 2	1/21/2013	$50.00	$5.12	$0.00	March	1125	Yes	$44.88
27	Therapeutic Activity D	1/20/2013	$82.00	$32.99	$0.00	March	1170	Yes	$49.01
37	Therap Proc 4	1/20/2013	$50.00	$12.86	$24.14	Michaels	1131	Yes	$13.00
40	Therapeutic Activity B	1/21/2013	$50.00	$32.24	$0.00	Michaels	1168	Yes	$17.76
41	Therapeutic Activity D	1/17/2013	$82.00	$40.00	$0.00	Michaels	1172	Yes	$42.00
48	Therap Proc 3	1/19/2013	$50.00	$19.93	$24.14	Sonna	1145	Yes	$5.93
51	Therapeutic Activity Tec	1/18/2013	$82.00	$40.00	$30.00	Sonna	1176	Yes	$12.00
52	Manual Therapy Tec	1/27/2013	$75.00	$46.52	$22.78	Toloes	1177	Yes	$5.70
54	Therap Proc 1	1/24/2013	$43.00	$25.81	$13.75	Toloes	1163	Yes	$3.44
60	Therapeutic Activity B	1/21/2013	$50.00	$18.00	$15.00	Toloes	1137	Yes	$17.00
64									

Dates are between 1/15 and 1/31

Using more than one rule when conditionally formatting data

You can apply conditional formatting to table cells in the same way that you can format a range of worksheet data. You can add multiple rules by clicking the Home tab, clicking the Conditional Formatting button in the Styles group, then clicking New Rule for each additional rule that you want to apply. You can also add rules using the Conditional Formatting Rules Manager, which displays all of the rules for a data range. To use the Rules Manager, click the Home tab, click the Conditional Formatting button in the Styles group, click Manage Rules, then click New Rule for each rule that you want to apply to the data range. After you have applied conditional formatting such as color fills, icon sets, or color scales to a numeric table range, you can use AutoFilter to sort or filter based on the colors or symbols.

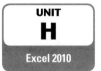
Filtering a Table with the Advanced Filter

If you would like to see more specific information in a table, such as date and insurance information for a specific procedure or procedures, then the Advanced Filter command is very helpful. Using the Advanced Filter, you can specify data that you want to display from the table using And and Or conditions. Rather than entering the criteria in a dialog box, you enter the criteria in a criteria range on your worksheet. A **criteria range** is a cell range containing one row of labels (usually a copy of the column labels) and at least one additional row underneath the row of labels that contains the criteria you want to match. Placing the criteria in the same row indicates that the records for which you are searching must match both criteria; that is, it specifies an **And condition**. Placing the criteria in the different rows indicates that the records for which you are searching must match only one of the criterion; that is, it specifies an **Or condition**. With the criteria range on the worksheet, you can easily see the criteria by which your table is sorted. You can also use the criteria range to create a macro using the Advanced Filter feature to automate the filtering process for data that you filter frequently. Another advantage of the Advanced Filter is that you can move filtered table data to a different area of the worksheet or to a new worksheet, as you will see in the next lesson. Tony wants to identify procedures performed before 1/15/2013 by the provider named Michaels. He asks you to use the Advanced Filter to retrieve these records. You begin by defining the criteria range.

STEPS

1. **Select table rows 1 through 6, click the Insert list arrow in the Cells group, click Insert Sheet Rows; click cell A1, type Criteria Range, then click the Enter button ✔ on the Formula bar**

   Six blank rows are added above the table. Excel does not require the label "Criteria Range", but it is useful to see the column labels as you organize the worksheet and use filters.

2. **Select the range A7:I7, click the Copy button ▣ in the Clipboard group, click cell A2, click the Paste button in the Clipboard group, then press [Esc]**

   Next, you want to insert criteria that will display records for only those procedures scheduled before January 15, 2013 performed by the provider Michaels.

3. **Click cell B3, type <1/15/2013, click cell F3, type Michaels, then click ✔**

   You have entered the criteria in the cells directly beneath the Criteria Range labels, as shown in Figure H-6.

4. **Click any cell in the table, click the Data tab, then click the Advanced button in the Sort & Filter group**

   The Advanced Filter dialog box opens, with the table (list) range already entered. The default setting under Action is to filter the table in its current location ("in-place") rather than copy it to another location.

5. **Click the Criteria range text box, select the range A2:I3 in the worksheet, then click OK**

   You have specified the criteria range and used the filter. The filtered table contains eight records that match both criteria—the date is before 1/15/2013 and the provider is Michaels, as shown in Figure H-7. You'll filter this table even further in the next lesson.

FIGURE H-6: **Criteria in the same row**

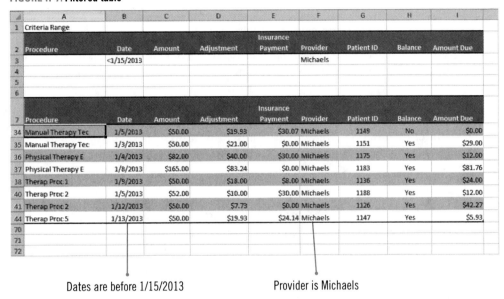

Filtered records will
match these criteria

FIGURE H-7: **Filtered table**

Dates are before 1/15/2013   Provider is Michaels

Using advanced conditional formatting options

You can emphasize top- or bottom-ranked values in a field using conditional formatting. To highlight the top or bottom values in a field, select the field data, click the Conditional Formatting button in the Styles group on the Home tab, point to Top/Bottom Rules, select a Top or Bottom rule, if necessary enter the percentage or number of cells in the selected range that you want to format, select the format for the cells that meet the top or bottom criteria, then click OK. You can also format your worksheet or table data using icon sets and color scales based on the cell values. A **color scale** uses a set of two, three, or four fill colors to convey relative values. For example, red could fill cells to indicate they have higher values and green could signify lower values. To add a color scale, select a data range, click the Home tab, click the Conditional

Formatting button in the Styles group, then point to Color Scales. On the submenu, you can select preformatted color sets or click More Rules to create your own color sets. **Icon sets** let you visually communicate relative cell values by adding icons to cells based on the values they contain. An upward-pointing green arrow might represent the highest values, and downward-pointing red arrows could represent lower values. To add an icon set to a data range, select a data range, click the Conditional Formatting button in the Styles group, then point to Icon Sets. You can customize the values that are used as thresholds for color scales and icon sets by clicking the Conditional Formatting button in the Styles group, clicking Manage Rules, clicking the rule in the Conditional Formatting Rules Manager dialog box, then clicking Edit Rule.

Extracting Table Data

Whenever you take the time to specify a complicated set of search criteria, it's a good idea to extract the matching records, rather than filtering it in place. When you **extract** data, you place a copy of a filtered table in a range that you specify in the Advanced Filter dialog box. This way, you won't accidentally clear the filter or lose track of the records you spent time compiling. To extract data, you use an Advanced Filter and enter the criteria beneath the copied field names, as you did in the previous lesson. You then specify the location where you want the extracted data to appear. Tony needs to filter the table one step further to reflect only the Therap Proc 1 and Therap Proc 2 procedures in the current filtered table. He asks you to complete this filter by specifying an Or condition, which you will do by entering two sets of criteria in two separate rows. You decide to save the filtered records by extracting them to a different location in the worksheet.

STEPS

1. **In cell A3, enter** Therap Proc 1, **then in cell A4, enter** Therap Proc 2

   The new sets of criteria need to appear in two separate rows, so you need to copy the previous filter criteria to the second row.

2. **Copy the criteria in B3:F3 to** B4:F4

   The criteria are shown in Figure H-8. When you use the Advanced Filter this time, you indicate that you want to copy the filtered table to a range beginning in cell A75, so that Tony can easily refer to the data, even if you use more filters later.

3. **If necessary, click the** Data tab, **then click** Advanced **in the Sort & Filter group**

4. **Under Action, click the** Copy to another location option button **to select it, click the** Copy to text box, **then type** A75

   The last time you filtered the table, the criteria range included only rows 2 and 3, and now you have criteria in row 4.

QUICK TIP

Make sure the criteria range in the Advanced Filter dialog box includes the field names and the number of rows underneath the names that contain criteria. If you leave a blank row in the criteria range, Excel filters nothing and shows all records.

5. **Edit the contents of the** Criteria range text box **to show the range** $A$2:$I$4, **click** OK, **then if necessary scroll down until row 75 is visible**

   The matching records appear in the range beginning in cell A75, as shown in Figure H-9. The original table, starting in cell A7, contains the records filtered in the previous lesson.

6. **Press** [Ctrl][Home], **add your name to the center section of the footer, then scale the worksheet width to print on one page**

7. **Save the workbook**

FIGURE H-8: **Criteria in separate rows**

	A	B	C	D	E	F	G	H	I
1	Criteria Range								
2	Procedure	Date	Amount	Adjustment	Insurance Payment	Provider	Patient ID	Balance	Amount Due
3	Therap Proc 1	<1/15/2013				Michaels			
4	Therap Proc 2	<1/15/2013				Michaels			
5									
6									

Criteria on two lines indicates an OR condition

FIGURE H-9: **Extracted data records**

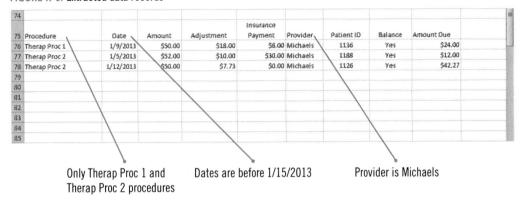

	A	B	C	D	E	F	G	H	I
74									
75	Procedure	Date	Amount	Adjustment	Insurance Payment	Provider	Patient ID	Balance	Amount Due
76	Therap Proc 1	1/9/2013	$50.00	$18.00	$8.00	Michaels	1136	Yes	$24.00
77	Therap Proc 2	1/5/2013	$52.00	$10.00	$30.00	Michaels	1188	Yes	$12.00
78	Therap Proc 2	1/12/2013	$50.00	$7.73	$0.00	Michaels	1126	Yes	$42.27
79									
80									
81									
82									
83									
84									
85									

Only Therap Proc 1 and Therap Proc 2 procedures   Dates are before 1/15/2013   Provider is Michaels

Understanding the criteria range and the copy-to location

When you define the criteria range and the copy-to location in the Advanced Filter dialog box, Excel automatically creates the range names Criteria and Extract for these ranges in the worksheet. The Criteria range includes the field names and any criteria rows underneath them. The Extract range includes just the field names above the extracted table. You can select these ranges by clicking the Name box list arrow, then clicking the range name. If you click the Name Manager button in the Defined Names group on the Formulas tab, you will see these new names and the ranges associated with each one.

Looking Up Values in a Table

The Excel VLOOKUP function helps you locate specific values in a table. VLOOKUP searches vertically (V) down the far left column of a table, then reads across the row to find the value in the column you specify, much as you might look up a number in a phone book: You locate a person's name, then read across the row to find the phone number you want. Tony wants to be able to find a procedure by entering the procedure code. You will use the VLOOKUP function to accomplish this task. You begin by viewing the table name so you can refer to it in a lookup function.

STEPS

QUICK TIP

You can change table names to better represent their content so they are easier to use in formulas. Click the table in the list of names in the Name Manager text box, click Edit, type the new table name in the Name text box, then click OK.

1. **Click the Lookup sheet tab, click the Formulas tab in the Ribbon, then click the Name Manager button in the Defined Names group**

   The named ranges for the workbook appear in the Name Manager dialog box, as shown in Figure H-10. The Criteria and Extract ranges appear at the top of the range name list. At the bottom of the list is information about the three tables in the workbook. Table1 refers to the table on the First Quarter sheet, Table2 refers to the table on the Lookup sheet, and Table3 refers to the table on the Subtotals worksheet. The Excel structured reference feature automatically created these table names when the tables were created.

2. **Click Close**

   You want to find the procedure name represented by the Procedure code 675Y. The VLOOKUP function lets you find the procedure name for any procedure code. You will enter a procedure code in cell L2 and a VLOOKUP function in cell M2.

3. **Click cell L2, enter 675Y, click cell M2, click the Lookup & Reference button in the Function Library group, then click VLOOKUP**

   The Function Arguments dialog box opens, with boxes for each of the VLOOKUP arguments. Because the value you want to find is in cell L2, L2 is the Lookup_value. The table you want to search is the table on the Lookup sheet, so its assigned name, Table2, is the Table_array.

QUICK TIP

If you want to find only the closest match for a value, enter TRUE in the Range_lookup text box. However, this can give misleading results if you are looking for an exact match. If you use FALSE and Excel can't find the value, you see an error message.

4. **With the insertion point in the Lookup_value text box, click cell L2, click the Table_array text box, then type Table2**

   The column containing the information that you want to find and display in cell M2 is the second column from the left in the table range, so the Col_index_num is 2. Because you want to find an exact match for the value in cell L1, the Range_lookup argument is FALSE.

5. **Click the Col_index_num text box, type 2, click the Range_lookup text box, then enter FALSE**

   Your completed Function Arguments dialog box should match Figure H-11.

6. **Click OK**

   Excel searches down the far-left column of the table until it finds a trip code that matches the one in cell L2. It then looks in column 2 of the table range and finds the procedure for that record, Physical Therapy E, and displays it in cell M2. You use this function to determine the procedure for one other procedure code.

7. **Click cell L2, type 439U, then click the Enter button ✔ on the formula bar**

   The VLOOKUP function returns the value of Therap Proc 5 in cell M2.

8. **Press [Ctrl][Home], then save the workbook**

Finding records using the DGET function

You can also use the DGET function to find a record in a table that matches specified criteria. For example, you could use the criteria of L1:L2 in the DGET function. When using DGET, you need to include [#All] after your table name in the formula to include the column labels that are used for the criteria range.

FIGURE H-10: Named ranges in the workbook

Created by Advanced Filter

Tables in the workbook

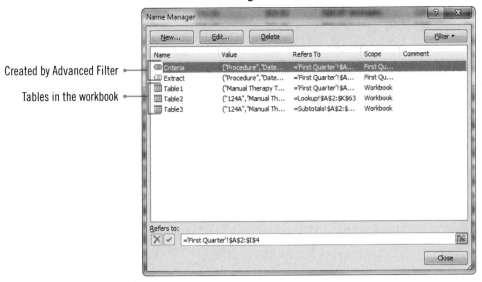

FIGURE H-11: Completed Function Arguments dialog box for VLOOKUP

Location of value for which you want to search

Range name of table to search

Number of column to search

Finds exact match

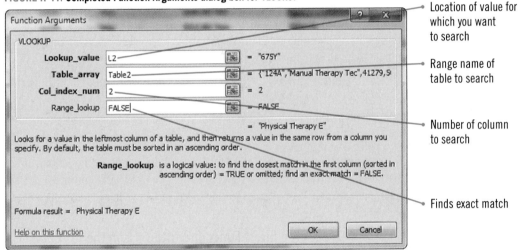

Using the HLOOKUP and MATCH functions

The VLOOKUP (Vertical Lookup) function is useful when your data is arranged vertically, in columns. When your data is arranged horizontally in rows, use the HLOOKUP (Horizontal Lookup) function. HLOOKUP searches horizontally across the upper row of a table until it finds the matching value, then looks down the number of rows you specify. The arguments for this function are identical to those for the VLOOKUP function, with one exception. Instead of a Col_index_ number, HLOOKUP uses a Row_index_number, which indicates the location of the row you want to search. For example, if you want to

search the fourth row from the top of the table range, the Row_index_number should be 4. You can use the MATCH function when you want the position of an item in a range. The MATCH function uses the syntax: MATCH (lookup_value,lookup_array,match_ type) where the lookup_value is the value you want to match in the lookup_array range. The match_type can be 0 for an exact match, 1 for matching the largest value that is less than or equal to lookup_ value, or –1 for matching the smallest value that is greater than or equal to the lookup_value.

Summarizing Table Data

Because a table acts much like a database, database functions allow you to summarize table data in a variety of ways. When working with insurance information, for example, you can use Excel to total the number of procedures performed by a provider or the total amount due for a provider's patients. Table H-1 lists database functions commonly used to summarize table data. ▓▓▒▒ Tony is reviewing the procedures performed in the first quarter of 2013. He needs your help in determining the number of procedures performed by certain providers as well as the amount owed by their patients.

STEPS

1. **Review the criteria range for the provider named March in the range L4:L5**

   The criteria range in L4:L5 specifies "March" is in the Provider column. The functions will be in cells N6 and N7. You use this criteria range in a DSUM function to sum the amount due for March's patients only.

2. **Click cell N6, click the Insert Function button in the Function Library group, in the Search for a function text box type database, click Go, click DSUM under Select a function, then click OK**

   The first argument of the DSUM function is the table, or database.

QUICK TIP

Because the DSUM formula uses the column headings to locate and sum the table data, the header row needs to be included in the database range.

3. **In the Function Arguments dialog box, with the insertion point in the Database text box, move the pointer over the upper-left corner of cell A1 until the pointer becomes ⬊, click once, then click again**

   The first click selects the table's data range, and the second click selects the entire table, including the header row. The second argument of the DSUM function is the label for the column that you want to sum. You want to total the amount due. The last argument for the DSUM function is the criteria that will be used to determine which values to total.

QUICK TIP

You can move the Function Arguments dialog box if it overlaps a cell or range that you need to click. You can also click the Collapse Dialog Box button [icon], select the cell or range, then click the Expand Dialog box button [icon] to return to the Function Arguments dialog box.

4. **Click the Field text box, then click cell J1, Amount Due; click the Criteria text box and select the range L4:L5**

   Your completed Function Arguments dialog box should match Figure H-12.

5. **Click OK**

   The result in cell N6 is 286.58. Excel totaled the information in the Amount Due column for those records that meet the criterion of Provider equals March. The DCOUNT and the DCOUNTA functions can help you determine the number of records meeting specified criteria in a database field. DCOUNTA counts the number of nonblank cells. You will use DCOUNTA to determine the number of procedures scheduled.

6. **Click cell N7, click the Insert Function button 𝑓ₓ on the formula bar, in the Search for a function text box type database, click Go, select DCOUNTA from the Select a function list, then click OK**

7. **With the insertion point in the Database text box, move the pointer over the upper-left corner of cell A1 until the pointer becomes ⬊, click once, click again to include the header row, click the Field text box and click cell B1, click the Criteria text box and select the range L4:L5, then click OK**

   The result in cell N7 is 13, and it indicates that there are 13 procedures performed by March. You also want to display the total amount due and number of procedures performed by Sonna.

8. **Click cell L5, type Sonna, then click the Enter button ✓ on the formula bar**

   Figure H-13 shows that the amount due for Sonna's patients is 195.09 and Sonna performed ten procedures.

FIGURE H-12: Completed Function Arguments dialog box for DSUM

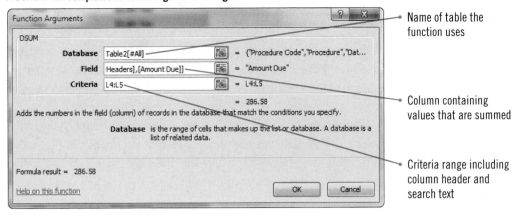

Name of table the function uses

Column containing values that are summed

Criteria range including column header and search text

FIGURE H-13: Result generated by database functions

	Insurance Payment	Provider	Patient ID	Balance	Amount Due	Authorization		Procedure Code	Procedure		
1											
2	$30.07	Michaels	1149	No	$0.00	Yes		439U	Therap Proc 5		
3	$50.00	Sonna	1156	No	$0.00	Yes					
4	$0.00	Sonna	1155	Yes	$50.00	No		**Provider**			
5	$30.00	Appleton	1173	Yes	$12.00	Yes		Sonna			
6	$30.00	March	1174	Yes	$12.00	Yes		Amount Due		195.09	
7	$0.00	Michaels	1151	Yes	$29.00	No		Number of procedures		10	
8	$0.00	March	1154	Yes	$25.00	No					
9	$13.75	March	1161	Yes	$3.44	Yes					

Information for provider Sonna

TABLE H-1: Common database functions

function	result
DGET	Extracts a single record from a table that matches criteria you specify
DSUM	Totals numbers in a given table column that match criteria you specify
DAVERAGE	Averages numbers in a given table column that match criteria you specify
DCOUNT	Counts the cells that contain numbers in a given table column that match criteria you specify
DCOUNTA	Counts the cells that contain nonblank data in a given table column that match criteria you specify

Validating Table Data

When setting up tables, you want to help ensure accuracy when you or others enter data. The Excel data validation feature allows you to do this by specifying what data users can enter in a range of cells. You can restrict data to whole numbers, decimal numbers, or text. You can also specify a list of acceptable entries. Once you've specified what data the program should consider valid for that cell, Excel displays an error message when invalid data is entered and can prevent users from entering any other data that it considers to be invalid. Tony wants to make sure that information in the Authorization column is entered consistently in the future. He asks you to restrict the entries in that column to two options: Yes and No. First, you select the table column you want to restrict.

STEPS

1. **Click the top edge of the Authorization column header**
   The column data is selected.

QUICK TIP

To specify a long list of valid entries, type the list in a column or row elsewhere in the worksheet, then type the list range in the Source text box.

2. **Click the Data tab, click the Data Validation button in the Data Tools group, click the Settings tab if necessary, click the Allow list arrow, then click List**
   Selecting the List option lets you type a list of specific options.

3. **Click the Source text box, then type Yes,No**
   You have entered the list of acceptable entries, separated by commas, as shown in Figure H-14. You want the data entry person to be able to select a valid entry from a drop-down list.

TROUBLE

If you get an invalid data error, make sure that cell K1 is not included in the selection. If K1 is included, open the Data Validation dialog box, click Clear All, click OK, then begin with Step 1 again.

4. **Click the In-cell dropdown check box to select it if necessary, then click OK**
   The dialog box closes, and you return to the worksheet.

5. **Click the Home tab, click any cell in the last table row, click the Insert list arrow in the Cells group, click Insert Table Row Below, click the last cell in the Authorization column, then click its list arrow to display the list of valid entries**
   The drop-down list is shown in Figure H-15. You could click an item in the list to have it entered in the cell, but you want to test the data restriction by entering an invalid entry.

6. **Click the list arrow to close the list, type Maybe, then press [Enter]**
   A warning dialog box appears and prevents you from entering the invalid data, as shown in Figure H-16.

7. **Click Cancel, click the list arrow, then click Yes**
   The cell accepts the valid entry. The data restriction ensures that records contain only one of the two correct entries in the Authorization column. The table is ready for future data entry.

8. **Delete the last table row, add your name to the center section of the footer, scale the worksheet width to print on one page, then save the workbook**

Restricting cell values and data length

In addition to providing an in-cell drop-down list for data entry, you can use data validation to restrict the values that are entered into cells. For example, if you want to restrict cells to values less than a certain number, date, or time, click the Data tab, click the Data Validation button in the Data Tools group, and on the Settings tab, click the Allow list arrow, select Whole number, Decimal, Date, or Time, click the Data list arrow, select less than, then in the bottom text box, enter the maximum value. You can also limit the length of data entered into cells by choosing Text length in the Allow list, clicking the Data list arrow and selecting less than, then entering the maximum length in the Maximum text box.

FIGURE H-14: Creating data restrictions

Restricts entries to a
list of valid options

List of valid options

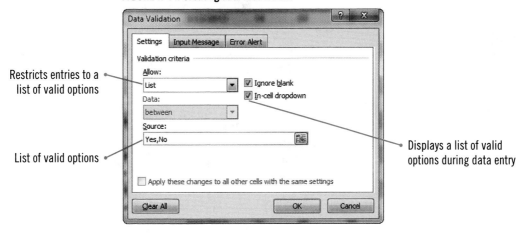

Displays a list of valid
options during data entry

FIGURE H-15: Entering data in restricted cells

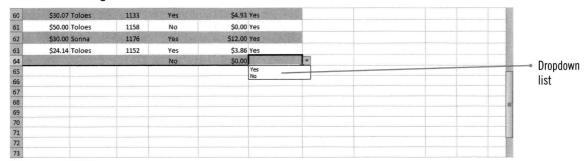

Dropdown
list

FIGURE H-16: Invalid data warning

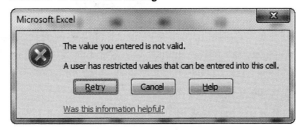

Adding input messages and error alerts

You can customize the way data validation works by using the two other tabs in the Data Validation dialog box: Input Message and Error Alert. The Input Message tab lets you set a message that appears when the user selects that cell. For example, the message might contain instructions about what type of data to enter. On the Input Message tab, enter a message title and message, then click OK. The Error Alert tab lets you set one of three alert levels if a user enters invalid data. The Information level displays your message with the information icon but allows the user to proceed with data entry. The Warning level displays your information with the warning icon and gives the user the option to proceed with data entry or not. The Stop level, which you used in this lesson, displays your message and only lets the user retry or cancel data entry for that cell.

Creating Subtotals

In a large range of data, you will often need ways to perform calculations that summarize groups within the data. For example, you might need to subtotal the amount due by providers listed in a table. The Excel Subtotals feature provides a quick, easy way to group and summarize a range of data. It lets you create not only subtotals using the SUM function, but other statistics as well, including COUNT, AVERAGE, MAX, and MIN. However, subtotals cannot be used in an Excel table, nor can it rearrange data. Before you can add subtotals to table data, you must first convert the data to a range and sort it. Tony wants you to group data by provider, with subtotals for the insurance payments and the amount due for the procedures. You begin by converting the table to a range.

STEPS

1. **Click the** Subtotals sheet tab, **click any cell inside the table, click the** Table Tools Design tab, **click the** Convert to Range button **in the Tools group, then click** Yes

   Before you can add the subtotals, you must first sort the data. You decide to sort it in ascending order, first by provider and then by date.

2. **Click the** Data tab, **click the** Sort button **in the Sort & Filter group, in the Sort dialog box click the** Sort by list arrow, **click** Provider, **then click the** Add Level button, **click the** Then by list arrow, **click** Date, **verify that the order is** Oldest to Newest, **then click** OK

   You have sorted the range in ascending order, first by provider, then by date.

3. **Click any cell in the data range, then click the** Subtotal button **in the Outline group**

   The Subtotal dialog box opens. Here you specify the items you want subtotaled, the function you want to apply to the values, and the fields you want to summarize.

4. **Click the** At each change in list arrow, **click** Provider, **click the** Use function list arrow, **click** Sum; **in the "Add subtotal to" list, click the** Insurance Payment **and** Amount Due check boxes **to select them, if necessary, then click any other selected check boxes to deselect them**

5. **If necessary, click the** Replace current subtotals **and** Summary below data check boxes **to select them**

   Your completed Subtotal dialog box should match Figure H-17.

6. **Click** OK, **then scroll down so you can see row 70**

   The subtotaled data appears, showing the calculated subtotals and grand total in columns F and J, as shown in Figure H-18. Excel displays an outline to the left of the worksheet, with outline buttons to control the level of detail that appears. The button number corresponds to the detail level that is displayed. You want to show the second level of detail, the subtotals and the grand total.

7. **Click the** outline symbol 2

   Only the subtotals and the grand total appear.

8. **Add your name to the center section of the footer, preview the worksheet, click the** Custom Scaling list arrow, **click** Fit Sheet on One Page **to scale the worksheet to print on one page, then save the workbook**

9. **Close the workbook, exit Excel, then submit the workbook to your instructor**

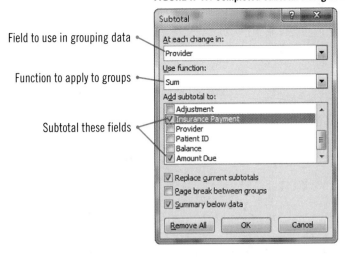

FIGURE H-17: **Completed Subtotal dialog box**

Field to use in grouping data

Function to apply to groups

Subtotal these fields

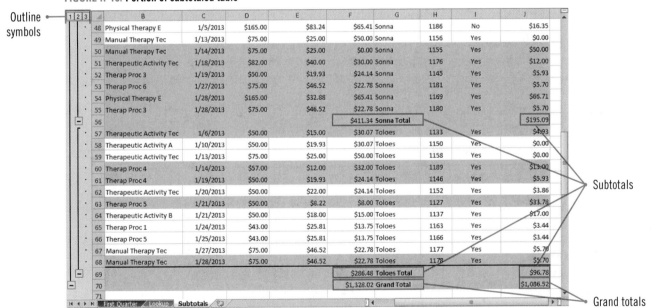

FIGURE H-18: **Portion of subtotaled table**

Outline symbols

Subtotals

Grand totals

Practice

Concepts Review

For current SAM information, including versions and content details, visit SAM Central (http://www.cengage.com/samcentral). If you have a SAM user profile, you may have access to hands-on instruction, practice, and assessment of the skills covered in this unit. Since various versions of SAM are supported throughout the life of this text, check with your instructor for the correct instructions and URL/Web site for accessing assignments.

FIGURE H-19

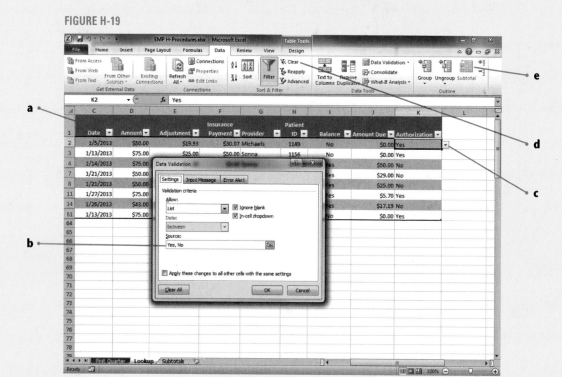

1. **Which element would you click to remove a filter?**
2. **Which element points to an in-cell drop-down list arrow?**
3. **Which element do you click to group and summarize data?**
4. **Which element points to a field's list arrow?**
5. **Where do you specify acceptable data entries for a table?**

Match each term with the statement that best describes it.

6. **Extracted table**
7. **Table_array**
8. **Criteria range**
9. **Data validation**
10. **DSUM**

  a. Cell range when Advanced Filter results are copied to another location
  b. Range in which search conditions are set
  c. Restricts table entries to specified options
  d. Name of the table searched in a VLOOKUP function
  e. Function used to total table values that meet specified criteria

Select the best answer from the list of choices.

11. **The _____ logical condition finds records matching both listed criteria.**
  a. And
  b. Or
  c. True
  d. False

12. **What does it mean when you select the Or option when creating a custom filter?**
  a. Either criterion can be true to find a match.
  b. Neither criterion has to be 100% true.
  c. Both criteria must be true to find a match.
  d. A custom filter requires a criteria range.

Skills Review

1. Filter a table.

a. Start Excel, open the file EMP H-2.xlsx from the drive and folder where you store your Data Files, then save it as **EMP H-Salary Summary**.

b. With the Compensation sheet active, filter the table to list only records for employees in the Radiology Department.

c. Clear the filter, then add a filter that displays the records for employees in the Radiology and Cardiology Departments.

d. Redisplay all employees, then use a filter to show the three employees with the highest annual salary.

e. Redisplay all the records.

2. Create a custom filter.

a. Create a custom filter showing employees hired before 1/1/2010 or after 12/31/2010.

b. Create a custom filter showing employees hired between 1/1/2010 and 12/31/2010.

c. Enter your name in the worksheet footer, then preview the filtered worksheet.

d. Redisplay all records.

e. Save the workbook.

3. Filter and extract a table with the Advanced Filter.

a. You want to retrieve a list of employees who were hired before 1/1/2011 and who have an annual salary of more than $70,000 a year. Define a criteria range by inserting six new rows above the table on the worksheet and copying the field names into the first row.

b. In cell D2, enter the criterion **<1/1/2011**, then in cell G2 enter **>70000**.

c. Click any cell in the table.

d. Open the Advanced Filter dialog box.

e. Indicate that you want to copy to another location, enter the criteria range **A1:J2**, verify that the List range is **$A$7:$J$17**, then indicate that you want to place the extracted list in the range starting at cell **A20**.

f. Confirm that the retrieved list meets the criteria as shown in Figure H-20.

g. Save the workbook, then preview the worksheet.

FIGURE H-20

4. Look up values in a table.

a. Click the Summary sheet tab. Use the Name Manager to view the table names in the workbook, then close the dialog box.

b. You will use a lookup function to locate an employee's annual compensation; enter the Employee Number **2214** in cell A17.

c. In cell B17, use the VLOOKUP function and enter **A17** as the Lookup_value, **Table2** as the Table_array, **10** as the Col_index_num, and **FALSE** as the Range_lookup; observe the compensation displayed for that employee number, then check it against the table to make sure it is correct.

d. Enter another Employee Number, **4177**, in cell A17, and view the annual compensation for that employee.

e. Format cell B17 with the Accounting format with the $ symbol and no decimal places.

f. Save the workbook.

5. Summarize table data.

a. You want to enter a database function to average the annual salaries by department, using the Emergency Medicine as the initial criterion. In cell E17, use the DAVERAGE function, and click the upper-left corner of cell A1 twice to select the table and its header row as the Database, select cell G1 for the Field, and select the range D16:D17 for the Criteria. Verify that the average Emergency Medicine salary is 91480.

b. Test the function further by entering the text **Radiology** in cell D17. When the criterion is entered, cell E17 should display 58500.

Skills Review (continued)

   c. Format cell E17 in Accounting format with the $ symbol and no decimal places.

   d. Save the workbook.

6. Validate table data.

   a. Select the data in column E of the table, and set a validation criterion specifying that you want to allow a list of valid options.

   b. Enter a list of valid options that restricts the entries to **Radiology**, **Cardiology**, and **Emergency Medicine**. Remember to use a comma between each item in the list.

   c. Indicate that you want the options to appear in an in-cell drop-down list, then close the dialog box.

   d. Add a row to the table. Go to cell E12, then select Cardiology in the drop-down list.

   e. Select the data in column F in the table, and indicate that you want to restrict the data entered to only whole numbers. In the Minimum text box, enter **1000**; in the Maximum text box, enter **10000**. Close the dialog box.

   f. Click cell F12, enter **15000**, then press [Enter]. You should get an error message.

   g. Click Cancel, then enter **7000**.

   h. Complete the new record by adding an Employee Number of **1112**, a First Name of **Caroline**, a Last Name of **Schissel**, a Hire Date of **2/1/2013**, and a Retirement Contribution of **1000**. Format the range F12:J12 as Accounting with no decimal places and using the $ symbol. Compare your screen to Figure H-21.

FIGURE H-21

	A	B	C	D	E	F	G	H	I	J
1	Employee Number	First Name	Last Name	Hire Date	Department	Monthly Salary	Annual Salary	Retirement Contribution	Benefits Dollars	Annual Compensation
2	1210	Maria	Lawson	2/12/2010	Radiology	$ 4,600	$ 55,200	$ 1,350	$ 12,696	$ 69,246
3	4510	Laurie	Warton	4/1/2011	Cardiology	$ 5,900	$ 70,800	$ 5,700	$ 16,284	$ 92,784
4	4177	Donna	Donnolly	5/6/2009	Emergency Medicine	$ 7,500	$ 90,000	$ 15,000	$ 20,700	$ 125,700
5	2571	Maria	Marlin	12/10/2010	Radiology	$ 8,500	$ 102,000	$ 18,000	$ 23,460	$ 143,460
6	2214	John	Greeley	2/16/2012	Radiology	$ 2,900	$ 34,800	$ 570	$ 8,004	$ 43,374
7	6587	Peter	Erickson	3/25/2010	Cardiology	$ 2,775	$ 33,300	$ 770	$ 7,659	$ 41,729
8	2123	Erin	Mallo	6/23/2009	Cardiology	$ 3,990	$ 47,880	$ 2,500	$ 11,012	$ 61,392
9	4439	Martin	Meng	8/3/2012	Emergency Medicine	$ 6,770	$ 81,240	$ 5,000	$ 18,685	$ 104,925
10	9807	Harry	Rumeriz	9/29/2011	Emergency Medicine	$ 8,600	$ 103,200	$ 14,000	$ 23,736	$ 140,936
11	3944	Joyce	Roberts	5/12/2010	Radiology	$ 3,500	$ 42,000	$ 900	$ 9,660	$ 52,560
12	1112	Caroline	Schissel	2/1/2013	Cardiology	$ 7,000	$ 84,000	$ 1,000	$ 19,320	$ 104,320
13										
14										
15										
16										
17	Employee Number	Annual Compensation		Department		Average Annual Salary				
18	4177	$ 125,700		Radiology		$ 58,500				
19										
20										

   i. Add your name to the center section of the footer, save the worksheet, then preview the worksheet.

7. Create subtotals.

   a. Click the Subtotals sheet tab.

   b. Use the Department field list arrow to sort the table in ascending order by department.

   c. Convert the table to a range.

   d. Group and create subtotals of the Annual Compensation data by department, using the SUM function.

   e. Click the 2 outline button on the outline to display only the subtotals and the grand total. Compare your screen to Figure H-22.

   f. Enter your name in the worksheet footer, save the workbook, then preview the worksheet.

FIGURE H-22

	A	B	C	D	E	F	G	H	I	J
1	Employee Number	First Name	Last Name	Hire Date	Department	Monthly Salary	Annual Salary	Retirement Contribution	Benefits Dollars	Annual Compensation
5					Cardiology Total					$ 195,905
9					Emergency Medicine Total					$ 371,561
14					Radiology Total					$ 308,640
15					Grand Total					$ 876,107
16										
17										
18										

   g. Save the workbook, close the workbook, exit Excel, then submit your workbook to your instructor.

Independent Challenge 1

As the manager of Miami Dental, a dental supply company, you spend a lot of time managing your inventory. To help with this task, you have created an Excel table from which you can extract information using filters. You also need to add data validation and summary information to the table.

   a. Start Excel, open the file EMP H-3.xlsx from the drive and folder where you store your Data Files, then save it as **EMP H-Dental**.

   b. Using the table data on the Inventory sheet, create a filter to display information about only the product bond refill. Clear the filter.

Independent Challenge 1 (continued)

c. Use a Custom Filter to generate a list of products with a quantity greater than 20. Clear the filter.

d. Copy the labels in cells A1:F1 into A16:F16. Type **Bond Refill** in cell A17, and type **Small** in cell C17. Use the Advanced Filter with a criteria range of A16:F17 to extract a table of small bond refills to the range of cells beginning in cell A20. Enter your name in the worksheet footer, save the workbook, then preview the worksheet.

e. Click the Summary sheet tab, select the table data in column B. Open the Data Validation dialog box, then indicate you want to use a validation list with the acceptable entries of **Berkley**, **Bromen**, **Lincoln**, **Mallory**. Make sure the In-cell dropdown check box is selected.

f. Test the data validation by trying to change a cell in column B of the table to **Loring**.

g. Using Figure H-23 as a guide, enter a function in cell E18 that calculates the total quantity of bond refill available in your inventory. Enter your name in the worksheet footer, preview the worksheet, then save the workbook.

h. On the Subtotals sheet, sort the table in ascending order by product. Convert the table to a range. Insert subtotals by product using the subtotal function, then select Quantity in the "Add subtotal to" box. Remove the check box for the Total field, if necessary. Use the appropriate button on the outline to display only the subtotals and grand total. Save the workbook, then preview the worksheet.

FIGURE H-23

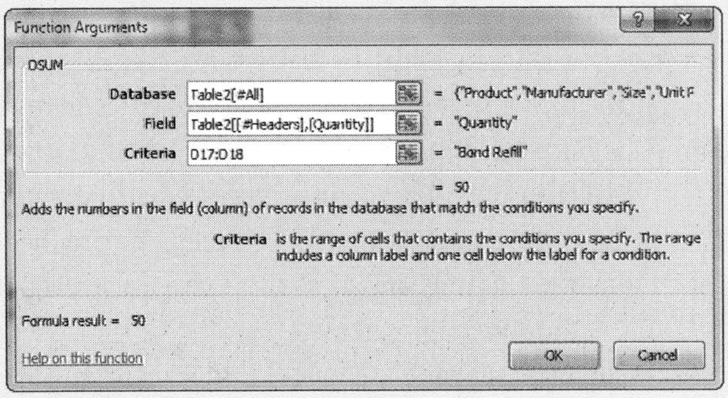

Advanced Challenge Exercise

ACE

- Clear the subtotals from the worksheet.
- Use conditional formatting to add icons to the quantity field using the following criteria: quantities greater than or equal to 20 are formatted with a green check mark, quantities greater than or equal to 10 but less than 20 are formatted with a yellow exclamation point, and quantities less than 10 are formatted with a red x. Use Figure H-24 as a guide to adding the formatting rule, then compare your Quantity values to Figure H-25. (*Hint*: You may need to click in the top Value text box for the correct value to display for the red x.)
- Save the workbook then preview the worksheet.

i. Submit the workbook to your instructor. Close the workbook, then exit Excel.

FIGURE H-24

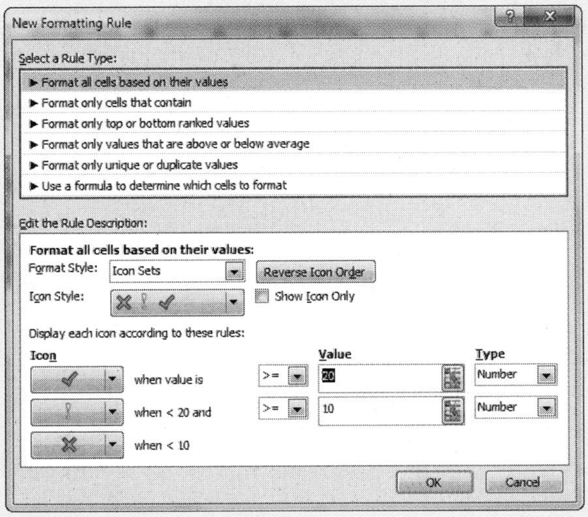

FIGURE H-25

	A	B	C	D	E	F
1	Product	Manufacturer	Size	Unit Price	Quantity	Total
2	Bond Refill	Berkley	Small	$6.55	! 12	$78.60
3	Bond Refill	Bromen	Medium	$10.25	! 11	$112.75
4	Bond Refill	Lincoln	Small	$6.25	✔ 21	$131.25
5	Bond Refill	Mallory	Small	$6.75	✖ 6	$40.50
6	Composite Kit	Berkley	Medium	$33.99	! 11	$373.89
7	Composite Kit	Mallory	Medium	$34.19	✔ 24	$820.56
8	Composite Syringe	Berkley	Small	$21.97	✖ 5	$109.85
9	Composite Syringe	Lincoln	Small	$21.88	✔ 31	$678.28
10	Masking Agent	Bromen	Small	$30.39	! 12	$364.68
11	Masking Agent	Lincoln	Medium	$42.99	! 18	$773.82
12	Mixing Well	Lincoln	Medium	$25.19	! 15	$377.85
13	Mixing Well	Mallory	Small	$19.99	✖ 8	$159.92

Excel 2010

Independent Challenge 2

You work for a medical supply company called Boston Medical Supplies based in Massachusetts. The business sells medical supplies to area clinics and hospitals. Customers order from sales representatives in the main Boston office as well as the newer Salem location. You have put together an invoice table to track sales for the month of October. Now that you have this table, you would like to manipulate it in several ways. First, you want to filter the table to show only invoices over a certain amount with certain order dates. You also want to subtotal the total order amount for each office. To prevent data entry errors you will restrict entries in the Order Date column. Finally, you would like to add database and lookup functions to your worksheet to efficiently retrieve data from the table.

a. Start Excel, open the file EMP H-4.xlsx from the drive and folder where you store your Data Files, then save it as **EMP H-Medical Supplies**.

b. Use the Advanced Filter to show invoices with amounts more than $3,000.00 ordered before 10/15/2013, using cells A27:B28 to enter your criteria and extracting the results to cell A33. (*Hint*: You don't need to specify an entire row as the criteria range.) Enter your name in the worksheet footer.

c. Use the Data Validation dialog box to restrict entries to those with order dates between 10/1/2013 and 10/31/2013. Test the data restrictions by attempting to enter an invalid date in cell D25.

d. Enter **23721** in cell D28. Enter a VLOOKUP function in cell E28 to retrieve the total based on the invoice number entered in cell D28. Make sure you have an exact match with the invoice number. Test the function with the invoice number **23718**.

e. Enter the date **10/1/2013** in cell G28. Use the database function, DCOUNT, in cell H28 to count the number of invoices for the date in cell G28. Save the workbook, then preview the worksheet.

f. On the Subtotals worksheet, sort the table in ascending order by Office, then convert the table to a range. Create subtotals showing the totals for the Boston and Salem offices. Adjust the column widths if necessary to display the totals. (*Hint*: Sum the Total field.) Display only the subtotals for the Boston and Salem offices along with the grand total. Enter your name in the worksheet footer.

g. Save the workbook, preview the worksheet, close the workbook, then exit Excel. Submit the workbook to your instructor.

Independent Challenge 3

As the office manager for an occupational therapy clinic, you keep track of the patients' reimbursement data. The therapists work on teams at the clinic and you have been asked to supply information for each team on a monthly basis. You begin by creating a table for the January appointments which you will manipulate using database functions and subtotals to provide each team with a summary of its reimbursements.

a. Start Excel, open the file EMP H-5.xlsx from the drive and folder where you store your Data Files, then save it as **EMP H-OT Clinic**.

b. Create an advanced filter that extracts records with the following criteria to cell A42: reimbursed amounts greater than $2,000 having Beginning Dates either before 1/10/2013 or after 1/24/2013. (*Hint*: Recall that when you want records to meet one criterion or another, you need to place the criteria on separate lines.) Enter your name in the worksheet footer.

c. Use the DSUM function in cell H2 to let worksheet users find the total reimbursed amounts for the team entered in cell G2. Format the cell containing the total reimbursed amount using the Accounting format with the $ symbol and no decimals. Test the DSUM function using the D Team. (The sum for the D Team should be $7,880.) Preview the worksheet.

d. Use data validation to create an in-cell drop-down list that restricts team entries to A, B, C, or D. Use the Error Alert tab of the Data Validation dialog box to set the alert level to the Warning style with the message "Data is not valid." Test the validation in the table with valid and invalid entries. Save the workbook, then preview the worksheet.

e. Using the Subtotals sheet, sort the table by team in ascending order. Convert the table to a range, and add Subtotals to the reimbursed amounts by team. Adjust column widths as necessary to see all of the totals and labels.

f. Use the outline to display only team names with subtotals and the grand total. Enter your name in the worksheet footer.

Independent Challenge 3 (continued)

Advanced Challenge Exercise

- Clear the subtotals from the worksheet.
- Conditionally format the Reimbursed Amount data using Top/Bottom Rules to emphasize the cells containing the top 10 percent with yellow fill and dark yellow text.
- Add another rule to format the bottom 10 percent in the Reimbursed Amount column with a light red fill.

g. Save the workbook, then preview the worksheet.

h. Close the workbook, exit Excel, then submit the workbook to your instructor.

Real Life Independent Challenge

You decide to organize your business and personal contacts using the Excel table format to allow you to easily look up contact information. You want to include addresses and a field documenting whether the contact relationship is personal or business. You enter your contact information in an Excel worksheet that you will convert to a table so you can easily filter the data. You also use lookup functions to locate phone numbers when you provide a last name in your table. Finally, you restrict the entries in the Relationship field to values in drop-down lists to simplify future data entry and reduce errors.

a. Start Excel, open a new workbook, then save it as **EMP H-Contacts** in the drive and folder where you store your Data Files.

b. Use the structure of Table H-2 to enter at least six of your personal and business contacts into a worksheet. (*Hint*: You will need to format the Zip column using the Zip Code type of the Special category.) In the Relationship field, enter either Business or Personal. If you don't have phone numbers for all the phone fields, leave them blank.

TABLE H-2

Last name	First name	Cell phone	Home phone	Work phone	Street address	City	State	Zip	Relationship

c. Use the worksheet information to create a table. Use the Name Manager dialog box to edit the table name to **Contacts**.

d. Create a filter that retrieves records of personal contacts. Clear the filter.

e. Create a filter that retrieves records of business contacts. Clear the filter.

f. Restrict the Relationship field entries to Business or Personal. Provide an in-cell drop-down list allowing the selection of these two options. Add an input message of **Select from the dropdown list**. Add an Information-level error message of **Choose Business or Personal**. Test the validation by adding a new record to your table.

g. Below your table, create a phone lookup area with the following labels in adjacent cells: **Last name**, **Cell phone**, **Home phone**, **Work phone**.

h. Enter one of the last names from your table under the label Last name in your phone lookup area.

i. In the phone lookup area, enter lookup functions to locate the cell phone, home phone, and work phone numbers for the contact last name that you entered in the previous step. Make sure you match the last name exactly.

j. Enter your name in the center section of the worksheet footer, save the workbook, then preview the worksheet.

k. Close the workbook, exit Excel, then submit the workbook to your instructor.

Visual Workshop

Open the file EMP H-6.xlsx from the drive and folder where you save your Data Files, then save it as **EMP H-Schedule**. Complete the worksheet as shown in Figure H-26. An in-cell drop-down list has been added to the data entered in the Room field. The range A18:G21 is extracted from the table using the criteria in cells A15:A16. Add your name to the worksheet footer, save the workbook, preview the worksheet, then submit the workbook to your instructor.

FIGURE H-26

	A	B	C	D	E	F	G	H
1				Wellness Clinic Yoga Classes				
2								
3	Class Code	Class	Time	Day	Room	Fee	Instructor	
4	Y100	Basics	8:00	Monday	Mat Room	$10	Martin	
5	Y101	Power	9:00	Tuesday	Equipment Room	$15	Grey	
6	Y102	Hatha	10:00	Wednesday	Mat Room	$10	Marshall	
7	Y103	Kripalu	11:00	Monday	Mat Room	$10	Bradley	
8	Y104	Basics	1:00	Friday	Mat Room	$10	Pauley	
9	Y105	Power	2:00	Saturday	Equipment Room	$15	Dash	
10	Y106	Hatha	3:00	Tuesday	Mat Room	$10	Robinson	
11	Y107	Power	4:00	Monday	Equipment Room	$15	Walsh	
12	Y108	Basics	5:00	Tuesday	Mat Room	10	Matthews	
13					Please select Mat Room or Equipment Room			
14								
15	Class							
16	Power							
17								
18	Class Code	Class	Time	Day	Room	Fee	Instructor	
19	Y101	Power	9:00	Tuesday	Equipment Room	$15	Grey	
20	Y105	Power	2:00	Saturday	Equipment Room	$15	Dash	
21	Y107	Power	4:00	Monday	Equipment Room	$15	Walsh	
22								
23								
24								
25								

Working with Windows Live and Office Web Apps

If the computer you are using has an active Internet connection, you can go to the Microsoft Windows Live Web site and access a wide variety of services and Web applications. For example, you can check your e-mail through Windows Live, network with your friends and coworkers, and use SkyDrive to store and share files. From SkyDrive, you can also use Office Web Apps to create and edit Word, PowerPoint, Excel, and OneNote files, even when you are using a computer that does not have Office 2010 installed. ▰▰▰ You work in the Vancouver branch of Quest Specialty Travel. Your supervisor, Mary Lou Jacobs, asks you to explore Windows Live and learn how she can use SkyDrive and Office Web Apps to work with her files online.

(*Note*: SkyDrive and Office Web Apps are dynamic Web pages, and might change over time, including the way they are organized and how commands are performed. The steps and figures in this appendix were accurate at the time this book was published.)

OBJECTIVES

Explore how to work online from Windows Live

Obtain a Windows Live ID and sign in to Windows Live

Upload files to Windows Live

Work with the PowerPoint Web App

Create folders and organize files on SkyDrive

Add people to your network and share files

Work with the Excel Web App

Exploring How to Work Online from Windows Live

You can use your Web browser to upload your files to Windows Live from any computer connected to the Internet. You can work on the files right in your Web browser using Office Web Apps and share your files with people in your Windows Live network. You review the concepts and services related to working online from Windows Live.

DETAILS

- ## What is Windows Live?

  Windows Live is a collection of services and Web applications that you can use to help you be more productive both personally and professionally. For example, you can use Windows Live to send and receive e-mail, to chat with friends via instant messaging, to share photos, to create a blog, and to store and edit files using SkyDrive. Table WEB-1 describes the services available on Windows Live. Windows Live is a free service that you sign up for. When you sign up, you receive a Windows Live ID, which you use to sign in to Windows Live. When you work with files on Windows Live, you are cloud computing.

- ## What is Cloud Computing?

  The term **cloud computing** refers to the process of working with files online in a Web browser. When you save files to SkyDrive on Windows Live, you are saving your files to an online location. SkyDrive is like having a personal hard drive in the cloud.

- ## What is SkyDrive?

  SkyDrive is an online storage and file sharing service. With a Windows Live account, you receive access to your own SkyDrive, which is your personal storage area on the Internet. On your SkyDrive, you are given space to store up to 25 GB of data online. Each file can be a maximum size of 50 MB. You can also use SkyDrive to access Office Web Apps, which you use to create and edit files created in Word, OneNote, PowerPoint, and Excel online in your Web browser.

- ## Why use Windows Live and SkyDrive?

  On Windows Live, you use SkyDrive to access additional storage for your files. You don't have to worry about backing up your files to a memory stick or other storage device that could be lost or damaged. Another advantage of storing your files on SkyDrive is that you can access your files from any computer that has an active Internet connection. Figure WEB-1 shows the SkyDrive Web page that appears when accessed from a Windows Live account. From SkyDrive, you can also access Office Web Apps.

- ## What are Office Web Apps?

  Office Web Apps are versions of Microsoft Word, Excel, PowerPoint, and OneNote that you can access online from your SkyDrive. An Office Web App does not include all of the features and functions included with the full Office version of its associated application. However, you can use the Office Web App from any computer that is connected to the Internet, even if Microsoft Office 2010 is not installed on that computer.

- ## How do SkyDrive and Office Web Apps work together?

  You can create a file in Office 2010 using Word, Excel, PowerPoint, or OneNote and then upload the file to your SkyDrive. You can then open the Office file saved to SkyDrive and edit it using your Web browser and the corresponding Office Web App. Figure WEB-2 shows a PowerPoint presentation open in the PowerPoint Web App. You can also use an Office Web App to create a new file, which is saved automatically to SkyDrive while you work. In addition, you can download a file created with an Office Web App and continue to work with the file in the full version of the corresponding Office application: Word, Excel, PowerPoint, or OneNote. Finally, you can create a SkyDrive network that consists of the people you want to be able to view your folders and files on your SkyDrive. You can give people permission to view and edit your files using any computer with an active Internet connection and a Web browser.

FIGURE WEB-1: SkyDrive on Windows Live

Browser window

SkyDrive - Windows Live tab

By default, one folder is available on SkyDrive; you can create additional folders

The name of the person who signed into Windows Live and SkyDrive appears here

Monitors the amount of space still available on your SkyDrive

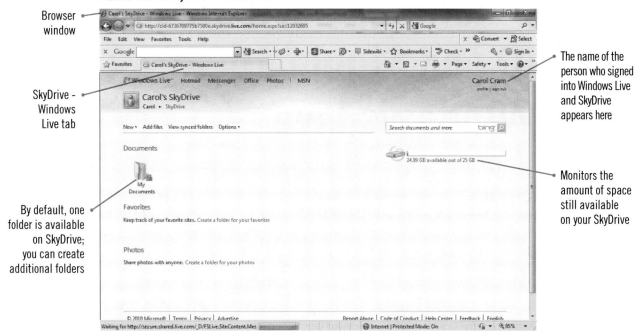

FIGURE WEB-2: PowerPoint presentation open in the PowerPoint Web App

Browser window

Ribbon available in PowerPoint Web App

The presentation in PowerPoint Web App maintains the same look and feel as the same presentation in the desktop version of PowerPoint

Name of PowerPoint presentation open in PowerPoint Web App

TABLE WEB-1: Services available via Windows Live

service	description
E-mail	Send and receive e-mail using a Hotmail account
Instant Messaging	Use Messenger to chat with friends, share photos, and play games
SkyDrive	Store files, work on files using Office Web Apps, and share files with people in your network
Photos	Upload and share photos with friends
People	Develop a network of friends and coworkers, then use the network to distribute information and stay in touch
Downloads	Access a variety of free programs available for download to a PC
Mobile Device	Access applications for a mobile device: text messaging, using Hotmail, networking, and sharing photos

Obtaining a Windows Live ID and Signing In to Windows Live

To work with your files online using SkyDrive and Office Web Apps, you need a Windows Live ID. You obtain a Windows Live ID by going to the Windows Live Web site and creating a new account. Once you have a Windows Live ID, you can access SkyDrive and then use it to store your files, create new files, and share your files with friends and coworkers. ██████ Mary Lou Jacobs, your supervisor at QST Vancouver, asks you to obtain a Windows Live ID so that you can work on documents with your coworkers. You go to the Windows Live Web site, create a Windows Live ID, and then sign in to your SkyDrive.

STEPS

QUICK TIP

If you already have a Windows Live ID, go to the next lesson and sign in as directed using your account.

1. **Open your Web browser, type home.live.com in the Address bar, then press [Enter]**

   The Windows Live home page opens. From this page, you can create a Windows Live account and receive your Windows Live ID.

2. **Click the Sign up button** *(Note: You may see a Sign up link instead of a button)*

   The Create your Windows Live ID page opens.

3. **Click the Or use your own e-mail address link under the Check availability button or if you are already using Hotmail, Messenger, or Xbox LIVE, click the Sign in now link in the Information statement near the top of the page**

4. **Enter the information required, as shown in Figure WEB-3**

   If you wish, you can sign up for a Windows Live e-mail address such as yourname@live.com so that you can also access the Windows Live e-mail services.

TROUBLE

The code can be difficult to read. If you receive an error message, enter the new code that appears.

5. **Enter the code shown at the bottom of your screen, then click the I accept button**

   The Windows Live home page opens. The name you entered when you signed up for your Windows Live ID appears in the top right corner of the window to indicate that you are signed in to Windows Live. From the Windows Live home page, you can access all the services and applications offered by Windows Live. See the Verifying your Windows Live ID box for information on finalizing your account set up.

6. **Point to Windows Live, as shown in Figure WEB-4**

   A list of options appears. SkyDrive is one of the options you can access directly from Windows Live.

TROUBLE

Click I accept if you are asked to review and accept the Windows Live Service Agreement and Privacy Statement.

7. **Click SkyDrive**

   The SkyDrive page opens. Your name appears in the top right corner, and the amount of space available is shown on the right side of the SkyDrive page. The amount of space available is monitored, as indicated by the gauge that fills with color as space is used. Using SkyDrive, you can add files to the existing folder and you can create new folders.

8. **Click sign out in the top right corner under your name, then exit the Web browser**

   You are signed out of your Windows Live account. You can sign in again directly from the Windows Live page in your browser or from within a file created with PowerPoint, Excel, Word, or OneNote.

FIGURE WEB-3: Creating a Windows Live ID

Click to sign in using a Hotmail, Messenger, or Xbox Live account

Once your registration is complete, you will be asked to verify your ID

A different code will appear on your screen

Type your e-mail address

You can choose to get a Windows Live e-mail address

Enter the information required

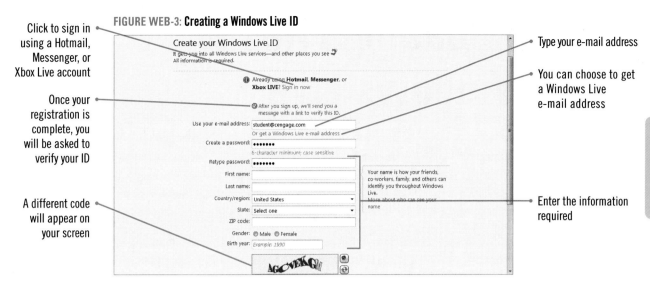

FIGURE WEB-4: Selecting SkyDrive

SkyDrive in the list of Windows Live options

Information about your Windows Live network

Your name appears here

Click to quickly add people to your network

An advertisement appropriate for your location appears here

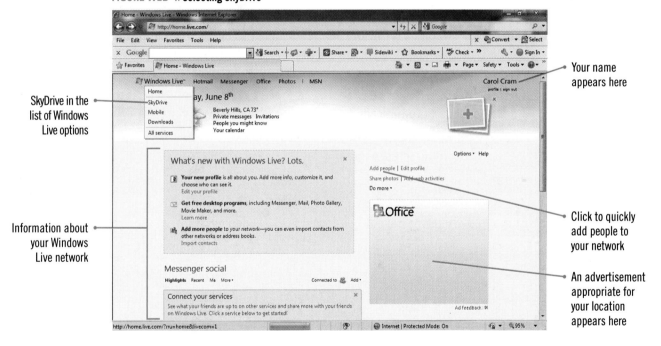

Verifying your Windows Live ID

As soon as you accept the Windows Live terms, an e-mail is sent to the e-mail address you supplied when you created your Windows Live ID. Open your e-mail program, and then open the e-mail from Microsoft with the Subject line: Confirm your e-mail address for Windows Live. Follow the simple, step-by-step instructions in the e-mail to confirm your Windows Live ID. When the confirmation is complete, you will be asked to sign in to Windows Live, using your e-mail address and password. Once signed in, you will see your Windows Live Account page.

Uploading Files to Windows Live

Once you have created your Windows Live ID, you can sign in to Windows Live directly from Word, PowerPoint, Excel, or OneNote and start saving and uploading files. You upload files to your SkyDrive so you can share the files with other people, access the files from another computer, or use SkyDrive's additional storage. ███████ You open a PowerPoint presentation, access your Windows Live account from Backstage view, and save a file to SkyDrive on Windows Live. You also create a new folder called Cengage directly from Backstage view and add a file to it.

STEPS

1. **Start PowerPoint, open the file WEB-1.pptx from the drive and folder where you store your Data Files, then save the file as WEB-QST Vancouver Presentation**

2. **Click the File tab, then click Save & Send**

   The Save & Send options available in PowerPoint are listed in Backstage view, as shown in Figure WEB-5.

3. **Click Save to Web**

QUICK TIP

Skip this step if the computer you are using signs you in automatically.

4. **Click Sign In, type your e-mail address, press [Tab], type your password, then click OK**

   The My Documents folder on your SkyDrive appears in the Save to Windows Live SkyDrive information area.

5. **Click Save As, wait a few seconds for the Save As dialog box to appear, then click Save**

   The file is saved to the My Documents folder on the SkyDrive that is associated with your Windows Live account. You can also create a new folder and upload files directly to SkyDrive from your hard drive.

6. **Click the File tab, click Save & Send, click Save to Web, then sign in if the My Documents folder does not automatically appear in Backstage view**

7. **Click the New Folder button in the Save to Windows Live SkyDrive pane, then sign in to Windows Live if directed**

8. **Type Cengage as the folder name, click Next, then click Add files**

9. **Click select documents from your computer, then navigate to the location on your computer where you saved the file WEB-QST Vancouver Presentation in Step 1**

10. **Click WEB-QST Vancouver Presentation.pptx to select it, then click Open**

    You can continue to add more files; however, you have no more files to upload at this time.

11. **Click Continue**

    In a few moments, the PowerPoint presentation is uploaded to your SkyDrive, as shown in Figure WEB-6. You can simply store the file on SkyDrive or you can choose to work on the presentation using the PowerPoint Web App.

12. **Click the PowerPoint icon 🖾 on your taskbar to return to PowerPoint, then close the presentation and exit PowerPoint**

FIGURE WEB-5: Save & Send options in Backstage view

PowerPoint file

Save & Send area in Backstage view

Save to Web option

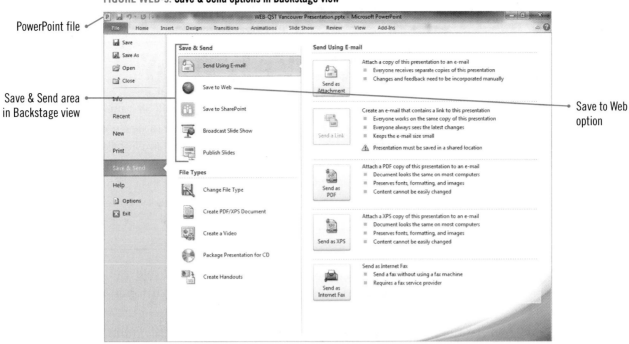

FIGURE WEB-6: File uploaded to the Cengage folder on Windows Live

Browser window

Path to file

Current folder menu bar

Uploaded file

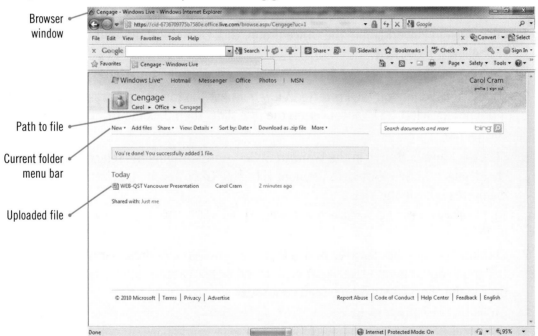

Web Apps

Working with the PowerPoint Web App

Once you have uploaded a file to SkyDrive on Windows Live, you can work on it using its corresponding Office Web App. **Office Web Apps** provide you with the tools you need to view documents online and to edit them right in your browser. You do not need to have Office programs installed on the computer you use to access SkyDrive and Office Web Apps. From SkyDrive, you can also open the document directly in the full Office application (for example, PowerPoint) if the application is installed on the computer you are using. ▰▰▰ You use the PowerPoint Web App to make some edits to the PowerPoint presentation. You then open the presentation in PowerPoint and use the full version to make additional edits.

STEPS

1. **Click the** WEB-QST Vancouver Presentation **file in the Cengage folder on SkyDrive**

   The presentation opens in your browser window. A menu is available, which includes the options you have for working with the file.

2. **Click** Edit in Browser, **then if a message appears related to installing the Sign-in Assistant, click the** Close button ☒ **to the far right of the message**

   In a few moments, the PowerPoint presentation opens in the PowerPoint Web App, as shown in Figure WEB-7. Table WEB-2 lists the commands you can perform using the PowerPoint Web App.

3. **Enter your name where indicated on Slide 1, click** Slide 3 (New Tours) **in the Slides pane, then click** Delete Slide **in the Slides group**

   The slide is removed from the presentation. You decide to open the file in the full version of PowerPoint on your computer so you can apply WordArt to the slide title. You work with the file in the full version of PowerPoint when you want to use functions, such as WordArt, that are not available on the PowerPoint Web App.

4. **Click** Open in PowerPoint **in the Office group, click** OK **in response to the message, then click** Allow **if requested**

   In a few moments, the revised version of the PowerPoint slide opens in PowerPoint on your computer.

5. **Click** Enable Editing **on the Protected View bar near the top of your presentation window if prompted, select** QST Vancouver **on the title slide, then click the** Drawing Tools Format tab

6. **Click the** More button ⚎ **in the WordArt Styles group to show the selection of WordArt styles, select the WordArt style** Gradient Fill - Blue-Gray, Accent 4, Reflection, **then click a blank area outside the slide**

   The presentation appears in PowerPoint as shown in Figure WEB-8. Next, you save the revised version of the file to SkyDrive.

7. **Click the** File tab, **click** Save As, **notice that the path in the Address bar is to the Cengage folder on your Windows Live SkyDrive, type** WEB-QST Vancouver Presentation_Revised. pptx **in the File name text box, then click** Save

   The file is saved to your SkyDrive.

8. **Click the** browser icon **on the taskbar to open your SkyDrive page, then click** Office **next to your name in the SkyDrive path, view a list of recent documents, then click** Cengage **in the list to the left of the recent documents list to open the Cengage folder**

   Two PowerPoint files now appear in the Cengage folder.

9. **Exit the Web browser and close all tabs if prompted, then exit PowerPoint**

FIGURE WEB-7: Presentation opened in the PowerPoint Web App from Windows Live

Browser window

Name of Web App

PowerPoint Web App Ribbon

URL is the file location

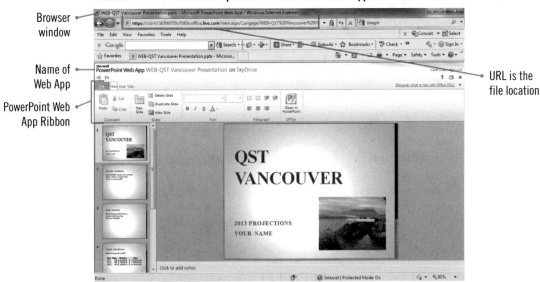

FIGURE WEB-8: Revised PowerPoint presentation

PowerPoint title bar

PowerPoint Ribbon

Presentation title enhanced using full version of PowerPoint

Name added using PowerPoint Web App

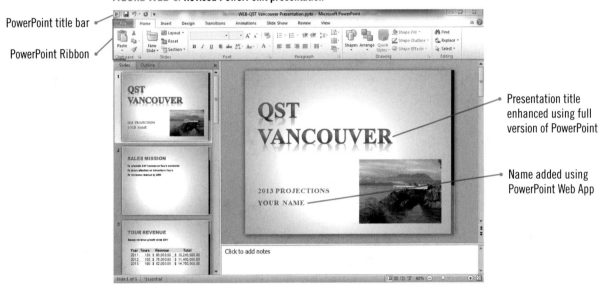

TABLE WEB-2: Commands on the PowerPoint Web App

tab	commands available
File	• Open in PowerPoint: select to open the file in PowerPoint on your computer • Where's the Save Button?: when you click this option, a message appears telling you that you do not need to save your presentation when you are working on it with PowerPoint Web App. The presentation is saved automatically as you work. • Print • Share • Properties • Give Feedback • Privacy • Terms of Use • Close
Home	• Clipboard group: Cut, Copy, Paste • Slides group: Add a New Slide, Delete a Slide, Duplicate a Slide, and Hide a Slide • Font group: Work with text: change the font, style, color, and size of selected text • Paragraph group: Work with paragraphs: add bullets and numbers, indent text, align text • Office group: Open the file in PowerPoint on your computer
Insert	• Insert a Picture • Insert a SmartArt diagram • Insert a link such as a link to another file on SkyDrive or to a Web page
View	• Editing view (the default) • Reading view • Slide Show view • Notes view

Creating Folders and Organizing Files on SkyDrive

As you have learned, you can sign in to SkyDrive directly from the Office applications PowerPoint, Excel, Word, and OneNote, or you can access SkyDrive directly through your Web browser. This option is useful when you are away from the computer on which you normally work or when you are using a computer that does not have Office applications installed. You can go to SkyDrive, create and organize folders, and then create or open files to work on with Office Web Apps. ▓▓▓ You access SkyDrive from your Web browser, create a new folder called Illustrated, and delete one of the PowerPoint files from the My Documents folder.

STEPS

TROUBLE
Go to Step 3 if you are already signed in.

TROUBLE
Type your Windows Live ID (your e-mail) and password, then click Sign in if prompted to do so.

1. **Open your Web browser, type home.live.com in the Address bar, then press [Enter]**
   The Windows Live home page opens. From here, you can sign in to your Windows Live account and then access SkyDrive.

2. **Sign into Windows Live as directed**
   You are signed in to your Windows Live page. From this page, you can take advantage of the many applications available on Windows Live, including SkyDrive.

3. **Point to Windows Live, then click SkyDrive**
   SkyDrive opens.

4. **Click Cengage, then point to WEB-QST Vancouver Presentation.pptx**
   A menu of options for working with the file, including a Delete button to the far right, appears to the right of the filename.

5. **Click the Delete button ☒, then click OK**
   The file is removed from the Cengage folder on your SkyDrive. You still have a copy of the file on your computer.

6. **Point to Windows Live, then click SkyDrive**
   Your SkyDrive screen with the current selection of folders available on your SkyDrive opens, as shown in Figure WEB-9.

7. **Click New, click Folder, type Illustrated, click Next, click Office in the path under Add documents to Illustrated at the top of the window, then click View all in the list under Personal**
   You are returned to your list of folders, where you see the new Illustrated folder.

8. **Click Cengage, point to WEB-QST Vancouver Presentation_Revised.pptx, click More, click Move, then click the Illustrated folder**

9. **Click Move this file into Illustrated, as shown in Figure WEB-10**
   The file is moved to the Illustrated folder.

FIGURE WEB-9: **Folders on your SkyDrive**

Current location

Folders currently available

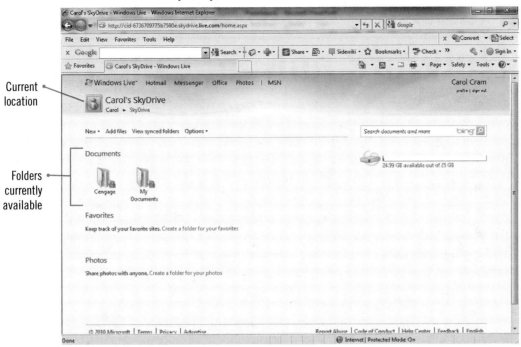

FIGURE WEB-10: **Moving a file to the Illustrated folder**

Click to move file to this location

Be sure to rename a file before moving it if you are moving it to a location where another copy of the same file exists

Name of file to be moved

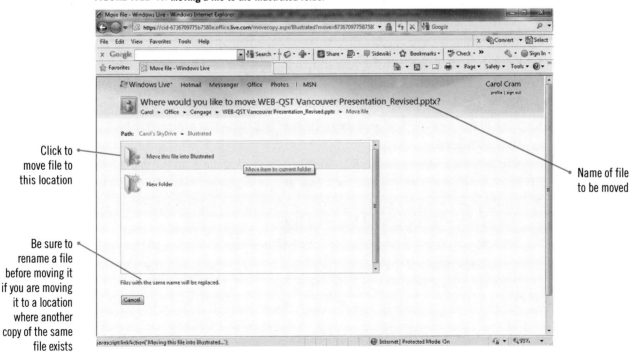

Adding People to Your Network and Sharing Files

One of the great advantages of working with SkyDrive on Windows Live is that you can share your files with others. Suppose, for example, that you want a colleague to review a presentation you created in PowerPoint and then add a new slide. You can, of course, e-mail the presentation directly to your colleague, who can then make changes and e-mail the presentation back. Alternatively, you can save time by uploading the PowerPoint file directly to SkyDrive and then giving your colleague access to the file. Your colleague can edit the file using the PowerPoint Web App, and then you can check the updated file on SkyDrive, also using the PowerPoint Web App. In this way, you and your colleague are working with just one version of the presentation that you both can update. ▆▆▆▆ You have decided to share files in the Illustrated folder that you created in the previous lesson with another individual. You start by working with a partner so that you can share files with your partner and your partner can share files with you.

STEPS

TROUBLE

If you cannot find a partner, read the steps so you understand how the process works.

1. **Identify a partner with whom you can work, and obtain his or her e-mail address; you can choose someone in your class or someone on your e-mail list, but it should be someone who will be completing these steps when you are**

2. **From the Illustrated folder, click** Share

3. **Click** Edit permissions

   The Edit permissions page opens. On this page, you can select the individual with whom you would like to share the contents of the Illustrated folder.

4. **Click in the** Enter a name or an e-mail address **text box, type the** e-mail address **of your partner, then press [Tab]**

   You can define the level of access that you want to give your partner.

5. **Click the** Can view files **list arrow shown in Figure WEB-11, click** Can add, edit details, and delete files, **then click** Save

   You can choose to send a notification to each individual when you grant permission to access your files.

6. **Click in the** Include your own message **text box, type the message shown in Figure WEB-12, then click** Send

   Your partner will receive a message from Windows Live advising him or her that you have shared your Illustrated folder. If your partner is completing the steps at the same time, you will receive an e-mail from your partner.

TROUBLE

If you do not receive a message from Windows Live, your partner has not yet completed the steps to share the Illustrated folder.

7. **Check your e-mail for a message from Windows Live advising you that your partner has shared his or her Illustrated folder with you**

   The subject of the e-mail message will be "[Name] has shared documents with you."

QUICK TIP

You will know you are on your partner's SkyDrive because you will see your partner's first name at the beginning of the SkyDrive path.

8. **If you have received the e-mail, click** View folder **in the e-mail message, then sign in to Windows Live if you are requested to do so**

   You are now able to access your partner's Illustrated folder on his or her SkyDrive. You can download files in your partner's Illustrated folder to your own computer where you can work on them and then upload them again to your partner's Illustrated shared folder.

9. **Exit the browser**

FIGURE WEB-11: Editing folder permissions

Folder permissions
will be changed for
the Illustrated folder

Click to select network
permission options

Type email address to
continue to add people

Person whose
permission status
will change

Click to select
person from list
of contacts

Click to select
permission option

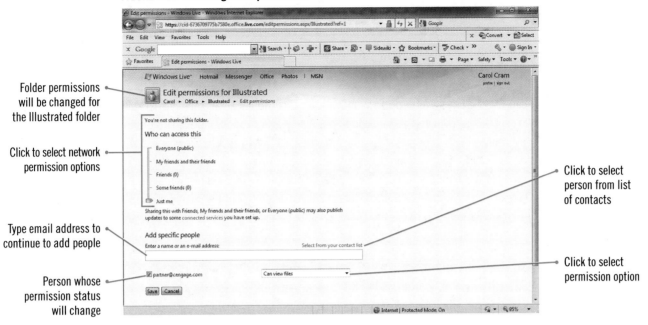

FIGURE WEB-12: Entering a message to notify a person that file sharing permission has been granted

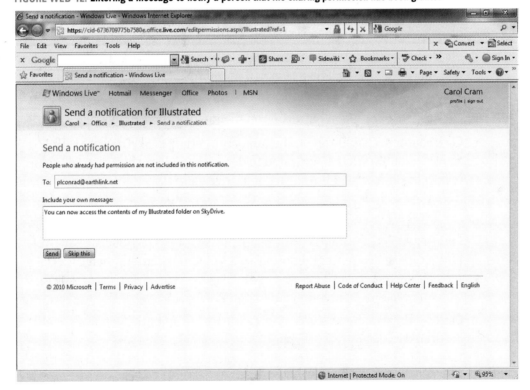

Sharing files on SkyDrive

When you share a folder with other people, the people with whom you share a folder can download the file to their computers and then make changes using the full version of the corresponding Office application.

Once these changes are made, each individual can then upload the file to SkyDrive and into a folder shared with you and others. In this way, you can create a network of people with whom you share your files.

Working with the Excel Web App

You can use the Excel Web App to work with an Excel spreadsheet on SkyDrive. Workbooks opened using the Excel Web App have the same look and feel as workbooks opened using the full version of Excel. However, just like the PowerPoint Web App, the Excel Web App has fewer features available than the full version of Excel. When you want to use a command that is not available on the Excel Web App, you need to open the file in the full version of Excel. ~~■■■■~~ You upload an Excel file containing a list of the tours offered by QST Vancouver to the Illustrated folder on SkyDrive. You use the Excel Web App to make some changes, and then you open the revised version in Excel 2010 on your computer.

STEPS

1. **Start Excel, open the file WEB-2.xlsx from the drive and folder where you store your Data Files, then save the file as WEB-QST Vancouver Tours**

   The data in the Excel file is formatted using the Excel table function.

TROUBLE
If prompted, sign in to your Windows Live account as directed.

2. **Click the File tab, click Save & Send, then click Save to Web**

   In a few moments, you should see three folders to which you can save spreadsheets. My Documents and Cengage are personal folder that contains files that only you can access. Illustrated is a shared folder that contains files you can share with others in your network. The Illustrated folder is shared with your partner.

3. **Click the Illustrated folder, click the Save As button, wait a few seconds for the Save As dialog box to appear, then click Save**

QUICK TIP
Alternately, you can open your Web browser and go to Windows Live to sign in to SkyDrive.

4. **Click the File tab, click Save & Send, click Save to Web, click the Windows Live SkyDrive link above your folders, then sign in if prompted**

   Windows Live opens to your SkyDrive.

5. **Click the Excel program button ▣ on the taskbar, then exit Excel**

6. **Click your browser button on the taskbar to return to SkyDrive if SkyDrive is not the active window, click the Illustrated folder, click the Excel file, click Edit in Browser, then review the Ribbon and its tabs to familiarize yourself with the commands you can access from the Excel Web App**

   Table WEB-3 summarizes the commands that are available.

7. **Click cell A12, type Gulf Islands Sailing, press [TAB], type 3000, press [TAB], type 10, press [TAB], click cell D3, enter the formula =B3*C3, press [Enter], then click cell A1**

   The formula is copied automatically to the remaining rows as shown in Figure WEB-13 because the data in the original Excel file was created and formatted as an Excel table.

8. **Click SkyDrive in the Excel Web App path at the top of the window to return to the Illustrated folder**

   The changes you made to the Excel spreadsheet are saved automatically on SkyDrive. You can download the file directly to your computer from SkyDrive.

9. **Point to the Excel file, click More, click Download, click Save, navigate to the location where you save the files for this book, name the file WEB-QST Vancouver Tours_Updated, click Save, then click Close in the Download complete dialog box**

   The updated version of the spreadsheet is saved on your computer and on SkyDrive.

10. **Exit the Web browser**

FIGURE WEB-13: **Updated table in the Excel Web App**

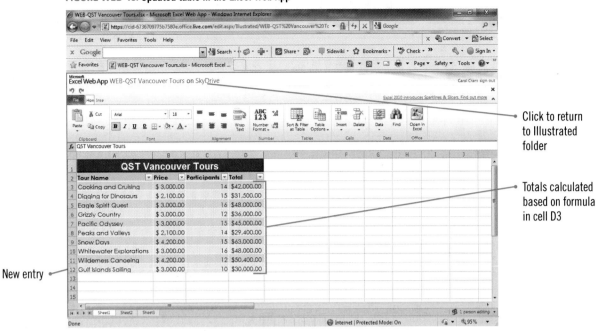

Click to return to Illustrated folder

Totals calculated based on formula in cell D3

New entry

TABLE WEB-3: **Commands on the Excel Web App**

tab	commands available
File	• Open in Excel: select to open the file in Excel on your computer • Where's the Save Button?: when you click this option, a message appears telling you that you do not need to save your spreadsheet when you are working in it with Excel Web App; the spreadsheet is saved automatically as you work • Save As • Share • Download a Snapshot: a snapshot contains only the values and the formatting; you cannot modify a snapshot • Download a Copy: the file can be opened and edited in the full version of Excel • Give Feedback • Privacy Statement • Terms of Use • Close
Home	• Clipboard group: Cut, Copy, Paste • Font group: change the font, style, color, and size of selected labels and values, as well as border styles and fill colors • Alignment group: change vertical and horizontal alignment and turn on the Wrap Text feature • Number group: change the number format and increase or decrease decimal places • Tables: sort and filter data in a table and modify Table Options • Cells: insert and delete cells • Data: refresh data and find labels or values • Office: open the file in Excel on your computer
Insert	• Insert a Table • Insert a Hyperlink to a Web page

Exploring other Office Web Apps

Two other Office Web Apps are Word and OneNote. You can share files on SkyDrive directly from Word or from OneNote using the same method you used to share files from PowerPoint and Excel. After you upload a Word or OneNote file to SkyDrive, you can work with it in its corresponding Office Web App. To familiarize yourself with the commands available in an Office Web App, open the file and then review the commands on each tab on the Ribbon. If you want to perform a task that is not available in the Office Web App, open the file in the full version of the application.

In addition to working with uploaded files, you can create files from new on SkyDrive. Simply sign in to SkyDrive and open a folder. With a folder open, click New and then select the Web App you want to use to create the new file.

Windows Live and Microsoft Office Web Apps Quick Reference

To Do This	Go Here
Access Windows Live	From the Web browser, type **home.live.com**, then click Sign In
Access SkyDrive on Windows Live	From the Windows Live home page, point to Windows Live, then click SkyDrive
Save to Windows Live from Word, PowerPoint, or Excel	File tab | Save & Send | Save to Web | Select a folder | Save As
Create a New Folder from Backstage view	File tab | Save & Send | Save to Web | New Folder button
Edit a File with a Web App	From SkyDrive, click the file, then click Edit in Browser
Open a File in a desktop version of the application from a Web App: Word, Excel, PowerPoint	Click Open in [Application] in the Office group in each Office Web App
Share files on Windows Live	From SkyDrive, click the folder containing the files to share, click Share on the menu bar, click Edit permissions, enter the e-mail address of the person to share files with, click the Can view files list arrow, click Can add, edit details, and delete files, then click Save

Glossary

3-D reference A worksheet reference that uses values on other sheets or workbooks, effectively creating another dimension to a workbook.

Absolute cell reference In a formula, a cell address that refers to a specific cell and does not change when you copy the formula; indicated by a dollar sign before the column letter and/or row number. *See also* Relative cell reference.

Active The currently available document, program, or object; on the taskbar, when more than one program is open, the button for the active program appears slightly lighter.

Active cell The cell in which you are currently working.

Alignment The placement of cell contents in relation to a cell's edges; for example, left-aligned, centered, or right-aligned.

And condition A filtering feature that searches for records by specifying that all entered criteria must be matched.

Argument Information necessary for a formula or function to calculate an answer.

Arithmetic operators In a formula, symbols that perform mathematical calculations, such as addition (+), subraction (–), multiplication (*), division(/), or exponentiation (^).

Ascending order In sorting an Excel field (column), the order that begins with the letter A or the lowest number of the values in the field.

AutoFill Feature activated by dragging the fill handle; copies a cell's contents or continues a series of entries into adjacent cells.

AutoFill Options button Button that appears after using the fill handle to copy cell contents; enables you to choose to fill cells with specific elements (such as formatting) of the copied cell if desired.

AutoFilter A table feature that lets you click a list arrow and select criteria by which to display certain types of records; *also called* filter.

AutoFilter list arrows *See* Filter List arrows.

AutoFit A feature that automatically adjusts the width of a column or the height of a row to accommodate its widest or tallest entry.

Backstage view View available in all Microsoft Office programs that allows you to perform many common tasks, such as opening and saving a file, printing and previewing a document, and protecting a document before sharing it with others.

Backward-compatible Software feature that enables documents saved in an older version of a program to be opened in a newer version of the program.

Banding Worksheet formatting in which adjacent rows and columns are formatted differently.

Calculated columns In a table, a column that automatically fills in cells with formula results, using a formula entered in only one other cell in the same column.

Calculation operators Symbols in a formula that indicate what type of calculation to perform on the cells, ranges, or values.

Category axis Horizontal axis in a chart, usually containing the names of data categories; in a 2-dimensional chart, also known as the x-axis.

Cell The intersection of a column and a row in a worksheet or table.

Cell address The location of a cell, expressed by cell coordinates; for example, the cell address of the cell in column A, row 1 is A1.

Cell pointer Dark rectangle that outlines the active cell.

Cell styles Predesigned combinations of formats based on themes that can be applied to selected cells to enhance the look of a worksheet.

Chart sheet A separate sheet in a workbook that contains only a chart, which is linked to the workbook data.

Charts Pictorial representations of worksheet data that make it easier to see patterns, trends, and relationships; *also called* graphs.

Clip A media file, such as a graphic, sound, animation, or movie.

Clip art A graphic image, such as a corporate logo, a picture, or a photo, that can be inserted into a document.

Clipboard A temporary Windows storage area that holds the selections you copy or cut.

Cloud computing When data, applications, and resources are stored on servers accessed over the Internet or a company's internal network rather than on users' computers.

Color scale In conditional formatting, a formatting scheme that uses a set of two, three, or four fill colors to convey relative values of data.

Column heading Identifies the column letter, such as A, B, etc.; located above each column in a worksheet.

Combination chart Two charts in one, such as a column chart combined with a line chart, that together graph related but dissimilar data.

Comparison operators In a calculation, symbols that compare values for the purpose of true/false results.

Compatibility The ability of different programs to work together and exchange data.

Complex formula A formula that uses more than one arithmetic operator.

Conditional formatting A type of cell formatting that changes based on the cell's value or the outcome of a formula.

Consolidate To combine data on multiple worksheets and display the result on another worksheet.

Contextual tab Tab on the Ribbon that appears when needed to complete a specific task; for example, if you select a graphic, the Picture Tools Format tab appears.

Criteria range In advanced filtering, a cell range containing one row of labels (usually a copy of column labels) and at least one additional row underneath it that contains the criteria you want to match.

Data entry area The unlocked portion of a worksheet where users are able to enter and change data.

Data marker A graphical representation of a data point in a chart, such as a bar or column.

Data point Individual piece of data plotted in a chart.

Data series The selected range in a worksheet whose related data points Excel converts into a chart.

Delimiter A separator such as a space, comma, or semicolon between elements in imported data.

Descending order In sorting an Excel field (column), the order that begins with the letter Z or the highest number of the values in the field.

Dialog box launcher An icon available in many groups on the Ribbon that you can click to open a dialog box or task pane, offering an alternative way to choose commands. *Also called* launcher.

Digital signature A signature that can be added to a workbook to establish its validity and prevent it from being changed.

Document window The portion of a program window in which you create the document; displays all or part of an open document.

Dynamic page breaks In a larger workbook, horizontal or vertical dashed lines that represent the place where pages print separately. They also adjust automatically when you insert or delete rows or columns, or change column widths or row heights.

Edit To make a change to the contents of an active cell.

Electronic spreadsheet A computer program used to perform calculations and analyze and present numeric data.

Embedded chart A chart displayed as an object in a worksheet.

Exploding Visually pulling a slice of a pie chart away from the whole pie chart in order to add emphasis to the pie slice.

External reference indicator The exclamation point (!) used in a formula to indicate that a referenced cell is outside the active sheet.

Extract To place a copy of a filtered table in a range you specify in the Advanced Filter dialog box.

Field In a table (an Excel database), a column that describes a characteristic about records, such as first name or city.

Field name A column label that describes a field.

File An electronic collection of stored data that has a unique name, distinguishing it from other files, such as a letter, video, or program.

Filter To display data in an Excel table that meet specified criteria. *See also* AutoFilter.

Filter arrows *See* Filter list arrows.

Filter list arrows List arrows that appear next to field names in an Excel table; used to display portions of your data. *Also called* AutoFilter list arrows.

Font The typeface or design of a set of characters (letters, numbers, symbols, and punctuation marks).

Font size The size of characters, measured in units called points.

Font style Format such as bold, italic, and underlining that can be applied to change the way characters look in a worksheet or chart.

Format The appearance of a cell and its contents, including font, font styles, font color, fill color, borders, and shading. *See also* Number format.

Formula A set of instructions used to perform one or more numeric calculations, such as adding, multiplying, or averaging, on values or cells.

Formula bar The area above the worksheet grid where you enter or edit data in the active cell.

Formula prefix An arithmetic symbol, such as the equal sign (=), used to start a formula.

Freeze To hold in place selected columns or rows when scrolling in a worksheet that is divided in panes. *See also* Panes.

Function A special, predefined formula that provides a shortcut for a commonly used or complex calculation, such as SUM (for calculating a sum) or FV (for calculating the future value of an investment).

Gallery A visual collection of choices you can browse through to make a selection. Often available with Live Preview.

Graphs *See* Charts.

Gridlines Evenly spaced horizontal and/or vertical lines used in a worksheet or chart to make it easier to read.

Group (n.) In a Microsoft program window's Ribbon, a section containing related command buttons.

Group (v.) To combine multiple objects into one object.

Header row In a table, the first row that contains the field names.

HTML (Hypertext Markup Language) The format of pages that a Web browser can read.

Hyperlink An object (a filename, a word, a phrase, or a graphic) in a worksheet that, when clicked, displays another worksheet or a Web page called the target. *See also* Target.

Icon sets In conditional formatting, groups of images that are used to visually communicate relative cell values based on the values they contain.

Insertion point A blinking vertical line that appears when you click in the formula bar or in an active cell; indicates where new text will be inserted.

Instance A worksheet in its own workbook window.

Integrate To incorporate a document and parts of a document created in one program into another program; for example, to incorporate an Excel chart into a PowerPoint slide, or an Access table into a Word document.

Interface The look and feel of a program; for example, the appearance of commands and the way they are organized in the program window.

Intranet An internal network site used by a group of people who work together.

Keywords Terms added to a workbook's Document Properties that help locate the file in a search.

Labels Descriptive text or other information that identifies data in rows, columns, or charts, but is not included in calculations.

Landscape Page orientation in which the contents of a page span the length of a page rather than its width, making the page wider than it is tall.

Launch To open or start a program on your computer.

Legend In a chart, information that identifies how data is represented by colors or patterns.

Linking The dynamic referencing of data in the same or in other workbooks, so that when data in the other location is changed, the references in the current location are automatically updated.

List arrows *See* Filter list arrows.

Live Preview A feature that lets you point to a choice in a gallery or palette and see the results in the document without actually clicking the choice.

Lock To secure a row, column, or sheet so that data in that location cannot be changed.

Logical conditions Using the operators And and Or to narrow a custom filter criteria.

Logical formula A formula with calculations that are based on stated conditions.

Logical test The first part of an IF function; if the logical test is true, then the second part of the function is applied; if it is false, then the third part of the function is applied.

Macros Programmed instructions that perform tasks in a workbook.

Major gridlines In a chart, the gridlines that represent the values at the tick marks on the value axis.

Metadata Information that describes data and is used in Microsoft Windows document searches.

Minor gridlines In a chart, the gridlines that represent the values between the tick marks on the value axis.

Mixed reference Cell reference that combines both absolute and relative cell addressing.

Mode indicator An area on the left end of the status bar that indicates the program's status. For example, when you are changing the contents of a cell, the word 'Edit' appears in the mode indicator.

Multilevel sort A reordering of table data using more than one column at a time.

Name box Box to the left of the formula bar that shows the cell reference or name of the active cell.

Navigate To move around in a worksheet; for example, you can use the arrow keys on the keyboard to navigate from cell to cell, or press [Page Up] or [Page Down] to move one screen at a time.

Normal view Default worksheet view that shows the worksheet without features such as headers and footers; ideal for creating and editing a worksheet, but may not be detailed enough when formatting a document.

Number format A format applied to values to express numeric concepts, such as currency, date, and percentage.

Object Independent element on a worksheet (such as a chart or graphic) that is not located in a specific cell or range; can be moved and resized and displays handles when selected.

Office Web Apps Versions of the Microsoft Office applications with limited functionality that are available online from Windows Live SkyDrive. Users can view documents online and then edit them in the browser using a selection of functions. Office Web Apps are available for Word, PowerPoint, Excel, and One Note.

Online collaboration The ability to incorporate feedback or share information across the Internet or a company network or intranet.

Or condition The records in a search must match only one of the criterion.

Order of precedence Rules that determine the order in which operations are performed within a formula containing more than one arithmetic operator.

Page Break Preview A worksheet view that displays a reduced view of each page in your worksheet, along with page break indicators that you can drag to include more or less information on a page.

Page Layout view Provides an accurate view of how a worksheet will look when printed, including headers and footers.

Panes Sections into which you can divide a worksheet when you want to work on separate parts of the worksheet at the same time; one pane freezes, or remains in place, while you scroll in another pane until you see the desired information.

Paste Options button Button that appears onscreen after pasting content; enables you to choose to paste only specific elements of the copied selection, such as the formatting or values, if desired.

Plot area In a chart, the area inside the horizontal and vertical axes.

Previewing Prior to printing, seeing onscreen exactly how the printed document will look.

Point A unit of measure used for font size and row height. One point is equal to 1/72nd of an inch.

Portrait Page orientation in which the contents of a page span the width of a page, so the page is taller than it is wide.

Print area A portion of a worksheet that you can define using the Print Area button on the Page Layout tab; after you select and define a print area, the Quick Print feature prints only that worksheet area.

Print title In a table that spans more than one page, the field names that print at the top of every printed page.

Properties File characteristics, such as the author's name, keywords, or the title, that help others understand, identify, and locate the file.

Publish To place an Excel workbook or worksheet on a Web site or an intranet in HTML format so that others can access it using their Web browsers.

Quick Access toolbar A small toolbar on the left side of a Microsoft application program window's title bar, containing icons that you click to quickly perform common actions, such as saving a file.

Range A selection of two or more cells, such as B5:B14.

Record In a table (an Excel database), data that relates to an object or a person.

Reference operators In a formula, symbols which enable you to use ranges in calculations.

Relative cell reference In a formula, a cell address that refers to a cell's location in relation to the cell containing the formula and that automatically changes to reflect the new location when the formula is copied or moved; default type of referencing used in Excel worksheets. *See also* Absolute cell reference.

Return In a function, to display a result.

Ribbon In many Microsoft application program windows, a horizontal strip near the top of the window that contains tabs (pages) of command buttons, organized into groups, that you click to interact with the program.

Scope In a named cell or range, the worksheet(s) in which the name can be used.

Screen capture An electronic snapshot of your screen, as if you took a picture of it with a camera, which you can paste into a document.

Scroll bars Bars on the right edge (vertical scroll bar) and bottom edge (horizontal scroll bar) of the document window that allow you to move around in a document that is too large to fit on the screen at once.

Search criterion In a workbook or table search, the text you are searching for.

Secondary axis In a combination chart, an additional axis that supplies the scale for one of the chart types used.

Shared workbook An Excel workbook that several users can open and modify.

Sheet tab scrolling buttons Allow you to navigate to additional sheet tabs when available; located to the left of the sheet tabs.

Sheet tabs Identify the sheets in a workbook and let you switch between sheets; located below the worksheet grid.

Single-file Web page A Web page that integrates all of the worksheets and graphical elements from a workbook into a single file in the MHTML file format, making it easier to publish to the Web.

Sizing handles Small series of dots at the corners and edges of a chart indicating that the chart is selected; drag to resize the chart.

SkyDrive An online storage and file sharing service. Access to SkyDrive is through a Windows Live account. Up to 25 GB of data can be stored in a personal SkyDrive, with each file a maximum size of 50 MB.

SmartArt graphics Predesigned diagram types for the following types of data: List, Process, Cycle, Hierarchy, Relationship, Matrix, and Pyramid.

Sort To change the order of records in a table according to one or more fields, such as Last Name.

Sparkline A quick, simple chart located within a cell that serves as a visual indicator of data trends.

Stated conditions In a logical formula, criteria you create.

Status bar Bar at the bottom of the Excel window that provides a brief description about the active command or task in progress.

Structured reference Allows table formulas to refer to table columns by names that are automatically generated when the table is created.

Suite A group of programs that are bundled together and share a similar interface, making it easy to transfer skills and program content among them.

Tab A page in an application program's Ribbon, or in a dialog box, that contains a group of related settings.

Table An organized collection of rows and columns of similarly structured data on a worksheet.

Table styles Predesigned formatting that can be applied to a range of cells or even to an entire worksheet; especially useful for those ranges with labels in the left column and top row, and totals in the bottom row or right column. *See also* Table.

Table total row A row you can add to the bottom of a table for calculations using the data in the table columns.

Target The location that a hyperlink displays after the user clicks it.

Template A predesigned, formatted file that serves as the basis for a new workbook; Excel template files have the file extension .xltx.

Text annotations Labels added to a chart to draw attention to or describe a particular area.

Text concatenation operators In a formula, symbols used to join strings of text in different cells.

Theme A predefined set of colors, fonts, line and fill effects, and other formats that can be applied to an Excel worksheet and give it a consistent, professional look.

Tick marks Notations of a scale of measure on a chart axis.

Title bar Bar at the top of every program window that displays the document and program name. In Internet Explorer, usually contains the name of the Web page currently displayed in the Web browser's active tab window.

Track To identify and keep a record of who makes which changes to a workbook.

User interface A collective term for all the ways you interact with a software program.

Value axis In a chart, the axis that contains numerical values; in a 2-dimensional chart, also known as the y-axis.

Values Numbers, formulas, and functions used in calculations.

View A set of display or print settings that you can name and save for access at another time. You can save multiple views of a worksheet.

Watermark A translucent background design on a worksheet that is displayed when the worksheet is printed. Watermarks are graphic files that are inserted into the document header.

What-if analysis A decision-making tool in which data is changed and formulas are recalculated in order to predict various possible outcomes.

Wildcard A special symbol that substitutes for unknown characters in defining search criteria in the Find and Replace dialog box. The most common types of wildcards are the question mark (?), which stands for any single character, and the asterisk (*), which represents any group of characters.

Windows Live A collection of services and Web applications that people can access through a login. Windows Live services include access to e-mail and instant messaging, storage of files on SkyDrive, sharing and storage of photos, networking with people, downloading software, and interfacing with a mobile device.

Workbook A collection of related worksheets contained within a single file.

Worksheet A single sheet within a workbook file; also, the entire area within an electronic spreadsheet that contains a grid of columns and rows.

Worksheet window Area of the program window that displays part of the current worksheet; the worksheet window displays only a small fraction of the worksheet, which can contain a total of 1,048,576 rows and 16,384 columns.

Workspace An Excel file with an .xlw extension containing information about the identity, view, and placement of a set of open workbooks. Rather than opening each workbook individually, you can open the workspace file instead.

X-axis The horizontal axis in a chart; because it often shows data categories, such as months or locations, *also called* category axis.

XML Acronym that stands for eXtensible Markup Language, which is a language used to structure, store, and exchange information.

Y-axis The vertical axis in a chart; because it often shows numerical values, *also called* value axis.

Z-axis The third axis in a true 3-D chart, lets you compare data points across both categories and values.

Zooming in A feature that makes a document appear larger but shows less of it on screen at once; does not affect actual document size.

Zooming out A feature that shows more of a document on screen at once but at a reduced size; does not affect actual document size.

Index

KEY TO PAGE NUMBER ABREVIATIONS

Excel   EX
Office   OFF
WEB   Web Apps

SPECIAL CHARACTERS

- (subtraction) operator, EX 7
! (exclamation point), EX 110
error value, EX 113
#DIV/0! error value, EX 113
#NA error value, EX 113
#NAME? error value, EX 113
#NULL! error value, EX 113
#NUM! error value, EX 113
#REF! error value, EX 113
#VALUE! error value, EX 113
$ (dollar sign), EX 38
% (percent) operator, EX 7
* (asterisk) wildcard, EX 160, 180
* (multiplication) operator, EX 7
/ (division) operator, EX 7
? (question mark) wildcard, EX 160, 180
^ (exponent) operator, EX 7
+ (addition) operator, EX 7
< (less than) operator, EX 117
<= (less than or equal to) operator, EX 117
<> (not equal to) operator, EX 117
= (equal to) operator, EX 117
> (greater than) operator, EX 117
>= (greater than or equal to) operator, EX 117
3-D charts, EX 3, 87
3-D Clustered Column chart, EX 86–87
3-D references, EX 110

A

absolute cell references
     copying formulas with, EX 38–39
     overview, EX 34–35
Access, OFF 2, 5
access permissions, EX 138
Accounting number format, EX 52–53
active cells, EX 4–5, 11

active content, EX 142
active documents, OFF 4
active printer, EX 16
Add View dialog box, EX 134–135
addition (+) operator, EX 7
address bar, Save As dialog box, OFF 9
Advanced Filter, EX 182–185
alert levels, error, EX 191
alignment
     of axis labels and titles, EX 90
     changing, EX 56–57
Alignment tab, Format Cells dialog box, EX 57
AND function, EX 118–119
And logical condition, EX 180, 182
annotating, EX 92–93
Area charts, EX 81
arguments, EX 8
arithmetic operators, EX 7, 12, 26–27
Arrange Windows dialog box, EX 130–131
arrow keys, EX 9
arrow shapes, EX 92–93
ascending sort order, EX 164–165
asterisk (*) wildcard, EX 160, 180
Auto Fill, EX 26
Auto Fill Options button, EX 9, 36–37
AutoFilter, EX 178, 180
AutoFilter list arrows, EX 178
AutoFit Column Width command, EX 58
AutoFit feature, EX 58
AutoFit Row Height command, EX 59
AutoRecover feature, EX 10
AVERAGEIF function, EX 108
AVERAGEIFS function, EX 108
axis labels, EX 90
axis titles, EX 90

B

Back button, Quick Access toolbar, EX 140
backgrounds, worksheet, EX 136–137
Backstage view
     creating folders from, WEB 16
     opening, OFF 6
     overview, OFF 7

Print tab, EX 16–17
Save & Send options, WEB 6–7
selecting templates, EX 41
worksheets in, EX 17
backups of tables, EX 164
backward compatibility, OFF 10
Banded Rows option, Table Styles Options group, EX 157
banding, EX 157
Bar charts, EX 81
Between dialog box, EX 64–65
bold font style, EX 56–57
borders
adding to chart objects, EX 88
applying, EX 62–63

C

calculated columns feature, EX 166
calculating payments, EX 120–121
calculation operators, EX 12
callouts, EX 92
Cancel button, EX 10
capitalization, sorting by, EX 164
Case sensitive box, Sort dialog box, EX 164
category axis, EX 80
cell address, EX 4–5
cell pointer, EX 4–5
cells
absolute references, EX 34–35
copying formulas with, EX 38–39
overview, EX 34–35
copying entries in, EX 32–33
copying formulas with absolute references, EX 38–39
copying formulas with relative references, EX 36–37
defined, EX 4–5
deleting, EX 33
editing entries in, EX 10–11
filling with sequential text, EX 39
formatting, EX 52–53
inserting, EX 33
locking, EX 132
mixed references, EX 35
moving entries in, EX 32–33
named, EX 114
referencing, EX 12
relative references
copying formulas with, EX 36–37
overview, EX 34–35
rotating text in, EX 57
styles of, EX 62–63
Center button, EX 56–57
Change Chart Type dialog box, EX 86–87
chart sheets, EX 82

Chart Tools
creating charts with, EX 82–83
Design tab, EX 86
editing charts with, EX 84
Format tab, EX 88, 90–91
Layout tab, EX 88–89, 92
charts, EX 79–104
adding borders to objects, EX 88
adding data labels to, EX 87
adding shadow effect, EX 86
annotating, EX 92–93
changing design, EX 86–87
changing layout, EX 88–89
combination, EX 86
creating, EX 82–83
creating pie charts, EX 94–95
drawing on, EX 92–93
editing text in, EX 88
formatting, EX 90–91
moving, EX 84–85
overview, EX 2, 79
planning, EX 80–81
previewing, EX 94
printing, EX 94
resizing, EX 84–85
checking spelling, EX 68–69
circular references, EX 113
Clear button, EX 56
clearing
filters, EX 178
formats, EX 56
clip art, EX 55
Clipboard, EX 32–33, OFF 9, 13
cloud computing, EX 5, OFF 5, WEB 2
Clustered Bar chart, EX 86–87
Clustered Column chart, EX 82–83
collaboration tools
comments, EX 61
Document Inspector, EX 138
online, OFF 2
overview, EX 2
shared workbooks, EX 139
tracking changes, EX 139
Collapse Dialog box button, EX 106
color
in charts, EX 90
sorting tables by, EX 178
of tabs, EX 66–67
in worksheets, EX 62–63
color scales, EX 183
Column charts, EX 81–83
Column resize pointer, EX 11
Column Width command, EX 58

Column Width dialog box, EX 58
columns
    adjusting width of, EX 58–59, 156
    deleting, EX 60–61
    formatting commands, EX 58
    freezing, EX 133
    headings of, EX 58
    hiding, EX 60
    inserting, EX 60–61
    planning table structure, EX 154–155
    unhiding, EX 60
combination charts, EX 86
Comma Style format, EX 52
commands
    Excel Web App, WEB 15
    PowerPoint Web App, WEB 9
comments
    adding, EX 61
    editing, EX 61
comparison operators, EX 12, 117
compatibility, Office suite, OFF 2
Compatibility Checker dialog box, EX 142
compatibility mode, EX 142–143, OFF 10
complex formulas, EX 26–27
CONCATENATE function, EX 106
conditional formatting
    applying, EX 64–65, 181
    color scales, EX 183
    highlighting top- or bottom-ranked values, EX 183
    icon sets, EX 183
    sorting tables, EX 164, 178
Conditional Formatting Rules Manager dialog box, EX 64, 181, 183
conditions
    stated, EX 116
    summing data ranges based on, EX 108–109
consolidating data
    using formulas, EX 110–111
    using named ranges, EX 114
contextual tabs, OFF 6
Convert Text to Columns feature, EX 106–107
Copy Cells option, EX 37
Copy pointer, EX 11
copying
    cell entries, EX 32–33
    formulas
        with absolute cell references, EX 38–39
        overview, EX 26
        with relative cell references, EX 36–37
    worksheets, EX 67
copy-to location, Advanced Filter dialog box, EX 185
COUNT function, EX 30
COUNTA function, EX 30
COUNTIF function, EX 108

COUNTIFS function, EX 108
Create Names from Selection dialog box, EX 12
Create Sparklines dialog box, EX 83
Create your Windows Live ID page, WEB 4–5
criteria range, EX 182, 184–185
currency formats, EX 52
Custom AutoFilter dialog box, EX 180–181
custom cell borders, EX 62
custom filters, EX 180–181
custom sort orders, EX 165
Custom Views dialog box, EX 134
custom views of worksheets, EX 134–135

D

data
    adding, EX 158–159
    consolidating
        using formulas, EX 110–111
        using named ranges, EX 114
    deleting, EX 162–163
    finding and replacing, EX 160–161
    inserting, EX 158–159
    sorting, EX 164–165
data bars, EX 64–65
data entry area, EX 132
data labels, chart, EX 87
data markers, EX 80–81
data points, EX 80–81, 94
data ranges, EX 108–109
data series, EX 80–81
Data Validation dialog box, EX 190–191
database functions, EX 188–189
date, inserting, EX 14
date sequences, EX 39
DAVERAGE function, EX 189
DCOUNT function, EX 189
DCOUNTA function, EX 189
default file extensions, OFF 8
Default Width command, EX 58
Delete dialog box, EX 33
deleting
    cells, EX 33
    columns, EX 60–61
    rows, EX 60–61
    table data, EX 162–163
    worksheets, EX 66
delimiters, EX 106
descending sort order, EX 164–165
design, chart, EX 86–87
Design tab
    Chart Tools, EX 86
    Header & Footer Tools, EX 136–137

DGET function, EX 186, 189
Diagonal resizing pointer, EX 85
dialog box launcher, OFF 6–7
dictionary, EX 68
digital signatures, EX 144
distribution, preparing workbooks for, EX 138–139
division (/) operator, EX 7
Document Inspector, EX 138–139
Document Properties Panel, EX 138–139
Document Recovery task pane, OFF 15
document window, OFF 6–7
dollar sign ($), EX 38
downloads, WEB 3
drag-and-drop feature, EX 32–33
Draw pointer, EX 85
drawing, on charts, EX 92–93
drop shadow, EX 86
DSUM function, EX 188–189
duplicate records, deleting, EX 162–163
dynamic page breaks, EX 135

E

Edit Formatting Rule dialog box, EX 64
Edit mode, EX 10
Edit permissions page, Windows Live, WEB 12–13
editing
   cell entries, EX 10–11
   comments, EX 61
   files, WEB 16
   text in charts, EX 88
electronic spreadsheet, EX 2
e-mail
   sending workbooks by, EX 68
   via Windows Live, WEB 3
embedded charts, EX 82, 85
Enter button, EX 10
equal to (=) operator, EX 117
Equation Tools Design tab, EX 119
equations, inserting, EX 119
Error Alert tab, Data Validation dialog box, EX 191
error values, EX 113
errors in formulas, EX 112–113
Excel
   opening and renaming files in, OFF 10
   overview, OFF 2
Excel 2010 window, EX 4–5
Excel 97 – 2003 workbook format, EX 143
Excel macro-enabled template format, EX 143
Excel template format, EX 143
Excel Web App, WEB 14–15
exclamation point (!), EX 110

exiting programs, OFF 4–5
Expand Dialog box button, EX 106
Exploded pie in 3-D button, EX 94
exploding data points, EX 94–95
exponent (^) operator, EX 7
external reference indicator, EX 110
extracting table data, EX 184–185

F

fields, EX 154–156
file extensions, default, OFF 8
File tab
   Excel Web App, WEB 15
   PowerPoint Web App, WEB 9
files
   closing, OFF 14–15
   creating, OFF 8–9
   defined, OFF 8
   editing with Web apps, WEB 16
   formats of, EX 142–143
   names of, OFF 8
   opening, OFF 10–11
   opening from Web apps, WEB 16
   organizing on SkyDrive, WEB 10–11
   printing, OFF 12–13
   saving, OFF 8–11
   sharing on networks, WEB 12–13
   sharing on Windows Live, WEB 16
   viewing, OFF 12–13
Fill Color list arrow, EX 62–63
Fill Down option, EX 36–37
Fill Formatting Only option, EX 37
fill handle, EX 11, 39
Fill Without Formatting option, EX 37
filter list arrows, EX 156, 178
filtering tables
   with Advanced Filter, EX 182–183
   creating custom filters, EX 180–181
   overview, EX 178–179
Find & Select button, EX 161
Find and Replace dialog box, EX 68–69, 160–161
Fit to option, Page Setup dialog box, EX 17
folders
   creating from Backstage view, WEB 16
   creating on SkyDrive, WEB 10–11
Font Color list arrow, EX 62–63
Font Size list arrow, Mini toolbar, EX 54
fonts
   changing, EX 54–55
   color of, EX 62–63
   size of, EX 54–55
   styles of, EX 56–57

footers
  adding to tables, EX 168
  changing information in, EX 14
Format Axis dialog box, EX 90
Format Axis Title dialog box, EX 90
Format Cells dialog box
  Alignment tab, EX 57
  applying colors, patterns, and borders with, EX 62
  custom conditional formatting, EX 64
  font list in, EX 54–55
  formatting values with, EX 52–53
  Protection tab, EX 132–133
Format Chart Area dialog box, EX 87
Format Chart Title dialog box, EX 86
Format Data Point dialog box, EX 94–95
Format Data Series dialog box, EX 86
Format Painter, EX 56
Format tab, Chart tools, EX 88, 90–91
formatting. *See also* formatting worksheets
  charts, EX 90–91
  clearing, EX 56
  commands for columns, EX 58
  data using text functions, EX 106–107
  keyboard shortcuts, EX 56
  tables, EX 156–157
  themes, EX 63
  values, EX 52–53
formatting worksheets, EX 51–78
  alignment, EX 56–57
  borders, EX 62–63
  checking spelling, EX 68–69
  colors, EX 62–63
  columns
    deleting, EX 60–61
    inserting, EX 60–61
    width, adjusting, EX 58–59
  conditional formatting, EX 64–65
  font
    changing, EX 54–55
    size of, EX 54–55
    styles of, EX 56–57
  formatting values, EX 52–53
  moving worksheets, EX 66–67
  overview, EX 51
  patterns, applying, EX 62–63
  renaming worksheets, EX 66–67
  rows
    deleting, EX 60–61
    inserting, EX 60–61
Formula AutoComplete feature, EX 30
formula bar
  canceling entries in, EX 8
  overview, EX 4–5

formula prefix, EX 12
formulas, EX 25–50, 105–128
  absolute cell references
    copying formulas with, EX 38–39
    overview, EX 34–35
  consolidating data using, EX 110–111
  copying cell entries, EX 32–33
  creating complex, EX 26–27
  editing, EX 12–13
  entering, EX 12–13
  errors, checking for, EX 112–113
  formatting data using text functions, EX 106–107
  AND function, building with, EX 118–119
  hiding, EX 132
  IF function, building with, EX 116–117
  inserting functions, EX 28–29
  moving cell entries, EX 32–33
  overview, EX 6–7, 25, 105
  PMT function, calculating payments with, EX 120–121
  printing, EX 16
  relative cell references
    copying formulas with, EX 36–37
    overview, EX 34–35
  rounding values with functions, EX 40–41
  summing data ranges based on conditions, EX 108–109
  in tables, EX 166–167
  toggling in worksheets, EX 112
  typing functions, EX 30–31
  using named ranges, EX 114–115
freezing panes, EX 133
Function Arguments dialog box
  AVERAGE function, EX 28–29
  COUNTIF function, EX 108–109
  DSUM function, EX 188–189
  IF function, EX 116
  moving, EX 106
  VLOOKUP function, EX 186
functions. *See also* specific functions by name
  defined, EX 8, 28
  inserting, EX 28–29
  rounding values with, EX 40–41
  typing, EX 30–31
FV (Future Value) function, EX 121
Fv argument, EX 120

G

gallery, OFF 6
Get a Digital ID dialog box, EX 144
Go to Special dialog box, EX 161
graphs. *See* charts
greater than (>) operator, EX 117
greater than or equal to (>=) operator, EX 117

gridlines
    major, EX 88
    minor, EX 88
    overview, EX 80–81
    printing, EX 16
    removing from chart, EX 88–89
    viewing, EX 14
Gridlines Print check box, Page Layout tab, EX 16
grouping worksheets, EX 144–145
groups, command, OFF 6

H

Header & Footer Tools Design tab, EX 14, 136–137
header row, EX 154
Header Row option, Table Styles Options group, EX 157
headers
    adding to tables, EX 168
    changing information in, EX 14–15
heading, column, EX 58
Help system, OFF 14–15
Help window, Word, OFF 14–15
Hide & Unhide command, EX 58, 60
hiding
    columns, EX 60
    formulas, EX 132
    rows, EX 60
    table headings and gridlines, EX 168
    worksheets, EX 130
Highlight Cells Rules submenu, EX 64
Highlight Changes dialog box, EX 139
HLOOKUP (Horizontal Lookup) function, EX 187
Home tab
    Excel Web App, WEB 15
    PowerPoint Web App, WEB 9
Horizontal resizing pointer, EX 85
HTML format, EX 142
hyperlinks, inserting, EX 140–141

I

I-beam, EX 11, 85
Icon Sets, EX 64, 183
IF function, EX 116–117
IFERROR function, EX 112
images, inserting, EX 55
indenting cell entries, EX 57
Information Rights Management (IRM) feature, EX 138
Input Message tab, Data Validation dialog box, EX 191
Insert dialog box, EX 33, 60–61
Insert Function dialog box, EX 28–29, 40
Insert Hyperlink dialog box, EX 140–141
Insert Options button, EX 60–61

Insert tab
    Excel Web App, WEB 15
    PowerPoint Web App, WEB 9
Insert Table dialog box, EX 156–157
inserting
    cells, EX 33
    clip art, EX 55
    columns, EX 60–61
    data in tables, EX 158–159
    dates, EX 14
    equations in worksheets, EX 119
    functions, EX 28–29
    hyperlinks, EX 140–141
    images, EX 55
    rows, EX 60–61
    text boxes, EX 92
    worksheets, EX 66
insertion point, EX 10–11, OFF 8–9
instances, EX 130
instant messaging, WEB 3
integration, Office suite program, OFF 2
interfaces, OFF 2
intranet, publishing documents to, EX 142
Invalid data warning, EX 190–191
IRM (Information Rights Management) feature, EX 138
italic font style, EX 56–57

K

keyboard shortcuts
    for creating tables, EX 156
    formatting, EX 56
keywords, EX 138

L

labels, EX 8–9
landscape orientation, EX 16
layout, chart, EX 88–89
Layout tab, Chart Tools, EX 88–89, 92
legend, EX 80–81, 84
less than (<) operator, EX 117
less than or equal to (<=) operator, EX 117
Line charts, EX 81
linking workbooks, EX 110–111
list arrows, EX 178
Live Preview feature, OFF 6–7
locking cells, EX 132
logical conditions, EX 180
logical formulas
    building with AND function, EX 118–119
    building with IF function, EX 116–117
logical test, EX 116

logos on backgrounds, EX 136
looking up table values, EX 186–187
LOWER function, EX 107

M

macros, EX 143
major gridlines, EX 88
marker, data, EX 80
MATCH function, EX 187
MAX function, EX 30–31
Merge & Center button, EX 56–57
metadata, EX 138
MHT format, EX 142
MHTML format, EX 142
Microsoft Access. *See* Access
Microsoft Excel. *See* Excel
Microsoft Office. *See* Office, Microsoft
Microsoft Office Web Apps. *See* Web Apps, Microsoft Office
Microsoft PowerPoint. *See* PowerPoint
Microsoft Windows Live. *See* Windows Live
Microsoft Word. *See* Word
MIN function, EX 30
Mini toolbar, EX 54
minor gridlines, EX 88
mixed references, EX 35
mobile devices, Windows Live apps for, WEB 3
mode indicator, EX 4–5, 8, 11
Move Chart dialog box, EX 85
Move pointer, EX 11, 85
moving
    cell entries, EX 32–33
    charts, EX 84–85
    worksheets, EX 66–67
multilevel sort, EX 164
multiplication (*) operator, EX 7

N

Name box, EX 4–5
Name Manager dialog box, EX 115, 186–187
named ranges
    consolidating data using, EX 114
    constructing formulas using, EX 114–115
    overview, EX 12
names, table, EX 186
navigating worksheets, EX 9
networks
    adding people to, WEB 12–13
    sharing files on, WEB 12–13
    via Windows Live, WEB 3
New Name dialog box, EX 12, 114–115
New Table Quick Style dialog box, EX 157
Normal pointer, EX 11

Normal view, EX 14
not equal to (<>) operator, EX 117
NOT logical function, EX 118
Number Format list arrow, EX 52
number sequences, EX 39

O

object pointers, EX 85
objects, EX 84
Office, Microsoft, OFF 1–16
    closing files, OFF 14–15
    creating files, OFF 8–9
    exiting programs, OFF 4–5
    Help system, OFF 14–15
    opening files, OFF 10–11
    overview, OFF 2–3
    saving files, OFF 8–11
    starting programs, OFF 4–5
    user interface, OFF 6–7
    viewing and printing documents, OFF 12–13
Office Clipboard, EX 32–33, OFF 9, 13
Office Open XML format, EX 143
Office Web Apps, Microsoft. *See* Web Apps, Microsoft Office
OneNote Web App, WEB 15
online collaboration, OFF 2
Open as Copy option, Open dialog box, OFF 11
Open dialog box, EX 4, OFF 10–11
Open Read Only option, Open dialog box, OFF 11
OpenDocument spreadsheet format, EX 143
operators
    arithmetic, EX 7, 12, 26–27
    comparison, EX 117
    formulas with multiple, EX 7
    order of precedence, EX 26
    types of, EX 12
Or logical condition, EX 180, 182
OR logical function, EX 118
order of precedence, EX 26
orientation, print, EX 16–17

P

Page Break Preview, EX 14–15, 135
Page Layout tab, EX 16
Page Layout view, EX 14–15
Page Setup dialog box, EX 17, 168–169
panes, EX 131, 133
parentheses, EX 6, 40
Paste Options button, EX 36–37
Paste Preview feature, EX 36
Paste Special dialog box, EX 36
patterns, EX 62–63
payments, calculating, EX 120–121

PDF format, EX 142–143

percent (%) operator, EX 7

permissions

    Excel, EX 138

    Windows Live, WEB 12–13

photo sharing, WEB 3

pie charts, EX 81, 94–95

planning tables, EX 154–155

plot area, EX 80–81

PMT function, EX 120–121

pointers, EX 11

points (font), EX 54

points, data, EX 80

portable document format (PDF), EX 142–143

portrait orientation, EX 16–17

PowerPoint, OFF 2, 6–7

PowerPoint Web App, WEB 3, 8–9

precedence, order of, EX 26

prefix, formula, EX 12

previews

    charts, EX 94

    Word document, OFF 12

    worksheets, EX 110

print area, EX 16, 169

Print Layout view, Word, OFF 12

print orientation, EX 16–17

Print tab

    Backstage view, EX 16–17

    Word, OFF 12–13

print title, EX 168

printer, active, EX 16

printing

    charts, EX 86, 94

    files, OFF 12–13

    gridlines, EX 16

    options for, EX 16–17

    selected areas, EX 169

    tables, EX 168–169

    worksheet formulas, EX 16

PROPER function, EX 106

properties, EX 138

Protect Sheet dialog box, EX 132–133

protecting worksheets, EX 132–133

Protection tab, Format Cells dialog box, EX 132–133

publishing documents, EX 142

Q

question mark (?) wildcard, EX 160, 180

Quick Access toolbar

    Back button, EX 140

    overview, OFF 6–7

    Quick Print button, EX 16, OFF 12

Quick Print button, EX 16, OFF 12

quick reference

    to Office Web Apps, WEB 16

    to Windows Live, WEB 16

R

ranges

    formatting, EX 52–53

    named, EX 12, 114–115

    selecting, EX 4–5

read-only format, EX 132

records

    defined, EX 154

    deleting, EX 162–163

    filtering, EX 178–181

    finding, EX 160–161, 186

    sorting, EX 164–165

    using Advanced Filter with, EX 182–183

recovered files, OFF 15

reference indicator, external, EX 110

reference operators, EX 12, 26

references

    circular, EX 113

    relative cell

        copying formulas with, EX 36–37

        overview, EX 34–35

    structured, EX 167

referencing cells, EX 12

relative cell references

    copying formulas with, EX 36–37

    overview, EX 34–35

Remove Duplicates dialog box, EX 162–163

renaming worksheets, EX 66–67

Replace tab, Find and Replace dialog box, EX 160–161

replacing table data, EX 160–161

reports, EX 3

Research task pane, EX 141

resizing

    charts, EX 84–85

    tables, EX 158–159

restrictions, data, EX 190

returns, AND function, EX 118

Ribbon, OFF 6–7

rotating text, EX 57

ROUND function, EX 40

rounding values, EX 40–41

Row Height command, EX 59

rows

    deleting, EX 60–61

    freezing, EX 133

    height of, EX 59

    hiding, EX 60

inserting, EX 60–61

planning table structure, EX 154–155

unhiding, EX 60

rulers, EX 14

rules, conditional formatting, EX 64

Rules Manager, EX 64, 181

S

Save & Send options, Backstage view, WEB 6–7

Save As command, OFF 10

Save As dialog box

Excel, EX 4, 142, OFF 10–11

PowerPoint, OFF 8

Word, OFF 9

saving

AutoRecover feature, EX 10

Custom Views of worksheets, EX 134–135

files

creating and, OFF 8–9

with new names, OFF 10–11

to Windows Live, WEB 16

workbooks for distribution, EX 142–143

workspaces, EX 145

Scale to Fit options, Page Layout tab, EX 16

scaling, EX 17, 136

Scatter charts, EX 81

scope, name, EX 114

screen capture, OFF 13

Screen Clipping button, EX 137

screenshots, EX 137

ScreenTips, OFF 14

scroll bars, EX 4–5

search criterion, EX 178

secondary axis, EX 86

Select a function list, Insert Function dialog box, EX 28

selecting table elements, EX 159

sensitive data, removing, EX 138–139

sequential text, EX 39

series, data, EX 80

Series dialog box, EX 39

shadow effect, chart, EX 86

shape styles, EX 90

Shapes gallery, EX 92

shared workbooks, EX 139

sharing files

on networks, WEB 12–13

on Windows Live, WEB 16

Sheet Background dialog box, EX 136

sheet tab scrolling buttons, EX 4–5, 66

sheet tabs, EX 4–5

shortcut keys, OFF 4

Show Formulas button, Formulas tab, EX 16

Signature Setup dialog box, EX 144

signatures, digital, EX 144

simple formula

editing, EX 12–13

entering, EX 12–13

single-file Web page, EX 142–143

sizing handles, chart, EX 82–83

SkyDrive, Windows Live, OFF 5

SmartArt graphics, EX 93

Snipping Tool, Windows 7, OFF 13

software, spreadsheet, EX 2–3

Sort dialog box, EX 164–165

sorting data, EX 3, 164–165

sparklines, EX 83

spelling, checking, EX 68–69

Spelling: English (U.S.) dialog box, EX 68–69

splitting worksheets, EX 131

spreadsheet software, EX 2–3

Start menu, OFF 5

starting programs, OFF 4–5

stated conditions, EX 116

status bar, EX 4–5

structured reference feature, EX 166–167

styles

cell, EX 62–63

font, EX 56–57

shape, EX 90

table, EX 53, 156

WordArt, EX 90

SUBSTITUTE function, EX 107

Subtotals feature, EX 192–193

subtraction (-) operator, EX 7

suite, OFF 2

Sum button, EX 8–9

SUM function, EX 8–9, 28

Sum list arrow, Ribbon, EX 28

SUMIF function, EX 108–109

SUMIFS function, EX 108

summarizing table data, EX 188–189

summing data ranges, EX 108–109

switching worksheet views, EX 14–15

Synchronous Scrolling button, EX 130

T

Tab Color palette, EX 66–67

Table of Contents pane, Word Help window, OFF 14

table styles, EX 53, 156

Table Styles gallery, EX 53

Table Styles Options group, EX 157

table total row, EX 166

tables, EX 153–200
  adding data to, EX 158–159
  creating, EX 156–157
  deleting data in, EX 162–163
  extracting data from, EX 184–185
  filtering
    with Advanced Filter, EX 182–183
    creating custom filters, EX 180–181
    overview, EX 178–179
  finding and replacing data in, EX 160–161
  formatting, EX 156–157
  looking up values in, EX 186–187
  overview, EX 153, 177
  planning, EX 154–155
  printing, EX 168–169
  selecting elements in, EX 159
  sorting data in, EX 164–165
  Subtotals feature, EX 192–193
  summarizing data in, EX 188–189
  using formulas in, EX 166–167
  validating data in, EX 190–191
tabs, OFF 6–7
target documents, EX 140–141
taskbar property settings, OFF 4
templates
  creating workbooks with, EX 41
  defined, EX 2
text
  annotations, EX 92–93
  applying WordArt styles, EX 90
  editing in charts, EX 88
text boxes, inserting, EX 92–93
text concatenation operators, EX 12
themes
  Excel, EX 63
  Word, OFF 2–3
Themes gallery, EX 63
thesaurus, EX 141
three-dimensional charts, EX 87
tick marks, EX 80–81
tiled graphics, EX 136
title, print, EX 168
title bar, OFF 6–7
titles, chart, EX 82–83, 86, 88
toggling worksheet formulas, EX 112
Total Row option, Table Styles Options group, EX 157
tracking changes, EX 139
Type argument, EX 120
typing functions, EX 30–31

U

underline font style, EX 56–57
underscores, EX 114

Undo button, EX 10
Undo Calculated Column option, EX 166
Unhide dialog box, EX 130
unhiding
  columns, EX 60
  rows, EX 60
uploading files to Windows Live, WEB 6–7
UPPER function, EX 107
user interface, OFF 6–7

V

validating table data, EX 190–191
value axis, EX 80
values
  defined, EX 8–9
  formatting, EX 52–53
  looking up table, EX 186–187
  restricting, EX 190
  rounding with functions, EX 40–41
  using HLOOKUP function, EX 187
  using MATCH function, EX 187
verifying Windows Live ID, WEB 5
Vertical Lookup (VLOOKUP) function, EX 186–187
Vertical resizing pointer, EX 85
View Side by Side button, EX 130
View tab
  Excel, EX 14
  PowerPoint Web App, WEB 9
viewing worksheets, EX 14–15, 130–131
views, OFF 12
VLOOKUP (Vertical Lookup) function, EX 186–187

W

watermark, EX 136
Web Apps, Microsoft Office
  Excel Web App, WEB 14–15
  overview, EX 5, OFF 5, WEB 2, 8
  PowerPoint Web App, WEB 8–9
quick reference to, WEB 16
Web Layout view, Word, OFF 12–13
Web page format, EX 143
Web pages, linking to, EX 140
what-if analysis, EX 2–3, 38–39
wildcards, EX 160, 180. *See also* specific wildcards by name
Windows Live, WEB 1–16
  creating folders and organizing files on SkyDrive, WEB 10–11
  Excel Web App, WEB 14–15
  obtaining Windows Live IDs, WEB 4–5
  overview, EX 5
  PowerPoint Web App, WEB 8–9
  quick reference, WEB 16
  sharing files, WEB 12–13

signing in to, WEB 4–5
uploading files to, WEB 6–7
working online from, WEB 2–3
Windows Live SkyDrive, OFF 5
Word
Help window, OFF 14–15
overview, OFF 2
printing documents, OFF 12
Save As dialog box, OFF 9
themes, OFF 2–3
viewing documents, OFF 12
Word Web App, WEB 15
WordArt styles, EX 90
workbooks. *See also* worksheets
adding digital signatures to, EX 144
creating with templates, EX 41
defined, EX 2
e-mailing, EX 68
inserting hyperlinks, EX 140–141
linking data between, EX 110–111
managing names of, EX 115
preparing for distribution, EX 138–139
saving for distribution, EX 142–143
shared, EX 139
worksheets. *See also* workbooks
adding backgrounds, EX 136–137
arranging, EX 130–131
copying, EX 67
defined, EX 2–3
formatting
alignment, EX 56–57
borders, EX 62–63
checking spelling, EX 68–69
colors, EX 62–63
columns, EX 58–61
conditional formatting, EX 64–65
font, EX 54–57
formatting values, EX 52–53

moving worksheets, EX 66–67
overview, EX 51
patterns, applying, EX 62–63
renaming worksheets, EX 66–67
rows, EX 60–61
grouping, EX 144–145
hiding, EX 130
inserting equations in, EX 119
moving, EX 66–67
moving embedded charts to, EX 85
navigating, EX 9
printing formulas on, EX 16
protecting, EX 132–133
renaming, EX 66–67
saving custom views of, EX 134–135
scaling, EX 136
simple formulas in, EX 13
splitting into panes, EX 131
switching views, EX 14–15
viewing, EX 130–131
workspace, EX 145

X

x-axis, EX 80
.xls extension, EX 142
.xlsx extension, EX 41, 142
.xltx extension, EX 41
.xlw extension, EX 145
XML paper specification format, EX 143

Y

y-axis, EX 80

Z

z-axis, EX 80, 87
Zoom tools, OFF 6